MAIMONIDES THE RATIONALIST

THE LITTMAN LIBRARY OF
JEWISH CIVILIZATION

Dedicated to the memory of
LOUIS THOMAS SIDNEY LITTMAN
who founded the Littman Library for the love of God
and as an act of charity in memory of his father
JOSEPH AARON LITTMAN
and to the memory of
ROBERT JOSEPH LITTMAN
who continued what his father Louis had begun
יהא זכרם ברוך

'Get wisdom, get understanding:
Forsake her not and she shall preserve thee'
PROV. 4: 5

The Littman Library of Jewish Civilization is a registered UK charity
Registered charity no. 1000784

MAIMONIDES THE RATIONALIST

◆

HERBERT A. DAVIDSON

The Littman Library of Jewish Civilization
in association with Liverpool University Press

The Littman Library of Jewish Civilization
in association with Liverpool University Press
4 Cambridge Street, Liverpool L69 7ZU, UK

www.liverpooluniversitypress.co.uk/littman

Managing Editor: Connie Webber

Distributed in North America by
Oxford University Press Inc., 198 Madison Avenue,
New York, NY 10016, USA

First published in hardback 2011
First published in paperback 2015

Catalogue records for this book are available from the
British Library and the Library of Congress

ISBN 978-1-906764-77-7

Publishing co-ordinator: Janet Moth
Index: Herbert A. Davidson
Design: Pete Russell, Faringdon, Oxon.
Typeset by John Saunders Design & Production, Eastbourne

Printed in Great Britain by
CPI Group (UK) Ltd., Croydon, CR0 4YY

For Mark M., Margaret, Claire, Nathaniel, and Sophia

Preface and Acknowledgements

MAIMONIDES was not the first rabbinic scholar to take an interest in philosophy. He was preceded by a small contingent of rabbinic scholars in Iraq who dabbled in the subject, the best known being Sa'adiah Gaon. But except for Sa'adiah's *Beliefs and Opinions*, their writings, the rabbinic as well as the philosophical—and it is only with indulgence that any of the latter may be granted the label *philosophical*—have been relegated to the rare book shelves of research libraries. Maimonides, by contrast, not merely interested himself in rabbinics as well as philosophy; he was a towering figure in each. His law code, the *Mishneh torah*, stands with Rashi's commentary on the Babylonian Talmud as one of the two most influential and intensely studied rabbinic works coming out of the Middle Ages, and his *Guide for the Perplexed* is the most influential and widely read Jewish philosophical work ever written. His accomplishments in both areas are, still today, the object of endless attention.

He moreover expressed unreserved commitment to both a rabbinic and a philosophical world-view. Yet each is hegemonic, and they are commonly thought to be mutually exclusive. Admirers as well as critics have consequently arrived at wildly divergent perceptions of the man. At one extreme, we are given a Maimonides who understood God to be wholly impersonal—if He exists at all—and who accordingly denied the possibility of communication between God and man, individual providence, and personal immortality; a man who lavished decades and boundless energy on his rabbinic writings, repeatedly going back to correct them, with no other aim than to create a smokescreen for concealing, and a vehicle for advancing, a radical philosophical ideology. At the other, we find a pious religious teacher who performed the invaluable service of identifying the principles of the Jewish faith and the 613 commandments that God communicated to Moses at Sinai, who instructed his co-religionists on the proper way to observe the commandments of the Written Torah and *halakhot* of the Oral Torah, and who was himself meticulous in observing the precepts of both. Observers of the latter persuasion often symbolize their picture of Maimonides by using his Hebrew name even when writing or speaking in a western language. They do not call him 'Maimonides', a European coinage, but, instead, 'Rambam', the Hebrew acronym for Rabbenu Mosheh ben Maimon.

The full gamut includes Maimonides the atheist or agnostic, Maimonides the sceptic, Maimonides the deist, Maimonides the Aristotelian, Averroist, or proto-

Kantian, Maimonides who was seduced by the blandishments of 'accursed philosophy', Maimonides who sowed the seeds that led to Spanish Jews' loss of faith and mass apostasy and was therefore responsible for the demise of the glorious Spanish Jewry, Maimonides who incorporated philosophical elements into his rabbinic works and wrote the weighty *Guide for the Perplexed* not because he was committed to what he says there but in order to rescue errant souls seduced by philosophy, Maimonides the defender of the faith, who defined the articles of the Jewish creed for all time—not to speak of such weird aberrations as Maimonides the kabbalist and Maimonides the mystic.

A pair of traditional scholars, working independently, made a stunning discovery: the philosopher and the rabbinist were two different men. In the sixteenth century, Joseph Ashkenazi, the earlier to gain the insight, contended that Maimonides, the author of the *Guide for the Perplexed*, could not possibly have written the admirably 'strict' *Mishneh torah*; the *Mishneh torah* must be the work of his father, which Maimonides appropriated to himself. Two centuries later, Rabbi Jacob Emden came to the reverse conclusion. He determined that Maimonides, the author of the 'holy' *Mishneh torah*, could not possibly have written the 'drivel' purveyed by the *Guide for the Perplexed*; the *Guide* must be the creation of some slyboots who affixed Maimonides' name to his own 'fetid stupidities, raising a stench like ordure' in order to further their acceptance. It happens that Maimonides' name was a powerful magnet and pulled into its orbit dozens of minor works—far outnumbering the authentic writings—from a variety of pens and claiming him as their author. Nevertheless, Joseph Ashkenazi and Jacob Emden cannot be taken seriously. Maimonides makes abundantly clear that it was he who wrote both the *Mishneh torah* and the *Guide for the Perplexed.*

If we take the unconventional step of granting Maimonides himself the say on who he was, the one-sided perceptions go up in smoke. He did not see himself exclusively as a dedicated philosopher or exclusively as a devoted rabbinist; he saw himself as both. Nor would he concede that two irreconcilable personas jostled within him, each struggling for dominance like Esau and Jacob in their mother's womb. If we accept him at his word, he visualized philosophy and the Written and Oral Torahs as a single harmonious domain. The harmony, he would have us believe, was embraced and lived by the prophets and rabbis of old but was forgotten during the millennium-long exile. He was the instaurator who re-established it for himself and for other men of understanding.

Six of the chapters in the present book grew out of essays published in a range of forums over the years. Chapter 2 is a light revision of the article on which it is based, but in the other instances, the originals have been rewritten. The articles out of which the six chapters have grown and the forums in which they were published are as follows:

CHAPTER 1: 'The Study of Philosophy as a Religious Obligation', in Sh. Goitein (ed.), *Religion in a Religious Age* (Cambridge, Mass.: Association for Jewish Studies, 1974).

CHAPTER 2: 'The First Two Positive Commandments in Maimonides' List of the 613 Believed to Have Been Given to Moses at Sinai', in R. Elior and P. Schaefer (eds.), *Creation and Re-Creation in Jewish Thought* (Joseph Dan Festschrift) (Tübingen: Mohr Siebeck, 2005).

CHAPTER 4: 'Maimonides' *Shemonah Peraqim* and Alfarabi's *Fusul al-Madani*', *Proceedings of the American Academy for Jewish Research*, 31 (1963).

CHAPTER 6: 'Maimonides on Metaphysical Knowledge', *Maimonidean Studies*, 3 (1992–3).

CHAPTER 7 incorporates and revises sections from 'Further on a Problematic Passage in *Guide for the Perplexed* 2:24', *Maimonidean Studies*, 4 (2000), and from 'The Problematic Passage in *Guide for the Perplexed* 2:24', *Aleph*, 8 (2008).

CHAPTER 8: 'The Middle Way in Maimonides' Ethics', *Proceedings of the American Academy for Jewish Research*, 54 (1987).

All the publishers have kindly given permission for use of material that appeared under their auspices.

My wife Kinneret read the manuscript three times. As in the past, she has helped clarify numerous points and saved me from innumerable embarrassing slips in both content and style.

Contents

Publisher's Note on Transliteration

Hebrew

The transliteration of Hebrew in this book reflects consideration of the type of book it is, in terms of its content, purpose, and readership. The system adopted therefore reflects a broad approach to transcription, rather than the narrower approaches found in the *Encyclopaedia Judaica* or other systems developed for text-based or linguistic studies. The aim has been to reflect the pronunciation prescribed for modern Hebrew, rather than the spelling or Hebrew word structure, and to do so using conventions that are generally familiar to the English-speaking reader.

In accordance with this approach, no attempt is made to indicate the distinctions between *alef* and *ayin*, *tet* and *taf*, *kaf* and *kuf*, *sin* and *samekh*, since these are not relevant to pronunciation; likewise, the *dagesh* is not indicated except where it affects pronunciation. Following the principle of using conventions familiar to the majority of readers, however, transcriptions that are well established have been retained even when they are not fully consistent with the transliteration system adopted. On similar grounds, the *tsadi* is rendered by 'tz' in such familiar words as bar mitzvah. Likewise, the distinction between *ḥet* and *khaf* has been retained, using *ḥ* for the former and *kh* for the latter; the associated forms are generally familiar to readers, even if the distinction is not actually borne out in pronunciation, and for the same reason the final *heh* is indicated too. As in Hebrew, no capital letters are used, except that an initial capital has been retained in transliterating titles of published works (for example, *Shulḥan arukh*).

Since no distinction is made between *alef* and *ayin*, they are indicated by an apostrophe only in intervocalic positions where a failure to do so could lead an English-speaking reader to pronounce the vowel-cluster as a diphthong—as, for example, in *ha'ir*—or otherwise mispronounce the word.

The *sheva na* is indicated by an *e*—*perikat ol*, *reshut*—except, again, when established convention dictates otherwise.

The *yod* is represented by *i* when it occurs as a vowel (*bereshit*), by *y* when it occurs as a consonant (*yesodot*), and by *yi* when it occurs as both (*yisra'el*).

Names have generally been left in their familiar forms, even when this is inconsistent with the overall system.

Arabic

Standard academic transliteration has been used for Arabic.

Hamza and *'ayn* are indicated by ʾ and ʿ respectively (apart from initial *hamza*, which is omitted). The letter *tha'* is indicated by *th*, *dhal* by *dh*, *kha'* by *kh*, and *shin* by *sh*. The definite article is represented throughout as *al-*, with no attempt to indicate elision, either following a vowel or preceding a sun letter. *Ta' marbuta* is indicated by *a*, except in the construct (*idafa*), when it is represented as *at*.

All Arabic words, apart from proper names standing alone, are italicized. When proper names occur within a transliterated phrase, they are italicized and written with the initial letter in lower case.

Abbreviations and Note on Sources

BT	Babylonian Talmud
JT	Jerusalem Talmud
MN	*Moreh nevukhim*
MT	*Mishneh torah*
ShP	*Shemonah perakim*
SM	*Sefer hamitsvot* (Maimonides)

The best available translation of the Babylonian Talmud is that in the Schottenstein edition of the text with English translation. The best available translations of the *Mishneh torah* are those in the Yale Judaica series. At the current writing, the series includes all but Book 1 of the *Mishneh torah*. A translation of that book is found in Moses Maimonides, *Mishneh Torah*, Book 1, ed. and trans. M. Hyamson (New York, 1937). Unless noted otherwise, citations of the *Moreh nevukhim* are from S. Munk's edition of the Arabic original, as republished with minor corrections, and with Munk's pagination indicated, by I. Joel.

Where a particular edition of a work is not specified, any standard edition may be consulted.

When quoting from the Hebrew Bible, I have, as far as possible, used the old Jewish Publication Society translation, which is based on the King James version. In instances where Maimonides understands a verse differently from the JPS translation, I have made adjustments to reflect his reading of the verse.

Except for quotations from the Hebrew Bible, all the translations are my own.

ONE

The Study of Philosophy as a Religious Obligation

He who thinks about God and talks about Him at length without scientific knowledge . . . does not truly talk about God and think about Him. For what he has in his imagination and talks about . . . is merely a figment of his imagination.

MAIMONIDES
Moreh nevukhim, iii. 51

He that believes, without having any reason for believing, may be in love with his own fancies, but neither seeks truth as he ought nor pays the obedience due to his Maker, who would have him use those discerning faculties He has given him, to keep him out of mistake and error.

LOCKE
Essay Concerning Human Understanding, iv. 17. 24

MEDIEVAL JEWISH PHILOSOPHY is sometimes viewed as a response to a threat. The writers known as Jewish philosophers, so the thinking goes, were exposed to Greek philosophy, sensed a challenge to their religious beliefs from that quarter, and manned the ramparts in order to fend it off.

Philosophy was undoubtedly regarded as a threat by many medieval thinkers, Jewish as well as Muslim. In the Jewish milieu, the perceived threat was reinforced by a deep-seated antipathy towards all alien literature that is evidenced in classic rabbinic writings; the antipathy, with noteworthy exceptions made for medicine, and, in recent years, technology, gained strength in medieval rabbinic circles and today remains as potent as ever on the right wing of the religious spectrum. There was, nonetheless, a minority of medieval Jewish thinkers who did not regard philosophy as a menace. They saw it as an opportunity.

Imagine a scenario in which the consensus of mainstream biologists did not dismiss the presence of teleology in nature with contempt—as biologists today dismiss with contempt the strident theory of *intelligent design*—but actually found grounds for endorsing it in, let us say, a Bergsonian version. There would be religious thinkers who would regard the notion of an impersonal force immanent in nature and driving evolution as a danger to their faith. Yet some of equally theistic convictions might think otherwise. Granted that an impersonal and immanent driving force was not what they meant by God, they might nonetheless find that it goes a fair distance in the right direction and that their concept of God is, moreover, enriched and strengthened by the teachings of biology. The medieval Jewish rationalist's reaction to the teachings of philosophy was analogous.

He is open-minded enough to face theoretical issues and address them in an analytic manner yet remains a sincere adherent of the religion of his fathers; the existence of clandestine atheists and agnostics among medieval Jewish and Muslim thinkers, at least among those whose writings have been preserved, is an invention of modern scholars. He shares the mentality of his age in the important sense of lacking a progressive view of human culture: he cannot imagine that people in ancient rabbinic times looked at the universe very differently from the way he does. By the same token, he does not question that one or another school of philosophy had already achieved, definitively, the most accurate description of the universe possible for the unaided human mind.

And the encounter with Greek philosophy bodes no ill for him. On the contrary, he finds that the tools provided by philosophy enable him to reconceptualize key elements in the Jewish religion in a form that is more satisfactory and attractive than non-reflective faith—more satisfactory and attractive precisely from a religious standpoint. He becomes convinced that there is a religious obligation to study philosophy.

The paragraphs that follow do not reproduce the thinking of any single individual but instead weave a composite figure out of a number of writers who dipped their toes in philosophy or plunged in head first. The picture to be limned is pieced together from the writings of Sa'adiah Gaon, Samuel ben Hofni, Hefets ben Yatsliah, Bahya ibn Pakuda, Abraham Ibn Ezra, Joseph Ibn Tsadik, Abraham ibn Daud, Maimonides, David Kimhi, Jacob Anatoli, Shem Tov Falaquera, Isaac Albalag, Joseph Ibn Kaspi, Moses Narboni, David Hakokhavi, Joseph Albo, Elijah Del Medigo, and Obadiah Sforno; Sforno's birth and education barely squeeze him in before the conventional terminus of the Middle Ages. Were we to pursue the subject beyond the Middle Ages, writers could be cited who think along similar lines at least until Isaac Reggio in the nineteenth century. If the subject were extended to Karaites, we could include someone like Aaron ben Elijah.

Most of the authors just named cannot, by a stretch of the imagination, be deemed profound thinkers or genuine philosophers—a circumstance, I would suggest, that strengthens rather than weakens the thesis I am advancing. It therefore is preferable to call them medieval Jewish *rationalists*, and not, narrowly, medieval Jewish *philosophers*.

They were aware of belonging to a select band that the majority in the scholarly community, whom they tended to consider benighted, looked upon with suspicion. As a consequence, their writings often sound a polemic note. One author refers to a real or fictional discussion he had with a man 'who laid claim to being knowledgeable in the science of the Law' and rejected the author's enlightened approach to religion. Another sets his thoughts down in the guise of an imagined debate between an advocate of philosophical study and an opponent of such study; after a few sharp exchanges, the opponent obligingly softens, and the debate ends with the advocate's winning his adversary over. A third writes what he calls an *apologia* in defence of the study of philosophy.[1]

I shall focus on the rationalist approach to the existence of God, the love of God, and the obligation to study the Torah. The writers from whom I draw are not all cut from the same cloth and would not all agree with everything to be said here. There would be demurrals, especially regarding the proposition—to be taken up in the last part of the chapter—that philosophy formed an integral component of the rabbinic curriculum. The composite portrait nevertheless captures the overall attitude of the segment of the medieval Jewish spectrum that qualifies as rationalist.

Our composite thinker is, to begin, sure that an essential, if not the most essential element in the Jewish religion is belief in the existence of a single God. There are recent theologians who maintain that a religion without a deity is not only possible but is an advanced and enlightened form. Whether or not that is the case, medieval thinkers were less sophisticated. It went without saying for them, as for the generality of medieval Jews, that the Jewish religion, and indeed Jewish identity, is meaningless without belief in the existence of God.[2] But what the act of believing consists in, and what belief in the existence of God *should* consist in, was not obvious. Asking the question 'In what does belief consist?' was one outgrowth of the direct or indirect encounter with Greek thought.[3] Once the question was asked, the answer took on a momentum of its own.

[1] Bahya ibn Pakuda, *Ḥovot halevavot* (Kafah), introd., 25; *Ḥovot halevavot* (Ibn Tibbon), introd., 13; Falaquera, *Epistle of the Debate*; Bedersi, *Igeret hitnatselut*.

[2] Cf. e.g. Bahya ibn Pakuda, *Ḥovot halevavot*, 1: 1; Halevi, *Kuzari*, i. 11; *MT*, 'Hilkhot yesodei hatorah', 1: 1; Nahmanides, *Hasagot* on *SM*, positive commandment 1, negative commandment 5; Crescas, *Or hashem*, introd., 3*a*; Sforno, *Or amim*, 412.

[3] Cf. Wolfson, *Philosophy of the Church Fathers*, 112–19.

It seemed clear that belief is not a matter of speech, and adequate belief in the existence of God is more than saying the words 'God exists'. The notion that belief consists solely in uttering words had to be ruled out, because an eccentric school of Muslim theology did in fact make belief a matter exclusively of the 'tongue' and not of the 'heart'.[4] For most men of intelligence, equating belief with uttering a few words would debase it, indeed render it paradoxical: a person may say things to which he gives no heed or that he does not in fact believe.[5]

Our thinker accordingly reasons that belief has to start with a 'conception in the soul' and it presupposes something further. Belief is 'the conviction that what one conceives exists outside the mind as it is conceived in the mind', the conviction that one's conception mirrors reality.[6] Now, a belief consisting in nothing more than a conviction of that sort may obviously be mistaken. A pauper may be convinced without justification that he has money in his pocket; the man who has a mortal enemy may be convinced without justification that his enemy has died.[7] Such beliefs are not merely open to error. They can be fatal. To let religion rest on nothing but an unfounded belief about the existence of God would be to build on sand, and anyone who thinks the subject through will want a sounder foundation for his religion.

For the conviction that God exists to be satisfactory, it must also carry certainty. Belief is certain when 'there exists in the mind no possibility of rejecting it or supposing that things might be contrary [to what the mind believes them to be]'. But when the mind successfully ascertains that things cannot possibly be otherwise than as it conceives them, it not only believes them to be so. It knows them to be so.[8] Analysis leads to the conclusion that belief at its best, belief carrying certainty and not merely certitude, is knowledge. The belief in the existence of God needed for placing religion on a sound basis is *knowledge* of the existence of God.[9]

In the Middle Ages, several ways were recognized whereby knowledge can be acquired,[10] but there were only two ways for ordinary people to acquire knowledge of the existence of a being that lies beyond the reach of the five senses. Ordinary people, who lack access to supernatural and superrational

[4] Ashʿari, *Maqālāt al-islāmiyīn*, 141.

[5] *MN* i. 50. Cf. Bahya ibn Pakuda, *Ḥovot halevavot*, 1: 2.

[6] *MN* i. 50. Cf. Sa'adiah, *Emunot vede'ot*, introd., §4; Bahya ibn Pakuda, *Ḥovot halevavot*, 1: 2; Albo, *Ikarim*, i. 19 (p. 165).

[7] Sa'adiah, *Emunot vede'ot*, introd., §4.

[8] Aristotle, *Posterior Analytics*, 1.2, 71b, 9–16, makes knowing that a thing cannot be other than it is a mark of scientific knowledge.

[9] *MN* i. 50; Ibn Kaspi, *Sefer hamusar*, 140. Cf. Sa'adiah, *Emunot vede'ot*, introd., §4; Bahya ibn Pakuda, *Ḥovot halevavot*, 1: 2.

[10] See Sa'adiah, *Emunot vede'ot*, introd., §5; *Milot hahigayon*, ch. 8; Albo, *Ikarim*, i. 19.

channels, can acquire knowledge of the existence of a being beyond the grasp of sense perception either through a rational demonstration of that being's existence; or through reports of some extraordinary event that confirms the being's existence, when those reports have been transmitted from one unimpeachable source to another until they reach the person who wishes to know.[11]

Placing implicit reliance on trustworthy reports as the route to knowledge of the existence of God was tempting. The reliability of traditions going back to the theophany that took place in the presence of the multitude at Mount Sinai and were then handed down from one trustworthy link in the chain of tradition to another had long been part of the very pith of the Jewish religion. Yet transmitted reports have drawbacks.

To rely on them is to relegate oneself to secondary status, for the believer through reliable reports has someone else attain the primary belief, and he, the recipient of the report, is dependent on that other person and trails after him. There is, moreover, the possibility that ostensibly trustworthy reports are erroneous. Believers on the basis of reliable reports are like 'blind men' walking in single file, 'each with his hand on the shoulder of the man preceding'. If by chance the leader of the line is negligent or if someone in the middle of the line should stumble, all who follow after will go astray. They may even 'fall into a pit'.[12] Reliable reports by themselves therefore do not meet the highest standard. Wholly adequate, that is to say, certain, belief in the existence of God as demanded precisely by religion consists in the ability 'to adduce proofs for [the existence of God] . . . in a theoretical manner and by the use of rational syllogism [*qiyās ʿaqlī*]'—in the ability to frame rational demonstrations of the existence of God.[13]

An adequate belief in the existence of God is, then, a matter not solely of 'the tongue', but also of 'the heart'.[14] It consists not in the conviction that God exists, but in the certainty that He does. To be certain of something to the point where the thing could not be otherwise than it is, is to have knowledge, and the most adequate way of knowing that God exists is by demonstrating

[11] Albo, *Ikarim*, i. 10 (p. 99).

[12] Bahya ibn Pakuda, *Ḥovot halevavot*, 1: 2–3. Cf. *MN* iii. 51; Falaquera, *Epistle of the Debate*, 23–4, 29, 61–2, 65.

[13] Bahya ibn Pakuda, *Ḥovot halevavot*, 1: 2–3. Cf. Samuel ben Hofni, in Sklare, *Samuel ben Ḥofni Gaon*, Arabic section, 16, English section, 230–1; Bahya ibn Pakuda, *Ḥovot halevavot* (Kafah), introd., 25; *Ḥovot halevavot* (Ibn Tibbon), introd., 13; Ibn Ezra, *Commentary on the Pentateuch*, Exod. 20: 2; Joseph Ibn Tsadik, *Olam katan*, 21, 43–4, 60; Abraham ibn Daud, *Emunah ramah*, 47; *MT*, 'Hilkhot yesodei hatorah', 1: 1–6; *MN* i. 50, iii. 51; Anatoli, *Malmad hatalmidim*, 25*b*, 158*b*–159*a*; Falaquera, *Sefer hama'alot*, 34; Ibn Kaspi, *Sefer hamusar*, 139–40; Albalag, *Tikun hade'ot*, 2–3; Kokhavi, *Sefer habatim*, 21–3; Del Medigo, *Beḥinat hadat*, 77; Sforno, *Or amim*, 412. A contrary position is taken by Halevi: see *Kuzari*, i. 13, 25.

[14] Bahya ibn Pakuda, *Ḥovot halevavot*, 1: 2; cf. *MN* i. 50.

His existence rationally. The train of thought, it should be noted, was well established in medieval Islam.[15] It struck a chord with tenth-century Jewish authors who encountered it there, and they imported it into Jewish literature.

How is one to go about framing a demonstration of the existence of God? The answer is again evident: Greek philosophical literature already provides such proofs. They, together with supplementary proofs growing out of adaptations of Greek philosophy, are consequently embraced by thinkers of a rationalist bent. The proofs vary. Although they all reason from the universe to a cause of the universe, some, as will appear in the next chapter, are more sophisticated than others. The upshot, however, is the same. Philosophical proofs are an indispensable component of fully sound *religion*.

Our composite thinker is a sincere adherent of the religion of his fathers and has no intention of constructing a new religion; he considers himself an expositor of the ancient one. He is, moreover, aware of the antipathy towards non-Jewish literature that had struck root in rabbinic circles. Having arrived at his position on a philosophical and scientific faith in God—faith at the level where it is tantamount to knowledge—he asks himself whether the stance he is taking conforms to the teachings of the sacred texts.

As he peruses Scripture he finds that it repeatedly summons mankind to knowledge of the Lord. It instructs readers: 'Know this day . . . that the Lord is God' (Deut. 4: 39). 'Know ye that the Lord He is God; it is He that hath made us, and we are His' (Ps. 100: 3). David instructed his heir: 'Solomon my son, know thou the God of thy father and serve Him [with a whole heart and a willing soul]' (1 Chr. 28: 9). The prophets looked forward to a time when 'the earth shall be full of the knowledge of the Lord, as the waters cover the sea' (Isa. 11: 9), a time when 'they shall all know me, from the least of them unto the greatest of them, saith the Lord' (Jer. 31: 34). One biblical verse, as read in the Middle Ages, explicitly teaches: 'Glory only in this, in *intellectual* understanding and knowledge' of God (Jer. 9: 23).[16] Other verses echo the theme.[17]

[15] See Rosenthal, *Knowledge Triumphant*, 29–30, 98–108; Hourani, *Islamic Rationalism*, 17–18; and especially the wealth of material cited in Frank, 'Knowledge and *Taqlīd*'.

[16] *Haskel vayado'a oti*; *sekhel* had become the established term for intellect.

[17] One or more of the verses quoted here are cited in order to make the point by Sa'adiah, *Emunot vede'ot*, introd., §2; ch. 3, §1; Samuel ben Hofni, in Sklare, *Samuel ben Ḥofni Gaon*, Arabic section, 14; English section, 225; Hefets ben Yatsliah, *Book of Precepts*, 31, 35; Bahya ibn Pakuda, *Ḥovot halevavot*, 1: 3; Ibn Ezra, *Yesod mora*, ch. 1, pp. 83–4; Joseph Ibn Tsadik, *Olam katan*, 1: 21; Abraham ibn Daud, *Emunah ramah*, 46; *MT*, 'Hilkhot melakhim', 12: 4–5; *MN* iii. 51 (124*b*–125*a*); Anatoli, *Malmad hatalmidim*, 17*a*, 158*b*; Falaquera, *Epistle of the Debate*, 34, 69; Kokhavi, *Sefer habatim*, 23; Del Medigo, *Beḥinat hadat*, 76; Sforno, *Or amim*, 412, 418. Halevi, *Kuzari*, v. 21, refers to, and rejects, a Karaite interpretation of the verse from Chronicles as commanding study of philosophy. Mendelssohn, *Jerusalem*, 71, and Krochmal, *Moreh nevukhei hazeman*, 313–15, still cite verses of this sort as mandating rational knowledge of God.

The inference is plain. Scripture exhorts mankind to know the Lord, and analysis has shown that the best path to knowledge of the existence of God is through scientific and philosophical demonstration. The Bible corroborates the obligation to demonstrate the existence of God rationally.

Support was forthcoming from the aggadic branch of rabbinic literature as well. There the patriarch Abraham is pictured as having discovered the existence of God through a process of enquiry. Abraham was like a wayfarer who sees a castle lit up and asks: 'Can the castle have no governor?'; like the wayfarer, he asked: 'Can the world have no governor?' And only after initiating the enquiry was he vouchsafed converse with the deity.[18] If one approaches the aggadic passage persuaded that establishing the existence of God through enquiry means mastering a rational proof, the conclusion is inescapable. More than a millennium before the birth of philosophy among the Greeks, the father of the Jewish people already framed a demonstration of the existence of God.[19]

Midrashic compilations that circulated in the Middle Ages add details. One day, the compilations relate, Abraham took note of the sun's beneficial effects and prayed to it. When the sun set and thereby revealed that it is not the sole governor of the world, Abraham directed his prayers to the moon. When the moon set and revealed that it too is not the sole governor of the world, he concluded that the heavenly bodies have 'a master above them' and he began to worship the invisible being transcending the heavens who is the true deity.[20] Although the preserved Hebrew sources are late, the story itself is fairly early, for versions appear in Jubilees, Philo, and the Qur'an.[21]

To someone familiar with Greek philosophy, the implication is clear. Abraham not only discovered the existence of God, but was led to that discovery by observing the movements of the heavenly bodies. When translated from picturesque to scientific language, the story tells us that Abraham contemplated the movements of the heavens, asked himself 'How can it be possible for the celestial sphere to move continually without a mover?', and concluded that there 'exists one God who moves the sphere and created everything'. In other words, he demonstrated the existence of God from the motion of the celestial spheres and framed the very proof that would be framed—rediscovered—by

[18] *Genesis Rabbah* 39: 1.

[19] Ibn Tsadik, *Olam katan*, 21; Judah ben Barzilai, *Commentary on Sefer yetsirah*, 2–3. Halevi, *Kuzari*, iv. 27, gives the Abraham story a different twist.

[20] Jellinek, *Beit hamidrash*, vol. ii, pp. xxxiv, 118; *Midrash hagadol*, Genesis, 204–5, 210 (apparently influenced by Maimonides); *Sefer hayashar*, 68; Ginzberg, *Legends of the Jews*, v. 210. Cf. McCarthy, *Theology of Al-Ash'arī*, 11.

[21] Jubilees 12: 16–18; Philo, *De Abrahamo*, §§70–8; Qur'an, 6: 76–80.

Aristotle centuries later.[22] To place belief in the existence of God on a rational foundation with the help of Greek philosophy is to retrace the path trod by the father of the Israelite nation.

The argument I have been making, that rationalists adduced philosophical proofs of the existence of God for purely religious reasons, can be extended to the unity and incorporeality of God. Medieval Jews did not have the slightest doubt that the Jewish religion rests on belief not just in the existence of God but also in a single God. An adequate belief in the unity of God must consist in true and certain knowledge; such knowledge rests on the ability to demonstrate the unity of God; and the requisite demonstrations are furnished by philosophy.[23]

It had moreover become established among rationalists and non-rationalists alike that the Jewish religion presupposes the incorporeality of God, though one would be hard put to unearth the concept of incorporeality anywhere in Scripture or ancient rabbinic literature;[24] the incorporeality of God is in fact the most significant legacy bequeathed by medieval philosophy to the Jewish religion. The train of reasoning that we have been following applies to incorporeality too, and the requisite demonstrations of the incorporeality of God are again supplied by the philosophical literature.[25]

Philosophy, in short, sustains the three legs on which a complete belief in the existence of God rests: His existence, unity, and incorporeality.

The Hebrew Bible repeatedly instructs its adherents to 'love the Lord', and the obligation to love God pervades rabbinic religion and the liturgy. When attempts to enumerate the 613 God-given commandments began to be made, love of God was regularly included among the positive commandments. Unlike Spinoza, the medieval rationalist whom we are envisaging has little to say about the meaning of love;[26] he takes it for granted. Yet his analysis of having God as the object of love leads him in a direction that is pertinent for us.

He posits that a person cannot love something unknown. The religious

[22] *MT*, 'Hilkhot avodah zarah', 1: 3; Falaquera, *Epistle of the Debate*, 32–3, 68; Ibn Kaspi, *Sefer hamusar*, 142–3; Abba Mari, *Minḥat kenaot*, 251–3 (pointed out by G. Freudenthal). Averroes too understood that Abraham was a philosopher. See *On the Harmony of Religion and Philosophy*, 45; *Tafsīr mā baʿda al-ṭabīʿa*, 1634; *Tahāfut al-tahāfut*, 416. For Aristotle's proof from motion, see *Physics*, 8; *MN* ii. 1.

[23] Bahya ibn Pakuda, *Ḥovot halevavot*, 1: 2; Abraham ibn Daud, *Emunah ramah*, 47, 49; *MT*, 'Hilkhot yesodei hatorah', 1: 7; *MN* i. 50; Anatoli, *Malmad hatalmidim*, 158*b*; Sforno, *Or amim*, 414. Cf. Wolfson, *Studies in the History of Philosophy and Religion*, ii. 433–57.

[24] Wolfson, *Philo*, ii. 152. For non-philosophers and critics of philosophy, see Eleazar of Worms, *Hasod, hayiḥud, veha'emunah*, 143; Halevi, *Kuzari*, i. 89; Crescas, *Or hashem*, i. 3: 6.

[25] *MT*, 'Hilkhot yesodei hatorah', 1: 7–8; Sforno, *Or amim*, 414.

[26] Vajda, *L'Amour de Dieu*, 165, quotes a quasi-definition from Jacob Anatoli: 'the approach of the minds of two individuals to one another'.

commandment to love God 'includes . . . knowledge; for no one can experience enormous love [such as that due the deity] without knowing the object of his love.' 'Love of God establishes itself in a man's heart . . . only through the knowledge that he has of Him'.[27]

The proposition is far-reaching. To start, it dictates that the existence of God, the object of love, be known, since sensible people do not love things that they do not know exist. The obligation to love thus joins with the obligation to believe; it too mandates knowledge, and not merely a conviction, of the existence of God. Yet knowing that something exists is plainly not enough. The proposed object of love must be known to be of a kind that deserves and inspires love, and that requirement opens into a wide-ranging cognitive enterprise.

It was a commonplace among philosophers in the Middle Ages that the essence of God, as distinct from His existence, is unknowable. The breadth of knowledge of God that will serve as a basis for love must consequently be acquired indirectly. Rather than trying to do the impossible and comprehend God's essence, one must look at the manner in which His essence manifests itself, and ascertain what that reveals about Him.

A subsidiary procedure is to 'contemplate and examine the commands' that God promulgates;[28] from what He commands and hence wants, man can get a notion of the sort of being He is. God's commands are learned, of course, through the reliable chain of transmission beginning with the reception and recording of the word of God by Moses.

But the primary procedure for creating a basis for love of God is through contemplating God's 'actions'.[29] Although God possesses no characteristics distinct from His unitary essence, and His essence is beyond man's grasp, an understanding of what He does affords a glimpse of what He is; and knowing what He is, to the extent that this is possible, arouses love: the obligation to love God requires man to 'know His wondrous attributes and His actions', all with the realization that the 'attributes are known only through the relationship of His actions to Him'; that is to say, they are what are termed attributes of action.[30] 'When one knows God's attributes and actions, an indescribable love is imprinted in one's heart.' The human subject is flooded with supreme 'pleasure'. By contemplating the infinite wisdom manifested in what God has made, a person 'immediately loves . . . God and experiences a powerful desire

27 Ibn Daud, *Emunah ramah*, 100; *MT*, 'Hilkhot teshuvah', 10: 6. Cf. Sa'adiah, *Emunot vede'ot*, 2: 13; Falaquera, *Sefer hama'alot*, 34; Kokhavi, *Sefer habatim*, 51; Sforno, *Or amim*, 412.

28 *SM*, positive commandment 3.

29 *SM*, positive commandment 3.

30 Ibn Ezra, *Commentary on the Pentateuch*, Exod. 31: 18; Abraham ibn Daud, *Emunah ramah*, 100; *MN* i. 54.

to know Him'; knowledge leading to love of God breeds a thirst for additional knowledge.[31]

Since God has been shown to be the author of the entire universe, everything that can be learned about the universe expands knowledge of God's actions, adds to man's glimpse of God, and contributes to love of God. 'When a man contemplates God's handiwork and His great, marvellous creatures, when he discerns God's infinite wisdom in them . . . man immediately loves, praises, and exalts God'.[32] To accomplish the task, recourse must be had to natural science, and there are degrees. 'Knowledge and love go hand in hand; when there is less of the first, there is less of the second, and when there is more, there is more. Consequently, a man should, as far as humanly possible, devote himself to exercising his intellect in mastery of the sciences . . . that lead to knowledge of God.'[33] The greater a person's mastery of the natural sciences, the greater his knowledge of the kind of being the author of nature is and the greater his love.

Scriptural support was forthcoming too, for the Bible enjoins: 'Thou shalt love the Lord thy God with all thy heart and all thy soul' (Deut. 6: 5). Since the heart was generally understood to be a metonym for the human intellect,[34] an obvious reading of the verse suggested itself. The scriptural injunction to love God with 'all thy heart' requires man to ground his love of God in 'knowledge of the entire universe . . . and in discerning God's wisdom in it'.[35]

Rational love of God—what Spinoza later would call intellectual love of God[36]—thus goes several strides beyond rational faith: it mandates scientific knowledge not only of God's existence but also of the kind of being He is, and the mandate is satisfied by the broadest possible scientific knowledge of the universe. Grounding love of God in scientific knowledge did not, of course, satisfy the religious needs of every medieval Jewish thinker. But the notion, for those who subscribed to it, arose out of an analysis of the religious precept to love God and served a religious end, and there is little reason to doubt that scriptural support was adduced ingenuously.[37]

[31] Ibn Daud, *Emunah ramah*, 100; Ibn Ezra, *Commentary on the Pentateuch*, Exod. 31: 18; *SM*, positive commandment 3; *MT*, 'Hilkhot yesodei hatorah', 2: 2.

[32] *MT*, 'Hilkhot yesodei hatorah', 2: 2; Ibn Ezra, *Commentary on the Pentateuch*, Exod. 31: 18.

[33] *MT*, 'Hilkhot teshuvah', 10: 6. Cf. *MN* iii. 51 (125*a*); iii. 52, (130*b*); Albo, *Ikarim*, iii. 35 (p. 318).

[34] Ibn Ezra, *Commentary on the Pentateuch*, Deut. 6: 5; *MN* i. 39; Kokhavi, *Sefer habatim*, 51.

[35] *MN* iii. 28. Cf. Sa'adiah, *Emunot vede'ot*, 2: 13; Ibn Ezra, *Commentary on the Pentateuch*, Deut. 6: 5; Ibn Daud, *Emunah ramah*, 46, 100; *SM*, positive commandment 3; *MT*, 'Hilkhot yesodei hatorah', 2: 2; 'Hilkhot teshuvah', 10: 6.

[36] Spinoza, *Ethics* v, propositions 32–3. Spinoza too associates intellectual love of God with the highest pleasure.

[37] Support was also adduced from the literature of the Oral Law. Cf. Maimonides' interpretation of the rabbinic description of Abraham's love of God, *SM*, positive commandment 3.

Jewish texts typically link love of God with fear, or awe, of God, and the rationalist construes fear of God as a lesser facet of love. We saw that recognition of the infinite wisdom present in God's marvellous handiwork leads man to love of God. When man does not focus immediately on the divine wisdom reflected in God's creatures but instead 'takes account of the creatures themselves, he immediately recoils, is struck with awe and fear, and recognizes that he is a small, insignificant, obscure creature' standing in the presence of the creator. That is awe in the presence of God.[38]

Genuine worship likewise presupposes an 'intellectual conception', that is, scientific knowledge, of 'God and His actions'. One can scarcely worship what one does not know,[39] and the greater one's knowledge, the 'greater the worship'. A person who, by contrast, 'thinks about God and talks about Him at length without scientific knowledge, following nothing but some imaginative concept [of God] or a belief received on the authority of someone else, such a person in my view is . . . not only distant [from God]; he does not truly talk about God and think about Him at all'. What he talks about 'corresponds to nothing whatsoever that exists and is merely a figment of his imagination'.[40] The unenlightened, who lack the benefit of philosophy and science, do not worship God. They worship something that their imagination has fabricated.

The obligation to study the Torah is prescribed by Scripture, and the classic rabbinic texts, although not monolithic, repeatedly elevate study of the Written and Oral Torah into the paramount human activity.[41] The other side of the coin is the antipathy of rabbinic texts towards other subjects of study, one of which is called *higayon* (a term that in the Middle Ages came to mean *logic*) and another, 'Greek wisdom'.[42] The concern was not so much the danger of heretical opinions as time: since it is axiomatic that all available time should be devoted to God's word, study of other subjects becomes a misuse of the most precious human resource.[43] The commitment to philosophy accordingly had to be squared with the obligation to study only the double Torah.

In the Middle Ages, as in the classic rabbinic period, more attention was

[38] *MT*, 'Hilkhot yesodei hatorah', 2: 2. Cf. Sa'adiah, *Emunot vede'ot*, 2: 13; Falaquera, *Sefer hama'alot*, 37; Sforno, *Or amim*, 412.

[39] Kimhi, *Commentary on Hosea*, 6: 3.

[40] *MN* iii. 51 (124*a*–*b*). Cf. Isaac Israeli in Altmann and Stern, *Isaac Israeli*, 124; Sa'adiah, *Emunot vede'ot*, 2: 13; Bahya ibn Pakuda, *Ḥovot halevavot* (Kafah), 1: 2 (p. 48), 3: 3; *Ḥovot halevavot* (Ibn Tibbon), 1: 2 (pp. 27–8); Ibn Tsadik, *Olam katan*, 21 (repeating the language of *Ḥovot halevavot*, 1: 2), 43–4.

[41] e.g. Mishnah *Ḥag.* 1: 6; *Avot* 3: 18.

[42] Mishnah *Sot.* 9: 14; BT *Ber.* 28*b*; *BK* 82*b*–83*a*. For the general attitude of medieval talmudists, see Isaac ben Sheshet, *Responsa*, no. 45; Moses Isserles' gloss on Jacob ben Asher, *Arba'ah turim*, 'Yoreh de'ah', no. 246, n. 9; For interpretations of the prohibitions in a manner sympathetic to the study of philosophy, see Maimonides, *Commentary on the Mishnah*, *Sot.* 9: 14 (15); Lieberman, *Hellenism in Jewish Palestine*, 100–5.

[43] Ibid. 100–1.

lavished on the Oral Torah than on the Written, and study of the Oral Torah primarily meant mastering the intricacies of marriage regulations, torts, ritual impurity, and the like.[44] Yet common sense would suggest that additional subjects, especially the nature of God and His relationship to the world, are no less deserving of attention.[45] It was not only rationalists who were of that opinion. The assumption that knowledge of God and His manifestations has at least the religious value of immersing oneself in ritual and civil law, even God-given ritual and civil law, animates kabbalah as well.

The classic sources themselves supply the resolution. While they repeatedly stress that only the Torah is worthy of study, they—it is often forgotten—include certain theological subjects in their Oral Law. Three terms in particular come into play: *pardes*, the supernal 'pleasure garden'; *ma'aseh vereshit*, 'the account of creation'; and *ma'aseh merkavah*, 'the account of the chariot'.

A well-known talmudic anecdote tells of four rabbinic scholars who 'entered the pleasure garden [*pardes*]'. Entry into the pleasure garden has commonly been taken to be a dramatic depiction of initiation into an esoteric doctrine relating to the supernal realm,[46] although the content of the doctrine was then and remains today a riddle wrapped in a mystery. The anecdote does disclose that dangers lurked, as it were, in the garden, for three of the four men who entered were overwhelmed by what they beheld. Rabbi Akiva, the fourth, nevertheless 'came out in peace', or, in another version, 'descended in peace'—in other words, he suffered no harm from exposure to the esoteric doctrine, whatever it was.[47]

Rabbi Akiva's role and the literary contexts in which the anecdote appears make clear that the pleasure garden, albeit sensitive and reserved for persons who are properly qualified, is of the utmost value. Medieval philosophers, for their part, regarded the metaphysical, and to some extent the physical, branches of philosophy as sensitive and reserved for persons who are properly qualified.[48] It was a small jump to the conclusion that physical science and metaphysics 'are what the ancient scholars call the pleasure garden'.[49] The rabbinic sources do not expressly classify the garden as a formal subject of

[44] Cf. BT *Kid.* 30*a*, and Rabbenu Tam's comment.

[45] Bahya ibn Pakuda, *Ḥovot halevavot* (Kafah), introd., 23, 3: 4 (p. 150); *Ḥovot halevavot* (Ibn Tibbon), introd., 12, 3: 4 (p. 93); Ibn Ezra, *Yesod mora*, ch. 1, p. 83; Ibn Daud, *Emunah ramah*, 46; Maimonides, *Commentary on the Mishnah*, *Ber.* 9: 7; *MN* iii. 51. I am not familiar with a medieval argument to the effect that studying God-given ritual and civil law will permit inferences about the nature of the divine legislator.

[46] Rabenu Hananel on BT *Ḥag.* 14*b*; Nathan ben Jehiel, *Arukh hashalem*, s.v. *avnei shayish*.

[47] BT *Ḥag.* 14*b*, and parallels.

[48] Cf. *MN*, introd. Averroes took a similar position; see *Kitāb al-kashf*, 27; *Tahāfut al-tahāfut*, 527–8.

[49] *MT*, 'Hilkhot yesodei hatorah', 4: 13. Cf. Ibn Daud, *Emunah ramah*, 2; Albalag, *Tikun hade'ot*,

study, but our rationalist determines that 'the topics called the pleasure garden'—the study of physics and metaphysics—'fall under the subheading of [rabbinic study known as] *talmud*'.[50]

Analysis of the *account of creation* and the *account of the chariot* leads to a similar result. In the strict sense, the account of creation is the story of creation in the book of Genesis and the account of the chariot, the vision of a celestial chariot in the book of Ezekiel. But both the creation story and Ezekiel's chariot attracted esoteric exegesis, and it is sometimes the rabbinic exegeses of the two scriptural sections, not the sections themselves, that are known as the account of creation and account of the chariot. The rabbinic sources expressly treat the esoteric exegeses as part of the Oral Torah, and a noteworthy passage in the Babylonian Talmud characterizes the account of the chariot as 'a great matter', in contrast to talmudic legal disputations, which it characterizes as 'a small matter'.[51]

Besides emphasizing that only the elite should be initiated into the exegesis of the two accounts,[52] surviving rabbinic texts say little about it.[53] It is another riddle, and for that reason and because of its sensitivity, it has been almost entirely ignored by talmudic students through the centuries. There was again, however, an obvious course for a rationalist interpretation to take: the creation story in Genesis describes the stages in the fashioning of the world inhabited by man, and it begins with references to earth, water, and wind. They sound strikingly like three of the four basic elements in Aristotelian physics, and with a little ingenuity, a reference to fire, the fourth element, can likewise be found in the opening verses of Genesis.[54] The account of the chariot in the book of Ezekiel depicts the supernal realm, giving a good deal of attention to the wheels that support the chariot and to the 'living creatures' that accompany the wheels. It did not take much imagination to connect the wheels and living beings with the celestial spheres and the incorporeal intelligences that maintain the spheres in motion.[55]

36; Twersky, 'Some Non-Halakic Aspects of the *Mishneh Torah*', 111. Katz, *Divine Law in Human Hands*, 73, points out that Moses Cordovero, using a different exegetical tactic, incorporates kabbalistic study into the rabbinic curriculum.

[50] *MT*, 'Hilkhot talmud torah', 1: 11–12. Cf. Anatoli, *Malmad hatalmidim*, unpaginated introd., pp. 10–11.

[51] BT *Suk.* 28*a* and *BB* 134*a*.

[52] Mishnah *Ḥag.* 2: 1.

[53] What they do say is so anticlimactic that it is hard to see what the to-do was about. For example, Ezek. 1: 4 reads: 'I looked, and behold . . . the colour of electrum [came] out of the midst of the fire.' BT *Ḥag.* 13*a* represents electrum, *ḥashmal*, as so sensitive a term that a young boy who deciphered it was consumed by fire. BT *Ḥag.* 13*b* then quotes a *baraita* that interprets *ḥashmal* as meaning: sometimes silent (*ḥash*) and sometimes talking (*mal*). That is to say, the angels are silent when speech issues from God's mouth and talk when speech does not issue from His mouth.

[54] *MN* ii. 30.

[55] Kimhi, *Commentary on Ezekiel*, appendix. Cf. Ibn Daud, *Emunah ramah*, 43; *MT*, 'Hilkhot yesodei hatorah', 2: 11–12. Maimonides reads the Aramaic translation of Ezekiel as identifying the

Now, a fully developed and systematic description of the physical universe is what is known as the science of physics; and a fully developed and systematic description of the structure of the supernal realm is what is known as metaphysics.[56] Another small jump leads to the conclusion that the rabbinic exegesis of the account of creation was the ancient rabbis' version of the science of physics, and the rabbinic exegesis of the account of the chariot, their version of the science of metaphysics.[57] The native formulations have unfortunately been lost with the passage of time, but a reliable science of physics and metaphysics, constructed by unaided human reason, is available. It is called philosophy.

Philosophy thus restores the lost parts of the Oral Torah that relate to the account of creation and account of the chariot. Far from falling under restrictions on study, philosophy astonishingly turns out to be a central part of the full Torah curriculum. By replacing the rabbinic account of the chariot, which is a 'great matter', philosophy in fact stands higher in the Torah curriculum than the dialectical give-and-take of the Babylonian Talmud, which is merely a 'small matter'.[58]

Through furnishing ostensibly certain knowledge of the existence, unity, and incorporeality of God, through teaching how truly to love, fear, and worship God, and through filling a gap in the study of the divine Law, philosophy enables the medieval rationalist to establish, or, as he sees it, to re-establish, a much more satisfactory form of religion than the form in which his non-reflective co-religionists are mired. The next chapter will show how philosophy was called upon for aid in fulfilling the first two positive commandments that God was believed to have given to Moses and Israel at Sinai.

wheels with the celestial spheres, but in the *MN* he prefers to take the four wheels as an allusion to the four elements underlying all existence in the lower world, and the living creatures as symbols of the spheres. See *MN* iii. 2, 4.

[56] To be more precise, one of the divisions of metaphysics.

[57] Maimonides, *Commentary on Mishnah*, *Ḥag.* 2: 1; *MT*, 'Hilkhot yesodei hatorah', 2: 11, 4: 13; *MN*, introd., 3*b*. Cf. the implication in Ibn Ezra, *Yesod mora*, ch. 10; *Commentary on the Pentateuch*, Gen. 3: 23; the allusion to BT *Suk.* 28*a* in Ibn Daud, *Emunah ramah*, 2; Anatoli, *Malmad hatalmidim*, unpaginated introd., pp. 10–11; Meiri, *Ḥidushim*, BT *Ḥag.* 11*b*; Moses Narboni, introd. to commentary on *MN*, in Hayoun, *Mosheh Narboni*, 125. Cf. Heschel, *Heavenly Torah*, pp. xxi–xxiii; Twersky, 'Some Non-Halakhic Aspects of the *Mishneh Torah*', 112–16.

[58] See also Bahya ibn Pakuda, *Ḥovot halevavot* (Kafah), introd., 13–14; *Ḥovot halevavot* (Ibn Tibbon), introd., 6–7; Ibn Ezra, *Yesod mora*, ch. 1, p. 83; id., *Commentary on Proverbs*, 9: 10; Anatoli, *Malmad hatalmidim*, unpaginated introd., pp. 10–11.

TWO

The First Two Positive Divine Commandments

The first of the positive commandments is to know that God exists.

MAIMONIDES
Mishneh torah, introduction, list of commandments

1. The 613 Commandments

THERE ARE DIVERSE WAYS of telling the story of the 613 commandments believed to have been given to Moses at Sinai, but they all start from the same point. The starting-point is a dictum cited by the Babylonian Talmud in the name of Rabbi Simlai, a Palestinian rabbi active about the end of the third and beginning of the fourth centuries. He was not a member of the circle that wielded authority in the ritual and legal sphere.

According to the printed editions of the Babylonian Talmud, 'Rabbi Simlai taught [*darash*]: 613 commandments were stated to Moses: 365 negative commandments, paralleling the number of days of the [solar] year, and 248 positive commandments, paralleling the number of discrete segments [*avarim*] in [the body of] a human being.'[1] No manuscript variants are known to me, but even without them it is easy to see that the talmudic dictum took different forms. The standard edition of *Ein ya'akov*, the sixteenth-century work that extracts all of the aggadic—that is to say, non-legal—material from the Babylonian Talmud, makes a small addition. In place of the words '613 commandments were stated to Moses', it reads: '613 commandments were stated to Moses at Sinai', and that is the form in which Maimonides and Nahmanides quote the dictum.[2] *Sefer halakhot gedolot* quotes Rabbi Simlai as having taught that '*Israel* were commanded regarding 613 commandments'[3] and at another spot it

[1] BT *Mak.* 23*b*.

[2] *SM* (Kafah), rule 1, p. 9; *SM* (Heller), p. 5 n. 1. Nahmanides, *Hasagot*, rule 1, p. 13.

[3] *Halakhot gedolot* (Traub), introd., 2*b*; *Halakhot gedolot* (N. Hildesheimer), iii, appendix, p. 13, apparatus.

refers, perhaps now speaking in its own voice and not quoting, to '613 commandments that Israel received at Sinai'.[4]

A good deal is left open. It is unclear whether we are being informed that each and every one of the 613 commandments is explicit in the Written Torah or whether some can only be known thanks to the enhancement of the Written Torah through the Oral Torah. It is not even clear whether we are to understand that all 613 were preserved and handed down to posterity. The Babylonian Talmud in one place speaks of hundreds or even thousands of *halakhot* and dialectical inferences that were lost when Moses died.[5] If matters are considered from wholly within the rabbinic framework, it is thus conceivable that many of the 613 commandments have disappeared forever.

No mention of, or allusion to, 613 commandments received by Moses, or by the people of Israel, is made in the Mishnah. None is found in the body of Mishnah-style material known as the Tosefta. The midrashic compilation *Mekhilta*, which is understood to belong to the same period as the Mishnah and Tosefta, contains a passage explaining why God did not give the Torah to the gentiles. In the printed editions, the passage reads: Inasmuch as the gentiles proved themselves incapable of observing even the seven commandments incumbent on descendants of Noah, '*a fortiori* [will they be incapable of observing] the 613 commandments'. The manuscripts have a different reading, however, one that Horovitz's critical edition of the *Mekhilta* deems preferable. It states: '*a fortiori* [will they be incapable of observing] *all* the commandments of the Torah'. No number is given.[6]

The midrashic compilation *Sifrei* on Deuteronomy, which belongs to the same period, raises the question why Scripture stresses so strongly that man must 'be *steadfast* in not eating blood' despite the commandment's being extremely easy to observe. In some versions of *Sifrei*, refraining from eating blood is characterized as the easiest of the '365 negative commandments of the Torah', but the best versions characterize it as the easiest of the '300 positive commandments'.[7] Perhaps someone in the line of transmission thought it awkward to classify the instruction *not* to eat blood as a positive, rather than a negative, commandment and emended the text.

Works from the mishnaic period—the Mishnah, the Tosefta, midrashic compilations, including the best versions of *Mekhilta* and *Sifrei*—do not, then, know the number 613.

Besides the passage recorded in Rabbi Simlai's name, three other passages

[4] *Halakhot gedolot* (Traub), introd., 3*b*; *Halakhot gedolot* (N. Hildesheimer), iii, appendix, p. 112 (with slight variations).

[5] BT *Tem.* 15*b*–16*a*.

[6] *Mekhilta de rabi yishma'el*, 'Baḥodesh' §5, p. 222.

[7] *Sifrei on Deuteronomy*, §76, p. 141, and note.

in the Babylonian Talmud—two of which occur twice—refer to 613 commandments, and in each instance the number is treated as something commonly known.[8] The three passages are non-halakhic in character and none carries an attribution to a rabbinic figure, which may be a sign that they belong to the final redaction of the Babylonian Talmud. References to 613 commandments are found in *Genesis Rabbah*,[9] which belongs roughly to the period when the Babylonian Talmud was being redacted, as well as in aggadic midrashic compilations that are still later.[10] Neither the Babylonian Talmud nor the midrashic works make any effort to identify and list the 613 commandments nor, with the exception of two key commandments to be discussed below, do they suggest in any way what they might comprise.

The Jerusalem Talmud knows nothing of the number 613. What is particularly significant, one of the passages where the Babylonian Talmud speaks of 613 commandments occurs almost verbatim in the Jerusalem Talmud, but without the critical words '613 commandments'.[11] It looks suspiciously as if the passage did not originally have those words, which were introduced at one of the stages in the transmission and redaction of the Babylonian Talmud.

It looks, indeed, very much as if Rabbi Simlai, or the tradition reported in his name, did not arrive at the figure 613 empirically and a posteriori, so to speak; that he—or it—did not painstakingly seek out each and every commandment communicated by God to Moses, count them, and discover that they come to 613. The figure appears to have been fixed a priori, through adding the number of segments of the human body to the number of days in the solar year; tractate *Oholot* of the Mishnah enumerates 248 segments in the human body.[12] The object of the dictum would be hortative. Each Jew, the preacher would be exhorting his listeners or readers, must scrupulously observe God's prohibitions every day of the year. Each must mobilize every inch of his body in the fulfilment of God's positive commands. Several medieval Jewish writers expressed reservations as to whether the commandments given by God to Moses amount to exactly 613, and two—Moses Nahmanides and Simon ben Tsemah Duran—carried impeccable scholarly credentials.[13] The number 613 nevertheless became ingrained in the Jewish

[8] BT *Shab.* 87*a*; *Yev.* 47*b*, 62*a* (which is identical to BT *Shab.* 87*a*); *Ned.* 25*a*; *Shev.* 29*a* (which is essentially identical to BT *Ned.* 25*a*).

[9] *Genesis Rabbah* 24: 5.

[10] See *Yefeh einayim* on BT *Mak.* 23*b*; Rabinowitz, *Taryag*, 40.

[11] The passage in BT *Shab.* 87*a*, and *Yev.* 62*a* which refers to the 613 commandments, appears in JT *Ta'an.* 4: 8, 68*c* without the number.

[12] Mishnah *Ohol.* 1: 8.

[13] Judah ibn Balam, on Deut. 30: 2, in Fuchs, *Studien über Abu Zakaria Jachja Ibn Bal'ām*, p. xxiii (pointed out by Halper in his introduction to Hefets ben Yatsliah, *Book of Precepts*, 7); Bahya ibn Pakuda, as quoted below. Ibn Ezra, *Yesod mora*, ch. 2, p. 92 (quoting Ps. 119: 96, which was a key proof text for Bahya); Nahmanides, *Hasagot*, rule 1 (pp. 13–16); Duran, *Zohar rakia*, 59*a*.

consciousness, and the notion of 613 divine commandments has been axiomatic in traditional Jewish circles until today.[14]

Immediately after recording the dictum of Rabbi Simlai, the Babylonian Talmud supports it with a proof text cited in the name of Rav Hamnuna; he could be Hamnuna II, a Babylonian teacher who was more or less contemporaneous with Rabbi Simlai and who enjoyed authority in both halakhah and aggadah, in both the legal and non-legal areas.[15] The pertinent passage as it appeared in the talmudic text used by Maimonides reads: 'Rav Hamnuna said: What is the scriptural proof [for the number 613? The answer:] "Moses commanded us *torah*, an inheritance of the congregation of Jacob". But is that the numerical value of [the letters in the word] *torah*? The numerical value of *torah* is 611.' To which the solution is given: 'They heard "I am the Lord thy God [who brought thee out of the land of Egypt]" and "Thou shalt have no [other gods before Me]" from God's mouth.'[16] The first person pronouns in the two opening sentences of the Decalogue—'I am the Lord your God', 'Thou shalt have no other gods before Me'—as well as in the following few verses, which expand on the prohibition against having other gods, show that God Himself was speaking. When the two sentences that the people of Israel heard directly from God's mouth are added to the 611 commandments represented by the numerical value of the letters in the word *torah* and received by Moses, we arrive at the desired sum of 613.

The proposition that Moses or Israel received exactly 613 commandments from God naturally led to attempts to identify them. What seems to be the oldest preserved attempt is incorporated into the homiletic introduction to *Sefer halakhot gedolot*, an influential code of Jewish law composed in Iraq and attributed to a little-known ninth-century rabbinic scholar, Simon Kayara.[17]

[14] Much of the foregoing owes a debt to Perla, *Sefer hamitsvot*, 1: 5–7, and Urbach, *Sages*, 342–4. Urbach examined the same rabbinic sources as Perla but arrived at a different, and to my mind the correct, conclusion, namely, that no ancient tradition prior to the Babylonian Talmud sets the number of commandments given to Moses or Israel at 613.

[15] Bacher, *Die Aggada der babylonischen Amoräer*, 73–4.

[16] BT *Mak.* 23*b*–24*a*, as quoted in *Halakhot gedolot* (Traub), introd., 2*b*; Hefets ben Yatsliah, 'New Extracts' (Heb.), 14; *SM*, positive commandment 1; Nahmanides, *Hasagot*, rule 1 (p. 13) (with a slight variation); and Crescas, *Or hashem*, 3*a* (with the same slight variation). In the standard printed editions of the Talmud, the passage is constructed a little differently, but the outcome is the same. The biblical verses are Deut. 33: 4 and Exod. 20: 2–3 (= Deut. 5: 6–7). BT *Hor.* 8*a* also states that 'I am the Lord your God' and 'Thou shalt have no [other gods before Me]' were heard directly from God's mouth, but it makes no mention of 613 commandments.

[17] It has, however, been argued that the commandments were enumerated in liturgical pieces preceding *Halakhot gedolot*; see Guttmann, *Beḥinat hamitsvot*, 9–10. The argument is most plausible in the case of the composition beginning with the words *Atah hinḥalta torah le'amekha*, which has a primitive look to it in both organization and style (see n. 23 below).

Halakhot gedolot, as already seen, states that '*Israel* were commanded regarding 613 commandments'.[18]

The list in *Halakhot gedolot* reveals a swarm of problems. In place of the clear-cut division of divine commandments into two categories, the positive and the negative, as Rabbi Simlai's dictum would require, *Halakhot gedolot* chooses a clumsy arrangement. It distinguishes four categories: infringements subject to the several classes of death penalties; infringements punishable by a whipping; positive commandments; and sixty-five 'chapters [*parashiyot*] of statutes and ordinances for which the community is responsible'. Some commandments crop up under more than one rubric and are counted more than once. It is not always clear where one commandment stops and the next begins. For instance, *Halakhot gedolot* records, under the rubric of positive commandments, the obligation 'to study, to teach, to keep, and to do' God's word; readers have construed the sentence as enumerating one, two, or four distinct commandments.[19] The list includes such items as reading the Esther scroll on Purim and lighting candles on Hanukah, both obviously post-Mosaic, as well as chanting the Hallel prayer in its entirety on nineteen occasions during the year and reciting a hundred blessings of God each day, obligations that are likewise generally classified in rabbinic circles as post-biblical. The problems go on.

Halakhot gedolot was followed by poetic compositions known as *azharot*, or 'admonitions', designed for recitation in the synagogue on Shavuot, the Festival of Weeks. By post-talmudic times, Shavuot had come to be recognized throughout the Jewish world as the holiday commemorating the giving of the Law at Sinai, and the poetic compositions designed for the festival undertook to spell out the 613 commandments that God gave His people on that occasion.

Maimonides speaks of 'the numerous *azharot* composed among us in Andalus' and dismisses their authors as 'poets and not rabbinic scholars [Arab.: *fuqahāʾ*]'.[20] Nahmanides is kinder. He merely speaks of the 'very many' *azharot* written by 'the scholars of Spain [Heb.: *ḥakhemei sefarad*] . . . in the land of Andalus'; and, he adds, compositions belonging to the genre had also been produced 'in other venues in every corner of the diaspora'.[21] I. Davidson identifies fifty *azharot* and poems 'on the [subject of the] 613 commandments'.[22]

[18] The list of commandments in the introduction to *Halakhot gedolot* does not necessarily come from the author of the body of the book, and for that matter, the entire homiletic introduction, which exists in at least three different versions, could well be the work of someone other than the author of *Halakhot gedolot*. See the literature cited in *Halakhot gedolot* (N. Hildesheimer), iii, appendix, introd., 9 n. 1.

[19] *Halakhot gedolot* (N. Hildesheimer), iii, appendix, 74 n. 336.

[20] *SM* (Kafah), 5.

[21] Nahmanides, *Hasagot*, rule 1 (p. 13).

[22] I. Davidson, *Thesaurus of Mediaeval Poetry*, iv. 493.

Eight of the early *azharot* are currently accessible in printed form,[23] and they stem, as Nahmanides writes, from a range of Jewish communities. Among the authors were Sa'adiah Gaon, who composed two—which seem to have been unknown to Maimonides[24]—and Solomon Ibn Gabirol.

With a couple of exceptions, the eight compositions employ the cumbersome classification of commandments in *Halakhot gedolot*. One exception is a piece known by its opening words, *Atah hinḥalta torah le'amekha*, where no classification or arrangement of the commandments can be detected; it has been conjectured that the stylistically primitive composition may even pre-date *Halakhot gedolot*. The other exception is the second of Sa'adiah's efforts, in which the 613 commandments are subsumed under the Ten Statements—the Hebrew term for what in the Western languages are called the Ten Commandments. Although the *azharot* differ from one another in details, the eight that I have been able to examine reflect the enumeration in *Halakhot gedolot* in ways going beyond the cumbersome classification. Most notably, they all include commandments regarded by rabbinic consensus as post-Mosaic.

The pages that follow will not be concerned with the tangle of problems raised by the lists of commandments in *Halakhot gedolot* and the *azharot*. My concern will be with two precepts that Maimonides places at the head of his list of positive commandments given by God at Sinai. These are the obligation that he finds embodied in the opening statement of the Decalogue, 'I am the Lord thy God', which is grammatically a declarative sentence and not an imperative, yet is marked by the Rav Hamnuna passage in the Babylonian Talmud as the first of the 613 commandments; and the obligation he finds embodied in the scriptural verse that occupies the most prominent place in the Jewish liturgy: 'Hear O Israel, the Lord our God, the Lord is one' (Deut. 6: 4).

The enumeration of commandments in the introduction to *Halakhot gedolot* has been preserved and published in three versions,[25] and two of them recognize the second of the Ten Statements in the Decalogue, 'Thou shalt have no other gods before Me', as a negative commandment.[26] None of the versions

[23] (1) *Atah hinḥalta torah le'amekha*, of unknown authorship, which is incorporated into the repetition of the Musaf Amidah in Shavuot prayer books used by a number of communities; it is rarely recited today. See *Maḥazor shavuot*, 615–43. The *azharot* of: (2) Yitshak ben Reuven, in *Netiv mitsvotekha*, 15*a*–105*b*; (3) Ibn Gabirol, in Duran, *Zohar rakia*; (4) and (5) Sa'adiah, who composed two *azharot*, in Sa'adiah, *Sidur*, 157–216; (6) Ibn Gikatilla, in Zulai, '*Azharot*' (Heb.), 161–76; (7) Binyamin Paytan, in Fleischer, 'The *Azharot* of R. Benjamin Paytan' (Heb.); (8) Elijah Hazaken, in *Maḥazor shavuot*, 652–95, and in id., *Shirat hamitsvot*.

[24] He would hardly have dismissed Sa'adiah as a poet and not a rabbinic scholar.

[25] *Halakhot gedolot* (J. Hildesheimer), iii, 8–16; *Halakhot gedolot* (Traub), introd., 2*b*–6*a*; *Halakhot gedolot* (N. Hildesheimer), iii, appendix, 25–112.

[26] See the comparative table in *Halakhot gedolot* (N. Hildesheimer), iii, appendix, introd., 31.

takes 'I am the Lord thy God' to be a commandment. Since the Rav Hamnuna passage in the Babylonian Talmud marks both sentences at the beginning of the Decalogue—'I am the Lord thy God' and 'Thou shalt have no other gods'—as commandments belonging to the privileged 613, commentators have struggled to explain how *Halakhot gedolot* could have omitted the first of the two. Nahmanides' solution was that *Halakhot gedolot* read the Rav Hamnuna passage as stating not that the verses 'I am the Lord thy God' and 'Thou shalt have no other gods' each embodies a commandment, but rather that the pair of verses together contain two. The two commandments heard directly from God and completing the figure of 613 are, on Nahmanides' reading of *Halakhot gedolot*, both packed into what in Jewish circles is usually numbered as the second of the Ten Statements; they are: 'Thou shalt have no other gods before Me' and 'Thou shalt not bow down to them nor serve them'.[27] The eight accessible *azharot* compositions fall into line behind *Halakhot gedolot* in failing to mark 'I am the Lord thy God' as one of the 613 commandments.

Nor do *Halakhot gedolot* and the *azharot* compositions find a commandment in the verse 'Hear O Israel, the Lord our God, the Lord is one'. As a matter of course, they mark the obligation that Jewish males have to recite the 'Hear O Israel' passage every evening and every morning as a divine commandment. They tie that obligation not to the words 'Hear O Israel' but to the injunction, which comes a few verses later in Scripture, to 'talk of' these 'words, which I command thee this day . . . when thou liest down and when thou risest up' (Deut. 6: 7).[28] Sa'adiah in both of his *azharot* seems, in fact, to discern not just one, but two commandments in the words 'when thou liest down and when thou risest up'—the obligation to recite 'Hear O Israel, the Lord our God, the Lord is one' when lying down in the evening, and a separate obligation to recite the declaration when rising in the morning. But Sa'adiah too recognizes no commandment in the 'Hear O Israel' verse itself that is distinct from the ritual obligation to recite the verse twice daily.[29]

In short, *Halakhot gedolot* and the *azharot* following in its wake do not locate a divine commandment in either the first sentence of the Decalogue or the 'Hear O Israel' verse.

[27] Nahmanides, *Hasagot*, positive commandment 1, with reference to Exod. 20: 3–5. Both of these negative commandments appear in the *Halakhot gedolot* list. Abraham Ibn Ezra knew of persons who maintained that 'Thou shalt have no other gods before Me' is the first commandment and 'Thou shalt not make unto thee a graven image' is the second. He rejects their position. See his *Commentary on the Pentateuch*, Exod. 20: 1–2.

[28] Mishnah *Ber.* 1: 3.

[29] In Mark 12: 28–30, Jesus identifies Deut. 6: 4–5, 'Hear O Israel. . . . And thou shalt love the Lord thy God', as 'the first' of the commandments. Love of God is enumerated as one of the formal positive commandments from *Halakhot gedolot* onward.

2. Four Writers on the Commandments Prior to Maimonides

Samuel ben Hofni, Hefets ben Yatsliah, Bahya ibn Pakuda, and Abraham Ibn Ezra contributed to the portrait of the composite medieval rationalist limned in the previous chapter. Each subscribed, expressly or tacitly, to the proposition that satisfactory belief in the existence of God as demanded specifically by religion is certain belief, certain belief is tantamount to knowledge, and the requisite knowledge is furnished by philosophy. That proposition is reflected in their several accounts of the divine commandments.

Samuel ben Hofni, who served as *gaon* of the Sura academy in Iraq in the late tenth century, some fifty or sixty years after Sa'adiah held the office, wrote a substantial Arabic work on the religious commandments, only fragments of which have survived. He treats a range of issues, for instance: the terms used by Scripture to designate positive and negative commands; the question whether performance of a commandment must be accompanied by the conscious intent to perform it as such or whether the act, without conscious intent to do it as a commandment, fulfils one's religious obligation; which commandments were received by Israel before the theophany at Sinai; which are incumbent on every adult member of the nation and which only on segments, such as males, females, priests, Levites, prophets, and slaves; which apply to the poor, and which to the wealthy; which are in effect during the day, and which at night; and so on.[30]

A good part of the book turns on the distinction between *intellectual* (Arab.: *ʿaqliyya*) and *promulgated* or *revealed* (Arab.: *samʿiyya*) *commandments* (Heb.: *mitsvot*; Arab.: *sharāʾiʿ*; *farāʾiḍ*).[31] The intellectual are defined by Samuel as commandments known through the exercise of man's intellect independently of an enactment by the divine legislator, and the promulgated, as commandments known solely because the divine legislator imposed them. The distinction goes back to a contrast drawn in Islamic religious literature between *dictates* of the intellect and divinely promulgated dictates.[32] As a distinction between two classes of *commandments* (*sharāʾiʿ ʿaqliyya*, *sharāʾiʿ samʿiyya*), it already appears in Sa'adiah.[33]

There are, Samuel ben Hofni determines, fifty-five intellectual commandments, whence he concludes that the remaining 558 are of the promulgated

[30] Sklare, *Samuel ben Ḥofni*, English section, 196–200.

[31] Ibid., Judaeo-Arabic section, 4, 16–18; English section, 198, 229, 233–4.

[32] See Tawḥīdī, *Baṣāʾir*, 742; German trans.: van Ess, *Theologie und Gesellschaft*, v. 172; *Kitāb maʿānī al-nafs*, editor's annotations, pp. 22*–23*; Goldziher, *Richtungen der islamischen Koranauslegung*, 136–7.

[33] Sa'adiah, *Emunot vede'ot*, 3: 2–3.

kind.[34] He carefully lists all the commandments that, in his opinion, fall under the former rubric; whether he undertook to do the same for the others is not clear from the preserved fragments of the book. Examples of intellectual commandments are: the obligations to long for and love God, to thank God for His beneficence, and to honour parents; and the prohibitions against swearing falsely in God's name, worshipping images, neglecting to pay one's employees on time, and failing to repay one's debts. Samuel supplies the 'intellectual proof' on which each of the intellectual commandments rests and he insists that man is required not only to recognize and do what is prescribed but also to master the proofs. He nevertheless holds that although the intellectual commandments can be known without the aid of revelation, they are mandated by Scripture as well, and he cites a verse from the Pentateuch for each of them; the prohibition against worshipping images is located by him in the verse 'Thou shalt have no other gods before Me'. And he takes up and answers the question why Scripture attaches its sanction to what the human intellect can, and should, grasp through its own powers.[35]

The commandment of interest to us is the first in the intellectual category—the obligation to engage in 'study [*naẓar*] leading to knowledge of God together with [knowledge of] His essential attributes and [attributes of] action, as is stated [in the scriptural verse]: "Know this day and lay it to thy heart [that the Lord, He is God in heaven above and upon the earth beneath; there is none else]"' (Deut. 4: 39). Samuel immediately adds, either as a corollary of the commandment to acquire knowledge of God or as a separate commandment in its own right,[36] the obligation to understand that God is 'one, without a second, as is stated [in the scriptural verse]: "Hear O Israel, the Lord our God, the Lord is one"'.[37]

The proof through which the human intellect fulfils the obligation to acquire rational knowledge of the existence and attributes of God reasons from 'the coming-into-existence of substances and accidents' to 'knowledge of their creator together with His essential attributes and attributes of action'. A few pages later, Samuel indicates that 'the coming-into-existence of bodies' also plays a role in the proof.[38] *Substance* is the Kalam term for *atom*; Samuel undoubtedly has in mind an argument for the creation of the world and hence

[34] Sklare, *Samuel ben Ḥofni*, Judaeo-Arabic section, 18; English section, 234.

[35] Ibid., Judaeo-Arabic section, 14–16; English section, 225–31 (to be harmonized with Judaeo-Arabic section, 6, and English section, 202–3).

[36] It is impossible to be sure whether it is a corollary or a separate commandment because he does not number the intellectual commandments or mark them in a consistent fashion.

[37] Sklare, *Samuel ben Ḥofni*, Judaeo-Arabic section, 14; English section, 225.

[38] Ibid., Judaeo-Arabic section, 14, 16; English section, 226, 231.

for the existence of a creator that was developed by the Islamic Kalam thinkers, who were atomists, and that is commonly called the proof *from accidents*.

What he writes indicates that the argument he is thinking of would run: accidents—such being the Kalam term for the characteristics of physical objects—reside in atoms, and every atom has accidents attached to it. Bodies consist of atoms, and hence they too have accidents attached to them. All accidents can be shown to come into existence after not having existed. Since—so the reasoning went—whatever is inescapably joined to things that come into existence perforce comes into existence as well, it follows that all atoms and bodies come into existence after not having existed. The physical world, which consists of atoms, accidents, and bodies, has therefore come into existence. It must consequently have a maker who brought it into existence; and the maker, or creator, is the being called God.[39] The further obligation to know the unity of God through an intellectual proof would be fulfilled by mastering one or more of the arguments for the unity of the creator with which the Kalam school supplemented the proof from accidents.[40]

Something radically new has been introduced here. The first intellectual commandment incumbent on Jews is, for Samuel ben Hofni, the obligation to study whatever is needed for acquiring rational knowledge of God's existence, and the obligation to acquire knowledge of God's unity is either part of that commandment or a commandment in its own right. Scripture confirms the two obligations through the verses 'Know this day and lay it to thy heart' and 'Hear O Israel'. No such divine commandment or commandments were recognized by *Halakhot gedolot* and the *azharot* dependent on it, and neither of the biblical verses was cited by them as containing a formal commandment.

What is even more revolutionary is that the initial intellectual commandment or commandments are fulfilled by studying and mastering proofs developed by an Islamic school of philosophy. Study of rational arguments of Islamic provenance has become an integral component in the performance of fundamental Jewish religious obligations, as mandated by both the human intellect and Scripture.

Hefets ben Yatsliah is a more obscure figure. Here and there, he seems to reflect statements in the writings of Sa'adiah Gaon and Samuel ben Hofni, and that would indicate that he lived at a date subsequent to them; yet not every-

[39] Wolfson, *Philosophy of the Kalam*, 392–406; H. Davidson, *Proofs for Eternity, Creation, and the Existence of God*, 134–41, and especially 140–1, 154–66.

[40] Sklare, *Samuel ben Ḥofni*, Judaeo-Arabic section, 14; English section, 225. For Kalam arguments for the unity of God, see H. Davidson, *Proofs for Eternity, Creation, and the Existence of God*, 166–71.

one who has looked at the evidence has been persuaded.[41] A document has been found that describes him as a 'man of Mosul';[42] otherwise it is not known where he lived and was active. Titles sometimes attached to his name establish that he held an official position in one of the rabbinic academies, but which academy is unknown.[43]

Hefets composed a work on the 613 commandments, again in Arabic, which like Samuel ben Hofni's book has been preserved only in part. He divided his book into sections, each of which dealt with a specific area of Jewish law—animal sacrifices, meal offerings, impurity law, vows, torts, and so forth. Under the headings, he lists the appropriate positive and negative commandments and devotes from a paragraph to a few pages to the legal niceties connected with each. The book must have been of considerable girth. On one extrapolation from what has survived, it reached 1,000 pages.[44]

A fragment that has been lost in the original Arabic but a Hebrew translation of which is preserved in a book by another medieval author sets forth what Hefets saw as the first two commandments of the divine Law.

The first commandment is the obligation to 'make God present in our heart' and to be convinced, 'without the slightest doubt or room for any other supposition, that He is the master of all . . . as is written: "Know this day and lay it to thy heart [that the Lord, He is God in heaven above and upon the earth beneath; there is none else]."' The ancient rabbis themselves instructed us to base that conviction on rational proofs when they said: 'Be diligent in studying Torah and *know* what to answer the sceptic [*epikoros*]' (Mishnah *Avot* 2: 14); they thereby taught 'that a person must learn proofs in order to be convinced that God is one [*yaḥid*] and there is none else'. Hefets accordingly furnishes a proof showing that God is 'one alone and the creator of all' and 'fixing in our mind . . . that God exists . . . and there is no similitude or likeness' by which we can represent Him 'except for the brilliance of His glory'.

His reasoning goes: all physical objects in our world are composed of fire, air, water, and earth, and those elements are not naturally at peace with one another; water, for example, extinguishes fire, and air dries up water. The circumstance that the elements nonetheless co-exist in composite physical objects shows that an external cause overcame the elements' mutual antagonism and compelled them to combine.[45] The heavenly bodies too must have a maker, for each of them 'possesses superiority and strength, whence we know that something other than they formed them and they were not created by themselves'.

[41] Hefets ben Yatsliah, *Book of Precepts*, 20–5; id., 'New Extracts' (Heb.), 8–10.

[42] Hefets ben Yatsliah, *Book of Precepts*, 12. [43] Ibid. 25–7. [44] Ibid. 50.

[45] The theme is found in Pseudo-Aristotle, *De mundo*, 5, 396b, 29–35.

It is, Hefets assures us, hereby established that the world has a 'maker and creator'; that He 'without doubt and question is the master of all; and He alone is God, to whom no likeness or similitude can be drawn, as is written: "To whom then will ye liken God, or what likeness will ye compare unto Him (Isa. 40: 18)?"'[46] The first part of his argument, which relates to physical objects formed out of the four elements, is an unsophisticated version of a medieval proof of the existence of God known as the proof *from composition*.[47] The second part, which relates to the heavenly bodies, is impossible to fathom. Some, although undoubtedly not all, of the blame may lie with the mediocre Hebrew translation from the original Arabic.

The second commandment recognized by Hefets is the obligation to 'affirm the unity of the creator and to believe in our heart and thoughts, with no shadow of a doubt, that He truly is one and nothing else is one except Him'. 'We must not suppose that He has any appearance or the likeness of any physical thing in the world'; when Scripture speaks of God's eyes, hand, and feet, it does so 'solely to liken [Him] to the language of man'. Again: 'We must believe, truly and with certainty, that God is one . . . without increase or diminution, without being joined [*ḥibur*] [with other objects] or being separated [*perud*], without change or motion'. By contrast, 'everything else that exists is subject to increase and diminution, to being divided . . . to being joined and being separated; and it has a beginning and an end. . . . Our creator is not affected by any of those qualities, as is written: "Hear O Israel, the Lord our God, the Lord is one"'.

Here too, Hefets furnishes an argument of sorts, which he copies or adapts from a Neopythagorean source and which he thinks proves that nothing else in existence is like God. Anyone, he writes, 'who wishes to discern that nothing whatsoever is one except God should examine the nature of the one and the many'. He will find that 'plural numbers come after the one, as the ancients showed. Since two, three, four, and so on, come after the one, it is evident that the one is prior to every number.' Hefets somehow concludes herefrom that there can be only a single *one*, that the truly one is not subject to increase, diminution, and the other qualities mentioned, and hence that God, who alone is one, is free of those qualities.[48]

There is no need to belabour the feebleness of the reasoning—supposing that it rises to a level where it deserves to be called reasoning—but that is of less interest than what Hefets has undertaken. He identifies the first two divine

[46] Hefets ben Yatsliah, *Book of Precepts*, 31–3, 35–7.

[47] Regarding proofs from composition, see Wolfson, *Philosophy of the Kalam*, 388–90; H. Davidson, *Proofs for Eternity, Creation, and the Existence of God*, 146–53, and especially 150–1.

[48] Hefets ben Yatsliah, *Book of Precepts*, 34–5, 38–40.

commandments as the obligations to be convinced of the existence and the unity of God. He finds scriptural proof texts for the two commandments in the same verses that Samuel ben Hofni cited: 'Know this day and lay it to thy heart' and 'Hear O Israel'. And, like Samuel, he instructs his co-religionists to fulfil the two divine commandments by mastering philosophical or quasi-philosophical arguments of non-Jewish provenance.

Bahya ibn Pakuda's *Ḥovot halevavot* enters the picture through the medium of his distinctive conception of the divine commandments.

The Arabic title of his book is *Kitāb al-hidāya ilā farā'iḍ al-qulūb*, that is: *Book of Guidance to the Farā'iḍ of Hearts*. Judah Ibn Tibbon, the medieval Hebrew translator, makes the title crisper by dropping the first half. Of greater moment is his choice of a Hebrew term to translate *farā'iḍ*. The term *farīḍa* (plural: *farā'iḍ*) means a divinely imposed obligation.

Samuel ben Hofni employed *farā'iḍ* as an Arabic equivalent of the Hebrew term *mitsvot*, commandments, and Bahya appears to have known Samuel's writings.[49] Ibn Tibbon nevertheless translates *farā'iḍ* as *ḥovot*, *duties*, and a long line of translations and studies of the book in modern languages has let itself be bound by that decision. The commonly accepted Hebrew title today is not *Mitsvot halevavot* but *Ḥovot halevavot*. The accepted English title is not *Commandments of the Heart* but *Duties of the Heart*.

The axis around which the book revolves is the distinction—going back to a similar distinction in Islamic literature[50]—between *farā'iḍ* of the limbs and *farā'iḍ* of the heart. The term *farā'iḍ* appears repeatedly throughout the book, and in a number of instances Ibn Tibbon and Kafah, the modern Hebrew translator, sensed that *ḥovot*, or *duties*, the word they chose to translate *farā'iḍ*

[49] Bahya ibn Pakuda, *Ḥovot halevavot* (Kafah), introd., 18, refers to a book by a rabbinic writer, entitled *Kitāb uṣūl al-dīn*, which appears to be a lost work of Samuel ben Hofni. It may be relevant or just a coincidence that Samuel ben Hofni also wrote a book entitled *Kitāb al-hidāya* (Book of Guidance). Regarding both works, see Sklare, *Samuel ben Ḥofni*, 58.

[50] There the distinction is commonly between *actions* performed by the heart and *actions* performed by limbs. See Shahrastani, *Al-milal wa-al-niḥal*, 35 (Abū Hudhayl); Goldziher, *Streitschrift*, 109 (Abū Hudhayl, Muḥāsibī, and others); van Ess, *Theologie und Gesellschaft*, iii. 248, iv. 197, 500 (Abū Hudhayl and Muḥāsibī). Muḥāsibī wrote a piece entitled *Questions regarding Works of Hearts and of Limbs*. Goldreich, 'Possible Arabic Sources' (Heb.), 196–8, has moreover found passages in Muḥāsibī that talk about *obligations* (*farḍ*, *farīḍa*) of the limbs and the heart.

Ch. 8 of Bahya ibn Pakuda's *Ḥovot halevavot* is entitled 'Man's Making a Reckoning with his Soul' (*Muḥāsabat al-insān nafsahu*), and one of Muḥāsibī's works is entitled *Making a Reckoning with One's Soul* (*Muḥāsabat al-nufūs*); see van Ess, *Theologie und Gesellschaft*, vi. 419. For additional background on the notion of making a reckoning with one's soul, see Makki, *Qūt al-qulūb*, i. 145; Goldziher, 'Zurechtweisung der Seele', 132; *Encyclopaedia of Islam*, s.v. *muḥāsaba*. For a couple of additional possible links between Muḥāsibī and Bahya ibn Pakuda, see Goldreich, 'Possible Arabic Sources' (Heb.), 198, 200, 204.

in the title, would not do. In those instances, they render *farā'iḍ* as *mitsvot, commandments*, instead. Neither translator seems to have been troubled by the inconsistency.

Consider a passage at the beginning of Bahya's introduction, in which he sets forth his premise:

Religious science has two parts: One is knowledge of the *farā'iḍ* of limbs . . . and the second is knowledge of the *farā'iḍ* of hearts. . . . The *farā'iḍ* of limbs have two parts, one, *farā'iḍ* that intellect makes obligatory even though Scripture does not, and the second, promulgated [*sam'iyya*] *farā'iḍ*, which intellect does not make obligatory or prohibit, such as the prohibition against eating meat and milk together. . . . The roots [*uṣūl*] of the *farā'iḍ* of hearts are, by contrast, all intellectual. . . . *Farā'iḍ* are, in general, divided into positive command and prohibition. There is no need for me to explicate this in the case of the *farā'iḍ* of limbs, since they are well known, but [as we proceed], I shall call attention to the positive commands and prohibitions in the case of the *farā'iḍ* of hearts.

An English translation of Ibn Tibbon's medieval Hebrew translation would read:

'Religious science has two parts: One is knowledge of the duties [*ḥovot*] of the limbs . . . and the second is knowledge of the duties [*ḥovot*] of hearts. . . . The duties [*ḥovot*] of limbs have two parts, one, commandments [*mitsvot*] that the intellect makes obligatory . . . and the second, promulgated commandments [*mitsvot*]*. . . . The foundations of the duties [*ḥovot*] of hearts are, by contrast, all from the intellect. . . . Commandments [*mitsvot*]* in general are divided into positive commands and negative commands. There is no need for me to explicate this in the case of the commandments [*mitsvot*] of the limbs . . . but [as we proceed], I shall call attention to the positive commands and negative commands in the case of duties [*ḥovot*] of hearts.'

In four instances, Ibn Tibbon translates *farā'iḍ* not as duties but as commandments. At the two places marked by asterisks, Kafah's modern Hebrew translation follows Ibn Tibbon and also renders *farā'iḍ* as 'commandments'; at the two other places where Ibn Tibbon translates *farā'iḍ* as 'commandments', Kafah has 'duties'. Both translators thus represent Bahya as zigzagging back and forth in the use of a term lying at the very core of his thought, all within the compass of a few lines.[51] The pattern repeats itself in their translations of other passages.[52]

A paragraph appearing a little later in Bahya's introduction to the book should have settled matters. He writes: 'The *farā'iḍ* of the limbs are circum-

51 Bahya ibn Pakuda, *Ḥovot halevavot* (Kafah), introd., 15–16; *Ḥovot halevavot* (Ibn Tibbon), introd., 7–8.

52 *Ḥovot halevavot* (Kafah), introd., 17–19, 3: 2 (p. 135), 3: 3 (p. 137), 3: 4 (pp. 144–5); *Ḥovot halevavot* (Ibn Tibbon), introd., 8–9, 3: 2 (p. 84), 3: 3 (pp. 85–6), 3: 4 (p. 90).

scribed in number at about 613 laws [*sharīʿa*], whereas the *farāʾiḍ* of the heart are very numerous [and virtually] infinite in their branches.'[53] As a proof text, Bahya cites Psalm 119: 96, which declares: 'I have seen an end to every measurement, but Thy commandment [*mitsvah*] is exceeding broad.' He reasons: since the *farāʾiḍ* of the limbs are circumscribed at about 613, 'Thy commandment' that is exceeding broad must be the other kind, the *farāʾiḍ* of the heart.

Both classes of *farāʾiḍ*—those numbering approximately 613 and those that the Psalmist designates as 'Thy commandment'—are plainly divine commandments for Bahya. Ibn Tibbon recognized as much in his translation, which reads: 'The commandments [*mitsvot*] of the limbs have a specific number, about 613 commandments, whereas the commandments [*mitsvot*] of the heart are very numerous, to the extent that their branches have no number.' Kafah's translation remains bound to the rendering of *farāʾiḍ* as duties and obscures Bahya's point. His translation reads: 'The duties of the limbs are circumscribed in number at about 613 laws, whereas the duties of the heart are very numerous.'[54]

In short, *commandments* is the correct translation of *farāʾiḍ* here and undoubtedly throughout the book. The English title of Bahya's book should be *Commandments of the Heart*, not *Duties of the Heart*.

Bahya's premise, then, is that the divine commandments fall into two categories. Some are performed with one's limbs; they may be either promulgated or intellectual and they number about 613. Others are performed in one's heart. These are all intellectual, form a class apart, are exceedingly broad, and surpass measurement. Bahya laments that rabbinic scholars of his day lavished their attention on the first, lesser class, while neglecting the second, and his book is designed to redress the oversight. He divides the book into ten chapters, each devoted to a commandment of the heart that is a 'root' (*aṣl*) from which additional commandments of the heart branch off.[55]

Chapter 1 opens by stating that 'the most solid pillar and root of our religion' and the 'crown of true religion' is 'unswerving affirmation of the existence of a single God'. When God addressed 'us at Mount Sinai', His opening words were accordingly 'I am the Lord thy God' and 'Thou shalt have no other gods', and those pronouncements were reinforced by Moses, the

[53] In *Ḥovot halevavot* (Kafah), 10: 7 (p. 427), Bahya speaks of 613 commandments without further qualification. They all appear to be commandments of the limbs.

[54] *Ḥovot halevavot* (Kafah), introd., 22–3, and cf. 3: 3 (p. 137); *Ḥovot halevavot* (Ibn Tibbon), introd., 11, and cf. 3: 3 (pp. 85–6). For the way I have translated Ps. 119: 96, see Ibn Ezra's commentary on the verse.

[55] *Ḥovot halevavot* (Kafah), introd., 35–6; *Ḥovot halevavot* (Ibn Tibbon), introd., 19–20.

messenger of God, when he addressed the Israelites and declared: 'Hear O Israel, the Lord our God, the Lord is one.'[56]

A few pages later, Bahya distinguishes different levels in affirming the existence of a single God. The highest is the level at which a person makes the affirmation not just with his tongue but with both his 'heart and tongue', after 'framing proofs [*istidlāl*] regarding God and His existence' and 'comprehending the true sense of His unity, through study [*naẓar*] and the use of intellectual syllogism[s]'. Scripture itself instructs us in several verses to go beyond merely mouthing belief and to acquire knowledge of God's existence and unity 'with our intellects'. Among the verses is '*Know* this day and lay it to thy heart that the Lord, He is God in heaven above and upon the earth beneath.' The ancient rabbis added their authority when they taught us to be 'diligent in learning what to answer the sceptic [*epikoros*]'. That we hear echoes of Hefets ben Yatsliah—a writer whom Bahya knew and refers to by name[57]—is confirmed by Bahya's exegesis of the verse '*Know* this day and lay it to thy heart', for he repeats distinctive phrases from Hefets's exegesis of the verse.[58]

Bahya provides readers with tools for fulfilling the first commandment of the heart properly. He offers rational proofs for the existence and unity of God.

The proof for the existence of God is a jumble of variations on the proof *from composition*. It begins by establishing the propositions that whatever is composite has come into existence and that nothing produces itself, and then goes on: the world resembles a mansion, the earth being the carpet; the heavens, the ceiling; the stars, the lamps; and so on. Man is the householder, and 'everything [in the world] is intended for the use and benefit of rational beings', that is, for the human species. The tenor thus far is unmistakably teleological, but Bahya infers merely that the world 'as a whole and in its parts . . . is plainly composite'.

He continues by taking up a motif that we encountered in Hefets: natural objects in the lower world are compounded of the elements fire, air, water, and earth; those elements stand in opposition to one another and resist combination; yet natural objects made of them, although not permanent, survive for considerable lengths of time. 'The agent who forcibly combines the elements against their natures must be their creator.' As Bahya nears his conclusion, he

[56] *Ḥovot halevavot* (Kafah), 1, introd., 44; *Ḥovot halevavot* (Ibn Tibbon) 1, introd., 25.

[57] *Ḥovot halevavot* (Kafah), introd., 18; *Ḥovot halevavot* (Ibn Tibbon), introd., 8.

[58] *Ḥovot halevavot* (Kafah), 1: 2–3 (pp. 50–1); *Ḥovot halevavot* (Ibn Tibbon), 1: 2–3 (pp. 28–9). Cf. Hefets ben Yatsliah, *Book of Precepts*, 31. Bahya cites the verse 'Know this day and lay it to thy heart' twice here and he also cites it earlier, *Ḥovot halevavot* (Kafah), introd., 27, as a proof text for the general obligation to apply one's intellect to the commandments of the heart.

oddly drops this motif too. He concludes only that 'combination and composition are thus clearly seen in the world as a whole and in all its parts . . . and the entire world must therefore have come into existence'. 'Since . . . nothing produces itself, the world must have a maker who brought it into existence.'[59]

As for sceptics who maintain that the world took shape purely by chance, Bahya deals with them by reverting to the teleological theme. He asks them to imagine a waterwheel (Arab.: *dawlāb*; Heb.: *galgal*) irrigating a field. No one would suppose that the waterwheel materialized by chance; how then can one suppose that the great all-encompassing wheel (*dawlāb*; *galgal*), the celestial sphere, which acts for the benefit of everything existing in the world, could have come about spontaneously? Alternatively, the sceptics should imagine a sheet of paper covered with legible writing. No one would suppose that ink accidentally spilled on the paper happened to arrange itself into lines of writing. How can anyone think that the infinitely more subtle structure of the world came about through chance?[60]

So much for God's existence. Bahya offers no fewer than seven arguments for the unity of God, and a remark he makes in the course of one of them repeats phraseology that we encountered in Hefets and shall presently encounter again. True unity, he writes, excludes similarity, multiplicity in any respect, as well as 'being joined [*ittiṣāl*] to anything' or 'being separated [*infiṣāl*] from anything'.[61]

Bahya has, with a twist of his own, trodden the rationalist path laid out by Samuel ben Hofni and Hefets ben Yatsliah: to fulfil the initial commandment of the heart at the highest level, one must acquire rational knowledge of God's existence and unity; and such knowledge, and the proper performance of the commandment, comes through mastering proofs of non-Jewish provenance. Scripture does not corroborate all commandments of the heart but does corroborate this one. The scriptural texts embodying the commandment are the first of the Ten Statements, or Ten Commandments: 'I am the Lord thy God', and the 'Hear O Israel' verse. Among the verses specifying that belief in the existence and unity of God should be grounded in rational proof is the familiar '*Know* this day and lay it to thy heart'.

[59] *Ḥovot halevavot*, 1: 5–6. Besides the echoes of Hefets ben Yatsliah, there may also be echoes of Sa'adiah's *Emunot vede'ot*, 1: 1, which presents an argument for creation from composition in the universe, supplemented (1: 2) by the proposition that nothing can bring itself into existence. In *Emunot vede'ot*, 2. 2, Sa'adiah cites the verse 'Know this day and lay it to your heart . . . there is none else' as a proof text for the unity of God. Sa'adiah's *Emunot vede'ot* is one of the works referred to by Bahya; see *Ḥovot halevavot* (Kafah), introd., 17–18; *Ḥovot halevavot* (Ibn Tibbon), introd., 8.

[60] *Ḥovot halevavot* (Kafah), 1: 6 (pp. 57–8); *Ḥovot halevavot* (Ibn Tibbon), 1: 6 (pp. 33–4).

[61] *Ḥovot halevavot* (Kafah), 1: 7 (p. 64).

Abraham Ibn Ezra—who was acquainted with Bahya's writings[62]—tried his hand at analysing and classifying the religious commandments in a small book, which is scarcely more than a pamphlet. At one spot, he distinguishes, as he does in his Bible commentary, between divine commandments that are performed in the heart, those performed with the mouth, and those performed through a physical act. The first of the three classes is the most basic, since commandments in the other two all presuppose beliefs.[63]

The initial commandment incumbent on the human heart is embodied in the opening sentence of the Decalogue: 'I am the Lord thy God [who brought thee out of the land of Egypt].' Every Jew is thereby obligated to 'believe with all his heart that the Lord, who brought him out of Egypt, is his God'. Additional verses expressing positive commandments for the heart are: 'Know this day and lay it to thy heart [that the Lord, He is God in heaven above and upon the earth beneath; there is none else]', and 'Hear O Israel, the Lord our God, the Lord is one'.[64] The 'Hear O Israel' verse plainly prescribes belief in the unity of God. What the verse 'Know this day and lay it to thy heart' prescribes in addition to belief in the existence of God, which is already enjoined by 'I am the Lord thy God', is not explained here. As usual, Ibn Ezra is chary of detail and terse to a fault.

His Bible commentary comes to our aid. In his exegesis of the Decalogue in the book of Exodus, he construes the 'first statement' (Heb.: *dibur*), 'I am the Lord thy God', as the obligation to 'believe, and cherish a belief in one's heart free of doubt, that the sublime name, which is written and not uttered'—the Tetragrammaton, conventionally translated into English as *Lord*—'is alone one's God'. That belief is the most fundamental of the commandments of the heart, the root (*ikar*) from which the 'nine following statements' issue forth. Inasmuch as the Ten Statements in the Decalogue are in their turn roots from which all other commandments flow, the first, belief in the existence of God, 'embraces' (*kolel*) the entire gamut of religious commandments whether of heart, mouth, or action.

Belief in the existence of God, Ibn Ezra goes on, is possible at different levels. At a lesser level, a person merely accepts what the Torah tells him. But at the loftiest level, he masters the natural sciences through 'apodictic proofs admitting no doubt' and arrives at the understanding that the sublunar world depends on the world of the spheres; the world of the spheres, on the world of intelligences; and the world of intelligences, on a transcendent first cause.

62 Ibn Ezra, *Yesod mora*, ch. 6, p. 126.

63 Ibid., ch. 7, p. 131. See Ibn Ezra, *Commentary on the Pentateuch*, Exod. 20: 1–2 and Deut. 30: 14.

64 Ibn Ezra, *Yesod mora*, ch. 7, pp. 142–3.

Knowledge of God's handiwork hence leads to knowledge of God. The verse 'Know this day and lay it to thy heart [that the Lord, He is God in heaven above and upon the earth beneath, there is none else]' teaches that 'apodictic knowledge' of God consists in 'man's laying to his heart until it becomes clear to him through [rational] proofs that God is alone'.[65]

'I am the Lord thy God', the opening statement in the Decalogue, is therefore the commandment to cherish a belief in the existence of God. The 'Hear O Israel' verse is a commandment to believe that God is one, that there is no other god apart from Him. The verse 'Know this day' is the injunction to acquire belief in the existence of God at the loftiest level, through rational proof. Ibn Ezra does not tell us which proof of the existence of God he has in mind.

When Maimonides appeared on the scene, he was provided with precedents for doing something that *Halakhot gedolot* and its school did not contemplate—construing belief in, or knowledge of, the existence of God as a formal commandment of the Law. He had precedents as well for the propositions that belief in the existence of God can be achieved at different levels and that belief at the supreme level rests on rational proof. Attempts at furnishing the requisite proofs had been made, although the results were not of a calibre that would appeal to Maimonides, even at this early stage of his career.

Samuel ben Hofni and Hefets ben Yatsliah found the commandment to acquire knowledge of the existence of God in the verse 'Know this day and lay it to thy heart that the Lord, He is God in heaven above and upon the earth beneath.' Bahya and Ibn Ezra found the commandment to believe in the existence of God in the first of the Ten Statements proclaimed by God at Sinai: 'I am the Lord thy God'. That was the statement that the Rav Hamnuna passage in the Babylonian Talmud marked as the first of the 613 commandments given to Moses and Israel. Bahya and Ibn Ezra followed Samuel ben Hofni and Hefets ben Yatsliah in taking the verse 'Know this day and lay it to thy heart' as a dictate to ground belief in the existence of God on rational proof.

Maimonides also had precedents for viewing belief in, or knowledge of, God's unity as a formal commandment, for locating that commandment in the 'Hear O Israel' verse, and for grounding knowledge of the unity of God in rational proof.

The introduction to his own *Sefer hamitsvot* (*Book of Commandments*), the Arabic work he devoted to the '613 commandments stated to Moses at Sinai',

[65] Ibn Ezra, *Commentary on the Pentateuch*, Exod. 20: 1–2. Ibn Ezra's comment on Deut. 4: 39 suggests a similar interpretation of 'Know this day and lay it to thy heart'.

mentions the 'author of the well-known *Book of Commandments*', and the reference is to Hefets ben Yatsliah.[66] Maimonides does not mention Samuel ben Hofni here, but elsewhere does reveal an acquaintance with Samuel's writings.[67] He never refers to Bahya or Ibn Ezra.[68] Whether he knew them or not, discussions of issues involving the Decalogue were in the air,[69] and he could have been exposed to views similar to those held by the two men without reading what they had written.

3. Maimonides

In the introduction to his *Sefer hamitsvot*, Maimonides relates that after completing his *Commentary on the Mishnah*, he wanted his next major work to be a comprehensive code of Jewish law. To guarantee that nothing would be overlooked, he needed a complete list of the 613 divine commandments.

As he pondered the subject, he became overcome by the 'grief' from which he 'had already suffered for years'. Earlier lists of the commandments contained mistakes 'the enormous odiousness' of which exceeded his ability to describe, the prime culprit being the author of *Halakhot gedolot*, in whose tracks others followed blindly. It was true that the 'author of the well-known *Book of Commandments*', that is, Hefets ben Yatsliah, avoided some of the errors in *Halakhot gedolot*; but he committed other, worse errors. The more Maimonides reflected on the mistakes that had been made and the manner in which one writer on the subject 'would follow another without thinking, the greater our misfortune appeared to' him. It was as if Isaiah's melancholy prophecy had once again been realized: 'And the vision of all this is become unto you as the words of a writing that is sealed, which men deliver to one that is learned, saying "Read this, I pray thee", and he saith "I cannot, for it is sealed"' (Isa. 29: 11). Even the learned were unable to penetrate the seal enveloping the commandments. As a prolegomenon to his code of Jewish law, Maimonides decided to draw up an accurate list, and the product is his *Sefer hamitsvot*.[70]

The errors perpetrated by *Halakhot gedolot* and its fellow travellers that Maimonides found so disturbing are such things as their inclusion of post-Mosaic commandments, which runs counter to the text of the Babylonian

66 Hefets ben Yatsliah, 'New Extracts' (Heb.), 9.

67 See Maimonides, *Responsa*, index.

68 Perla, *Sefer hamitsvot*, 1: 15–16, contends that Ibn Ezra's *Yesod mora* is reflected in Maimonides' *SM*, but he overstates the evidence.

69 Ibn Ezra, *Commentary on the Pentateuch*, Exod. 20: 1–2, refers to opinions held by others regarding the commandments. He relates that he and Judah Halevi discussed the reason why God declared 'I am the Lord thy God *who brought thee out of Egypt*' rather than *who made the heavens and the earth*.

70 *SM* (Kafah), 4–5.

Talmud known to him, where the 613 commandments are said to have been stated to Moses at Sinai; the inclusion of divine instructions of only temporary force; and the treating of broad, nonspecific exhortations as, for example, 'be ye holy', as formal commandments.[71] He says nothing about the failure of *Halakhot gedolot* to mark the verse 'I am the Lord thy God' as a commandment.

In his own enumeration, Maimonides remains faithful to the dichotomy of 248 positive and 365 negative commandments that the Babylonian Talmud transmits in the name of Rabbi Simlai. The first of the positive commandments and the one with which he begins the body of his *Sefer hamitsvot* is 'belief [*iʿtiqād*] in divinity [*rubūbiyya*]', in other words, 'that we believe a cause exists that produces all existent beings'. Scripture articulates the commandment in the words 'I am the Lord thy God', the verse that had been identified by the Babylonian Talmud as embodying one of the 613 commandments of the Law.[72] Maimonides ignores 'Know this day and lay it to thy heart that the Lord, He is God in heaven above and upon the earth beneath', although he does cite it elsewhere.

The second positive commandment is 'belief in [God's] unity', in other words, 'that we believe that He who produces existence and is its first cause is one'. Scripture articulates that commandment in the pronouncement: 'Hear O Israel, the Lord our God, the Lord is one.'[73]

Sefer hamitsvot, as just noted, is a prolegomenon to Maimonides' *Mishneh torah*, his law code. The latter locates the first two positive divine commandments in the same two biblical verses but makes a significant change. Book 1 of the *Mishneh torah*, which is appropriately entitled the 'Book of Knowledge', opens with the words: 'The most basic foundation [of religion] and pillar of the sciences is to *know* that there exists a first being who brings every [other] being into existence.' Several paragraphs later, Maimonides marks knowledge of the existence of God as 'a positive commandment, as stated [in Scripture]: "I am the Lord thy God."' And in the following paragraph, he makes *knowledge* of the unity of God 'a positive commandment, as stated [in Scripture]: "Hear O Israel, the Lord our God, the Lord is one."'[74] The commandments to believe, which stand at the head of *Sefer hamitsvot*, reappear in the same position in the *Mishneh torah*, but they are now commandments to know.

[71] *SM*, introd., rules 1, 3, and 4.

[72] *SM*, positive commandment 1. (Kafah's translation of *iʿtiqād* as 'knowledge' is unwarranted and misleading.) Maimonides seems to have come to the present position after writing his *Commentary on the Mishnah*, for he states there that the rational faculty of the soul does not have 'an activity to which the term 'commandment' or 'transgression' can be applied without qualification'. See *Commentary on the Mishnah*, introd. to *Avot*, ch. 2, p. 377.

[73] *SM*, positive commandment 2.

[74] *MT*, 'Hilkhot yesodei hatorah', 1: 1, 6, 7.

A rationale for the shift is provided by an analysis of belief that Maimonides gives in the *Moreh nevukhim* (*Guide for the Perplexed*). His train of thought was alluded to in the previous chapter.

The analysis begins with the sensible statement that words merely spoken do not qualify as belief (*iʿtiqād*). Belief occurs when a proposition is conceptualized (*mutaṣawwar*, *taṣawwur*) in the mind and the human subject has the conviction (*taṣdīq*) that the proposition in his mind reflects what exists in the external world. Should the human mind rise to a further level and determine that no alternative to the belief is possible and the mind can find no way of rejecting it, the belief acquires certainty.[75]

Now, if the mind can be certain that there is no alternative to accepting a proposition, it possesses not merely conviction but knowledge; in effect, belief at the highest level, certain belief, merges with knowledge. When Maimonides' *Sefer hamitsvot* identifies the first positive commandment of the Law as *belief* that God exists and the second as *belief* that He is one, it can be read as having the highest level of belief in view. *Sefer hamitsvot* can be read as dictating what the *Mishneh torah* does—*knowledge* of the existence and unity of God.

Maimonides goes on in the *Mishneh torah* to supply, albeit in barest outline, rational proofs whereby the two tenets can be known and the commandments mandating knowledge of the existence and unity of God can be fulfilled.

His proof of the existence of God is a simplified version of Aristotle's demonstration of the existence of a first mover of the heavens. Maimonides posits that 'the celestial sphere rotates continually, and it is impossible for it to move without a mover'. By a *mover* he means not an agent that sets the sphere in motion, but one that constantly maintains it in motion; ancient and medieval thinkers did not know Newton's first law of motion, the law of inertia. Since the rotation of the sphere never ceases, the cause maintaining the sphere in motion must possess 'an infinite power', and the infinitely powerful mover is the being known as God. 'Knowledge of the foregoing', which, the context shows, means knowledge by means of proof, 'is a positive commandment, as stated [in Scripture]: "I am the Lord thy God."'[76]

The proof of God's unity, for which Maimonides again offers the barest bones, carries the argument a step further. Fleshed out a little more fully than it is put in the *Mishneh torah*, the reasoning goes: corporeal beings are perforce

[75] *MN* i. 50, with an echo of Aristotle, *Posterior Analytics*, 1.2, 71b, 9–16, according to which knowing that something cannot be other than it is, is a mark of scientific knowledge. In the Arabic material studied by Wolfson, 'The Terms *Taṣawwur* and *Taṣdīq*', *taṣdīq* is a proposition, such as 'A is B', and *taṣawwur* is a component of the proposition, that is, 'A' or 'B'. As Maimonides uses the terms, *taṣawwur* is a proposition, and *taṣdīq* is the conviction or mental affirmation that the proposition in the mind reflects the reality outside the mind.

[76] *MT*, 'Hilkhot yesodei hatorah', 1: 5–6.

finite in their dimensions, and consequently finite in power. The mover of the celestial sphere, which must be infinite in power, is hence non-corporeal. But an old philosophical axiom posits that a plurality of beings wholly identical in their essence can be distinguished from one another and numbered only when they are present in matter; put more technically, matter is the principle of individuation. There can accordingly be no more than a single exemplar of any type of being that does not exist in matter. Inasmuch as the being whose nature it is to be the mover of the celestial sphere is non-corporeal, only a single exemplar of the class, a single mover of the sphere—by which Maimonides means the outermost sphere—can exist. 'Knowledge of the foregoing is a positive commandment, as stated [in the scriptural verse]: "Hear O Israel, the Lord our God, the Lord is one."'[77]

Maimonides does not spell his reasoning out in sufficient detail to enable someone unfamiliar with the subject to grasp all it involves. He moreover glides over such complications as the following: the proof from motion succeeds only if the world is eternal, for only then must the sphere's mover possess infinite power; in deploying the proof, Maimonides would therefore appear to abandon the doctrine of the creation of the world. He joins the consensus of medieval astronomers in recognizing a number of celestial spheres, each with its own motion. Since each sphere would have to have its own incorporeal mover,[78] the uniqueness of God seems to be compromised. Although these are matters to which Maimonides gave a good deal of attention in the *Moreh nevukhim*, it is by no means certain that, at the present stage of his career, he thought the argument, its presuppositions, and its implications through to the end. As will appear in the next chapter, he had little or no familiarity with Aristotle's writings when he wrote the *Mishneh torah*. He almost surely did not borrow the proof directly from Aristotle.

His choice of the proof from motion as the tool for fulfilling the commandments to know the existence and unity of God is nonetheless hardly accidental. When worked out properly the proof was more philosophically respectable, and more rigorous, than the arguments for the existence of God advanced by Samuel ben Hofni, Hefets ben Yatsliah and Bahya ibn Pakuda. Maimonides furthermore persuaded himself that the proof had originally been framed by the father of the Jewish people. Extrapolating from a piece of rabbinic aggadah,[79] he writes in the *Mishneh torah*: Abraham began at an early age to meditate 'day and night.

[77] *MT*, 'Hilkhot yesodei hatorah', 1: 7, 2: 5. Aristotle proved the existence of a first mover in both his *Physics* and *Metaphysics*, but he inferred the unity of the first mover from its incorporeality only in *Metaphysics*, 12.8.1074a, 33–7.

[78] *MT*, 'Hilkhot yesodei hatorah', 2: 5, explains how multiple incorporeal movers of the spheres can be distinguished from one another.

[79] See above, Ch. 1.

He marvelled: How can it be possible for the celestial sphere to move continually without a mover? What causes it to rotate, seeing that the sphere [being a body] cannot be the cause of its own rotation?' Abraham ultimately 'attained the true path . . . by the power of his sound intellect and concluded that there exists one God who moves the sphere and created everything. There is no god in existence except Him.'[80]

In a word, Abraham discovered the proof of the existence of God from the motion of the spheres a millennium and a half before Aristotle did. A flaw in the position of Maimonides' predecessors has hereby been repaired. The first two positive divine commandments are no longer to be fulfilled through proofs of non-Jewish provenance but rather through a proof that boasts an impeccable Israelite and Jewish lineage, going all the way back to the first of the patriarchs.

One more statement in the *Mishneh torah* should be noted. Maimonides writes: Inasmuch as it has been demonstrated that God is not a physical object, 'it is plain that none of the accidents affecting bodies can affect Him—neither being joined [*ḥibur*] nor being separated [*perud*], neither place nor measurement, neither going up nor going down, neither right nor left, front nor back. sitting nor standing'. God has neither a temporal 'beginning nor end' and is not subject to 'change'. When Scripture employs terms carrying those implications regarding God, it 'speaks in conformity with the language of men' (*kileshon benei adam*).[81]

Being *joined* and *separated* are not among the anthropomorphisms that medieval Jewish thinkers ordinarily warn against ascribing to God. The terms belong to the vocabulary of the Islamic Kalam, where they designate one of the most fundamental pairs of accidents, those such that no atom can be free of one or the other member of the pair: every atom, it was reasoned, must possess either the accident of *being contiguous* with other atoms or the accident of *being separated* from them.[82] Maimonides' *Mishneh torah* takes no cognizance of the Kalam, and while his *Commentary on the Mishnah*, which precedes the *Mishneh torah*, does have a few references to Kalam concepts, Maimonides there exhibits the disdain for the movement that was typical of the Arabic Aristotelians.[83] It would be strange for him to draw consciously from the vocabulary of the disreputable Kalam when making the point that anthropomorphisms must not be applied to God.

[80] *MT*, 'Hilkhot avodah zarah', 1: 3.

[81] *MT*, 'Hilkhot yesodei hatorah', 1: 11–12.

[82] Bāqillānī, *Kitāb al-tamhīd* 22; Baghdādī, *Kitāb uṣūl al-dīn*, 40–1; Wolfson, *Philosophy of the Kalam*, 386–7; Schwarz, 'Who Were Maimonides' Mutakillimūn?', i. 167–8; Dhanani, *Physical Theory of Kalām*, 147, 155.

[83] Maimonides, *Commentary on the Mishnah, Ber.* 9: 7.

In stating that God is exempt from being joined and being separated, Maimonides could be copying from Bahya, who wrote that the true One is free of both conditions. A more probable conjecture is that he is echoing Hefets ben Yatsliah. Hefets wrote: 'God is one . . . without being joined or being separated, without change or motion', he contrasted God to beings having 'a beginning and an end', and he remarked that when Scripture describes God anthropomorphically, it likens Him 'to the language of men'. The tell-tale phrases suggest that Hefets's book may have been among the factors helping to shape Maimonides' views on the first two positive divine commandments—though Maimonides would have dismissed Hefets's inept proofs for the existence and unity of God with derision. Here as elsewhere, Maimonides' originality consists in impressing his own stamp on materials supplied by his predecessors.

4. What Followed

In certain respects, Maimonides carried the day. Of all the attempts that have been made to identify the 613 commandments of the Law, his is by far the most widely studied and copied. Commentaries on it and adaptations of it are still being written. More to the point for us, lists of the commandments subsequent to Maimonides, and there are well over a hundred,[84] consistently list affirmation of the existence and the unity of God as positive commandments and identify 'I am the Lord thy God' and 'Hear O Israel' as the verses in which they are embodied. Although Maimonides was not the first to take the position, it was he who propagated it.

Nahmanides, in his *Hasagot* (*Animadversions*) on Maimonides' *Sefer hamitsvot*, does his best to defend *Halakhot gedolot* for its failure to recognize 'I am the Lord thy God' as a commandment. But after all has been said, he joins Maimonides in taking the verse as one of the 613; 'I am the Lord thy God' directs us, in Nahmanides' words, 'to believe' in God. Nahmanides' Bible commentary puts things a little differently. There he characterizes 'I am the Lord thy God' as 'a positive commandment . . . directing them [the members of the Israelite nation] to *know* and *believe* that the Lord exists and is their God. That is to say, He is an eternal being from whom everything [else] derives through the medium of will and power and He is their God, whom they have an obligation to worship.'[85] As for the 'Hear O Israel' verse, Nahmanides

[84] Jellinek, *Kuntres taryag*, lists 144 'poems, books, and treatises, on the [subject of the] 613 commandments of the Law . . . in Hebrew, Spanish, Italian, and German'. About a hundred of Jellinek's entries postdate Maimonides, and since Jellinek's time the number has enjoyed a healthy expansion.

[85] Nahmanides, *Hasagot*, negative commandment 5; id., *Commentary on the Pentateuch*, Exod. 20: 2.

tacitly certifies it as a positive commandment by registering no reservation regarding Maimonides' having included it in his list.[86] Nahmanides thus follows Maimonides in identifying 'I am the Lord' and 'Hear O Israel' as the first two positive commandments. He says nothing about proofs.

The two most influential lists of commandments subsequent to Maimonides are *Sefer mitsvot gadol* (*Large Book of Commandments*) of Rabbi Moses of Coucy and *Sefer haḥinukh*, which is of uncertain authorship; the introductions to both expressly acknowledge the authors' debt to Maimonides. Trailing some distance behind in influence is Isaac of Corbeil's *Amudei golah* (*Pillars of the Diaspora*), commonly known as *Sefer mitsvot katan* (*Small Book of Commandments*). The two French authors lived in the thirteenth century, and *Sefer haḥinukh* appears to belong to the early fourteenth.

The list of 248 positive commandments in *Sefer mitsvot gadol* opens with the dictate 'to *believe* that He who gave us the Torah at Mount Sinai . . . is the Lord our God who took us out of Egypt'; God instructed the Israelites to believe in His existence when He proclaimed at Sinai: 'I am the Lord thy God'. The second positive commandment is the dictate 'to believe and to hear, that is to say, to accept, that He is one in the heavens, the earth, and the four corners [of the world], as is stated [in Scripture]: "Hear O Israel, the Lord our God, the Lord is one"'. Moses of Coucy provides a proof for the unity of God, but it is not the one Maimonides gave. Instead, he offers a proof of Kalam origin, which he found in Sa'adiah's *Sefer emunot vede'ot* (*Book of Beliefs and Opinions*); it reasons, in a nutshell, that if there were two or more gods, they would interfere with, and frustrate one another in the creation and governance of the world.[87] Moses continues: Sa'adiah 'expatiated at great length on the subject of divine unity, yet such length is unnecessary, for all Israel are firm in the belief that the creator of everything is one and unique'; they do not have to be convinced. The book cites several biblical proof texts for the unity of God in addition to the 'Hear O Israel' verse, and among them is: 'Know this day and lay it [to thy heart that the Lord, He is God in heaven above and upon the earth beneath; *there is none else*].'[88]

Moses of Coucy's first two positive commandments of the Law are, then, the two listed by Maimonides and they are located in the same scriptural

[86] In his commentary on Deut. 6: 4, Nahmanides writes of the 'Hear O Israel' verse that 'it too is a commandment'; he interprets it as an expansion on the unity of God, which, he maintains, is already present in the words 'I am the Lord thy God'. That does not necessarily identify 'Hear O Israel' as a formal commandment belonging to the 613; Nahmanides also writes of the two preceding verses in Deut. 6 that they 'command' the Israelites to do one thing or another, yet neither here nor in his *Hasagot* on Maimonides' *SM* does he recognize those verses as formal commandments.

[87] Sa'adiah, *Emunot vede'ot*, 1: 3.

[88] Moses of Coucy, *Sefer mitsvot gadol*, positive commandments 1 and 2.

verses. They have reverted, however, from obligations to know to obligations to believe, and the philosophical proofs that Maimonides provided for fulfilling them have been dropped. In their place, Moses offers a non-technical argument that he found in Sa'adiah, insisting that even this is superfluous. Although the verse 'Know this day and lay it to thy heart' has re-entered the arena, now as the dictate to know God's unity, it no longer is the obligation to conceptualize a rational proof. As far as rational proof is concerned, Maimonides' authority has met a brick wall.

Isaac of Corbeil's *Amudei golah* is a list not of all 613 commandments but only of those—320 in number—that he judged still to be in effect in the diaspora (*golah*) during his day. Because his book limits itself to little more than half of the commandments and, further, treats them briefly, it was dubbed *Sefer mitsvot katan*, the 'Small Book of Commandments', in contradistinction to its predecessor, *Sefer mitsvot gadol*, the 'Large Book of Commandments'.

The first commandment in Isaac of Corbeil's list is the obligation 'to *know* that He who created heaven and earth is the ruler above, below, and at the four corners [of the world], as is written: "I am the Lord thy God, etc." and "Know this day and lay it to thy heart that the Lord, He is God in heaven above and upon the earth beneath; there is none else"'. A subheading—at least in the published version of the book—tells us what we would in any event have realized: the author has drawn from Maimonides' *Mishneh torah* and from *Sefer mitsvot gadol*.

Isaac of Corbeil has formulated the first commandment as an obligation to know, but the knowledge that he has in view is not the knowledge Maimonides envisioned. In a bizarre gloss he informs us that the words 'to know' in his formulation are intended to 'rule out the position of the philosophers, who maintain that the world is controlled by the heavenly bodies, that it has no governor . . . and that even the splitting of the Red Sea and the exodus from Egypt . . . were brought about by the heavenly bodies'. He has taken the knowledge incorporated into the first commandment by Maimonides not as knowledge of the existence of God but rather as knowledge of the error in viewing the heavens as the ultimate cause of events in the lower world and in recognizing no spiritual being beyond them. If I have read him correctly, he had no glimmering of what philosophy signified in the Middle Ages or what Maimonides aimed to accomplish. At all events, he does not repeat Maimonides' proof, or offer any other proof, of the existence of God.

Isaac's second commandment, for which the published version of the book again cites the *Mishneh torah* and *Sefer mitsvot gadol* as sources, is the obligation to 'affirm the unity [*leyaḥed*] of God's name, as is stated [in Scripture]: "Hear O

Israel, the Lord our God, the Lord is one"'. This time, Isaac does offer a proof, but it is Sa'adiah's argument, which he copied from *Sefer mitsvot gadol*, that if there were two gods, they would interfere with each other's efforts.[89]

Sefer haḥinukh is apparently of Spanish origin, and the introduction reveals that the anonymous author, like other medieval Spanish Jewish intellectuals, was acquainted with the terminology of Arabic Aristotelian philosophy. He nevertheless distances himself from the thought that religion should look to philosophy and science for succour. Jewish faith, he maintains, rests not on an exercise of the human intellect, but on the testimony of the Israelites who were present at Sinai, experienced the theophany, and transmitted what they saw and heard to later generations. To him 'whose heart turneth away from the Lord our God' and 'enticeth us' to rely on the human intellect rather than on authoritative tradition, the author responds that 'through our speculation we can never arrive at an understanding of anything whatsoever about God'. Physical scientists are unable to solve such lesser mysteries as the 'peculiar properties of grasses and fruits, the properties of precious stones, and the reason why iron is drawn to the magnet'. How can we expect practitioners of the human intellect to guide us 'in the higher sciences and [help us] attain knowledge of God'?[90]

The author recognizes the dichotomy of 365 negative, and 248 positive commandments but he arranges the commandments differently from the way Maimonides did. He presents them according to the order in which—he understands—they appear in the Pentateuch. The obligation to affirm the existence of God accordingly does not stand at the head of his list. It makes its appearance only when the Decalogue is reached, at which point the author records the commandment 'to *believe* that the world has one God who brought every existent thing into existence . . . and that He brought us out of Egypt and gave us the Torah, as is stated at the beginning of the giving of the Torah [at Sinai]: "I am the Lord thy God who brought thee out of Egypt, out of the house of bondage."' The verse, on his interpretation, instructs the Israelite nation to: '*know* and *believe* that the world has a God. For the word "I" connotes existence. . . . This *belief* is the foundation of religion.' 'Should someone's . . . heart grasp . . . through apodictic demonstration that the belief he holds is true . . . and that nothing else is possible, he fulfils the positive commandment in the most excellent fashion.'[91] The author has meandered back and forth between belief and knowledge, and after having insisted that speculation can reveal nothing whatsoever about God, he finally and as a courtesy to

[89] Isaac of Corbeil, *Amudei golah*, commandments 1 and 2.

[90] *Sefer haḥinukh*, introd., 46–7.

[91] Ibid., commandment 25 (pp. 76–7).

Maimonides grants supererogatory value to mastering a rational demonstration of the existence of God. The value of such a demonstration is nonetheless not strong enough to induce him to furnish one.

When *Sefer haḥinukh* reaches the 'Hear O Israel' verse in Deuteronomy, it explains the verse as 'a positive commandment and not [mere] narrative'. Scripture here enjoins 'believing that God, He who produces all existence and is the ruler of all, is one, without an associate [literally: without association], as is stated: "Hear O Israel. . . ."' Among the particulars of the commandment (*midinei hamitsvah*) is the obligation incumbent on 'every member of the nation of Israel to give his life for the sake of the commandment of declaring [God's] unity', in other words, to suffer martyrdom, if necessary, rather than renounce his monotheistic faith.[92]

In short, the three most influential works on the commandments after Maimonides follow him in identifying the first sentence in the Decalogue as a commandment to believe—the term Maimonides uses in his *Sefer hamitsvot*—or even to know—the term he uses in the *Mishneh torah*—the existence of God. They follow him in identifying the 'Hear O Israel' verse as a commandment to believe in the unity of God. But they carefully drop the requirement that the commandments are fulfilled by mastering rational proofs of the existence and unity of God, and they ignore the proofs that Maimonides provided to help readers fulfil the commandments properly.

In addition to the three works just discussed, I examined thirty-nine compositions subsequent to Maimonides that undertake to enumerate the 613 commandments. I was not selective and simply took whichever printed works on the subject happened to be accessible; the majority are from the nineteenth and twentieth centuries, when the publication of rabbinic books of every genre proliferated. Most are naturally in Hebrew, but other languages are represented as well. I took no account of mere translations of Maimonides' list or of one of the others.

Among the compositions I examined are two enumerations of the commandments in Latin, one written in what can best be characterized as Ashkenazi Aramaic;[93] a list in Spanish;[94] and two in English.[95]

The two in Latin were composed and published in the sixteenth century by Paulus Ricius, a Jewish convert to Christianity, and by the Christian Hebraist Sebastian Münster. Münster, who relied extensively on Moses of Coucy's *Sefer*

92 Ibid., commandment 416 (pp. 528–9).

93 Kahana, *Birkehot ḥayim*.

94 Stepansky de Segal, *Preguntas y respuestas*, 412–64. The author follows Maimonides.

95 Margoliouth, *Fundamental Principles*; Kahan, *Taryag Mitsvos*.

mitsvot gadol, formulates the initial positive commandments as the obligations to 'believe that He who gave the Law to Moses at Mount Sinai is the Lord God'; and to 'believe that God is one in heaven and earth'. In support of the second of these commandments, he deploys the argument, which he found in Moses of Coucy and which the latter borrowed from Sa'adiah, that two gods are impossible since they would interfere with one another.[96] Ricius presents the commandments through the medium of pertinent biblical verses. The first positive commandment in his enumeration is: 'I am the Lord your God' and it mandates belief in God who made the world and provides for 'you'. The second positive commandment is expressed in the verse that—departing from the Vulgate—Ricius renders: *Audi israel deus [tetragrammaton] deus noster deus unus est*, that is: 'Hear O Israel, God [the tetragrammaton], our God, is one God'. It mandates the belief that God is one, while at the same time enabling 'the mystery of the trinity to shine forth clearly'[97] through the three appearances of the word *deus*.

The more interesting of the efforts in English is by Moses Margoliouth, a nineteenth-century Polish Jew who emigrated to England and there converted to Christianity. Margoliouth accompanies his exposition of the 613 commandments with the devout hope that his 'Jewish brethren', whom he holds in undiminished 'affection and admiration . . . for their genius, for their love of learning, and for their literature', would see the light. They would then throw off the heavy ritualistic and legalistic burden imposed by what he calls their 'most extravagant and superstitious religion', and embrace the true faith. At the head of the subscribers to his book stands 'His Royal Highness, The Prince Albert'. Prince Albert is joined by Their Graces, the Lord Archbishops of York and Armagh, seven bishops of the Church of England—two of whom magnanimously subscribed to '2 copies' each—a couple of hundred lesser clergymen, a smaller number of laymen, and 'His Majesty the King of Prussia'.[98]

Four of the enumerations that I examined are in German, namely: a list of the 613 commandments in that language interspersed with Hebrew by an eighteenth-century convert to Christianity,[99] an early nineteenth-century list with facing pages in Hebrew and in German printed in Hebrew characters,

[96] Münster, *Catalogus omnium praeceptorum*, positive commandments 1 and 2.

[97] Ricius, *De sexcentum et tredecim Mosaice sanctionis edictis*, 27a.

[98] Margoliouth, *Fundamental Principles*, pp. xvi–xviii, [i], 1–2, 32, 118, 168, 194, 226. Margoliouth's unhappiness with the Jewish observance of so many commandments must have extended to the commandment embodied in the 'Hear O Israel' verse. As he formulates it, in language adapted from *Sefer haḥinukh*, 528, it requires Jews 'to believe sincerely that God is the Creator of all things, that He is One, that there is no unity like His, and that without an associate, He is Lord of all'. Margoliouth, for his part, declares his faith in God's 'Son, Jesus Christ, the only Mediator between God and Man'.

[99] Leberecht, *Tariack Mitzwoth*.

designed for Jewish elementary schools in the Austro-Hungarian territories,[100] one by a prominent figure in the nineteenth-century German Reform movement, and one from the end of the nineteenth century by an American rabbi who had strong ties to American Reform Judaism.

Theodor Creizenach, the German advocate of Reform, does not commit himself to the accuracy of the figure of 613 Mosaic commandments. He nevertheless offers a standard table of 248 positive and 365 negative commandments, first, as a sort of summary of talmudic law, and then, somewhat inconsistently, in order to make the point that these observances alone are Mosaic, whence it follows that the remaining Jewish rituals and laws are man-made and not permanently binding. Creizenach is known, *inter alia*, for his part in the dispute over the observance of the Jewish festivals for two days outside the Land of Israel.[101] The book by the American rabbi, which was published—in Gothic type, no less—in Cincinnati, Ohio, is a conventional account of the commandments, supplemented by pertinent quotations from a variety of ancient, medieval, and contemporary sources. The foreword has five letters of approbation—'Gutachten'—naturally in German. They come from Isaac Mayer Wise, the guiding spirit of American Reform, and four Reform rabbis who held positions in Chicago, where the author also had served as a rabbi. Wise performs the duty with a palpable lack of enthusiasm, but the author's Chicago colleagues recommend him and his book warmly and without reservation.[102]

Perhaps most curious are a Samaritan enumeration of the 613 divine commandments that goes back at least to the sixteenth century and a composition by an eighteenth-century Karaite scholar, published a quarter of a century ago by a Karaite organization in Israel.

The Samaritan list, which is in Hebrew, contains the positive commandment to bind God's words 'for a sign upon thy hand' and, as a separate commandment, to have them 'for frontlets between thine eyes', that is, to fulfil the phylacteries obligation in some fashion; the commandment to 'write them upon the doorposts of thy house and upon thy gates', that is, to fulfil the *mezuzah* obligation; to 'number fifty days' from the time of bringing the 'sheaf of the waving . . . unto the morrow after the seventh week', that is, to count fifty days from Passover and then to celebrate the festival of Shavuot; and to perform the levirate marriage, that is, wedding the widow of a brother who

[100] Kadisch, *Otsar haḥayim*.

[101] Creizenach, *Thariag*, pp. xiii–xiv. Creizenach follows Moses of Coucy's list and appends that of Maimonides. Katz, *Divine Law in Human Hands*, 270–4, discusses Creizenach's role in the dispute over observing a second day of the Jewish festivals in the diaspora. Creizenach's son Theodor converted to Christianity.

[102] Grossmann, *613 Gesetze der mosaischen Lehre*.

died without issue (*yibum*).[103] The author is extremely concise, usually limiting himself to a pertinent biblical phrase for each item, and he does not explain how he thought the various commandments should be observed. Scholars who have studied Samaritan religious practices report that the sect took the 'sign', the 'frontlets', and the words written upon the doorpost as metaphors; it always had the Shavuot festival occur on a Sunday; and it required that someone other than the actual brother of a deceased married man perform the levirate marriage.[104]

The Karaite composition, which is written in fluent Hebrew, omits a few commandments that appear in the standard rabbinic enumerations but were not accepted by the sect—such as the wearing of phylacteries and the affixing of a parchment scroll containing the 'Hear O Israel' passage to doorposts[105]—and adds a few to fill out the number. In most instances, however, the author follows standard models, with an occasional substitution of Karaite rules for fulfilling a commandment. To take a couple of examples, he, like his rabbinic compeers, includes celebrating the Shavuot festival and performing the levirate marriage among the positive commandments. But he specifies, in opposition to rabbinic law, (1) that Shavuot must always occur on a Sunday; and (2) that the levirate marriage is to be observed 'solely in the Land of Israel' and must be performed by a close male relative of the deceased and not, 'God forbid', by an actual brother, since Scripture prohibits marriage with a brother's wife even after the brother's demise.[106]

[103] Gaster, 'Die 613 Gebote und Verbote der Samaritaner', 394, 396–7, and positive commandments 112, 182, 183, 184, 240. Gaster's theory that the list has its roots in the eleventh century, and hence is earlier than Maimonides, cannot be taken seriously.

[104] Regarding the 'sign', 'frontlets', and words on the doorpost, see Montgomery, *Samaritans*, 32, and Lowy, *Principles of Samaritan Bible Exegesis*, 68–9. Regarding the date for observing Shavuot, see Mishnah *RH* 2: 2, Montgomery, *Samaritans*, 40, and Thomson, *Samaritans*, 133. Regarding the levirate marriage, see Montgomery, *Samaritans*, 185, and Thomson, *Samaritans*, 138 ('the most intimate and trusted friend of the deceased is expected to make the widow his wife'). BT *Kid.* 75*b*–76*a* reports that the Samaritans required the levirate ceremony only in the case of women who were betrothed, and not of women who were married, to the deceased brother. Montgomery, *Samaritans*, 185, writes on the contrary he found Samaritans performing the ceremony in the case of married women. There happens to have been a minority opinion among Karaites that the ceremony should be restricted to women who were betrothed, and not married, to the deceased; see Aaron of Nicomedia, *Gan eden*, 159*b*.

[105] The Karaites took the sign upon the hand, the frontlets between the eyes, and the words written on doorposts (Deut. 6: 8–9) metaphorically and not as phylactery boxes and a parchment scroll.

[106] Luzki, *Torei zahav*. On p. 8 he refers to other Karaite authors who accepted the figure of 613 commandments. The festival of Shavuot is positive commandment 29 in his enumeration; the Karaites celebrated Shavuot on the fiftieth day after the sabbath that falls within the Passover week and hence invariably on a Sunday. See Bashyazi, *Aderet eliyahu*, 72*b*–73*b*. The levirate marriage is positive commandment 71. In rabbinic law the obligation to perform the levirate marriage takes precedence over the prohibition against marrying a brother's widow. In mainstream Karaite law, the

What is striking is that neither the converts to Christianity, the Samaritan and Karaite authors, nor the organization publishing the Karaite work, evinces the slightest discomfort with the conception of exactly 613 divine commandments, divided into 248 positive and 365 negative—a conception that is distinctively rabbinic and has its source in the stronghold of rabbinic law, the Babylonian Talmud.

Almost all of the forty-two writers whose compositions I examined acknowledge Maimonides' influence, the German and English converts to Christianity and the Samaritan writer being noteworthy exceptions. The writers are unanimous in construing the verse 'I am the Lord thy God' as embodying a commandment to affirm the existence of God. Some characterize the deity as the being who brought the world into existence, and others, as the being who took the Israelites out of the house of bondage and favoured them with His Torah at Mount Sinai. Most employ the terminology of belief in their exposition of the commandment, some employ the terminology of knowledge, and a few combine the two. There is even a small number of strained, scholastic attempts to justify the yoking of knowledge with belief. A few incorporate kabbalistic motifs.

Despite their differing orientations, the lists of commandments subsequent to Maimonides thus all agree that the opening sentence of the Decalogue prescribes either belief in or knowledge of God's existence. They are unanimous in construing the 'Hear O Israel' verse as embodying a commandment to 'believe' or to 'affirm' the unity of God. Apart, however, from the pair of works to which I turn now, none makes the fulfilment of the two commandments contingent on rational proof.

I could discover only two enumerations of the 613 commandments after Maimonides, both of them from the Middle Ages, that make knowledge through rational proof a condition for performing the initial positive commandments of the Torah properly. One was composed around the turn of the fourteenth century by David ben Samuel Hakokhavi, a writer who quotes copiously from Maimonides. The cognomen Hakokhavi, 'of the star', is a reference to Estella in Provence, where he was either born or lived.

Hakokhavi identifies the first positive commandment of the Law as the obligation 'to believe in divinity, that is, to believe that there is a cause who produces all existent beings', in accordance with God's declaration 'I am the

prohibition against marrying one's brother's widow takes precedence over the obligation to perform the levirate marriage, although Qirqisani followed the rabbanite position and required the actual brother to perform the marriage. See Aaron of Nicomedia, *Gan eden*, 159*a*–*b*; Bashyazi, *Aderet eliyahu*, 154*a*–*b*.

Lord thy God'. At a minimal level, the obligation is fulfilled without 'great investigation'. But at a higher level, in its 'true essence' and 'with completeness', it demands study of the sciences from the ground up and mastery of the proof of the existence of God from the motion of the celestial spheres. Scripture tells us as much in the verse 'Know this day and lay it to thy heart [that the Lord, He is God in *heaven* above and upon the earth beneath; there is none else]'.

The second positive commandment is the obligation to 'believe [God's] unity', as prescribed by the 'Hear O Israel' verse. Hakokhavi requires that, once a person acquires belief in the unity of God from the Written and Oral Laws, he validate it through 'the theoretical sciences', much as a person should validate his belief in the existence of God through scientific demonstration. As for the demonstration of God's unity that Hakokhavi envisages, I found only a soupçon: among the lessons taught by the 'Hear O Israel' verse, he includes the critical truth that, although the existence of God is established by the motion of the celestial spheres, God is not, in fact, their direct mover; God is distinct from, and transcends, the incorporeal movers of the spheres. Hakokhavi explains: after Maimonides set forth his demonstration of the existence of God as the mover of the heavens and characterized it as the strongest proof of the existence of God, he turned around and proved that in actuality God is distinct from the movers of the spheres—whence it follows that God is transcendent and unique.[107]

The other composition to accord rational proof a role in fulfilling the divine commandments is *Ma'amar haskel*, a medieval composition of unknown date, place, and authorship. The opening lines of the introduction to the book forewarn that it is intended 'solely for him who, to a greater or lesser extent, has familiarized himself with the works of our metaphysical philosophers', and these are: 'the great rabbi, Rabbenu Moses Maimonides; the great scholar, Rabbi Abraham Ibn Ezra; Nahmanides; the great man, Rabbenu Sa'adiah; and the other scholars of Spain'. Persons who have wasted 'their days in vanity' and failed to develop their intellect will derive no benefit from the book.[108]

Borrowings from Sa'adiah and Ibn Ezra can be detected here and there,[109] and the author refers a number of times to Nahmanides. Most frequent and substantial are the quotations and paraphrases from Maimonides, which are

[107] Kokhavi, *Sefer habatim*, 17, 22–5, 47–8, 284, 287–8; *MN* i. 70 (end), ii. 4. The proof for the existence of God as the mover of the outermost sphere is Aristotle's, whereas, the position that God transcends the movers of the spheres is Avicenna's, although Maimonides explicitly ascribes it to Aristotle. As will be seen later, he unwittingly read Avicenna's metaphysics as Aristotle's.

[108] *Ma'amar haskel*, author's introduction (unpaginated).

[109] For example, *Ma'amar haskel*, 1*a*–*b* (Ibn Ezra, not by name), 5*b*, 15*a* (Sa'adiah, by name).

not always labelled as such.[110] The author nevertheless also embraces ideas that are wholly foreign to Maimonides, such as astrological doctrines, the belief that the archangel Michael intercedes with God for Israel, and the proposition that the souls of the wicked are punished in hellfire after the death of their bodies.[111] To cap matters, he hints at kabbalistic secrets that are too deep for the human intellect to grasp, as, for example, transmigration of the soul.[112] The book is a pot-pourri.

The first positive commandment of the Law is, for *Ma'amar haskel*, embodied in the verse 'I am the Lord thy God who brought thee out of Egypt, out of the house of bondage.' Scripture there makes it incumbent on everyone 'to search, to speculate, to recognize his God, and to *know* that He is true, complete existence' and capable 'of bringing every existent being into existence'. The verse 'Know this day and lay it to thy heart that the Lord, He is God' imposes the same obligation, the obligation to acquire rational knowledge of the existence of God.[113]

The author is acquainted with the astronomical concepts out of which Maimonides fashioned his proof from the motion of the celestial spheres,[114] but when he himself comes to 'establish the truth of God's existence', he strikes out on his own. He reverts to a procedure that Maimonides sidestepped when expounding the commandment to know the existence of God in the *Mishneh torah* and expressly rejected in *Moreh nevukhim*, namely, the procedure of arguing first for the creation of the world and inferring the existence of a creator from creation.

The anonymous author starts, like Bahya, by establishing that nothing produces itself and he proceeds to a chain of vertiginous reasoning: 'What is composed of matter and form cannot be eternal.'[115] For 'whatever can possess accidents is a body, every body is linked to a place, place has come into existence [and is not eternal], and whatever is necessarily attached to what has come into existence has also come into existence'. Since the world is composed of matter and form it must therefore have come into existence and hence stand in need of an agent who brought it into existence. How the argument gets from 'what is composed of matter and form' to 'whatever can possess accidents' and what its grounds are for introducing the premise that 'place has come into existence' is unexplained.

110 A few of many instances: *Ma'amar haskel*, 3*b*: Maimonides' analysis of the issue of the creation of the world; 6*b*: Maimonides' theory of divine knowledge; 10*a*–*b*: his explanation, in the *Treatise on Resurrection*, of the reason why resurrection is not mentioned in the Pentateuch; 5*b*–6*a*: his theory of providence; 30*b*: his theory of prophecy; 15*a*, 17*b*–18*a*, *et passim*: his allegorical interpretations of Scripture.

111 *Ma'amar haskel*, 7*b*, 10*b*.

112 Ibid. 2*a*, 19*a*, 19*b*, *et passim*.

113 Ibid.

114 Ibid. 18*b*.

115 The sentence may also be read: 'What is eternal cannot be composed of matter and form.'

To clinch matters, the author expostulates: 'How foolish are they who think that the celestial sphere [*galgal*] turns through its own power!' If a person saw a waterwheel (*galgal*) irrigating a field or a sheet of paper covered with legible writing and was told that the wheel and the writing 'came into existence through themselves', he would laugh the speaker out of court. '*A fortiori*, the great sphere, which is responsible for rest and motion in the sublunar world', plainly has to be a 'body that came into existence by the power of a wise, powerful, eternal maker'.[116] Although *Ma'amar haskel* does not, as far as I could see, ever mention Bahya ibn Pakuda, it obviously is echoing a teleological argument that we met in Bahya.[117]

The second positive commandment identified by *Ma'amar haskel* is 'the affirmation of [God's] unity [as stated in the verse] "Hear O Israel, the Lord our God, the Lord is one"'. The commandment has three moments: recognition of God as our master and 'knowing that we are his servants'; 'knowing that He exists', as already embodied in the earlier verse 'I am the Lord thy God'; and 'knowing that He is the true one, simple, and free of composition'. 'We have the duty to examine and investigate' the unity of God 'by means of our intellect as well as on the basis of tradition, as Scripture says: "Know this day and lay it to thy heart, etc.".' 'Many books' have been written on the subject, according to our author, but he again tries his hand at a proof of his own.

He reasons: from our 'sensation that we exist, our intellect concludes' that something exists which brought us into existence; for 'it is impossible to conceive of a possibly existent being without a necessary being that brought it into existence'. 'By virtue of its necessity', the necessary being 'is conceived of as first'. If there were two such beings, they would have to possess 'something whereby they are distinguished'; the thing whereby they are distinguished would fall 'under the category of quality'; 'there would have to be something prior to both'; 'and neither of the two would therefore be perfect, since the truly perfect is such that nothing else can exist which is similar to it'.[118] Instead of quoting Maimonides' proof for the unity of God in the *Mishneh torah* or one of the proofs for God's unity in Maimonides' *Moreh nevukhim*, our author has taken threads from *Moreh nevukhim*[119] and woven them into a perfect hodgepodge.

The notion that the initial positive commandments of the law are obligations to affirm the existence and the unity of God infiltrated other literary genres. I again offer a couple of illustrations:

116 *Ma'amar haskel*, 13*a*.
117 See above, §2.
118 *Ma'amar haskel*, 13*b*–14*a*.
119 *MN* ii: 1 (*c*) and (*d*).

Joseph Ibn Kaspi, a devotee of Maimonides, suffered from a wanderlust that kept him away from his home in Provence for long periods of time, although without ever interfering with his putting pen to paper. In 1332, Ibn Kaspi was in Spain and preparing to visit a number of locations in that country before travelling on to Morocco. From Spain, he discharged his parental duties by sending his younger son, who was 12, a small book of ethical and religious advice. He counsels the boy to be scrupulous in observing the 613 commandments of the Torah, explains that the 'theoretical . . . commandments' relating to the existence and unity of God can be fulfilled through belief based on the authority of Scripture and tradition but are best fulfilled through rational demonstration, and directs the boy to study Aristotle's *Metaphysics* and Maimonides' *Moreh nevukhim* when he reaches the appropriate age. There he will learn the requisite demonstrations.[120]

Around the end of the fourteenth century, Maimonides was the target of a critique from outside the commandment genre. Hasdai Crescas contends that, in general, belief cannot be mandated; that recognition of the existence of God precedes divine commandments, since the notion of God's imposing obligations is meaningless until His existence is accepted; and that the verse 'I am the Lord thy God' consequently expresses something more fundamental than a commandment. Belief in God's existence is, for Crescas, the 'root and principle underlying the totality of beliefs of the Torah and the commandments' and hence not a commandment itself. Crescas, it happens, does offer a well-thought-out philosophical proof of the existence of God. In that respect, he came closer to Maimonides than the parade of authors who classified belief in the existence of God as one of the 613 divine commandments yet showed no interest in proving it rationally.[121]

It may be of interest that Moses Mendelssohn similarly maintained that the verse 'I am the Lord thy God' is not to be read as a commandment.[122]

Maimonides would scarcely have been pleased to behold the proliferation of works on the 613 commandments. He expected that his *Sefer hamitsvot* would settle the issue once and for all—as he expected that his *Mishneh torah* would

[120] Abrahams, *Hebrew Ethical Wills*, 130–2, 136, 141–2, 144–5.

[121] Crescas, *Or hashem*, 3*a*–*b*, i. 3: 2 (p. 22*a*), ii. 5: 5 (pp. 49*a*–50*b*). For an exposition of Crescas' position and Isaac Abrabanel's response on Maimonides' behalf, see Hyman, 'Rabbi Simlai's Saying and Beliefs Concerning God', 56–8. Another defence of Maimonides against Crescas comes from an unexpected quarter, M. Schick (Maharam), a pillar of 19th-cent. Hungarian Orthodoxy. He may have known of Crescas only through a secondary source, such as the commentaries *Lev same'aḥ* or *Kin'at soferim* on *SM* (Frankel), positive commandment 1. See Schick, *Al taryag mitsvot*, 12*a*.

[122] Mendelssohn, *Netivot hashalom*, Exod. 20: 2, in accordance with the conception of the Jewish religion that he advocates in *Jerusalem*, 71, 97.

be the last word in Jewish law codes. He might, perhaps, have derived some satisfaction from the regularity with which works on the subject of the commandments subsequent to his take the opening sentence of the Decalogue, 'I am the Lord thy God', as a commandment to affirm the existence of God, and the 'Hear O Israel' verse as a commandment to affirm divine unity. But even there, his satisfaction would have been soured by the almost universal refusal to make fulfilment of the two obligations contingent on knowledge through rational proof. The incoherence of one of the two pretences at grounding them in rational proof would hardly relieve the disillusionment.

In his *Moreh nevukhim*, Maimonides remarks that he would, if need be, write for one person in 10,000 and disregard the opinion of everyone else.[123] Whatever the percentage of co-religionists whom he was able to persuade that the most basic of God's commandments are properly fulfilled through knowledge of rational proofs, it was tiny. Still fewer mastered the proofs. By the same token, the broad enterprise of placing the Jewish religion on a wholly rational basis, sketched in the first chapter of the present book, remained the province of no more than a handful of medieval Jews. The vast majority continued to worship what Maimonides disparaged as a figment of their imagination.

So much from the medieval viewpoint. The state of astronomy since Copernicus and Newton, and the state of philosophy since Hume and Kant, would have completed Maimonides' disillusionment. Celestial motion no longer lends itself to a proof of the existence of an incorporeal being who constantly maintains the heavens in motion. Maimonides' *Moreh nevukhim* does supplement the proof for the existence of God from the motion of the spheres with other proofs, but no philosophical school of standing today recognizes them as apodictic demonstrations.

If Maimonides were alive, he would have to concede that he too was no longer able to fulfil the first two positive commandments of the divine Law in the manner he prescribed. More generally, he would have to concede that the ground on which he anchored love, fear, and worship of God had turned to sand.

[123] *MN* introd., 9*b*.

THREE

Maimonides' Knowledge of the Philosophical Literature in his Rabbinic Period

The goal of the human species is to conceive intelligible thoughts. . . . [It is attained by those who are] students of science and philosophize.

MAIMONIDES
Commentary on the Mishnah, introduction

1. Background

RABBINIC WORKS ARE NOT a place where one would expect to encounter philosophy. Although recent scholars have given us books bearing such titles as *The Philosophical Mishnah* and *The Philosophy of the Talmud*,[1] they use the term *philosophy* in the broad sense of the views or attitudes of a person or group. When *philosophy* is understood in the technical sense of the discipline practised by such figures as Plato, Aristotle, Kant, Wittgenstein, and their peers, rabbinic works have not been hospitable to it. The statement holds good for all strata of rabbinic literature—the Mishnah and Talmud corpuses, the classic midrashic compilations, post-talmudic law codes, commentaries on the Mishnah and Talmud, the *ḥidushim* (new interpretations) on the Talmud that are still being composed today. Except for a handful of kabbalistic customs that have been taken up by the law codes, kabbalah, despite the oddly warm reception it has received in traditional Jewish circles, has likewise been shut out of rabbinic literature. Jewish Bible commentaries, by contrast, have proved to be much more open to both philosophy and kabbalah.

Maimonides' *Commentary on the Mishnah* and his law code, the *Mishneh torah*, are striking exceptions. They incorporate a considerable amount of philosophy, an astonishing amount when the contexts are taken into account. One of the digressions with which the *Commentary on the Mishnah* is peppered states Maimonides' rationale.

[1] Neusner, *The Philosophical Mishnah*; Maccoby, *The Philosophy of the Talmud*.

At issue is a theological problem that he does not treat in depth because discussion of it by expert philosophers is 'abstruse and subtle, requiring numerous premisses and a training in the sciences'. He nonetheless permits himself the digression on the grounds that his 'aim is always to offer some explanation whenever a whiff of a statement involving belief comes up. For to give instruction regarding a root [or: principle (Arab.: *aṣl*)] is, for me, preferable to giving instruction regarding anything else'.[2] He is implying a contrast between beliefs, which are the roots, or principles, of the Jewish religion, and the legal and ceremonial side, which are the branches. Although laws and ceremonies are the primary subject of his rabbinic works, he is asserting that the underlying religious beliefs are even closer to his heart. As he makes his way through the formal subject matter of the *Commentary on the Mishnah* and of the *Mishneh torah*, he keeps his word. Where opportunities arise, he offers instruction regarding correct belief, and the instruction, more often than not, is philosophical in character.

As we have seen, Maimonides teaches that the two most basic of the 613 commandments given by God to Moses and Israel are fulfilled by mastering demonstrations of God's existence and unity. Love of God, a fundamental religious obligation and another of the 613 commandments in Maimonides' list, is contingent on rational knowledge not only of God's existence, but also of His nature, and knowledge of His nature is possible only through knowledge of His actions. Since God's handiwork is nothing less than the entire universe, the greater one's knowledge of the universe, the greater one's love of God. The classic rabbinic texts may appear to reject the study of science and philosophy, but Maimonides was convinced that the texts had been misunderstood. As he reads them, the rabbis made physics and metaphysics part of their study curriculum and viewed metaphysics as 'a great matter', in contrast to talmudic legal disputations, which they considered 'a small matter'.

In that spirit, he writes in the introduction to his *Commentary on the Mishnah*, prophets and philosophers agree that everything in the lower, physical world exists for the single purpose of bringing forth men who excel in 'knowledge and practice' (*ʿilm* and *ʿamal*). 'Practice' here means 'balance in natural matters . . . [that is,] taking from them only what contributes to the maintenance of the body and the improvement of one's qualities [*khulq*]'—in other words, tempering physical gratification in order to equip oneself for the acquisition of moral virtue. The knowledge that the prophets and philosophers had in view is the 'conceiving of the true essences [of things] . . . and the cognition [*idrāk*] of everything a man can know'. Should someone fail to grasp

[2] Maimonides, *Commentary on the Mishnah*, *Ber.* 9: 7.

the import, Maimonides removes any ambiguity a page later when he writes: 'The goal of the human species is to conceive intelligible thoughts', and that goal is attained by those who are 'students of science and philosophize'.[3]

In short, Maimonides maintained from an early period that knowledge of philosophy is a condition for fulfilling the most fundamental religious obligations; he believed that the prophets and ancient rabbis endorsed the philosophical ideal; he joins them in embracing it; and he commits himself to elucidating what he understands to be the philosophical roots of the Jewish religion whenever the context in his rabbinic works offers an appropriate opportunity.

Philosophy as pursued in the Middle Ages looked backwards to a greater extent than it does today; preparation consisted, to a greater extent, in mastering the writings of those who had gone before. Seeing that Maimonides regards philosophy as integral both to the goal of human life in general and to fulfilling the obligations of the Jewish religion, one might easily assume that he too steeped himself in the philosophical literature available at the time. Recent scholars have made this assumption.

The present chapter and the one that follows will undertake to ascertain how far his commitment to the philosophical ideal expressed itself in the study of the writings of earlier philosophers during the period when he composed his rabbinic works, that is to say, from his early twenties until the age of 40. Chapter 5 will do the same for the later period of his life, during which he composed *Moreh nevukhim.*

From today's vantage point, we can discern four distinct strands of philosophy that angled for adherents in Maimonides' milieu: the translations of Aristotle, Neoplatonism, Kalam, and Arabic Aristotelianism. I begin with Neoplatonism. The evidence is so scanty in its case that there would be little point in discussing Maimonides' early and later periods separately, and I accordingly treat them together.

2. Neoplatonism

Plotinus and his Greek followers saw themselves simply as students of Plato, and the terms *Neoplatonist* and *Neoplatonism* are modern coinages. It is hardly remarkable, therefore, that medieval Arabic thinkers looking at what we regard as Neoplatonic texts did not realize that they had to do with a distinct, well-defined school.

The main channels through which Neoplatonic thought reached the Arabic

[3] Ibid., introd., 42–3.

Middle Ages are three compositions, each of which paraphrases a different set of passages from Plotinus' *Enneads*. The paraphrases may have existed in Greek or Syriac before being translated into Arabic, but only the Arabic versions have survived. The name *Plotinus*, which barely penetrated medieval Arabic literature,[4] does not appear in any of the three. One names no author, a second names Alfarabi as its author, and the third and best known, *The Theology of Aristotle*, names Aristotle, with the comment that Porphyry also had a hand in putting it together.[5] Plotinus' student Porphyry did in fact mould the Greek text of the *Enneads* into its present shape.

The *Ennead* paraphrases were supplemented by excerpts, in Arabic, from Proclus, most importantly translations and paraphrases of a number of theorems from Proclus' *Elements of Theology*. Manuscripts of the excerpts from the *Elements of Theology* again name their authors in different ways. They report that 'Proclus is said to have excerpted it [that is, what they contain] from Plato's words'; that what they contain was 'composed by Proclus, who is said to have excerpted it from Plato'; that the author was Aristotle; or that the contents are 'what Alexander of Aphrodisias extracted from Aristotle's book called *Theologia*, which means: *Discourse on Divinity*'. Alexander preceded Proclus by two centuries.[6]

Alfarabi and Avicenna accepted the *Theology of Aristotle* as a genuine work of Aristotle's, and Avicenna wrote a commentary on it. Otherwise none of the paraphrases of sections from Plotinus or excerpts from Proclus have left an overt mark on the philosophical milieu in which Maimonides placed himself.

The paraphrases of sections from the *Enneads* assume the standard Neoplatonic emanation scheme. An incorporeal, utterly transcendent, and ineffable First Cause, the One, stands at the top. It is followed by the cosmic Intellect, which is the source of all intellect in the universe, the cosmic Soul, which is the source of all souls, and the physical world. Each successive stage emanates eternally and spontaneously from the one above it in such a manner that the emanating source loses nothing of itself in the process.

The cosmology is accompanied by a characteristic conception of the human soul: individual souls descend from the eternal cosmic Soul into the world of physical bodies, and that thesis gives rise to a series of questions. Why do souls leave the comfort of their supernal home and make the descent? Can a soul return to its source while still associated with a human body? Can it rise

[4] Rosenthal, 'Plotinus in Islam', repr. in his *Greek Philosophy in the Arab World*, item iv.

[5] Plotinus, *Opera*, vol. ii, has an English translation of the three paraphrases printed opposite corresponding passages in the *Enneads*.

[6] Van Ess, 'Jüngere orientalische Literatur zur neuplatonischen Überlieferung', 345; Endress, *Proclus Arabus*, 13–14, 18–19.

beyond its origin in the cosmic Soul and come into contact with the cosmic Intellect? And so on.

Maimonides, not surprisingly, never mentions the names Plotinus or Proclus. He never refers in any way to the paraphrases of the *Enneads* or excerpts from Proclus, and the *Theology of Aristotle* in particular has left no mark on his writings.[7] The most substantial medieval work of a Neoplatonic character that we might imagine him reading is Solomon Ibn Gabirol's *Fons vitae* (*Mekor ḥayim*), a book belittled by Abraham ibn Daud, Maimonides' older contemporary, because of its long-windedness and philosophical blunders.[8] Maimonides betrays no inkling of having seen or heard of the book.

He does provide a few tantalizing straws in a letter that he wrote to Samuel Ibn Tibbon in the late 1190s, that is, several years after completing *Moreh nevukhim*. Ibn Tibbon requested an evaluation of Greek, Islamic, and Jewish thinkers, and Maimonides complied.

Among those whom he evaluates for Ibn Tibbon is the Jewish writer Isaac Israeli. Maimonides observes, not very kindly, that Israeli's '*Book of Definitions* and *Book on the [Physical] Elements*' are 'inanities, wind, and vanities. For Israeli was . . . solely a physician' and not a philosopher.[9] Two of the terms taken up in the *Book of Definitions* are *soul* and *sphere*, and in defining them, Israeli alludes to the Neoplatonic emanation scheme.[10] If Maimonides caught the allusions, he lumps that emanation scheme together with the other inanities of which Israeli was guilty.

He also offers Ibn Tibbon his opinion of the 'works of Empedocles, Pythagoras, Hermes, and Porphyry', although he unfortunately says nothing about what those works contained.

Texts falsely ascribed to Empedocles and evincing a strong Neoplatonic colouring circulated in Arabic,[11] and there circulated at least one Arabic work attributed to the mythical Hermes that revolves around the Neoplatonic conception of the human soul.[12] There is thus a chance that Maimonides was exposed to a watered-down version of the Neoplatonic picture of the universe and conception of the soul. It is difficult even to guess what he might mean by the works of Pythagoras and Porphyry. The *Theology of Aristotle* comes to mind, since the Arabic title mentions Porphyry's name, but, as just noted,

[7] Ivry, 'Neoplatonic Currents in Maimonides', does a yeoman's job in trying to identify allusions to Plotinus' theories in Maimonides, but I cannot see that he succeeds.

[8] Ibn Daud, *Emunah ramah*, 2–3.

[9] Marx, 'Texts by and about Maimonides', 378.

[10] Altmann and Stern, *Isaac Israeli*, 41–2, 45–6.

[11] Kaufmann, *Studien über Salomon b Gabirol*; *Encyclopaedia of Islam*, s.v. *Anbāduḳlīs*.

[12] Pseudo-Hermes, *Hermes Trismegistus an die menschliche Seele*; *Hermetis Trismegisti . . . de Castigatione animae libellum*.

Maimonides discloses no evidence of ever having seen the *Theology*. The survey of the views of philosophers put together by Shahrastani—the Muslim historian of thought who preceded Maimonides by two generations—devotes sections to both Pythagoras and Porphyry.[13] Shahrastani describes Porphyry as a follower of Aristotle. His account of Pythagoras focuses on the latter's lucubrations concerning the numerals 1 to 10, which are the 'bases of existent beings'; along the way, however, he credits Pythagoras with what we know to be the Neoplatonic cosmic hierarchy, something that the historical Pythagoras of course never dreamed of.[14] In one way or another, Neoplatonic motifs were linked to the names of all four men.

Maimonides' opinion of the four is no more positive than his opinion of Isaac Israeli. He advises Ibn Tibbon that their writings are 'ancient philosophy' serving no function apart from wasting a person's time.[15] Whether he is offering his own judgement, growing out of his reading, or is relying on what he knew of the reputation of the four and the works attributed to them is uncertain.

Nothing, then, that Maimonides wrote at any stage of his career discloses a consciousness of a distinct Neoplatonic strand of philosophy, whether ancient or medieval. He never takes cognizance of the Neoplatonic cosmology or conception of the soul. In his later period he refers to a work of Isaac Israeli's that contains allusions to the Neoplatonic cosmology; to one or more pseudographical writings of Empedocles, which to judge from what is extant would have offered a watered-down Neoplatonic cosmology; and to one or more works ascribed to the mythical Hermes and reflecting the Neoplatonic concept of the soul. When he mentions Porphyry and Pythagoras, he could be thinking of Neoplatonic material ascribed to them in the Middle Ages. Whatever it was that he knew about these authors left him unimpressed, since he dismisses their writings as worthless.

Neoplatonism did make an indirect contribution to his thought insofar as threads extracted from it—most notably the concept of a first cause of the existence, and not merely the motion, of the universe; the unknowability of God's essence; and the concept of emanation—were appropriated by the Arabic Aristotelians, encountered by Maimonides in their writings, and taken by him to be authentically Aristotelian.

[13] Shahrastani, *Al-milal wa-al-niḥal*, 345; French trans.: *Livre des religions et des sectes*, 357 and n.

[14] Shahrastani, *Al-milal wa-al-niḥal*, 267–9; *Livre*, 203–6.

[15] Marx, 'Texts by and about Maimonides', 380.

3. Kalam

The Kalam was a school of Islamic thought—with a few Jewish adherents—that defended a set of theses regarding the universe with rational, albeit idiosyncratic, arguments. It can accordingly lay claim to classification as philosophy, although its adversaries dismissed it as undeserving of the honorific and the Kalam thinkers themselves were more than willing to forgo the distinction.

Alfarabi composed a work on the subject matters and methods of the various sciences and he devotes a section to the Kalam. He was unwilling, however, to grace it with the label of either *philosophy* or *science*, and pointedly calls it 'the *art* of Kalam'. With equal pointedness, he defines it not as a specifically Islamic system, but simply as unabashed apologetics—to use a modern term—deployed in defence of the basic beliefs of an established religion.[16]

In *Moreh nevukhim*, Maimonides drew from a different work of Alfarabi's, which is no longer extant, when offering an account of the history of what he does call 'the science of Kalam'. He traces the Kalam style of argumentation back to Greek and Syriac scholars who adopted the Christian religion and undertook to defend their new faith against the challenge of philosophy. They picked and chose premisses, he writes, not because the premisses were correct but because they would serve their apologetic purpose. Then, when Islam came on the scene and Muslim thinkers likewise sensed that philosophy posed a threat to their religion, they imitated their Christian predecessors and went further. They borrowed a theory of atomism from 'the early philosophers', the falseness of which was demonstrated by 'the later philosophers', and employed it for their own ends.[17]

The only rabbinic work of Maimonides in which I have found traces of the Kalam is his *Commentary on the Mishnah*.

Maimonides had a liking for introductions, and at a number of junctures in the *Commentary* stops and provides an introduction to the text that he is about to expound. The best known is his introduction to Mishnah *Avot*, the sole tractate in the Mishnah corpus the contents of which are wholly non-legal. *Avot* means *fathers*, and *Avot* is a collection of rabbinic maxims, most of them ethical in nature, reported in the names of the spiritual fathers of the Jewish nation—hence the title *Ethics of the Fathers* by which the tractate is commonly known in English. Maimonides' introduction to *Avot* is often separated from his full

[16] Alfarabi, *Catálogo de las Ciencias*, 100–7; English trans., 27–30. It is against the background of Alfarabi that Strauss speculates—partly with tongue in cheek—whether the *Guide* is a Kalam work; Strauss, *Persecution and the Art of Writing*, 40–1.

[17] *MN* i. 71.

Commentary on the Mishnah and treated as an independent composition, and since it happens to be divided into eight chapters, it is known, when standing alone, as *Shemonah perakim* (*Eight Chapters*).[18] Maimonides refers to the Kalam at three spots in *Shemonah perakim*, and as far as I could determine, his *Commentary on the Mishnah* contains one possible additional reference.

Human freedom of choice is among the topics he discusses in *Shemonah perakim*, and in connection with it, he considers the theological position that everything a man does, even sitting or standing, is determined by God. The proposition, he writes, is valid only in the sense that when God created man, He gave him a 'nature' enabling him to sit or stand as he chooses. Similarly, when God created the rest of the universe, He implanted in the nature of each kind of being the ability to act in certain ways. But the Kalam thinkers (*mutakallimūn*) were of 'a different opinion'. For, Maimonides writes, 'I have heard them maintain' that at every moment, God exercises His will and decides what is to occur.[19] God decides at every moment whether each individual human being will sit or stand, as well as everything else that occurs in the universe at that moment.

The thesis that God directly determines everything in the universe is a genuine Kalam position, although the Muʿtazilite branch of the school appended qualifications. When Maimonides writes that he 'heard' Kalam thinkers maintain it, the word could be no more than a *façon de parler*, but he could also be speaking advisedly. He could be reporting what he happened to have heard, as distinct from what he had learned from study and reading.

At another place in *Shemonah perakim*, Maimonides discusses the faculties of the human soul. In connection with the imaginative faculty, he calls attention to 'the enormous, reprehensible mistake on which they [the Kalam thinkers] built the foundation of their imposture', namely, the supposition that 'whatever can be imagined has the possibility [of existing]'. The Kalam, in other words, held that no imaginable state of affairs, such as—to take examples that Maimonides gives of fantasies concocted by the human imaginative faculty—an animal possessed of a thousand eyes or 'a ship made of iron that travels through the air', can be excluded on empirical grounds or because of physical laws.[20] In *Moreh nevukhim*, Maimonides characterized the proposition regarding imaginable states of affairs as one of the most fundamental premisses of the Kalam school, and we shall see that there are inaccuracies in the way he presents it.[21]

[18] Maimonides simply called it 'Introduction to *Avot*'. Cf. Rosin, *Die Ethik des Maimonides*, 31 n. 1.

[19] *ShP*, ch. 8, p. 399. *MN* iii. 17 (3) characterizes the thesis as a doctrine peculiar to the Asharite branch of Kalam.

[20] *ShP*, ch. 1, p. 375.

[21] *MN* i. 73 (10, excursus); below, Ch. 5, §1.

The third reference to the Kalam in *Shemonah perakim* occurs when Maimonides comments on Jewish writers who accepted the notion of 'intellectual commandments', that is, religious commandments that are discoverable by the human intellect independently of any enactment by the divine legislator.[22] Maimonides characterizes those writers as suffering from 'the sickness of the Kalam thinkers', and that is as much as he says.[23] He is probably referring to the position of the Muʿtazilite branch of Kalam, which was categorically rejected by the Asharite branch, that ethical truths are discoverable by the human intellect.

The remaining possible reference to the Kalam occurs in another part of the *Commentary on the Mishnah*. The discussion there leads Maimonides to mention and reject a contention of a '*mutakallim*' on the subject of divine providence and retribution. In the context, the term *mutakallim* could have the non-technical sense of 'a speaker', a sense that it actually has a few lines earlier on the same page. Maimonides could merely be remarking that someone or other had uttered the opinion in question. Nevertheless, since he immediately cites 'expert philosophers' as a counterweight to the *mutakallim*, he is probably using the word in the specific sense of a member of the Kalam school. Whatever his meaning, the passage tells us virtually nothing. All Maimonides says is that the contention he refers to is 'imagination and rhetoric resembling an argument' without being one.[24] We are left in the dark as to what the contention was.

A further detail is furnished by a highly born Muslim personage, Ibn Sanā' al-Mulk, who describes a disputation on the 'science of Kalam', which, he indicates, was held before an audience.[25] The participants were Ibn Sanā' al-Mulk himself, a second recognized Muslim scholar, and Maimonides; nothing that the participants said is recorded. Since Ibn Sanā' al-Mulk was born in 1155, we may conjecture that the event did not take place before, or much before, 1175. Its latest possible date would seem to be the end of 1186 or beginning of 1187, because there is a report that the second Muslim scholar died at that time. In 1175 Maimonides had long since finished his *Commentary on the Mishnah* and had been working for six or seven years on the *Mishneh torah*. By 1187 he had completed the latter and was well along in writing *Moreh nevukhim*.

In sum, Maimonides refers to three Kalam tenets during the period when he composed his *Commentary on the Mishnah*. Of one, he writes that he 'heard'

[22] See above, Ch. 2, §2.
[23] *ShP*, ch. 6, p. 392.
[24] Maimonides, *Commentary on the Mishnah*, *Ber.* 9: 7.
[25] Rosenthal, 'Maimonides and a Discussion of Muslim Speculative Theology', 110.

Kalam thinkers maintain it; of a second that Kalam thinkers 'built the foundation of their imposture on it', although, as we shall see later, that is not wholly accurate; and of a third that it was held by the 'Kalam thinkers' although, if I understood the allusion correctly, it was embraced by only one of the two branches and rejected by the other. The evidence establishes some familiarity with the movement but not very much. Between about 1175 and the beginning of 1187, that is to say, after he had completed the *Commentary on the Mishnah* and perhaps the *Mishneh torah* as well, his grasp of Kalam thought was at a level where he could dispute the subject with Muslim scholars.

As for his opinion of the Kalam, it reflects the jaundiced view of the school that was standard among the Arabic Aristotelians.

4. Aristotle

Although the philosophical material in Maimonides' two main rabbinic works is virtually the same in content, their modes of presentation are different. In the *Commentary on the Mishnah*, philosophical notions are scattered, and the fragments have to be pieced together for a picture to be obtained. The *Mishneh torah* sketches a concise and systematic philosophical picture of the universe in its opening chapters, and the book is so designed that the sketch is called for at just that point.

Furthermore, the *Mishneh torah* mentions even its Jewish sources in summary fashion, as part of an overall introduction. Aside from a few general references to Muslim and Greek astronomy,[26] it scrupulously avoids any mention of non-Jewish literature. The *Commentary on the Mishnah*, by contrast, makes no bones about borrowing from non-Jewish sources. The *Commentary* makes only one reference to a philosopher by name, an explicit reference to Aristotle. But at various junctures, it cites: 'the philosopher', 'the pre-eminent figure in philosophy', 'the philosophers', 'the statements of ancient and recent philosophers', 'expert philosophers', 'philosophers who are perfect', 'the statements of the philosophers who are expert in philosophy', 'metaphysical [literally: divine] philosophers', 'the philosophers' belief', 'the philosophy of Greece', 'metaphysics', 'divine science, that is to say, metaphysics', 'first philosophy', which again means metaphysics, and philosophical matters that are 'abstruse' and 'subtle'.[27] In medieval Arabic literature, *philosopher* in the singular generally means Aristotle. *Philosophers* in the plural usually means members of the

[26] *MT*, 'Hilkhot yesodei hatorah', 3: 5; 'Hilkhot kidush haḥodesh', 11: 2, 3, 5, 17: 24.

[27] Maimonides, *Commentary on the Mishnah*, introd., 42; *Ber.* 9: 7; *RH* 2: 7 (p. 316); *San.* 10 (introd., pp. 204–5, 212); *AZ* 4: 7; *Avot* 3: 11, 3: 20, 5: 13; *Nid.* 3: 2; *ShP*, ch. 1, p. 372, ch. 4, p. 386, ch. 6, ch. 8, pp. 397, 405, 406.

Arabic Aristotelian school but may also designate persons who, in general, plied the philosophical craft.

The passages in the *Commentary on the Mishnah* that cite propositions in the name of the philosopher, the philosophers, or philosophy arrange themselves under five rubrics: human physiology, the human intellect, ethics, human free choice, and the nature of God. I take them up in turn, and that will require entering into some technical discussion.

Human Physiology

At two places in the *Commentary on the Mishnah*, Maimonides cites the *Problemata physica* (*Al-masāʾil al-ṭabīʿiyya*), a Greek work attributed in error to Aristotle and consisting of hundreds of pieces of miscellaneous information, particularly of a biological and physiological character. Maimonides knew it in an Arabic version that parallels about half of the preserved Greek text and is not, even in that half, a straightforward translation; somewhere in the process of transmission or translation, the text mutated.[28] Inasmuch as the contents are largely biological and physiological, the *Problemata* was employed by Arab physicians as a medical text,[29] and Maimonides may have read it as part of his medical education.

One of the passages in which he cites the *Problemata* elucidates a ruling in the Mishnah regarding deaf mutes. Maimonides observes that congenital deafness is accompanied by muteness because a child who is deaf from birth never hears speech and consequently never learns to speak himself, as was 'made clear in the *Problemata physica*'. He undoubtedly has in view an item in the Arabic *Problemata* stating that a child with congenital deafness has great difficulty learning to speak because he cannot learn from hearing the speech of others.[30] The second passage concerns the Mishnah's description of the high priest's preparation for the Day of Atonement. The high priest was not allowed to sleep on the eve of the holy day, lest he have a seminal emission, which would render him impure. One way that he kept awake was by standing on a cold floor. In his commentary, Maimonides explains that warm feet induce sleepiness, and the reason is 'made clear in the *Problemata physica*'. The *Problemata* does associate warm feet with sleepiness, although it does not, as far as I could see, say that they *induce* sleepiness.[31]

A third passage in the *Commentary on the Mishnah* may also derive from the *Problemata*. The mishnaic paragraph that now elicits Maimonides' comment

[28] *The Problemata Physica attributed to Aristotle*, pp. xvii–xxvi.

[29] Ullmann, *Die Medizin im Islam*, 93–4; *The Problemata Physica attributed to Aristotle*, pp. xliii–xliv.

[30] Maimonides, *Commentary on the Mishnah*, *Ter.* 1: 2; *The Problemata Physica attributed to Aristotle*, 528–31, expanding on *Problemata physica*, 11. 1.

[31] Maimonides, *Commentary on the Mishnah*, *Yoma* 1: 7; *The Problemata Physica attributed to Aristotle*, 260–3, paralleling and supplementing *Problemata physica*, 4. 5.

treats monstrous human births, such as offspring resembling fish, locusts, creeping things, animals, and birds; the ritual question is whether giving birth to creatures of this sort renders the mother ritually impure, as a normal birth does. Maimonides writes: 'Do not suppose that it is impossible, from the standpoint of nature, for a human being to give birth to everything stated [in the Mishnah paragraph]. . . . The *philosopher* has reported even stranger things than these.' He could be thinking of an item in the Arabic version of the *Problemata* that recognizes the possibility of a woman's giving birth to 'part of the [human] form, such as bone and pieces of flesh, without the natural shape's being perfected'.[32]

The *Problemata physica*, hardly a philosophic text, is thus a book with which Maimonides was acquainted.

Human Intellect

A pair of passages in the *Commentary on the Mishnah* tell us that statements made by the rabbis reflect what the philosophers teach about the human intellect. In one of the passages, Maimonides reads a mishnaic statement as the encapsulation of a 'philosophic matter' that is 'very subtle' and difficult to understand 'even from the books composed regarding it'. He makes the following brief points, which he concedes will be comprehensible only to those who have the proper background: when man 'acquires' intellect, that is, when the human intellect is in a state of actuality, it consists in cognition (*idrāk*) of the intelligible thought that it thinks. What it thinks can be the form of a physical object that 'we separate' from the object's material side. Alternatively, the intellect can have cognition of 'forms that are incorporeal [*mufāraq*; literally: 'separated'] in their being, without our rendering them intellect'.[33] Elucidation is plainly needed.

The part about forms of physical objects was later explained by Maimonides in the *Guide for the Perplexed*, where he offers the following illustration. Before a man acquires the concept of wood, his intellect is in a state of potentiality and the form of the piece of wood to which he directs his attention is a potential intellectual thought. By abstracting the form of wood from its material substratum and thinking it, the man renders his intellect actual and renders the form an actual thought. The intellect and the form of wood are then not 'two things', for actual human intellect is nothing 'other than what it thinks'. In taking the form abstracted from a piece of wood as a thought, the human intellect becomes identical with that form.[34]

[32] Maimonides, *Commentary on the Mishnah*, *Nid.* 3: 2; *The Problemata Physica attributed to Aristotle*, 276–7, which reworks *Problemata physica*, 4. 13.

[33] Maimonides, *Commentary on the Mishnah*, *Avot* 3: 20.

[34] *MN* i. 68 (86*b*–87*b*).

The passage from the *Commentary on the Mishnah* further says that the human intellect is able to think forms that already exist apart from matter and consequently do not have to be separated off and abstracted. When the intellect manages to have such a form as the concept it thinks—analogously to its having the form of wood as its concept—the intellect again becomes one with what it thinks. How a person can accomplish the extraordinary feat of getting a form that exists apart from matter to present itself to him is not taken up by Maimonides.

The human intellect can, in a word, have forms abstracted from matter as well as beings that already are forms free of matter as the thoughts it thinks. In each instance the intellect becomes identical with the abstracted or abstract form.

The second passage in the *Commentary on the Mishnah* that addresses the subject of human intellect introduces an additional flourish. In the course of a digression, Maimonides quotes a rabbinic portrayal of the righteous in the world to come as 'sitting with their crowns on their heads and enjoying the splendour of the divine presence'. The rabbis were not, in his view, indulging in colourful whimsy. They were offering an allegory for 'the permanence of the soul through the permanence of its object of knowledge and through their being one, as expert philosophers have stated, using arguments [*ṭuruq*] too long to expound here'. An explanation is again in order.

The human intellect, as seen from the first passage, may manage to have an incorporeal form as the thought it thinks and, in doing so, become one with that form. Maimonides now adds that since incorporeal forms are immune from destruction, a human intellect—which he loosely calls a 'soul'—becoming one with an incorporeal form will be equally indestructible. Having an immortal form as the thought it thinks renders the human intellect immortal.

Maimonides goes on: 'The ultimate end and eudaemonia [well-being]' for man, as well as the highest conceivable human pleasure, consists in attaining the intellectual level at which the soul has 'unending . . . permanence by reason of the permanence of the Creator, who is the cause of the soul's permanence thanks to the soul's having cognition [*idrāk*] of Him, as explained in first philosophy'.[35] Maimonides apparently is saying that the human soul—in other words, the human intellect—not only can have an incorporeal being as the thought it thinks. It can have God Himself, the highest incorporeal being, as the form it thinks. It not merely thinks *about* God, but becomes one with the divine form—that is to say, with God!—shares in God's permanence, and attains ultimate human eudaemonia and immortality. Leaving aside the

[35] Maimonides, *Commentary on the Mishnah*, *San.* 10, introd., 205.

extraordinariness of the notion, there is a problem in such a reading of Maimonides, for he insists in the *Commentary on the Mishnah* and elsewhere that human beings cannot know God's essence.[36] If man cannot know God's essence, which is His form, he can scarcely have the form and essence of God as the thought he thinks and thereby become one with it and with God.

Just before the lines I have quoted, Maimonides discourses on the immense pleasure enjoyed by the 'angels', that is, the incorporeal intelligences, and by the 'stars and spheres', that is to say, the intellects of the celestial spheres, through 'the intelligible thought that they have of the creator' (*bi-mā ʿaqalūhu min al bāriʾ*). By the same token, a human soul—an intellect—that 'purifies itself' will, after the death of the body, have an 'intelligible thought of the creator which is similar to, or exceeds, the intelligible thought achieved by the [intellects of the] supernal [celestial] bodies'; and the human intellect will then enjoy a proportionate level of pleasure.[37] Maimonides apparently is saying that there are levels in thinking the form of God, that the incorporeal intelligences attain one level, the intellects of the spheres attain another, and after death, a successful human intellect attains yet another. A statement in Maimonides' *Mishneh torah* likewise suggests that there are levels in an intellect's having God as the form it thinks.[38] But if God's essence is absolutely simple and non-composite, how can there be degrees in having it as a concept and becoming one with it?[39]

The only way I see out of the conundrum is to take Maimonides' intent to be not that the human intellect actually has God Himself as the form it thinks, but that the intellect thinks and becomes one with the form of an incorporeal being belonging to the supernal hierarchy headed by God.

The final rung in the incorporeal hierarchy, the active intellect, is the incorporeal being that plays a role in sublunar phenomena[40] and specifically in the development of the human intellect. Maimonides merely touches on the subject of the active intellect in his rabbinic works. He writes, for example, in the *Commentary on the Mishnah* that men of superior natural qualities and perfected intellects may succeed in having their intellect 'conjoin . . . with the

[36] *Commentary on the Mishnah*, *Ber.* 9: 7; *ShP*, ch. 8, p. 406; *MT*, 'Hilkhot yesodei hatorah', 2: 8.

[37] Maimonides, *Commentary on the Mishnah*, *San.* 10, introd., 204.

[38] *MT*, 'Hilkhot yesodei hatorah', 2: 8: The incorporeal intelligences have knowledge of God that exceeds the ability of 'men, who are made of matter and form', to know Him; the intelligences vary in their ability to know God in 'accordance with their level' in the hierarchy; none achieves 'cognition of the true nature of God as it is' and know Him as he knows Himself.

[39] In *MN* i. 59, Maimonides also speaks of levels in knowing God, but he makes clear (p. 73*a*), that the human intellect cannot have cognition of God; only God has cognition of what He is. The levels in knowing God are different degrees of negation, that is, different degrees in comprehending what God is not.

[40] *MT*, 'Hilkhot yesodei hatorah', 4: 6.

active intellect, whereupon a noble emanation from the active intellect emanates upon them' and they attain the gift of prophecy.[41] That statement, the few references to the active intellect in the *Mishneh torah*, and the fuller account of the active intellect in the *Moreh nevukhim*[42] are wholly in the spirit of Arabic Aristotelian theories of intellect. And when Maimonides speaks of the 'philosophers', as he does in the second of the passages from the *Commentary on the Mishnah* that we are considering, the Arabic Aristotelians are as a rule those whom he has in view. A point on which the Arabic Aristotelians agreed was that fully developed human intellects, even of non-prophets, can enter into conjunction with the active intellect.

The incorporeal being that the human intellect is capable of having as the thought it thinks, thereby attaining permanent eudaemonia and immortality, is most likely not God Himself, but rather the active intellect, which is a kind of vicar of God on earth. Maimonides, it must be kept in mind, composed the *Commentary on the Mishnah* for non-philosophers and accordingly expresses himself loosely.

Much of what he writes in the first of the two passages I have quoted from the *Commentary on the Mishnah* ultimately goes back to Aristotle's *De anima*. The *De anima* states that the human intellect becomes one with what it thinks, that the intellect ordinarily thinks forms abstracted from matter, and that it sometimes may have 'what contains no matter' as the thought it thinks.[43] A subsequent sentence in the *De anima* promises, in the language of the Arabic translation, that 'we shall later investigate whether or not the intellect, while it is in the body, can know any [of the things] that are separated from bodies'.[44] The promise is not kept in Aristotle's preserved works.

What Aristotle intended by the intellect's having that which contains no matter as the form it thinks is far from clear. One scholarly opinion is that he was alluding to transcendental concepts, that is to say, concepts such as *the good* and *the beautiful*.[45] In the *Metaphysics*, he analyses *the good* and *the beautiful* and concludes that they are identical with *to be good* and *to be beautiful*, which seems to mean that they are identical with the essence of *good*, and the essence of *beautiful*.[46] The scholarly theory is that in the *De anima*, he envisions the possibility of the human intellect's taking hold of the essence of *the good* or the

[41] Maimonides, *Commentary on the Mishnah*, *San.* 10, introd., 212, sixth principle. Similarly in *MT*, 'Hilkhot yesodei hatorah', 7: 1.

[42] *MN* ii. 4 (14*a*), 6 (17*a*), 12 (25*a*).

[43] Aristotle, *De anima*, 3.4, 429a, 15–16, 429b, 31–430a, 7; medieval Arabic trans., 74.

[44] Aristotle, *De anima*, 3.7, 431b, 17–19; medieval Arabic trans., 78.

[45] See Ross's comment on Aristotle, *De anima*, 3.4, 429b, 12. Ross was not the first to suggest a connection between the *De anima* passage and the passage in the *Metaphysics*.

[46] Aristotle, *Metaphysics*, 7.6.

essence of *the beautiful* and having it as the object of its thought without needing to separate it from matter, something much easier to say than to comprehend. Whatever Aristotle meant, it was not that an incorporeal intelligence is the form that the human intellect may think and become one with, although later readers could of course have read him as meaning that.

The statement in the second passage from the *Commentary on the Mishnah*, to the effect that immortality results from the human intellect's having an incorporeal being as the thought it thinks, is entirely foreign to Aristotle.

Alexander of Aphrodisias' *De anima*, which was available in Arabic translation, Alfarabi's *Risāla fī al-ʿaql* (*Epistle Concerning Intellect*), and several works of Ibn Bājja follow Aristotle in explaining that the human intellect becomes one with the form it thinks, that the form it thinks is ordinarily abstracted from a material substratum, and that the human intellect can also think forms existing apart from matter by their very nature and not needing to be abstracted. By forms existing apart from matter, they, however, mean incorporeal beings.[47] Alexander and Ibn Bājja further construe human immortality as the outcome of the human intellect's having the active intellect—which is the deity itself for Alexander and the final rung in the supernal incorporeal hierarchy for Ibn Bājja—as the form it thinks and unites with.[48] Alfarabi gives a somewhat different account of the process whereby immortality is achieved, although he concurs that once the intellect does reach the immortal condition, it has the active intellect as the object of its thought.[49]

Alexander, although not his *De anima*, is mentioned by name in a couple of Maimonides' writings. The *Moreh nevukhim* refers to Alfarabi's *Risāla fī al-ʿaql*. It refers to Ibn Bājja a few times; at one juncture it comments on Ibn Bājja's distinctive conception of the immortality of the human intellect, and at another it makes a statement traceable to him concerning the active intellect's becoming the form that the human intellect thinks.[50]

The theses concerning human intellectual thought that Maimonides' *Commentary on the Mishnah* characterizes as a subtle philosophic matter, the

[47] Alexander of Aphrodisias, *De anima*, 86–8; Alfarabi, *Risala fī al-ʿaql*, 12–16, 20–1. See the next note for Ibn Bājja.

[48] Alexander, *De anima*, 90. Regarding Alexander's statements and the way he could have been understood by readers of the Arabic translation, see H. Davidson, *Alfarabi, Avicenna, and Averroes, on Intellect*, 36–8. Ibn Bājja, *Ittiṣāl al-ʿaql bi-al-insān* (Arabic text, 19–20; Spanish trans., 41–2); id., *Risālat al-wadāʿ* (Arabic text, 30, 37; Spanish trans., 69, 82); id., *Tadbīr al-mutawaḥḥid* (Arabic text, 61; Spanish trans., 100); and below, Ch. 6, §3.

[49] Alfarabi, *Al-madīna al-fāḍila*, 204–7, 262–5; id., *Al-siyāsa al-madaniyya*, 32, 35, 42, 82; id., *Risala fi al-ʿaql*, 22.

[50] See the index to Pines' translation of the *MN*, s.v. Alexander, al-Fārābī, and Ibn Bājja; *MN* i. 74 (7), and below, Ch. 6, §5.

position of expert philosophers, and a subject for first philosophy ultimately go back in part to Aristotle. They reflect the positions of Alexander and Ibn Bājja fully, and the views of Alfarabi to a considerable extent; the three are thinkers with whom Maimonides had an acquaintance at one or another stage of his career. In his rabbinic period, Maimonides thus demonstrates a familiarity with post-Aristotelian theorizing regarding the human intellect and its fate. Although the possibility that he read Aristotle's *De anima* cannot be entirely ruled out, his rabbinic works furnish no evidence that he did read it.

Ethics

In the sole instance known to me where Maimonides cites a philosopher by name in his rabbinic works, he quotes a 'statement of Aristotle's' to the effect that a 'friend is someone else who is you',[51] which appears to mean that a friend is someone who acts towards you, and towards whom you act, as if he and you were one. The saying can be traced to Aristotle's *Nicomachean Ethics*, where Ross translates the somewhat enigmatic Greek as: 'A friend is another self'.[52] What counts for us is not, however, the Greek text but the medieval Arabic translation, and it differs from what Maimonides writes in a small yet significant detail. It reads: A 'friend is someone else who is the same'. Averroes' commentary on the *Nicomachean Ethics* confirms the reading.[53] Whereas Aristotle in Arabic translation states that a friend is someone 'who is *the same*', Maimonides quotes Aristotle as saying that a friend is someone 'who is *you*'.

There circulated a medieval Arabic abridgement of the *Nicomachean Ethics*; it has not been preserved as such but is known through quotations, some extensive, in other Arabic works and through a medieval Latin translation, the *Summa alexandrinorum*. The Arabic quotations from the abridgement include a statement almost identical with Maimonides': 'He [that is, Aristotle] said: "*Your* friend is someone else who is you."'[54] Medieval Arabic writers also have the saying in that form.[55] A fictional life of Alexander the Great extant in Arabic represents Aristotle as observing: 'Your friend is *you*, except that he exists in a different person.'[56] Just where Maimonides came upon the saying cannot be determined from the information at hand, but we can safely assert that he does not quote it from the Arabic translation of Aristotle's *Nicomachean Ethics*.

[51] Maimonides, *Commentary on the Mishnah*, *Avot* 1: 6.

[52] Aristotle, *Nicomachean Ethics*, 9.4, 1166a, 31–2.

[53] Aristotle, *The Arabic Version of the Nicomachean Ethics*, 496–7, paralleling Aristotle, *Nicomachean Ethics*, 9.4, 1166a, 31–2. Averroes, *Middle Commentary on Aristotle's Nicomachean Ethics*, 301.

[54] Mubashshir b. Fātik, *Mukhtār al-ḥikam*, 213.

[55] S. Harvey, 'Sources of Quotations' (Heb.), 100 n. 45, supplemented by personal communications from Mr Harvey.

[56] Gutas, *Greek Wisdom Literature in Arabic Translation*, 405.

Then there are a couple of passages in Maimonides' *Commentary on the Mishnah* that cite the philosophers on the necessity of perfecting oneself morally before undertaking theoretical pursuits. One of the passages takes its departure from a maxim in the mishnaic tractate *Avot*: 'If a person's fear of sin precedes his wisdom [*ḥokhmah*], his wisdom endures; if his wisdom precedes his fear of sin, his wisdom does not endure.' Maimonides understands 'fear of sin' to be a rabbinic way of saying moral virtue, and writes that the rabbinic maxim, as he interprets it, is 'agreed upon by the philosophers as well'. For the philosophers explain that when someone acquires moral virtue before starting on the road to science (Heb.: *ḥokhmah*, Arab.: *ʿilm*), his desire for science, love for it, and motivation are all enhanced. When, on the contrary, a person first acquires evil qualities, those qualities make the pursuit of science burdensome for him, and he abandons the pursuit.[57]

Maimonides makes more or less the same point in the context where, as quoted earlier, he describes prophets and philosophers as agreeing that everything in the lower, physical world exists for the single purpose of bringing forth men who excel in 'knowledge and practice'. He proceeds there to cite 'the statement of the pre-eminent figure in philosophy: "God's [*Allah*'s] aim for us is to be knowledgeable [*nubalāʾ*] and good."' Being knowledgeable is, moreover, contingent on being good. For a person who ostensibly is 'knowledgeable [*ʿālim nabīl*]', yet is consumed by desire, lacks the 'beginning of knowledge [or: science; *ʿilm*]', which consists in 'partaking of physical pleasure only to the extent necessary for the maintenance of the human body'. A person who lacks the ethical prerequisite is therefore 'not truly knowledgeable [*ʿālim*]'.[58] The pursuit of knowledge, or science, must be preceded by, and rest on, an ethical foundation.

What Maimonides reports in the name of the 'pre-eminent figure in philosophy' looks like an actual quotation. The Arabic term *nabīl* (plural: *nubalāʾ*) ordinarily means *eminent*, *noble*, not *knowledgeable*, and since Maimonides understands it to have the latter meaning in the present context, he glosses it as equivalent to *ʿālim*, a term carrying the desired sense. When speaking in his own voice before and after the quotation, he uses the more common *ʿālim* rather than *nabīl*. If he were not quoting, we may assume that he would have avoided the unconventional usage of the term *nabīl* altogether.[59]

[57] Maimonides, *Commentary on the Mishnah*, *Avot* 3: 11.

[58] Ibid., introd., 42. Maimonides connects what he writes here with the passage from his commentary on *Avot* quoted in the previous paragraph.

[59] Blau, *Dictionary*, 680, gives the common definition 'noble, magnanimous, distinguished' for *nabīl*. Maimonides uses the word in the plural in his *Commentary on the Mishnah*, *Shab.* 16: 3, and Kafah translates it as *pikḥim*, 'smart'. (What Maimonides says there can be taken in a different way.) The term *nabīl* also appears in *MN* iii. 19, 40*a*, where Blau understands it to mean 'distinguished'.

A few lines later, Maimonides makes a further comment. He writes: A 'man who is God-fearing and abstinent, who rejects pleasures except for those necessary to sustain the body, who behaves . . . in accordance with moderation, and who possesses all the moral virtues, but does not possess science [*ʿilm*] . . . falls short of perfection. He nevertheless is more nearly perfect than the previously mentioned man', the one who is ostensibly knowledgeable but is a slave to physical desires.[60]

Maimonides maintains, then, that the pursuit of science presupposes the possession of moral virtue, that the person who possesses moral virtue but has no scientific achievements is closer to perfection than the ostensibly knowledgeable person who is immoral, and that the position he has taken is that of the 'pre-eminent figure in philosophy'. The expression *pre-eminent figure in philosophy* immediately brings Aristotle to mind, but it is not Aristotle, and, specifically, not the *Nicomachean Ethics*, that Maimonides is quoting. Aristotelian scholars have long debated the respective roles of behaviour, moral virtue, and intellectual virtue in the *Nicomachean Ethics*' conception of a perfect human life. However Aristotle's position in that work is construed, the necessity of preparing for knowledge and science by acquiring ethical virtue does not appear there.

Especially pertinent is the denouement of the *Nicomachean Ethics.* As Aristotle approaches the conclusion of the book, he returns to the pivotal question that he posed at the outset, namely: What constitutes human eudaemonia, man's true felicity? He determines now that the contemplative and theoretical life constitutes 'perfect' eudaemonia, whereas moral virtue is eudaemonia of a 'secondary' sort. Moral virtue, moreover, presupposes substantial material resources, since a person cannot, for example, exercise the virtues of liberality and justice unless he possesses the means for treating others liberally and justly. True eudaemonia, that is, eudaemonia of the contemplative kind, makes do with a lower level of material resources. To clinch the identification of the contemplative and theoretical life as the ultimate human goal, Aristotle offers a quasi-theological argument, which he undoubtedly did not intend *au pied de la lettre.* He writes that God or the gods—the Arabic like the Greek has the word in both the singular and the plural—may be assumed to love and be pleased with men who cultivate the aspect of themselves that most resembles the divine. Since the human intellect is the aspect in question, the favourite of the gods must be the person who cultivates his intellect.[61]

[60] Maimonides, *Commentary on the Mishnah*, introd., 43.

[61] Aristotle, *Nicomachean Ethics*, 10.7, 10. 8, 1178b, 21–3, 1197a, 24–32. Similarly in the *Summa alexandrinorum*; see Fowler, 'Manuscript Admont 608', 247–9.

The *Nicomachean Ethics* thus decides in the end that the contemplative and theoretical life, not a theoretical life built on moral goodness, is what the gods take pleasure in. Aristotle has no reservation about the enjoyment of material goods and indeed makes them a *sine qua non* for moral perfection. And the Arabic translation of the *Nicomachean Ethics* does not, as far as I could see, use the distinctive term *nabīl*. The *Nicomachean Ethics* is consequently not the source of the propositions that success in science presupposes moral virtue, that God's aim for human beings is for them to be both knowledgeable (*nubalāʾ*) and good, and that moral virtue involves limiting one's physical pleasure to what is necessary for the maintenance of the human body.

A concise introduction to the study of philosophy and Aristotle's philosophy in particular has been preserved that carries Alfarabi's name. It is closely modelled on late Greek introductions to philosophy and, like its models, devotes several paragraphs to identifying the starting place—in its words, the 'knowledge', or 'science' (*ʿilm*)—from which students of philosophy should begin. Among the different views it records, the pertinent one is credited to the school of Theophrastus and is bolstered with quotations from Plato and Hippocrates. Theophrastus' position is that the student of philosophy 'should begin with knowledge [or: the science] of perfecting moral qualities, for anyone who does not perfect his moral qualities cannot learn true science'.[62]

In a similar vein, Alfarabi's *Fuṣūl muntazaʿa*—a work from which, we shall presently see, Maimonides borrowed extensively when composing his *Commentary on the Mishnah*—compares two men, one of whom knows everything contained in Aristotle's books but acts in a fashion contrary to commonly accepted moral standards, whereas the other has no knowledge of science, but does behave in conformity with commonly recognized morality. The second man, Alfarabi submits, 'is closer to being a philosopher than the first'.[63]

Alfarabi's introduction to philosophy and *Fuṣūl muntazaʿa* could have allowed Maimonides to characterize the requirement that moral virtue precede theoretical activity as something 'agreed upon by the philosophers'. The contrast in the *Fuṣūl muntazaʿa* between the moral non-philosopher and the immoral student of Aristotle is echoed by Maimonides. Still, the unusual term *nabīl* does not appear in either of the Alfarabi statements. The data at hand

[62] Alfarabi, *Philosophische Abhandlungen*, 52; German trans., 87–8. Ibn al-Ṭayyib's commentary on Aristotle's *Categories* (a century after Alfarabi) records virtually the same opinion in the name of Theophrastus; see Gutas, 'Starting Point', 121.

[63] Alfarabi, *Fuṣūl muntazaʿa*, §98; §§97–100 are found in only one manuscript and appear to be an appendix to the book, but §97 is among the sections from which Maimonides borrows in his *Shemonah perakim*.

therefore do not permit identifying him as the pre-eminent figure who held that 'God's aim for us is to be knowledgeable and good'.

Whatever role Alfarabi may have played, Maimonides has attributed to Aristotle, to the philosophers, and to the pre-eminent figure in philosophy, propositions that are not found in the Arabic translation of the *Nicomachean Ethics.*

I have for now left aside the theory that the moral virtues are intermediate characteristics in the soul—that courage, for instance, is a characteristic in the soul lying midway between the vices of cowardice and foolhardiness. The theory of the middle way in ethics, which plays a prominent role in Maimonides' two main rabbinic works, has its origin in Aristotle's *Nicomachean Ethics*, and as a consequence, a number of scholars have jumped to the conclusion that Maimonides borrowed it from Aristotle. The next chapter will show in detail that he copied it not from the *Nicomachean Ethics*, but from Alfarabi's *Fuṣūl muntazaʿa*, a much less complex and more accessible work.

Human Free Choice

In *Shemonah perakim*, Maimonides rejects the 'inanities fabricated by the astrologers' who maintain that a person's character and the course of his life are ineluctably determined by the configuration of the heavenly bodies at the moment of his birth. Maimonides counters: 'It is something agreed upon by our Law and by the philosophy of Greece', it is supported by 'true arguments', and 'it is a truth about which there is no doubt, that a person's actions are all within his control [*maṣrūf ilayhi*]. If he wishes, he acts, and if he does not, he does not, there being no compulsion [*jabr*; *qahr*]' upon him. Human actions and the acquisition of virtue or vice are wholly a matter of 'choice' (*khiyār*, *ikhtiyār*), and nothing 'from without' determines how a person chooses.

In support, Maimonides adduces stock arguments that go back to post-Aristotelian Greek philosophy,[64] and some of which appear in Judah Halevi.[65] He contends that if a person's character and the course of his life were predetermined, the person would deserve no credit or reward for being good, and punishing him for being evil would be unjust. It would be senseless to command good behaviour and to prohibit bad behaviour. Since success and failure would be out of a person's hands, all human endeavour would be in vain.[66] How the arguments may have reached Maimonides, or whether he formulated them on his own, seeing that they are fairly obvious, can only be guessed.

[64] Alexander of Aphrodisias, *On Fate*, 10, 64–6, 150.
[65] Halevi, *Kuzari*, v. 20.
[66] *ShP*, ch. 8, pp. 396–7. Maimonides, *Commentary on the Mishnah*, *AZ* 4: 7, similarly states that the complex of beliefs surrounding astrology was completely alien to 'the philosophy of Greece'.

Astrology was not a concern of Aristotle's, at least in his preserved writings. Compositions carrying the names of Alfarabi and Avicenna[67] do refute the belief in astrology, and one of them even advances the argument that if events were predetermined, men would sit back and make no effort.[68]

The topic of human choice, by contrast, does receive attention in the *Nicomachean Ethics*. Aristotle posits there that some human acts and qualities (Greek: *pathē*, Arab.: *infiʿālāt*) are voluntary (*ṭawʿan*) and hence subject to praise or blame, whereas others are involuntary (*karhan*) and hence subject to neither. The involuntary ones are those that are compelled (*qasran*; *karhan*) by a factor 'from without' or performed through ignorance. A little later, when discussing matters about which human beings deliberate, Aristotle lays down the proposition that men deliberate only about what is 'within our power' (*ilaynā*).[69] There are general resemblances here to Maimonides' language, but the thrust of Maimonides' discussion is different: Aristotle's object is to delimit the areas in which human choice may or may not be operative, whereas Maimonides wants to show that men have freedom of choice in all their actions. While it is conceivable that Maimonides drew from the discussion of human choice in the *Nicomachean Ethics* and refers to it when crediting the philosophy of Greece with the truth that *all* of a person's actions are within the person's control, the evidence does not establish that such was the case.

The abridgement of the *Nicomachean Ethics* that circulated in Arabic also shows a similarity to Maimonides' language. It affirms that human actions lie within a person's 'power, will, and choice' and that it is 'within our power' to act or not to act.[70] None of Alfarabi's preserved writings address the issue of human choice, as far as I could see, but his lost commentary on the *Nicomachean Ethics*—which Maimonides cites at one point in the *Moreh nevukhim*—may have done so when it took up the pertinent chapters of the Aristotelian work.

The topic of human choice intertwines with an issue that comes up at a couple of junctures in the *Commentary on the Mishnah*. Early in the *Commentary*, Maimonides states: when the time comes for someone to be punished for his sins and crimes, God may bring the miscreant to a pass where he, willy-nilly, commits an additional misdeed serious enough to warrant the harsh punishment that God wants to mete out. Maimonides returns to the

[67] Druart, 'Astronomie et astrologie selon Farābī', 43–7; id., 'Le Second Traité de Farābī', 47–51; Avicenna, *Réfutation de l'astrologie*, Arabic section, 7–26, 38–44; French trans., 63–79, 83–107, 140–9.

[68] Alfarabi, *Philosophische Abhandlungen*, 106; German trans., 174.

[69] Aristotle, *Nicomachean Ethics*, 3.1, 1109b, 30–1110a, 2, 3.5, 1113b, 3–14; *The Arabic Version of the Nicomachean Ethics*, 184–5, 206–7.

[70] Fowler, 'Manuscript Admont 608', 210; Chiesa, 'Una fonte sconosciuta', 608. The phrase 'within our power' is my translation of the words '*in nobis*' in the Latin version of the abridgement. I assume that the Arabic had '*ilaynā*'.

issue in *Shemonah perakim* shortly after presenting his argument for human free choice. He discloses that his remarks earlier in the *Commentary* had the biblical Pharaoh in view. Pharaoh refused to release the Israelites from bondage, and the reason, Scripture relates, was that God hardened his heart to a level where he was unable to obey. His disobedience brought disaster upon him and the Egyptian nation.[71]

The question how a just God could prevent someone from obeying and then punish him for his disobedience is, Maimonides writes, 'lengthy and difficult, "exceeding deep, who can find it out?"'. All he ventures to say is that God is just, He rewards the righteous and punishes the wicked, and human minds are incapable of fathoming the workings of divine justice. Maimonides thereupon observes: the 'discussion of the matter by expert philosophers is very abstruse and subtle, requiring numerous premisses and a training in the sciences'.[72] He does not make clear exactly what is abstruse and subtle—whether the philosophers' solution to the problem of a sinner's being led to a pass where he brings about his own downfall or the philosophers' handling of the broader question of the manner in which divine control of events can be harmonized with human free will. God's control of events and the difficulty of harmonizing it with human free choice are not subjects that would occupy Aristotle, and I could discover nothing in Alfarabi that might qualify as a discussion of either issue.

Aristotle does state in the *Nicomachean Ethics* that vice sometimes becomes so ingrained that a person cannot extricate himself from it.[73] That notion suggests a possible explanation of the hardening of Pharaoh's heart: perhaps Pharaoh's vices had become so ingrained that he was unable to change. Such is not, however, the explanation that Maimonides gives. When he discusses the hardening of Pharaoh's heart in *Shemonah perakim*, he continues to insist that, as far as the laws of nature are concerned, 'every [human] situation can be changed from good to bad and from bad to good, for a man retains the power to choose' even though he may have sunk into vice.[74] Maimonides' solution of the Pharaoh puzzle is that as a punishment for prior crimes against the Israelites, God now overruled the laws of nature and miraculously deprived Pharaoh of the power to exercise his will.[75] We are on the verge here of a matter of sharp dispute; for, notwithstanding what Maimonides expressly and repeatedly affirms, some readers today are convinced that he did not believe in the possibility of miracles, that is, the possibility of God's intervening in

[71] Maimonides, *Commentary on the Mishnah*, *Ber.* 9: 7; *ShP*, ch. 8, pp. 401–2.

[72] Maimonides, *Commentary on the Mishnah*, *Ber.* 9: 7; see above, §1. The phrase 'exceeding deep, who can find it out' is from Eccles. 7: 24.

[73] Aristotle, *Nicomachean Ethics*, 3.5, 1114a, 3–21.

[74] *ShP*, ch. 8, p. 400.

[75] *ShP*, ch. 8, p. 402.

nature. At all events, the *Nicomachean Ethics* is plainly not the locus of the 'discussion . . . by expert philosophers' which is 'very abstruse and subtle, requiring numerous premisses and a training in the sciences'.

Maimonides' remarks about ethics and human choice have led us into byways, and it is worth recapitulating what is relevant for us. The 'statement of Aristotle's' to the effect that a 'friend is someone else who is you' undoubtedly has its origin in Aristotle's *Nicomachean Ethics*, but Maimonides does not quote it from there. The proposition that a person must perfect himself morally before undertaking theoretical pursuits, which Maimonides attributes to the 'pre-eminent figure in philosophy' and to philosophers in general, does not come from the *Nicomachean Ethics*. Alfarabi expresses sentiments along the same lines, but the similarities are in spirit, not language, and none of the known works of Alfarabi can be identified as Maimonides' source. When calling on the authority of the philosophy of Greece in his refutation of astrology, Maimonides could have compositions attributed to Alfarabi and Avicenna in view. He credits the philosophy of Greece with the proposition that human actions are a matter of human choice, and some of his language shows a general resemblance to phraseology in Aristotle's *Nicomachean Ethics*. His point regarding human choice is not, however, Aristotle's point, and the resemblance is scarcely sufficient to establish that he read and was borrowing from the *Nicomachean Ethics*. His reference to a 'very abstruse and subtle' discussion by 'expert philosophers' that relates to God's depriving a man of his freedom of choice is not traceable to Aristotle.

The evidence thus falls well short of showing that Maimonides was familiar with the *Nicomachean Ethics* during his early period. It is somewhat more likely that he used the Arabic abridgement of the *Nicomachean Ethics*.

The Nature of God

References to metaphysical philosophy in the *Commentary on the Mishnah* remain. We have already seen that Maimonides' description of the manner whereby the human intellect acquires immortality 'as explained in first philosophy', that is to say, in metaphysics, is not Aristotelian. Additional references to metaphysics revolve around yet one more question involving human choice.

At issue now is the apparent contradiction between man's freedom to act as he chooses and God's infallible foreknowledge of the way in which each individual man will act: if God knows what a person will do, the person will not be able to do otherwise. Maimonides resolves, or circumvents, the antinomy with the help of three propositions concerning God's attributes and essence.

He begins: 'It has been made clear in divine science [*ʿilm*], that is to say, in metaphysics, that God does not know through [an attribute of] knowledge [*ʿilm*].' If God had an attribute of knowledge, the consequence would be 'that God and His knowledge are two things as is the case with man and his knowledge; for man is not knowledge, and knowledge is not man; they are two [distinct things].' To assume that God has an attribute of knowledge would be to ascribe 'multiplicity' (*kathra*) to Him and impinge on His absolute unity. Rather, God's knowledge, in contrast to man's, is identical with Himself, as 'God's life is identical with Himself', and so on for other attributes. Because Maimonides foresaw readers with a limited background in philosophy, he refrains from a full demonstration of the point. The complete 'arguments and proofs are . . . very strong and demonstrative', but 'these are difficult matters, and you must not expect to grasp them completely from two or three lines' in a rabbinic commentary.

Maimonides continues: 'It has also been made clear in metaphysics [or: the *Metaphysics*] that our intellects are incapable of wholly comprehending God's being [*wujūd*] because of the perfection of God's being and the deficiency of our intellects.' To illustrate, Maimonides offers an analogy: 'The inability of our intellects to have cognition [*idrāk*] of God is like the inability . . . of vision to perceive [*idrāk*] the light of the sun, which is due not to the weakness of the sun's light, but to its being too strong' for human eyes to tolerate. 'He [that is to say, the author of metaphysics, or the *Metaphysics*] said a good deal on the present subject, and everything he said is true and clear.'

The upshot for the issue of divine foreknowledge and human choice is that inasmuch as God's knowledge is identical with Himself, and His being, that is, His essence, is beyond man's ability to comprehend, His knowledge is likewise beyond the human ability to comprehend. Since God's knowledge is beyond our understanding, no inference can be drawn regarding its compatibility or incompatibility with human free choice.[76]

What is pertinent for us is not the cogency of Maimonides' solution of the antinomy of divine foreknowledge and human free will but the three propositions he adduces on the authority of metaphysics, namely: God's attributes are identical with Himself; God's being, or essence, is unknowable; and the inability of the human intellect to know God is analogous to the inability of physical vision to have a direct perception of the light of the sun. When Maimonides remarks that 'he', that is to say, the author of metaphysics or of the *Metaphysics*, 'said a good deal on the present subject, and everything he said is true and

[76] *ShP*, ch. 8, pp. 405–6. The analogy between the unknowability of God and the inability of the human eye to look at the sun is repeated in *MN* i. 59 (73*a*).

clear', the names that immediately come to mind are Aristotle and Aristotle's *Metaphysics*.

The notion that God possesses no attributes is not Aristotelian. In the *Metaphysics*, Aristotle has no qualms about speaking about God's actual thought, life, and other qualities, and he neither asserts nor intimates that those qualities are to be construed as identical with the divine essence.[77] That the deity does not possess actual attributes is present, in germ, in Plotinus, who stresses that the One—his term for the deity—is utterly simple and indescribable, and nothing can be predicated of It.[78] The proposition then came into its own in medieval Arabic philosophical literature, both Islamic and Jewish, and Plotinus was forgotten.

To take a few examples: Ashʿari reports that 'most of the Muʿtazila' as well as members of other sects 'stated . . . that God knows [literally: is knowing], is powerful, and is living by virtue of Himself, not by virtue of [attributes of] knowledge, power, or life'.[79] Alfarabi writes that the First, which is his term for the deity, does not acquire knowledge from outside Himself. Insofar as He knows things outside Himself, it is by virtue of knowing Himself, and 'His knowledge of Himself is nothing distinct from His substance'.[80] Avicenna writes in the metaphysical part of his most comprehensive philosophical work that the 'life' of the Necessarily Existent by reason of itself—Avicenna's term for the deity—'is not distinct from His knowledge, and all this belongs to Him by virtue of Himself'.[81]

Ghazali, in one of his several guises, composed a summary of what he called the views of the 'philosophers'; the book is accordingly entitled *Maqāṣid al-falāsifa*, literally *The Intentions of the Philosophers*. The picture of the universe set forth there is in fact that of Avicenna and thinkers of a like persuasion, but a reader who had a limited familiarity with the history of philosophy might easily take the word 'philosophers' in the title and in Ghazali's introduction to the book as a reference to Aristotle and his school. Ghazali subsequently turned around and drew up a refutation, entitled *Tahāfut al-falāsifa* (*Destruction of the Philosophers*), of key philosophical theories that, in his opinion, clash with fundamental Islamic beliefs. In the *Tahāfut*, he expressly names Aristotle as the author of the unacceptable theories, with the qualification that he would treat

[77] Aristotle, *Metaphysics*, 12.7.

[78] Plotinus, *Enneads*, 5.3.13–14; Wolfson, 'Albinus and Plotinus on Divine Attributes', 116–17; Gerson, *Plotinus*, 15–16.

[79] Ashʿari, *Maqālāt al-islāmiyyīn*, 164. See further ibid. 164–7, 486; Wolfson, *Philosophy of the Kalam*, 180, 225; id., 'Avicenna, Algazali, and Averroes on Divine Attributes', 162.

[80] Alfarabi, *Al-madīna al-fāḍila*, 72–3; id., *Al-siyāsa al-madaniyya*, 45.

[81] Avicenna, *Shifāʾ*: *Ilāhiyyāt*, 295 (= id., *Najāt*, 250).

those theories as they had been transmitted and interpreted by Alfarabi and Avicenna.[82]

In the metaphysical part of the *Maqāṣid*, Ghazali represents the philosophers as maintaining that the Necessarily Existent's 'knowledge of Himself is not [something] added to Himself, which would carry the implication that He contains multiplicity [*kathra*], but *is* Himself'; and Ghazali goes on to offer a complicated argument designed to prove the point.[83]

In the *Tahāfut*, where he turns around and refutes theses supposedly held by Aristotle, he formulates one of the unacceptable theses as follows: 'It is inadmissible to affirm attributes added to the First Principle's essence in the way that, in the case of man, our knowledge and our power may be an attribute added to our essence'.[84] The proposition that God's knowledge and other ostensible attributes are identical with His essence also appears in Jewish writers preceding Maimonides.[85]

The unknowability of God is also not Aristotelian. It is a doctrine espoused by Plotinus regarding the One and before that, as Wolfson shows, by Philo of Alexandria.[86] It eventually became common coin among the Arabic Aristotelians, and Philo and Plotinus were forgotten.

As for the analogy between the inability of the human intellect to know God and the inability of the eye to look directly at the sun, it is a topos with an even longer history. In one version or another, it is found in the Babylonian Talmud,[87] in Alfarabi and Ghazali on the Islamic side,[88] and in Bahya ibn Pakuda, Joseph Ibn Tsadik, Judah Halevi, and Abraham ibn Daud, on the Jewish side.[89]

Aristotle's *Metaphysics* employs what at a casual glance may seem to be the same analogy. An early passage there muses about the difficulty facing thinkers who undertake an 'investigation of the truth'. Each individual, the *Metaphysics* acknowledges, can attain no more than a fragment; yet the cumulative efforts of all seekers do approach the full truth. The reason why attaining the truth is difficult lies not in the objects (Greek: *pragmata*, Arab.: *umūr*) that are investi-

[82] Ghazali, *Tahāfut al-falāsifa*, 3–4.

[83] Ghazali, *Maqāṣid al-falāsifa*, 152.

[84] Ghazali, *Tahāfut al-falāsifa*, 97.

[85] Al-Mukamis, as cited and elucidated in Wolfson, *Repercussions of the Kalam*, 8; Ibn Tsadik, *Olam katan*, 57–8; Sa'adiah, *Emunot vede'ot*, 2.5.

[86] Wolfson, 'The Knowability and Describability of God in Plato and Aristotle', 112–14; id., *Philo*, ii. 111–20; Plotinus, *Enneads*, 5.3.14.

[87] BT *Ḥul.* 59*b*–60*a*: R. Yehoshua instructs the emperor who wishes to *see* God to try first to look at the midday sun.

[88] See Wensinck, *La Pensée de Ghazzali*, 32–3; Alfarabi, *Al-madīna al-fāḍila*, 81.

[89] Bahya ibn Pakuda, *Ḥovot halevavot*, 1: 10; Halevi, *Kuzari*, iv. 3 (end); Ibn Tsadik, *Olam katan*, 57; Ibn Daud, *Emunah ramah*, 53 (as a 'bat' (*waṭwāṭ*) cannot look at the sun); German trans., 67.

gated but 'in ourselves'. For it is as difficult for the human intellect to grasp truths concerning the world that 'by nature are most evident of all' as it is for the 'eyes of the bat' to see in broad daylight.[90]

The *Metaphysics* compares the feebleness of eyes *vis-à-vis* bright light to the feebleness of the human intellect *vis-à-vis* objects of knowledge in general; it is not specifically the nature of God that overwhelms the human intellect with brightness. More importantly, the difficulty faced by the human intellect is not absolute. Each investigator into the nature of things contributes something, and individual discoveries accumulate into an increasingly complete account. Many a little makes a mickle.

There are thus three propositions in the *Commentary on the Mishnah* that Maimonides cites from metaphysics or indicates come from the author of the science of metaphysics: God's attributes are identical with Himself; His essence is unknowable; and the inability to know God's essence is analogous to the inability of the eye to look directly at the sun. None of the three is Aristotelian.

So far, we have been examining references to philosophers, philosophy, and the like, in Maimonides' *Commentary on the Mishnah*. There is one significant philosophical item that appears in his *Mishneh torah* and not in the *Commentary on the Mishnah*—a proof for the existence of a first cause of the motion of the celestial spheres.[91] Maimonides does not label it as a philosophical proof, but it is obviously a bare-bones version of the proof for a first cause of the motion of the heavens that Aristotle worked out in great detail in the *Physics* and stated briefly in *Metaphysics* 12. There were, in the Arabic Middle Ages, channels through which the proof could be learned without recourse to Aristotle.

It is put forward in the *Principles of the Universe*, a book attributed to Alexander of Aphrodisias and extant only in Arabic. Ghazali restates it in *Maqāṣid al-falāsifa*, his account of the views of the philosophers. And it is alluded to in a work of Alfarabi's.[92] Maimonides quoted and made considerable use of the *Principles of the Universe* in the *Guide for the Perplexed*, and, as just seen, there are indications that he was familiar with Ghazali's *Maqāṣid* in his rabbinic period.

Before setting forth the proof for a first mover of the spheres in the *Mishneh torah*, Maimonides makes a few preliminary remarks. One of them affirms the dependence of everything in the universe on 'the first being', whose existence he was about to demonstrate. He writes: 'If it should be supposed that He [the

[90] Aristotle, *Metaphysics*, 2.1.

[91] *MT*, 'Hilkhot yesodei hatorah', 1: 5, 7.

[92] Alexander, *Principles of the Universe*, §§44–7; Ghazali, *Maqāṣid al-falāsifa*, 209. The proof is alluded to in Alfarabi, *Falsafat arisṭūṭālīs*, 97.

first being] does not exist, nothing else could exist. If it should, by contrast, be supposed that everything existent apart from Him does not exist, He alone would exist.'[93]

Aristotle's *Metaphysics*, 12, contains the observation that 'the heaven and nature depend' on the first mover, but Aristotle does not elaborate and proceeds at once to another matter.[94] The *Principles of the Universe* makes a statement that is more apropos: if 'someone should assume as a hypothesis that one of these [eternal divine beings, that is, the celestial spheres and their mover] ceased to exist [*fasada*], he could not then maintain that beings in the lower world' continue to exist.[95] Most pertinent is Ghazali's *Maqāṣid*, which defines possible and necessary being in language that is very close to Maimonides' Hebrew wording. Possible being, Ghazali writes, is such that 'its existence depends on something other than itself; and if that other thing should be supposed not to exist [*qudira 'adam dhālika al-ghayr*], it [the possible being] would not exist'. Necessary being is such that 'if the non-existence of everything apart from it be supposed, its non-existence would not follow'.[96]

Since Maimonides connects the proof for the existence of a first mover to notions that apparently echo Ghazali's *Maqāṣid* or perhaps another composition belonging to the same milieu, he probably borrowed the proof from motion from there as well.

To summarize what can be garnered concerning Maimonides' acquaintance with Aristotle in his rabbinic period: even when he quotes a 'statement of Aristotle's' to the effect that a 'friend is someone else who is you', the wording reveals that he is quoting a recasting of what Aristotle wrote in the *Nicomachean Ethics* and not the *Nicomachean Ethics* itself. He does adduce two or three items from the Arabic recension of the pseudo-Aristotelian *Problemata physica*. There is a similarity between some of the terms he uses when discussing human choice and language in the *Nicomachean Ethics*' discussion of choice, although the similarity does not extend to what Aristotle wanted to bring out. His account of the immortality of the human intellect and the propositions of a metaphysical character that he adduces in the name of the philosophers are wholly foreign to Aristotle. When he cites the philosopher, the 'pre-eminent figure in philosophy', the author of the science of metaphysics, and the philosophy of Greece, and when he employs other designations that sound like references to Aristotle, there is hence no reliable evidence that it is Aristotle whom he is citing.

93 *MT*, 'Hilkhot yesodei hatorah', 1: 2–3; similarly in *Commentary on the Mishnah*, *San.* 10: 1, p. 210, first principle.

94 Aristotle, *Metaphysics*, 12.7, 1072b, 14.

95 Alexander, *Principles of the Universe*, §§82–3.

96 Ghazali, *Maqāṣid al-falāsifa*, 131–2.

A final suggestive item is furnished by Maimonides' *Sefer hamitsvot*, the third work he published in his rabbinic period and one that so far has had nothing to contribute to our analysis. Maimonides composed the *Sefer hamitsvot* in Arabic, and in his methodological introduction he calls attention to a peculiarity of the Arabic language. He writes: 'The students of the art of logic stated verbatim: the Arabic language does not have a general term that includes both *positive command* [*amr*] and *prohibition* [*nahy*]. To cover them both, we therefore have to use the term for one of the two [specific kinds of command], namely, the term for *positive command* [*amr*].' In other words, when an Arabic speaker wants to say *command*, without specifying whether the command is positive or negative, he has to fall back on the term *amr*, which strictly means *positive command*. The sentences that Maimonides says he is quoting verbatim from the students of the art of logic come directly from Alfarabi's *Epitome* of Aristotle's *De interpretatione*.[97] In the evaluation of various philosophers that Maimonides sent to Samuel Ibn Tibbon several decades later, he advised Ibn Tibbon that for logic, Alfarabi alone should be consulted. The quotation from the *Epitome* of the *De interpretatione* suggests that Maimonides was already relying on Alfarabi in matters of logic at the time when he wrote his rabbinic works.

Pines' introduction to his translation of the *Moreh nevukhim* makes the categorical assertion: 'There is no reason to doubt that Maimonides was acquainted with all the writings of Aristotle known in Moslem Spain. . . . It is, moreover, abundantly clear that, from an early age, Maimonides had lived with these texts and that they formed a notable part of his intellectual makeup.'[98] No documentation is offered, and examination of Maimonides' rabbinic works points in the very opposite direction. Apart from the *Problemata physica*, which is not authentically Aristotelian, and some additional questionable titbits, Maimonides shows no evidence of having, by the age of 40, read a line of Aristotle.

5. The Arabic Aristotelians

Put in a nutshell, the Arabic Aristotelians accepted the Aristotelian picture of the universe with the following emendations: Aristotle's first mover, which maintains the celestial spheres in constant circular motion, expands into a first cause that maintains the entire universe in existence. The essence of the first cause is unknowable. There follow nine or ten incorporeal intelligences—

[97] *SM*, rule 8 (p. 26). See Alfarabi, *Epitome of the De interpretatione*, 46–7; English trans.: *Commentary and Short Treatise on Aristotle's De interpretatione*, 227.

[98] *MN* (Pines), translator's introd., p. lxi.

known in religious parlance as angels—all but the last of which serve as movers of the celestial spheres. The first cause brings the first intelligence into existence through a process of emanation, and each intelligence emanates the sphere that it governs as well as the next intelligence in the series. The Aristotelian *active intellect*, the factor that enables human intellects to pass from potentiality to actuality, may or may not have been envisioned by Aristotle as an entity that exists independently of individual human souls; the Arabic Aristotelians have no doubt that it is an independently existent substance and they assign it a place in the supernal incorporeal hierarchy. It is an incorporeal being that emanates from the intelligence co-ordinated with the sphere of the moon and it now forms the final stage in the hierarchy. Besides its role as the cause of actual human thought, it takes on added functions in the sublunar world, which vary from one member of the Arabic Aristotelian school to another.

Maimonides' *Commentary on the Mishnah* and *Mishneh torah* say enough to show that he embraced the scheme. He views God as the cause that constantly maintains everything else in existence[99] and as a being whose essence is unknowable. He depicts a process of emanation starting from God and continuing down through a series of ten incorporeal beings, or angels, the last of which is the active intellect.[100] He understands that a constant emanation is broadcast, as it were, by the active intellect. That emanation is the source from which all natural objects in the sublunar world receive their forms and from which persons worthy of the gift of prophecy—with the exception of Moses, who communicated directly with God—receive their inspiration.[101]

6. Summary

Although a number of Maimonides' references to philosophers and philosophy cannot be traced, certain conclusions can be drawn.

Maimonides does not, in either his early or later period, disclose an acquaintance with the Arabic paraphrases of Plotinus and Proclus. He reveals no consciousness of a Neoplatonic school of philosophy. When he has the occasion to express an opinion about works in which a Neoplatonic colouring can be detected, he dismisses them as inanities, wind, vanities, and ancient philosophy having no function apart from wasting a person's time. Neoplatonic

[99] Maimonides, *Commentary on the Mishnah*, *San.* 10: 1, p. 210, first principle; *MT*, 'Hilkhot yesodei hatorah', 1: 1.

[100] *MT*, 'Hilkhot yesodei hatorah', 2: 6–7, 9. Maimonides uses the terms 'active intellect' and 'emanation' (*faiḍ*) in *Commentary on the Mishnah*, *San.* 10: 1, p. 212, sixth principle.

[101] Maimonides, *Commentary on the Mishnah*, *San.* 10: 1, sixth principle; *MT*, 'Hilkhot yesodei hatorah', 4: 6; 7: 1.

motifs play a role in his thought, but only insofar as they were adopted by the Arabic Aristotelians.

A few Kalam notions come up in Maimonides' *Commentary on the Mishnah*. They are basic and were well known, and his information is inexact. Shortly before, or soon after completing his *Mishneh torah*, he was, however, able to participate in a disputation on the Kalam.

There is no evidence that he had a direct acquaintance with a single genuine Aristotelian work.

His rabbinic writings subscribe to the Arabic Aristotelian picture of the universe, which he took for granted was authentically Aristotelian. He appears to have learned that scheme from straightforward and accessible works such as Alfarabi's writings and Ghazali's account of the views of the philosophers rather than from the heavier-going treatises of Avicenna. Reliance on Ghazali may also have been what led him to believe that he was reading an account of the genuine Aristotle: Ghazali's *Maqāṣid al-falāsifa* represents itself as a summary of the views of the 'philosophers', and his *Tahāfut al-falāsifa* takes up and refutes what it identifies as doctrines of Aristotle as they were transmitted and interpreted by Alfarabi and Avicenna.

During the period in which Maimonides acquired a breathtaking mastery of rabbinic literature and was busy with his rabbinic writings, he managed to acquire a thorough knowledge of astronomy and a good knowledge of medicine. Despite his unequivocal commitment to the philosophical ideal, he did not find the time needed for mastering the literature of philosophy and made do with short cuts instead.

FOUR

Maimonides' Shemonah perakim *and Alfarabi's* Fuṣūl Muntazaʿa

Listen to the truth from whoever speaks it.

MAIMONIDES
Shemonah perakim, introduction

THE MOST EXTENSIVE QUOTATIONS from a philosophical text in Maimonides' *Commentary on the Mishnah* occur when he arrives at tractate *Avot*. As an introduction to his commentary on *Avot*, Maimonides furnishes the background in psychology, ethical theory, and related matters that he thinks readers will need in order to understand the mishnaic tractate and his comments on it. As noted earlier, his introduction is divided into eight chapters and accordingly is known by the unimaginative title *Shemonah perakim* (*Eight Chapters*).

In his introduction to *Shemonah perakim*—in other words, his introduction to the introduction—Maimonides writes: the chapters (*fuṣūl*) that follow are fashioned from 'statements [*kalām*] of the rabbis . . . as well as from statements [*kalām*] of the ancient [*qudum*] and recent philosophers and from many [other] compositions. . . . Listen to the truth from whoever speaks it.' He continues: 'Sometimes, moreover, I copy an entire quotation verbatim from a well-known book.' He gives two reasons for not naming the source or sources of his extensive quotations. The first is trivial: if he named the person whom he quotes every time he offered a quotation, he would add unnecessarily to the length of the introduction. The second sounds like the real reason: the name of 'that person' could lead a narrow-minded reader to assume that the statement quoted is 'corrupt' and contains something 'evil'. Readers may not listen to the truth if they know who it is that speaks it.[1]

Although Maimonides refers to ancient and recent philosophers and to 'many' other compositions, all the identifiable quotations in *Shemonah perakim* can be traced to a single source, the well-known book that he mentions. The

[1] *ShP*, ch. 1, pp. 372–3.

book is not Aristotle's *Nicomachean Ethics*, as some have supposed, but a more straightforward and accessible work by Alfarabi that has been published under two titles: *Fuṣūl al-madanī* and *Fuṣūl muntazaʿa*, that is to say, *Fuṣūl for the Statesman* and *Excerpted Fuṣūl.*

Alfarabi's book comprises about 100 *fuṣūl*—the manuscripts differ slightly in their contents and in the way they divide the *fuṣūl*—which range in length from a sentence or two to a couple of pages but usually consist of a single paragraph. They are too short to be termed chapters in the accepted sense of the word today, in contrast to the eight *fuṣūl* making up Maimonides' *Shemonah perakim*, which are genuine chapters. And they are too long and matter-of-fact to qualify as *aphorisms*, though translators of the book into English have given it the title *Aphorisms of the Statesman* or *Selected Aphorisms*. The precise translation of the word is more prosaic—simply *sections*.[2]

Alfarabi opens by describing his book as 'excerpted sections, comprising numerous principles drawn from the ancients [*qudamāʾ*], regarding the manner whereby polities should be governed and rendered successful, whereby the behaviour of their citizens should be perfected, and whereby the citizens should be led to eudaemonia'.[3] The subject matter is human psychology, ethics, and statecraft, the presupposition being that a properly constructed polity will concern itself with its citizens' intellectual development; the ideal polity will thereby bring its citizens to eudaemonia, or felicity, and their fully developed intellects to immortality.[4] Maimonides draws from the sections on psychology and ethics and ignores those on statecraft.

Whether Alfarabi assembled and formulated the material by himself or copied some or all from an earlier work that had already done the job can only be conjectured. Whoever it was that composed and assembled the building blocks out of which the *Fuṣūl* is put together was familiar with Aristotle's *Nicomachean Ethics*; that is clear from the contents and terminology. The difference between the *Nicomachean Ethics* and Alfarabi's book is nonetheless striking. Aristotle's thought-provoking analysis and the nuances in which he excelled have been dropped, and the conclusions to which his analysis led are now stated as stark, cut and dried facts. The other side of the coin is that while Aristotle's train of thought is sometimes tortuous, Alfarabi's presentation is much easier to follow.

The framework allows Alfarabi opportunities to indulge in a favourite pastime, the disparagement of popular religion. He criticizes, for instance, what

[2] On *fuṣūl* as a literary genre, found, among others, in Maimonides himself, see Dunlop's observations in Alfarabi, *Fuṣūl al-madanī*, 9–10, 79.

[3] Alfarabi, *Fuṣūl muntazaʿa*, preface.

[4] Ibid., §§28, 81, 89.

he calls the 'shameful and hateful' belief that the first cause of the universe has knowledge of, and exercises providence over, individual human beings.[5] And he remarks casually: the accomplished philosopher who works out a set of rules for organizing society and the man who receives a set of such rules through revelation (*waḥy*) are perhaps both called knowledgeable; but the term 'knowledge' (or science: *ʿilm*) is predicated in the two instances 'equivocally'.[6] Put in plain words, a prophet who relies solely on revelation does not possess genuine knowledge. Maimonides could well have had *obiter dicta* of this sort in mind when he expressed the fear that readers might reject what he quotes as corrupt, should they know whom he was quoting.

I begin by setting a half dozen passages of *Shemonah perakim* side by side with corresponding passages in the *Fuṣūl muntazaʿa*. Maimonides is on the left.

1. The healer of souls must know the nature of the soul and its parts

Shemonah perakim	*Fuṣūl muntazaʿa*
You know that improving moral characteristics is what constitutes healing [*ʿilāj*] of the soul and its faculties. Now just as the physician [*ṭabīb*] who heals [*yuʿālij*] bodies must first know the body he is healing as a whole [*bi-asrihi*] and what the parts of the body are . . . and must moreover know which things make the body sick and are to be avoided and which make it healthy and are to be pursued, so he who treats the soul and wishes to correct its moral qualities must know the soul as a whole and its parts and what makes it sick and what makes it healthy. (ch. 1, p. 373)	The healer of bodies is the physician [*ṭabīb*], and the healer of souls is the statesman, who is also called the king. . . . Just as the physician who heals [*yuʿālij*] bodies must understand the body as a whole [*bi-asrihi*] and the body's parts, the diseases affecting the entire body and each of its parts . . . and the way to remove those diseases . . . so the statesman and king who heals souls must understand the soul as a whole and its parts, the defects and vices affecting it and each of its parts . . . the way to remove vices from the citizens of states, and tactics for inculcating [virtue] in the souls of the citizens. (§§4–5)

2. The parts of the soul

Shemonah perakim	*Fuṣūl muntazaʿa*
The parts of the soul are five: the nutritive [*ghādhī*], sense perceptive [*ḥāss*], imaginative [*mutakhayyil*], appetitive [*nuzūʿī*], and rational [*nāṭiq*]. (ch. 1, pp. 373–4)	The main parts and faculties of the soul are five: the nutritive [*ghādhī*], sense perceptive [*ḥāss*], imaginative [*mutakhayyil*], appetitive [*nuzūʿī*], and rational [*nāṭiq*]. (§7)

[5] Ibid., §§86–7.

[6] Ibid., §94 (p. 98).

3. The parts of the soul in which observance of the religious commandments takes place and the part in which the moral virtues are located

Shemonah perakim	*Fuṣūl muntazaʿa*
Know that disobedience and obedience in respect to the religious law belong to only two parts of the soul, the sense perceptive and the appetitive. All transgressions and the performance of all commandments are in those two parts. . . . As for virtues, they are of two sorts, moral virtues and rational virtues, and opposite them are two sorts of vice. The rational virtues are found in the rational part of the soul, and they are. . . . The moral virtues are found exclusively in the appetitive part, and in this instance, the sense perceptive part merely serves the appetitive part. The virtues of this part are very numerous, for example . . . (ch. 2, pp. 376–7)	Virtues are of two types, moral and rational. The rational are the virtues of the rational part, for example . . . The moral are the virtues of the appetitive part, for example. . . . Vices are divided in the same way. (§8)

4. Moral virtues and how they are inculcated

Shemonah perakim	*Fuṣūl muntazaʿa*
Actions that are good are actions that are balanced and lie midway between two extremes, both of which are bad, one of them going too far and the other falling short. Virtues are characteristics in the soul and habits that lie midway between two vile [*radītayn*] characteristics, one of them excessive and the other, defective . . . Know that these moral virtues and vices come about and are established in the soul by repeating the actions flowing from the pertinent trait, frequently, over a long period of time, and by accustoming ourselves to them. (ch. 4, pp. 379, 381)	Actions that are good are actions that are balanced and lie midway between two extremes, both of which are bad, one of them going too far and the other falling short. Similarly regarding virtues, for they are characteristics in the soul and habits that lie midway between two characteristics, both of which are vices [*radhīlatān*; alternative reading: *radītān*, vile], one of them excessive and the other, defective. . . . Moral virtues and vices come about and are established in the soul by repeating the actions flowing from the pertinent trait, frequently, and over a period of time, and by accustoming ourselves to them. (§§9, 18)

5. Health and sickness of the soul

Shemonah perakim

The ancients stated that the soul is subject to health and sickness just as the body is subject to health and disease. The health of the soul is a situation in which its characteristics [*hayʾāt*] and the characteristics of its parts are characteristics whereby it always does good things, fine things, and [performs] beautiful actions. Its disease is a situation in which its characteristics and the characteristics of its parts are characteristics whereby it always does bad things, evil things, and [performs] ugly actions. . . .

Just as in the case of those suffering from a disease of the body, the deterioration of their [physical] senses causes them to imagine that what is sweet is bitter and what is bitter is sweet, and they visualize what has a pleasant shape as unpleasant . . . so too those suffering from a disease of the soul, that is to say, those who are bad and have deficiencies, imagine that bad things are good things and good things are bad things . . . Those who suffer from a disease of the soul must consult with the wise, who are the physicians of the soul. (ch. 3, pp. 378–9)

Fuṣūl muntazaʿa

The soul is subject to health and sickness just as the body is subject to health and disease. The health of the soul is a situation in which its characteristics [*hayʾāt*] and the characteristics of its parts are characteristics whereby it always does good things, fine things, and [performs] beautiful actions. Its disease is a situation in which its characteristics and the characteristics of its parts are characteristics whereby it always does bad things, evil things, and [performs] ugly actions. (§1)

Just as in the case of those suffering from diseases of the body, the deterioration of their [physical] senses causes them to imagine [alternative reading: because of the deterioration of their senses and imagination they imagine] that what is sweet is bitter and what is bitter is sweet, and they visualize what has a pleasant shape as unpleasant, and what has an unpleasant shape as pleasant; so too inasmuch as those who are bad and possess deficiencies suffer from diseases of the soul, they imagine that bad things are good things and good things are bad things. (§41)

The healer of souls is the statesman, who is also called the king. (§4)

6. The difference between the self-controlled man and the virtuous man

Shemonah perakim

Regarding the difference between the virtuous man [*al-fāḍil*] and the self-controlled man [*al-ḍābiṭ li-nafsihi*]: The philosophers stated that although the self-controlled man performs virtuous actions, he does good things while desiring and longing for bad actions. He resists his desire and opposes in his action that towards which

Fuṣūl muntazaʿa

There is a difference between the self-controlled man [*al-ḍābiṭ li-nafsihi*] and the virtuous man [*al-fāḍil*]. For although the self-controlled man performs virtuous actions, he does good things while desiring and longing for bad actions. He resists his desire and opposes in his action that towards which his characteristic and his faculties, his longing, and the characteristic of his soul pull him. He does good things while suffering pain in doing them. The virtuous man, by contrast, follows in his action that towards which his longing and characteristic pull him. He does good things while desiring and longing for them. The consensus of the philosophers is that the virtuous man is more virtuous and perfect than the self-controlled man. They stated, however, that in many respects the self-controlled man can take the place of the virtuous man, although he is definitely inferior to him. . . . Now, when we investigate the words of the rabbis on the subject, we find them saying that he who desires and longs for sin is *more* virtuous and perfect than he who does not. (ch. 6, p. 391)

longing pull him. He does good things while suffering pain in doing them. The virtuous man follows in his action that towards which his characteristic and longing pull him. He does good things, while desiring and longing for them. . . . It is like the difference between the man who bears great pain . . . and the man who does not feel pain. Similarly, the temperate man [*ʿafīf*] and self-controlled man [*al-ḍābiṭ li-nafsihi*]; for the temperate man does what the rule requires . . . without having desire for more than it requires, whereas the desire of the self-controlled man is excessive and [he desires] something other than what the rule requires. He acts according to the rule while his desire is for the opposite. In many respects, however, the self-controlled man can take the place of the virtuous man. (§14)

There is more. After distinguishing the five parts of the human soul, Maimonides lists: seven distinct faculties within the nutritive part, the five senses constituting the sense-perceptive part, the functions performed by the imaginative part, the functions performed by the appetitive part and the actions that flow from it, the subdivisions of the rational part and the functions they perform. His account, which extends well over a page and includes several dozen technical terms, is copied virtually word for word from Alfarabi's *Fuṣūl muntazaʿa*.[7] Almost half of the opening chapter of *Shemonah perakim* thus comes directly from Alfarabi.

In the chapter partly translated above in item 4, Maimonides illustrates the proposition that each moral virtue is a characteristic in the soul, lying midway between a vice of excess and one of deficiency, by listing nine virtues and the corresponding vices. Temperance, for example, lies midway between the vices of gluttony and insensitiveness, generosity midway between stinginess and prodigality, courage midway between foolhardiness and cowardice. Maimonides includes a virtue—good-heartedness—not found in the preserved versions of the *Fuṣūl muntazaʿa*; in a couple of instances, he simplifies a little; he alters the terms for the extremes in two more; and he omits a virtue—friendliness—that

[7] *ShP*, ch. 1, pp. 374–6, paralleling Alfarabi, *Fuṣūl muntazaʿa*, §6.

Alfarabi includes. Otherwise, he copies the virtues and their respective vices from Alfarabi and presents them in the same order.[8]

Alfarabi writes in *Fuṣūl muntazaʿa*: A 'man cannot be formed from the outset naturally in possession of virtue or vice'; it is, moreover, 'rare and unusual [*ʿasīr wa-baʿīd*] for someone to exist who is disposed [*muʿadd*] by nature for [acquiring] all the virtues, both the moral and the rational'.[9] Maimonides similarly writes: 'A man cannot, from the outset, be naturally in possession of virtue or vice.'[10] 'The philosophers have stated: It is rare and unusual [*ʿasīr wa-baʿīd*] for someone to exist who is naturally disposed [*muʿadd*] for [acquiring] all the virtues, moral and rational.'[11]

On my calculation, about 5 per cent of *Shemonah perakim* is taken directly from the *Fuṣūl muntazaʿa* and well over half of the strictly philosophical passages are built around direct quotations from Alfarabi's book. The quotations form a complete ethical theory, including: the assertion that the practitioner who treats the soul must understand it just as the physician who treats the body must understand the body; a taxonomy of the parts and functions of the human soul; the distinction between moral and intellectual virtue; the principle that each moral virtue is an intermediate characteristic of the soul lying midway between an extreme of excess and an extreme of deficiency, both of which are vices; the proposition that moral virtue is health, and vice, illness; a list of moral virtues, each of which is shown to be a mean lying between two extremes; and the rule that a virtuous or vicious characteristic is instilled in the soul by the repeated performance of actions corresponding to the given characteristic.

To the above, Maimonides makes a couple of additions. He explains how non-virtuous characteristics in the soul can be cured. A person whose soul has a characteristic that is off-centre in one direction is to be instructed to perform actions corresponding to a characteristic lying in the opposite direction. For example, someone who is stingy is to be instructed to behave more prodigally than is ordinarily proper until he—or she—drags the characteristic of his soul to the centre and becomes generous.[12] The recommended therapy, it should be noted, is not an exception to the principle that moral virtues are means. It is actions departing from the mean that are prescribed therapeutically, whereas characteristics in the soul, not actions, are the locus of moral virtue. The actions departing from the mean are designed to reposition wayward characteristics of the soul precisely where they belong, at the mean.

[8] *ShP*, ch. 4, pp. 379–80, paralleling Alfarabi, *Fuṣūl muntazaʿa*, §18.

[9] Alfarabi, *Fuṣūl muntazaʿa*, §§10–11.

[10] *ShP*, ch. 8, p. 396.

[11] *ShP*, ch. 4, p. 386, and again in *Commentary on the Mishnah*, *Avot* 5: 13.

[12] Therapy along similar lines is prescribed in Avicenna, *Fī al-ʿahd*, 148.

Maimonides further recommends a form of ethical prophylaxis, which is a genuine exception to the principle of the mean. To protect himself against the more harmful of the two extremes that are, in each case, vices, the reader is advised to diverge slightly from the mean in the direction of the less harmful extreme. Since, for example, the characteristic of stinginess is the worse of the two extremes bracketing the virtue of generosity, it is advisable to move a little away from the centre and cultivate a characteristic that inclines slightly towards prodigality.[13] In his commentary on tractate *Avot*, Maimonides finds textual grounds in the tractate for applying the Hebrew term *ḥakham*, wise, to the man who combines rational virtue with standard, middle-way ethical virtue and the term *ḥasid*, pious, to the man who in addition moves slightly away from the midpoint as a form of prophylaxis.[14] I saw no basis in the *Fuṣūl muntazaʿa* for either the therapy or the prophylaxis that Maimonides recommends.

While Maimonides' reliance on the *Fuṣūl muntazaʿa* is beyond doubt, it remains to be asked whether he may have used Aristotle's *Nicomachean Ethics* as well. Averroes, a contemporary and a fellow Cordovan, reports that the first four books of the *Nicomachean Ethics* were available in Spain; they should therefore have been available to Maimonides. Averroes adds that he had the remaining books of the *Nicomachean Ethics* brought from abroad; in one version of his report he had them brought from Egypt.[15] Since Maimonides completed the *Commentary on the Mishnah*, of which *Shemonah perakim* is a part, in Egypt, he should have been able to consult the entire *Nicomachean Ethics* before publishing his *Commentary*. When he later wrote the *Moreh nevukhim* in Egypt, he did quote from both halves of the *Nicomachean Ethics*.

The definition of moral virtue as a mean and a list of virtues with their corresponding vices form a prominent part of the first four books of the *Nicomachean Ethics*, the books that should have been available to Maimonides in Spain. The contrast between the self-controlled and the virtuous man is traceable to Book 7, which Averroes tells us was not available in Spain but which Maimonides should have been able to see in Egypt. With a single conceivable exception, Maimonides' *Shemonah perakim* gives us reason to conclude that he did not consult the Aristotelian work.

The analogy between the health and disease of the body and health and disease of the soul is a topos going back at least to Plato.[16] Aristotle employs it in the *Nicomachean Ethics*, writing, for instance, that as the physician who treats

[13] *ShP*, ch. 4, p. 382.

[14] Maimonides, *Commentary on the Mishnah*, *Avot* 5: 6; 9.

[15] Averroes, *Middle Commentary on Aristotle's Nicomachean Ethics*, 354; Aristotle, *The Arabic Version of the Nicomachean Ethics*, 51.

[16] See Plato, *Gorgias*, 464B. Other instances: Philo, *Quod Omnis Probus Liber*, 2.12; Ikhwān al-Ṣafā', *Rasā'il*, iv. 457; Rosin, *Die Ethik des Maimonides*, 78 n. 4.

the eye or the body as a whole must have knowledge of the organ or organism he is treating, so the person responsible for the health of the human soul must have knowledge of the object of his ministrations. Aristotle, however, adds that the requisite knowledge need not be exhaustive.[17] The full account of the soul's subdivisions and functions, drawn up for the use of the physician of the soul, and the notable detail that a diseased soul confuses good and bad just as a diseased body confuses sweet with bitter, are taken by Maimonides from Alfarabi and not from Aristotle.

The *Nicomachean Ethics* recommends shamefacedness (*ḥayāʾ*) and locates it between two unacceptable extremes, but with the proviso that since it is a passion and not a characteristic in the soul, it is not strictly a virtue. 'Shamefacedness' (*ḥayāʾ*) is included in Alfarabi's list of moral virtues without qualification, and Maimonides too lists it, without qualification, as a moral virtue.[18] Aristotle classifies pride (*kibr al-nafs*) as a virtue. Alfarabi makes pride (*takabbur*; in one manuscript: *kibr*) and its opposite, self-abasement, a pair of vices, between which the virtue of humility (*tawāḍuʿ*) lies. Maimonides follows, classifying humility (*tawāḍuʿ*) as a virtue located midway between pride (*takabbur*) and self-abasement.[19] Aristotle's list of moral virtues includes 'wittiness' (*ẓarf*), which lies midway between the vices of buffoonery and boorishness. The *Fuṣūl muntazaʿa* feels a need to clarify. It states: 'Wittiness [*ẓarf*] is an intermediate in [matters of] joking [*hazl*], playfulness [*laʿb*], and the like, [lying] midway between wantonness [*khalāʿa*] and dullness [*fadāma*].' Maimonides drops *ẓarf*, 'wittiness', the term used by the Arabic translator of the *Nicomachean Ethics*, and replaces it with one of the terms that the *Fuṣūl* introduces to explain it. He writes: 'Playfulness [*laʿb*] is an intermediate between shamelessness [*jalāʿa*] and dullness [*fadāma*].'[20] In Arabic script, *khalāʿa*, the vice of excess according to the preserved text of the *Fuṣūl*, and *jalāʿa*, the vice of excess according to the preserved text of Maimonides' *Shemonah perakim*, are distinguished only by the placing of a dot.

There is one possible trace of Aristotle's *Nicomachean Ethics* in *Shemonah perakim*. In connection with the definition of moral virtue, Aristotle observes that determining the exact midpoint on the spectrum is difficult, and that of the two extremes bracketing a given virtue one may be worse than the other. He

[17] Aristotle, *Nicomachean Ethics*, 1.13, 1102a, 18–26. Jaeger, 'Aristotle's Use of Medicine', is an illuminating account of the analogy between medicine and ethics in the *Nicomachean Ethics*.

[18] Aristotle, *Nicomachean Ethics*, 4.9, 1128b, 10–11; *The Arabic Version of the Nicomachean Ethics*, 285; Alfarabi, *Fuṣūl muntazaʿa*, §18; *ShP*, ch. 4, p. 380.

[19] Aristotle, *Nicomachean Ethics*, 2.7, 1107b, 21–3; *The Arabic Version of the Nicomachean Ethics*, 177; Alfarabi, *Fuṣūl muntazaʿa*, §18; *ShP*, ch. 4, p. 380.

[20] Aristotle, *Nicomachean Ethics*, 2.7, 1108a, 23–6; *The Arabic Version of the Nicomachean Ethics*, 179; Alfarabi, *Fuṣūl muntazaʿa*, §18.

accordingly advises the person 'who aims at the mean' to 'distance himself from the extreme that is more opposed to the mean', even if he thereby goes beyond the midpoint in the direction of the other extreme. Thus if extreme X is more opposed to a given mean than its contrary, extreme Y, and hitting the midpoint is difficult, a person trying to avoid X, the greater vice, may be excused for going slightly beyond the virtuous midpoint in the direction of Y, the lesser vice. The situation, Aristotle writes, is similar to that in which someone straightens a crooked stick by bending it in the opposite direction. Such a course is not, however, the ideal. In the Arabic translation of the *Nicomachean Ethics*, Aristotle calls it the 'least possible evil' and rates it as of 'secondary rank'; the desideratum remains the mean.[21] I did not find the nuance about going slightly beyond the mean in the *Fuṣūl muntazaʿa*, although an echo of it, without the remark about lesser evil and secondary rank, is found in another of Alfarabi's works.[22] Aristotle's observation appears to be the ultimate, although not necessarily the immediate, seedbed out of which Maimonides' conception of ethical prophylaxis grew.

Alfarabi's *Fuṣūl muntazaʿa* describes itself as 'excerpted sections, comprising numerous principles drawn from the ancients', and at various junctures Alfarabi credits 'the ancients' as the source for what he writes.[23] Maimonides has accordingly treated the *Fuṣūl* as a reliable transcript of the views of the ancients. When he cites the statements of 'ancient and recent philosophers' regarding moral virtue he conveys what he found in the *Fuṣūl muntazaʿa* and not what he learned through his own study of ancient philosophy and of Aristotle in particular. He may have gathered bits of additional information from other sources, but there is no credible evidence that the *Nicomachean Ethics* was one of them and good reason to think that it was not.

Maimonides was not an automaton, and it should be no surprise that he does not follow Alfarabi blindly. He differs on the ever controversial subjects of religion and politics.

The *Fuṣūl muntazaʿa* is thoroughly deistic in spirit. It makes no bones about its dismissal of conventional religion and contains nothing that might identify the author as a Muslim. We have already encountered Alfarabi's comment on the 'shameful and hateful' belief that the first cause of the universe has knowledge of, and exercises providence over individual human beings. In the course of the *Fuṣūl*, Alfarabi grants the 'bearers of religion' (*dīn*) a role in the ideal

[21] Aristotle, *Nicomachean Ethics*, 2.9, 1109a, 30–1109b, 7; *The Arabic Version of the Nicomachean Ethics*, 181–3.

[22] Alfarabi, *L'Harmonie entre les opinions de Platon et d'Aristote*, §42.

[23] Alfarabi, *Fuṣūl muntazaʿa*, §§22, 36, 91.

state. But he groups them with 'rhetoricians, eloquent speakers, poets, musicians, and secretaries', persons whose skill lies in 'language', and he studiously excludes them from the ruling class, which is made up of the pre-eminent (*al-afāḍil*) members of the state, namely, 'the wise, persons of practical intelligence, and those who possess [correct] opinions on momentous matters'.[24] The modest role given the bearers of religion is restricted to the area of education and propaganda. They are excluded from governance of the polity and, most provocatively, from deciding matters of correct belief.

The framework into which Maimonides incorporates his quotations from Alfarabi is very different. He weaves what he takes into a work of religious law, offers corroboration with a flood of citations from Scripture and rabbinic literature, and mobilizes the theory of the ethical middle way as augmented by his conception of ethical prophylaxis for interpreting maxims in tractate *Avot*. *Shemonah perakim*, generally in translation, is to this day regarded in religious Jewish circles as a fount of moral edification.

The statement in *Fuṣūl muntazaʿa* to the effect that moral virtues are located in the appetitive faculty of the soul leads Maimonides to the question of the parts of the soul responsible for performing religious commandments. He accepts the principle that characteristics in the appetitive faculty and not the actions flowing from them are what constitute virtue and vice; a man can be virtuous whether or not his virtue expresses itself in action. Yet almost all the religious commandments require that the agent move, say, view, smell, hear, or eat something or that he scrupulously refrain from doing so. Maimonides accordingly concludes that the commandments of the religious law involve not only the appetitive part of the soul but the sense-perceptive part as well. Positive commandments are fulfilled when the appetitive faculty initiates, and the senses perform, the required acts. Negative commandments are fulfilled when the appetitive faculty instructs the senses not to act, and the senses obey.[25]

Religious commandments enter the discussion again in connection with the self-controlled man and the virtuous man. The Greek text of the *Nicomachean Ethics* contrasts the self-controlled man with the *temperate* man, that is to say, the possessor of the virtue lying between gluttony and insensitiveness; and Aristotle does not judge between the two. Because of a confusion in the Arabic translation of the *Nicomachean Ethics*, Alfarabi's *Fuṣūl muntazaʿa* presents the primary contrast as between the self-controlled man and the *virtuous* man in general, rather than the *temperate* man in particular. (A secondary contrast is drawn there between the self-controlled man and the *temperate* man, but

[24] Ibid., §§57, 66. [25] *ShP*, ch. 2, p. 376.

Maimonides takes no cognizance of it.) While Alfarabi indicates that the virtuous man is the more meritorious, he does not press the point.[26]

The contrast between the self-controlled and the virtuous man and their relative merits occupied Maimonides' attention not because of any philosophical significance it might have, but because of certain rabbinic sayings. The rabbis stated: 'When one man is greater than another, his evil inclination is likewise greater.' They maintained that struggling with temptation adds to one's merit: 'In accordance with the pain is the reward.' They went as far as to encourage a person to desire the forbidden, struggle with his desire, and overcome it: 'A man should not say "I have no desire to eat meat cooked in milk, I have no desire to wear garments made of wool and linen, I have no desire for sexual relations with women who are forbidden to me." He should rather say: "I have the desire, but what can I do? My father in heaven has enjoined me."'

On the one hand, the tenor of Alfarabi's *Fuṣūl* indicates to Maimonides that the 'consensus of the philosophers' ranks the virtuous man higher than the self-controlled man. On the other hand, the rabbis ranked the man who exercises self-control higher than the man who has no desire for what is forbidden. In good talmudic style, Maimonides resolves the conflict by drawing a distinction.

He finds that the positions of the philosophers and the rabbis are 'both true, and there is no discrepancy whatsoever between them'. The philosophers were talking about characteristics of the soul governing behaviour that is universally regarded as evil, such as murder, theft, chicanery, and the like. A virtuous soul does not desire such behaviour. When the rabbis assigned greater merit to overcoming desire than to being free of it, they had something else in view. They were talking about actions that are not intrinsically bad but are to be avoided solely because the divine law forbids them—actions prohibited by revealed commandments (*sharāʾiʿ samʿiyya*).[27] In that case, a person's motive should be that the divine law commands him to refrain from the actions, not that his appetitive faculty recoils from them.

The discrepancy between the consensus of the philosophers and the statements of the rabbis merits an entire chapter in Maimonides' *Shemonah perakim*, and he is palpably pleased with his solution. Alfarabi would have been bemused and amused to see a purported philosopher exercised over the prattle of ignorant prophets and clerics.

Then there is the matter of the state. It has been contended in recent years that political theory was a central philosophical concern of Maimonides and, more strongly, that the only fulfilling human life is life within a political frame-

[26] Alfarabi, *Fuṣūl muntazaʿa*, §15.

[27] *ShP*, ch. 6. On the term *sharāʾiʿ samʿiyya*, see above, Ch. 2, §2.

work.[28] *Shemonah perakim* allows us to assess the accuracy of the contention for the period during which Maimonides wrote his *Commentary on the Mishnah*.

At the beginning of the *Nicomachean Ethics*, Aristotle posits that, as the Arabic translation puts it, 'the art of governing polities' is the supreme discipline, that it overarches and directs all the other arts and sciences, including ethics.[29] When Aristotle sets forth the analogy between the care of bodies and the care of souls, he identifies the governor of the polity as the person responsible for the latter.[30]

Alfarabi's *Fuṣūl muntazaʿa* follows suit. It tells us that the 'healer of souls is the statesman, who is also called the king'; he is the person responsible for curing citizens' vices and training them in virtue.[31] Somewhat later, Alfarabi returns to the healing analogy, writing: the person who calculates where the midpoint and correct balance lie in regard to nutrition and medication is the physician. The person who calculates where the midpoint and correct balance lie in regard to 'moral qualities and actions is the governor of the city and the king'; and the art plied by the governor and king is 'the political art and kingly craft'.[32] From that juncture on, the *Fuṣūl* focuses on the organization and governance of polities, and particularly of the ideal state, which encourages men to develop their intellects, attain ultimate eudaemonia, and prepare their intellects for the higher existence into which intellects enter when they separate from their human bodies. Alfarabi warns readers against ignoring the good of the state and of their fellow citizens. He mandates that men cultivate moral virtue within the political framework and not privately, that they do not keep their virtue to themselves but express it in action, and that actions in accordance with virtue have as their object the good of the state and its citizens.[33] The organization of polities and particularly of the ideal state is a theme that repeatedly comes up in Alfarabi's writings.

As Maimonides draws from the *Fuṣūl muntazaʿa*, he makes no mention of political entities and the contributions men make to them, and he recommends moral virtue not for beneficial actions that might flow from it but because of its service to the possessor. Moral virtue serves the person who possesses it by enabling him to mobilize the powers of his soul in pursuit of the final goal of human life, the development of his intellect.

[28] Strauss, *Philosophie und Gesetz*, 58–60, 108–22; id., *Philosophy and Law*, 70–1, 120–33; Pines, 'The Limitations of Human Knowledge', 100; Berman, 'Political Interpretation', 59.

[29] Aristotle, *Nicomachean Ethics*, 1.2. Aristotle does not in fact use the term 'ethics'; see Burnet, *Ethics of Aristotle*, p. xxvi.

[30] Aristotle, *Nicomachean Ethics*, 1.13, 1102a, 23; *The Arabic Version of the Nicomachean Ethics*, 147–9. Aristotle is echoing Plato, *Gorgias*, 464.

[31] See above.

[32] Alfarabi, *Fuṣūl muntazaʿa*, §21.

[33] Ibid., §§27–8.

Maimonides goes beyond merely ignoring Alfarabi's statements on political theory. As we have seen, he makes only small stylistic changes in the material he borrows. There is a single substantive change. In copying the passage marked above as item 5, where Alfarabi states that 'the healer of souls is the statesman, who is also called the king', Maimonides writes: 'Those who suffer from a disease of the soul must consult with the *wise* [*ʿulamāʾ*], who are the physicians of the soul.' He does not specify who the wise are; he could mean philosophers, rabbis, or perhaps even the Pentateuch and the prophetic books of the Bible. Whoever they are, they replace Alfarabi's statesman and king as physicians of the human soul.

What we have found in connection with *Shemonah perakim* further confirms the findings of the previous chapter. Despite his commitment to the philosophical ideal, Maimonides chose not to plod through the Arabic translation of the *Nicomachean Ethics* in order to ascertain what the greatest philosopher who ever lived taught about ethics; he used a convenient short cut instead. When that short cut took positions that did not accord with his religious beliefs or were not to his taste, he ignored it and went his own way. His reliance on the *Fuṣūl muntazaʿa* as a source for what the ancient philosophers taught concerning ethics does not make him a 'disciple of Alfarabi'—to use a sobriquet coined by a recent scholar—at the time when he wrote the *Commentary on the Mishnah*, any more than reliance on one of the helpful introductions to Aristotle available today makes one a disciple of the person who wrote the introduction.

The evidence marshalled here comes from Maimonides' *Commentary on the Mishnah*, the first of his main rabbinic works. There is no reason to imagine that his study of philosophical works on ethics expanded appreciably over the next ten years, during which, he tells us, he 'laboured day and night' on the *Mishneh torah*, his rabbinic masterpiece.

FIVE

Maimonides' Knowledge of the Philosophical Literature in his Later Period

I studied the writings of the philosophers to the extent of my ability.

MAIMONIDES
Moreh nevukhim, i. 71

Take nothing on its looks; take everything on evidence. There's no better rule.

CHARLES DICKENS
Great Expectations

A GREATER FAMILIARITY WITH the philosophical literature is to be expected in Maimonides' philosophical opus, the *Moreh nevukhim*, which he began after finishing his rabbinic works and completed by 1191, when he was 53 or 54 years old. The present chapter examines the extent to which the evidence bears out the expectation. I have already shown that except for a few doubtful scraps there are no grounds for supposing knowledge of Neoplatonic literature on Maimonides' part during either his rabbinic or philosophical period. Here I begin with the Kalam and then proceed to Aristotle, the Greek commentators on Aristotle, other Greek philosophers, the Arabic philosophers, and medieval Jewish philosophers.

1. Kalam

Maimonides states in the *Moreh nevukhim* that he had studied the 'books of the Kalam thinkers as far as was feasible' for him to do so.[1] At one juncture he refers to 'lengthy books and better-known compositions' written by members of the school,[2] and although he does not name any of the compositions, he leaves the unmistakable implication that he had read them. He adduces Kalam opinions on major and minor issues,[3] and is cognizant of the divide between the Asharite and Muʿtazilite branches of the school.

[1] *MN* i. 71 (95*b*).

[2] *MN* i. 74 (118*a*).

[3] *MN* i. 50: thesis that God, although wholly one and simple in His essence, has essential attributes;

He thus distinguishes between the stance of the Asharites and that of the Muʿtazilites on divine providence. The former, he writes, maintained that God acts with untempered arbitrariness, determines every action a human being will perform, whether good or bad, yet rewards and punishes human beings for those very actions. The latter reserved for men some control over their behaviour and viewed God as a paragon of justice. They therefore held that, in the world to come, God will reward and punish every living creature, man as well as beast, in accordance with its deserts and will compensate His creatures for undeserved suffering in this life.[4] Maimonides has simplified a little regarding the Muʿtazilites but is reasonably faithful to the sources that have been preserved.

Most of what he has to say about the Kalam is concentrated in a sequence of four chapters that are devoted to Kalam arguments for the creation of the world and the existence, unity, and incorporeality of God. It is here that he speaks of having studied books by members of the Kalam school as far as was feasible. He characterizes some of the Kalam propositions that he discusses as having been embraced by all members of the school, others as positions of the majority, and still others as positions of the minority.[5] He categorizes several arguments as having been put forward by either 'early' or 'later' Kalam thinkers.[6] The signal he plainly conveys is that he knows whereof he speaks.

The first of the four chapters spells out and analyses twelve propositions that he reports members of the school used in their arguments for creation and the existence, unity, and incorporeality of God. The remaining chapters examine the arguments themselves. Almost all the arguments in the three chapters can be identified in preserved Kalam sources, and in their case, what Maimonides reports is more or less accurate.[7] It is the twelve propositions that concern us.

They turn out to be more than just premisses employed in the arguments; some do not appear to play a role in the arguments at all. The propositions encapsulate the Kalam picture of the universe, with particular attention to its atomism and occasionalism, and Maimonides' critique becomes in effect a critique of the entire system. Despite the fact that he does not name a single

i. 51 (58*a*–*b*): question whether atoms occupy space, and the sense in which man may be said to perform actions if the universe is completely controlled by divine omnipotence; i. 69 (88*b*): insistence on calling God an agent and not a cause; i. 71 (95*a*): God's eternal speech (see Munk's translation, *Guide des égarés*); iii. 10 (66*b*): thesis that the lack of a quality is itself a positive quality. Maimonides does not expressly name the Kalam in any of the instances.

[4] *MN* iii. 17 (3) and (4). [5] *MN.* i. 73 (5, 6, 7, 10, 11, 12). [6] *MN* i. 74 (6); i. 75 (3, 5).

[7] Evidence regarding the arguments is provided in H. Davidson, *Proofs for Eternity, Creation, and the Existence of God*, chs. 5 and 6.

thinker or work from which he drew, his account, in which he brings to bear his considerable analytical and systematizing gifts, is so clear and confident that more than one scholar has employed it as a prime source of information on the Kalam.[8] A recent meticulous and invaluable study by M. Schwarz has unfortunately shown that a number of the propositions have no basis in the large body of Kalam texts accessible today.

Maimonides states, for instance, that the Kalam thinkers[9] 'believe in the existence of the void', that is to say, the existence of regions of totally empty space within the physical universe. It happens that only two men, both belonging to the Muʿtazilite branch of the school, are known to have advocated the notion.[10] Maimonides represents 'their', that is, the Kalam, view as being that time is not a continuum but consists of 'moments . . . not subject to division because of the brevity of their duration'. Time, in other words, is made up of infinitesimal, discrete, and indivisible bits, just as bodies, in the Kalam universe, are made up of infinitesimal and indivisible atoms. Only a single figure associated with the movement can be identified who advocated such a view.[11] Maimonides ascribes two theories of soul to the Kalam: 'Most' members of the school held that the soul is an 'accident present in a single one of the totality of atoms' forming a living being. Some—or one—understood the soul to be 'a body consisting of [particularly] fine atoms' that are endowed with a variety of accident unique to themselves; the body made up of those soul-atoms interpenetrates the entire frame of a living being. In a similar vein, Maimonides writes: 'I saw them agreeing' that intellect is 'an accident present in one of the atoms' forming an intelligent being. The closest statement that has been found to the two views on soul is the opinion of a peripheral Kalam thinker who held that 'soul' is 'one of the accidents present in the body' of a living being. As for intellect, adherents of the Kalam, in studied contrast to their philosophical adversaries, showed little interest in it. What Maimonides portrays as a unanimous position on the nature of intellect cannot be traced to a single figure associated with the school.[12]

To take a final revealing example, Maimonides reports 'their assertion' that 'the senses deceive [or: are deceived] and many objects of perception elude

[8] A few are listed by Schwarz, 'Who Were Maimonides' Mutakallimūn?', i. 160 n. 1.

[9] *Al-uṣūliyyūn*, literally: 'those who deal with the fundamentals [of religion]'. In *MN* i. 71 (96*b*–97*a*), where Maimonides also uses the term *al-uṣūliyyūn*, he immediately glosses it as *al-mutakallimūn*, the Kalam thinkers. Munk, in a note to his translation, points out the implied contrast between those who deal with fundamentals and those who deal with the *branches* of religion, that is, with the legal side.

[10] *MN* i. 73 (2); Schwarz, 'Who Were Maimonides' Mutakallimūn?', i. 170–5.

[11] *MN* i. 73 (3); Schwarz, 'Who Were Maimonides' Mutakallimūn?', i. 176–81.

[12] *MN* i. 73 (5); Schwarz, 'Who Were Maimonides' Mutakallimūn?', i. 191–3.

them', hence what has been perceived by the senses 'may not be employed as premisses in a demonstration'. The unreliability of sense perception is, in his words, a 'proposition' for which 'the Kalam thinkers have fought'. A Kalam contemporary of Maimonides, as well as a writer associated with the school who lived more than a century and a half later, take note of attacks on the reliability of sense perception but they themselves do not endorse them.[13] Not a single Kalam figure is known to have subscribed to the sceptical stance on sense perception that Maimonides ascribes to the school as a whole, and prominent Kalam thinkers do not hesitate to rely on sense perception as a legitimate source of knowledge.[14]

The reason for Maimonides' missing the mark so badly in a number of instances can only be guessed, and none of the guesses that come to mind sparkles. The supposition that he drew not from the Kalam works available today but from an entirely different corpus is scarcely plausible. A treasure trove of Kalam writings has been published in recent years and they derive from the influential and better-known members of both the Asharite and Muʿtazilite branches; from whom else could Maimonides have drawn? It might be conjectured that he once read widely in Kalam literature but was relying on memory when he sat down to write the *Moreh nevukhim* in middle age, and that his memory, which reputedly was phenomenal in his youth, had now become porous and misled him. Yet, as was seen in Chapter 3, his rabbinic writings do not indicate that he studied Kalam texts in any depth during his earlier period. In the *Commentary on the Mishnah*, he spoke of having 'heard' a certain position maintained by the Kalam, and at least on one occasion he participated in a disputation on Kalam matters. Could he have drawn primarily from oral discussions and not from written texts?

Medieval Arabic philosophers sometimes allowed themselves to recreate the thought of their predecessors, and a tempting conjecture might be that Maimonides recorded not merely what he read or heard but also what he thought was required in order to render the system consistent.[15] Support for the suggestion might be drawn from his statement that a belief in the existence of a void follows from the belief in a universe made up of solid, indivisible atoms: since the atoms are impermeable and inflexible, if there were no areas of completely empty space, nothing could budge and movement would be impossible; the existence of empty space is consequently 'necessary' for the

[13] Van Ess, *Erkenntislehre des ʿAḍudaddīn al-Īcī*, 172–3.

[14] *MN* i. 73 (105*a*), and (12); Schwarz, 'Who Were Maimonides' Mutakallimūn?', ii. 169–72.

[15] Van Ess, *Erkenntislehre des ʿAḍudaddīn al-Īcī*, 179: 'One almost has the impression that he collected things from every corner in order to erect a sort of 'system'.

Kalam. Maimonides similarly finds the proposition that time is made up of discrete, infinitesimal moments to be 'necessarily' entailed by Kalam atomism. For Aristotle demonstrated in the *Physics* that movement, moving objects, distance traversed, and the time during which motion occurs must correlate;[16] either all of them are continuous and infinitely divisible or all consist of discrete, indivisible particles. The unreliability of sense perception is 'necessary' for the Kalam, inasmuch as the school recognizes phenomena that run counter to the reports of sense perception. Kalam atomism, for example, entails oddities that are below the visible threshold, such as motion that repeatedly stops and starts as objects lurch from one atom of space to the next, in one atom of time after another; Kalam occasionalism entails that objects lose their accident of colour after every atom of time and immediately have it restored to them in the next time-atom. Maimonides might, then, be read as reporting not what he actually found the school maintaining but what he saw as inescapable implications of the system.

Consider too a notion that Maimonides treated in his *Commentary on the Mishnah* and includes in his list of the twelve Kalam propositions, namely, as he puts it somewhat awkwardly: 'Everything imaginable is possible from the standpoint of reason [*ʿaql*].'[17] In the *Moreh nevukhim*, he calls this 'the pillar of the science of Kalam' and devotes more space to it than to any of the other propositions. He marks it and the impossibility of an infinite number as the two most fundamental Kalam principles, inasmuch as every Kalam argument for creation turns on either one or the other.[18]

The proposition that an infinite number is impossible was indeed generally accepted by members of the Kalam school.[19] The proposition that any state of affairs not hitherto observed could come to pass was likewise an authentically Kalam tenet, although not embraced as universally as Maimonides indicates. But not a single Kalam thinker is known to have formulated it as Maimonides does and to have maintained that everything *imaginable* is possible—although at least one key figure did write that whatever the human *intellect* deems possible is so.[20] Maimonides apparently formulates the notion as he does because, in his judgement, the Kalam picture of the universe presupposes an unfettered human imagination. He says in effect that the Kalam universe—where all physical existence is reducible to atoms and accidents; where accidents, which give atoms their character, constantly flicker out of existence and must constantly be restored; and where a completely different set of accidents could at any given

[16] Aristotle, *Physics*, 6.1–2.
[17] *MN* i. 73 (10).
[18] *MN* i. 73 (10), 74 (7).
[19] See Schwarz, 'Who Were Maimonides' Mutakallimūn?', ii. 166–8.
[20] See ibid. 156–63, supplemented by a personal communication from M. Schwarz.

moment be attached to a given atom, and objects could therefore change their character radically in the blink of an eye—makes whatever sense it does only when imagination is enthroned as the ultimate arbiter, and reason is relegated to the rank of second fiddle. Alfarabi, it happens, had remarked somewhat similarly in his *Risāla fī al-ʿaql* that when Kalam thinkers spoke of what 'intellect' (*ʿaql*) 'affirms . . . or negates . . . accepts . . . or does not accept', they were in actuality talking about a criterion inferior to intellect. They were talking only about what would occur to an ordinary person upon 'first consideration'.[21]

Undercutting every suggested explanation for Maimonides' attributing to Kalam writers positions held by no identifiable Kalam thinker is his remark that he read the literature as far as was feasible and his repeated assurance that he is conveying what members of the school maintained. They were, he writes, 'driven necessarily to affirm the [existence of a] void'. They 'undoubtedly' arrived at 'their statement' on the atomic character of time after 'they saw Aristotle's demonstrations', which establish that motion, moving objects, distance traversed, and time must correspond. They were forced by their system to 'assume' that time and the distance traversed are not continuous; and their misunderstanding of the nature of time may be forgiven, since even expert philosophers have had trouble in comprehending its nature. The Kalam writers 'enumerated' instances where the senses err, 'fought' for their position regarding the unreliability of the senses, and 'stated' that since the reports of the senses are unreliable, those reports cannot be used as premisses in demonstrations. 'Most' of the Kalam thinkers construed the soul as an accident in a single atom within the living organism; 'some'—or 'one'—took it to be a congeries of atoms. Members of the school 'agree' that the human intellect is an accident in one of the atoms making up a human being.[22]

Whatever the reason, the information that Maimonides imparts with confidence concerning the Kalam picture of the universe is badly flawed. That says something significant about Maimonides and should be kept in mind as we proceed.

2. Aristotle

At one spot in the *Moreh nevukhim*, Maimonides assures readers that he 'had studied the books of the philosophers to the extent of my ability', just as he had studied Kalam works as far as he could.[23] The gaps just observed in his knowledge of the Kalam may occasion some uneasiness about the assurance.

[21] Alfarabi, *Risala fi al-ʿaql*, 7–8, 12, cited by Maimonides in *MN* i. 73 (no. 10, p. 113*b*).
[22] *MN* i. 73 (2, 3, 5, 12).
[23] *MN* i. 71 (95*b*).

As for Aristotle in particular, Maimonides describes him in the *Moreh nevukhim* as the 'chief [*ra'īs*] of the philosophers'.[24] He expresses himself still more strongly when evaluating a number of philosophers in a letter to Samuel Ibn Tibbon. There he characterizes 'Aristotle's intellect' as the upper 'limit of human intellect, with the exception of those upon whom the divine emanation has poured forth',[25] that is to say, with the exception of the Hebrew prophets. The letter to Ibn Tibbon further confirms that Maimonides was acquainted with at least some of Aristotle in Arabic translation.

Ibn Tibbon was preparing to translate the *Moreh nevukhim* from Arabic into Hebrew, and Maimonides advises him to avoid the path, literal to the point of incomprehensibility, taken by Yaḥyā ibn Biṭrīq in translating Aristotle and Galen and to prefer instead the freer method of Ḥunayn ibn Isḥāq and Isḥāq ibn Ḥunayn. Because of the superiority of Isḥāq's translations of Aristotle, Maimonides writes: 'We use only them and reject others.' The obvious intimation is that he was acquainted with translations of Aristotle done by both men.[26]

More specific and solid evidence of an acquaintance with Aristotle is furnished by quotations from Aristotle and references to him in the *Moreh nevukhim* as well as in a few of Maimonides' other later writings. As far as I could determine, the *Moreh nevukhim* has five definite quotations from Aristotle, ranging from one to eleven lines, and taken from the *Physics*, *On the Heavens*, and *Nicomachean Ethics*. They and three additional ostensible quotations are as follows:

(*a*) In one of the chapters of the *Moreh nevukhim* devoted to the issue of the eternity or creation of the world, Maimonides quotes 'verbatim' (*naṣṣ kalām al-rajul*) from what he identifies as Aristotle's *On the Heavens*. The immediate context is Maimonides' attempt to establish that 'Aristotle had no demonstration of the eternity of the world . . . and was not unaware of the fact. That is, he realized that he had no demonstration', and whatever arguments he offered were intended not to demonstrate the eternity of the world but only to render eternity more plausible than the alternative. Maimonides' 'verbatim' quotation matches, with a few variants, a passage in the preserved medieval Arabic translation of *On the Heavens*, and where he diverges from the Arabic translation as it has been published, his version generally is superior. The printed edition of the translation is unreliable, even omitting an entire line (through homoeoteleuton, skipping from a word in one line to the same word in the next line).[27]

[24] *MN* i. 5, ii. 23 (51*a*).

[25] Marx, 'Texts by and about Maimonides', 380. A similar statement is made by Maimonides' contemporary Averroes, *Long Commentary on the De anima*, 433.

[26] Maimonides, *Igerot harambam*, 532–3.

[27] *MN* ii. 15 (32*b*), quoting *On the Heavens*, 1.10.279b, 4–12; medieval Arabic trans.: Aristotle, *De coelo et meteorologica*, 196.

Aristotle explains, in the passage Maimonides quotes, that he would begin his discussion of eternity and creation by giving opponents a fair hearing; for when readers would see what the opponents' arguments were, they would be better disposed towards his position and arguments.[28] Maimonides' contention is that if Aristotle deemed the eternity of the world to be demonstrable, he would not have taken the trouble to examine opposing arguments with such care, since they would be irrelevant. Whether Maimonides had an accurate appreciation of Aristotle's methodology need not concern us.

(*b*) In another chapter from the section of the *Moreh nevukhim* dealing with creation and eternity, Maimonides writes that he is quoting 'verbatim' (*naṣṣuhu*) from Aristotle but does not name the work from which he draws. The quotation again matches a passage in the medieval Arabic translation of Aristotle's *On the Heavens*, again with variants.

In *On the Heavens*, the passage serves as preface to a pair of anomalies in the structure of the celestial region, that is, aspects that are out of harmony with the overall structure of the heavens as Aristotle conceived it. Aristotle writes—according to the Arabic translation, which embellishes a little on the Greek—that he would explain the anomalies as well as he could; he asks readers to be indulgent and not condemn him as audacious for wading into an extremely difficult subject; and he suggests that he instead deserves praise for his efforts and his dedication to the philosophical enterprise. The statement is of utmost significance for Maimonides. Irregularities in the structure of the heavens are the data from which he fashions a series of arguments leading to the conclusion that the heavens must be the product of a voluntary cause, which exercised will and implanted the irregularities. Since voluntary causes act after not acting, the voluntary cause responsible for the existence of the heavens must have brought the heavens into existence after they did not exist; it, or He, must have created them. The anomalies Aristotle struggled with are among the irregularities adduced by Maimonides, and the fact that Aristotle was 'cognizant of the weakness' of his explanation of the anomalies is grist for Maimonides' mill.[29]

The same passage from *On the Heavens* appears in an earlier chapter of the *Moreh nevukhim*, and there too Maimonides identifies Aristotle as his source without naming the work from which he quotes. On the earlier occasion he gives the gist (*maʿnā*) of what Aristotle says rather than a verbatim quotation. His purpose is to portray Aristotle as a model of philosophical discretion and

[28] *MN* ii. 15 (32*a*).

[29] *MN* ii. 19 (42*b*), paralleling Aristotle, *De caelo*, 2.12.291b, 24–8, and id., *De coelo et meteorologica* (Arabic), 269–70.

to encourage readers to emulate him—to prepare themselves properly before entering into philosophical investigation, to recognize their limitations, and to avoid venturing beyond their depths.[30]

(*c*) In still another chapter from the discussion of eternity and creation, Maimonides, as in the previous instance, quotes a 'statement' of Aristotle's 'verbatim' (*naṣṣ kalāmihi*) without naming the work from which he draws. Except for minor variants, the quotation now matches a passage in the printed edition of Isḥāq b. Ḥunayn's medieval Arabic translation of Aristotle's *Physics*.[31] Aristotle there answered earlier thinkers who inconsistently recognized that plants and animals do not come into existence by chance and spontaneously—an olive tree, for example, always grows out of a certain kind of seed, and a man, from a certain kind of semen—yet supposed that the heavens and what they enclose came into existence spontaneously and 'through themselves'. The statement tells Maimonides that Aristotle affirmed a cause of the world's existence—a reading that the consensus of today's Aristotelian scholars would reject. Maimonides' aim is to prepare a foil against which to spell out his own position, which is that the world not only has a cause of existence but that its cause is endowed with will and hence brought the world into existence after its non-existence.

(*d*) In a later section of the *Moreh nevukhim*, which seeks to uncover the purposes for which God imposed the various scriptural commandments on the people of Israel, Maimonides records 'verbatim' (*qāla bi-hādhā al-naṣṣ*) what 'Aristotle stated in the [*Nicomachean*] *Ethics*'. His quotation matches a sentence in the medieval Arabic translation of that work.[32]

The sentence in the *Nicomachean Ethics* is a piece of *obiter dicta* that comes up in the course of a discussion of the role played by communities in human life. Aristotle remarks that in earlier times, religious sacrifices and communal gatherings were typically held after the harvest season, when farmers had leisure. The comment suggests to Maimonides a cultural framework for explaining Sukkot, the Tabernacles festival—the final harvest celebration, which occurs in the autumn.

(*e*) The *Moreh nevukhim* contains a second 'verbatim' (*bi-naṣṣihi*) quotation from the *Nicomachean Ethics*. Aristotle, Maimonides writes, stated that 'this sense is shameful for us': and, he explains, Aristotle was referring to the human

[30] *MN* i. 5.

[31] *MN* ii. 20 (45*a*), paralleling Aristotle, *Al-ṭabīʿa*, 114–15 (= *Physics* 2.4.196a, 24–35).

[32] *MN* iii. 43 (96*a*), quoting *Nicomachean Ethics*, 8.9.1160a, 25–8; Aristotle, *The Arabic Version of the Nicomachean Ethics*, 458–9. The Arabic version, which is used by Maimonides, adds a book after Book 6 and as a consequence designates as Book 9 what is properly Book 8.

sense of touch. The brief quotation exactly matches a sentence in the medieval Arabic translation of the *Nicomachean Ethics*.[33]

Maimonides continues: 'In his books, Aristotle calls people who have a predilection for sexual intercourse and tasty foods "base [*akhissā'*]"' and disparages and ridicules them, as 'you will find in his *Ethics* and *Rhetoric*'. The context where the *Nicomachean Ethics* makes the statement about the shamefulness of the sense of touch contains additional disparaging remarks about touch, and laughs at a certain gourmand who wished for a throat as long as a crane's in order to maximize his enjoyment of what he ate.[34] As for Aristotle's *Rhetoric*, Maimonides would seem to be thinking of a sentence there that characterizes desires relating to taste, sexual intercourse, and the sense of touch as 'irrational'. The *Rhetoric* does not, however, go as far as Maimonides seems to say it does and pour ridicule on those who indulge the pleasures of the sense of touch.[35]

Aristotle's disparagement of the sense of touch supports Maimonides' understanding of a class of divine commandments, those having the purpose, so he maintains, of training men to control their physical desires and especially their sexual drive. Aristotle enables him to observe that 'the philosophers' too warned against surrendering to the pleasures of the flesh. The notion that the sense of touch is shameful struck a chord with Maimonides. He cites it on three additional occasions in the *Moreh nevukhim*, once when encouraging readers to control their physical desires and twice when making such control a prerequisite for receiving the gift of prophecy.[36]

(*f*) One of the twenty-six propositions that Maimonides prefaces to his proofs for the existence of God records 'Aristotle's verbatim statement [*naṣṣ kalām*]: "Matter does not move itself."' I shall discuss the quotation later in the present chapter.

(g) In the chapter of the *Moreh nevukhim* where Maimonides contends that 'Aristotle had no demonstration of the eternity of the world . . . and was not unaware of the fact', he records 'verbatim' (*naṣṣuhu*) something that Aristotle 'states in the *Physics*', namely: 'All prior students of physics except Plato believe that motion is not subject to generation and destruction, whereas he [Plato] believes that motion *is* subject to generation and destruction and the heavens too are subject to generation and destruction.'[37] At another spot in his discus-

33 *MN* iii. 49 (117*a*), quoting *Nicomachean Ethics*, 3.10.1118b, 2; Aristotle, *The Arabic Version of the Nicomachean Ethics*, 226–7 .

34 Aristotle, *Nicomachean Ethics*, 3.10.1118a, 25–1118b, 4; id., *The Arabic Version of the Nicomachean Ethics*, 226–7 (defective).

35 Aristotle, *Rhetoric*, 1.11.1370a, 18–25; id., *Rhetorica in versione Arabica*, 51.

36 *MN* ii. 36 (79*a*), ii. 40 (87*a*), iii. 8 (12*b*).

37 *MN* ii. 15 (32*a*).

sion of eternity and creation, Maimonides writes more briefly: 'Aristotle relates in the *Physics* that Plato believes the heavens to be subject to generation and destruction.'[38]

The passage in the *Physics* to which Maimonides apparently refers reads in the medieval Arabic translation, as in the Greek: 'All except one are in agreement concerning time; they state that it is not generated. . . . Plato alone takes it to be generated. For he states that it came into existence together with the heavens and that the heavens are generated.'[39] Whereas Maimonides, ostensibly quoting verbatim, has Aristotle ascribe to Plato the proposition that *motion* is generated and subject to destruction, Aristotle in actuality ascribed to Plato the proposition that *time* is generated and made no mention of its destruction. Maimonides' purported quotation is in the spirit of Aristotelian physics, where everything generated is perforce subject to destruction, and where time and motion are inextricably linked. But the purported quotation does not accord with Plato's account, or myth, of creation. Plato—as Aristotle knew, but Maimonides does not—ascribed an irregular motion to the chaos that preceded the existence of the heavens and time. He said nothing about the irregular motion's not existing and then coming into existence.[40]

Maimonides therefore does not, despite his assertion, quote verbatim. He could be quoting from memory, relying on a notation of some sort that he once made, or borrowing from a writer who paraphrased what Aristotle wrote.[41] There is no way of telling.

Aristotle's citation of Plato enables Maimonides to reason, as he did in a previous instance, that if Aristotle considered eternity to be demonstrable, he would not have troubled himself with what earlier thinkers, including Plato, held. Their opinion would have been irrelevant. Maimonides' object is to garner more evidence for his contention that Aristotle made no pretence of offering a full-fledged demonstration of the eternity of the world.

(b) In the same chapter of the *Moreh nevukhim*, Maimonides quotes yet one more 'verbatim statement' (*naṣṣ kalāmihi, naṣṣuhu*) of Aristotle's without naming the work from which he is quoting. Aristotle, he writes, stated: 'In matters for which we have no argument [*ḥujja*] or that are [too] immense for us, it is difficult to say why it is so. An example is whether the world is eternal or not.'[42] The quotation matches a couple of sentences in Aristotle's *Topics*,[43] but those sentences also appear in Alfarabi's commentary on the *Topics*, and it would be

[38] *MN* ii. 13 (28*b*). [39] Aristotle, *Al-ṭabīʿa*, 810 (= *Physics*, 8.1.251b, 14, 16–19).

[40] Plato, *Timaeus*, 30A, 38B, 52D–53A.

[41] Maimonides is not following Ibn Bājja's commentary on the *Physics*.

[42] *MN* ii. 15 (33*b*). [43] Aristotle, *Topics*, 1.11.104b, 14–17; id., *Manṭiq arisṭū*, ii. 505.

no surprise to find Maimonides quoting Aristotle through the medium of Alfarabi rather than directly from the original. The *Topics* belongs to Aristotle's logical works, and, a few years later, Maimonides would advise Samuel Ibn Tibbon that only Alfarabi need be resorted to for the study of logic.[44]

There is reason to think that Maimonides is indeed quoting Aristotle through Alfarabi's commentary.

A comparison of Maimonides' version of the passage, Alfarabi's version, and the passage as it appears in the published edition of the medieval Arabic translation of Aristotle's *Topics*[45] reveals differences. All but one are tiny, and in the single significant parting of the ways, Maimonides aligns himself with Alfarabi against the Arabic translation. The preserved Arabic translation of the *Topics* is faithful to the Greek and reads: 'In matters for which we have no argument *because* [*idh*] they are [too] immense for us, it is difficult to say why it is so.' Alfarabi's version alters the italicized word and says: 'In matters for which we have no argument *or* [*aw*] that are [too] immense for us'. That is precisely Maimonides' version.[46]

After citing Aristotle, Maimonides addresses the reader: 'You know Alfarabi's interpretation' of Aristotle's statement, his 'utter rejection of the possibility that Aristotle doubted the eternity [*qidam*] of the world', and his 'total disdain for Galen' for having described the issue of the eternity or creation of the world as not amenable to demonstration.

The section of Alfarabi's commentary on the *Topics* that quotes the passage we are concerned with does explain away Aristotle's suggestion that the eternity of the world is an issue for which there is no effective argument; Alfarabi could not conceive that Aristotle doubted the eternity of the world. Alfarabi further takes note of Galen's having characterized the eternity of the world as not amenable to demonstration. Although he does not express the utter rejection and total disdain ascribed to him by Maimonides, it is hard to imagine that in talking about 'Alfarabi's interpretation' of Aristotle's statement',

[44] Marx, 'Texts by and about Maimonides', 379.

[45] I stress that this is the reading of the published edition of the Arabic translation because the words *idh* and *aw* would look very similar in a manuscript, and Badawi, who published the translation, did not follow western standards of editing. He may have corrected the manuscript reading in order to bring the Arabic translation into harmony with the Greek original.

[46] See the excerpt from Alfarabi's commentary on the *Topics* in Vajda, 'A propos d'une citation non identifée', 48–9. Alfarabi also refers to the passage from the *Topics*, although without quoting it, in *L'Harmonie entre les opinions de Platon et d'Aristote*, 126–9; English trans.: *The Political Writings*, 154 (assuming the attribution to Alfarabi to be correct). There he brands as 'reprehensible and unacceptable' the supposition that Aristotle doubted whether the world is or is not eternal (*qadīm*), for Aristotle undoubtedly did *not* believe the world to be eternal but instead agreed with Plato that it had 'been brought into existence [*muḥdath*] and had an agent'. If Alfarabi is indeed the author, the statement is disingenuous and means only that Aristotle did not doubt that the world has a cause of its existence.

Maimonides has some unknown work of Alfarabi's, and not the commentary on the *Topics*, in view.

Maimonides thus quotes the *Topics* passage in the form that Alfarabi does and he refers to the context in Alfarabi's commentary on the *Topics* where Alfarabi quotes the passage. The quotation may therefore very well have come to him through the medium of the *Commentary* on the *Topics* and not directly from Aristotle.

He considers the Aristotelian statement significant and cites it because he was struck by Aristotle's choice of the eternity of the world to exemplify issues 'for which we have no argument or that are [too] immense for us'. The example buttresses the point he has been hammering home: the greatest and most highly regarded of philosophers expressly acknowledged that the eternity of the world cannot be demonstrated.

With the quotation in item (*f*) set aside for now, and the quotations in items (*g*) and (*h*) placed in abeyance, we are left with five genuine quotations from Aristotle's *Physics*, *On the Heavens*, and *Nicomachean Ethics*. It is noteworthy that in each instance, Maimonides quotes Aristotle verbatim not for the purpose of unravelling a technical philosophical conundrum but rather to enlist support for a matter close to his heart—his position on the creation of the world or his interpretation of the reasons for which various divine commandments were promulgated.

Apart from the actual quotations, the *Moreh nevukhim* furnishes considerable evidence of a familiarity with Aristotle's *Physics*, *On the Heavens*, and *Nicomachean Ethics*.

To start, there is Maimonides' analysis of Aristotelian arguments for the eternity of the world. The arguments—which rest on the impossibility of a vacuum and on the nature of matter, motion, time, and the celestial spheres—are drawn from Aristotle's *Physics* and *On the Heavens*.[47]

Then there are the following statements appearing at various junctures in the *Moreh nevukhim*: 'Aristotle establishes the existence of motion and demonstrates the nonexistence of the atom.'[48] 'Aristotle proved in the *Physics*' that if the distance travelled by a moving body is continuous and infinitely divisible, time must likewise be continuous and infinitely divisible.[49] 'Aristotle demonstrates that what comes about by nature [*umūr ṭabīʿiyya*] does not come about by chance', his demonstration being that what comes about by nature occurs invariably or in the majority of cases, whereas what comes about by chance

[47] H. Davidson, *Proofs for Eternity, Creation, and the Existence of God*, 13, 17, 24, 27, 28.

[48] *MN* i. 51. See Aristotle, *Physics*, 6.1–2, 9.

[49] *MN* i. 73 (3). See Aristotle, *Physics*, 6.2.

occurs in neither fashion.[50] 'It is made clear in physical science that every natural object must have a purpose.'[51] 'Aristotle made clear that in natural objects' the formal cause, efficient cause, and final cause coincide and are the same.[52] 'It is stated in the *Physics*' that the person who removes a pillar is the cause of the downward motion of the object that rested on it.[53] 'Aristotle prefaced' a certain proof of the existence of God 'with a proposition stating: when something exists that is composed of two things and one of the two things exists by itself apart from the composite, then the existence of the other apart from the composite follows necessarily'.[54]

All the statements go back to Aristotle's *Physics*, although the last two do not exactly reproduce what Aristotle says there. On the removal of the pillar, Maimonides omits a qualification: Aristotle labels the removal of the pillar specifically as an *accidental* cause of the subsequent downward motion of what was resting on it. In the final item, the kernel goes back to Aristotle's *Physics*, but the formulation that Maimonides attributes to Aristotle is post-Aristotelian. The subject will come up again later in the present chapter.

The *Moreh nevukhim* also reports: Aristotle 'constantly' says that nature does nothing in vain.[55] 'One of Aristotle's premisses in physical science is that there is necessarily something stable [*thābit*] around which [circular] motion takes place; the earth must therefore be stable', since the celestial spheres rotate around it.[56] Aristotle offered a natural explanation for the circumstance that the outermost celestial sphere moves from east to west[57] and not in the opposite direction; the circumstance that some spheres rotate rapidly and some slowly, his explanation being that the inner ones vary in velocity in accordance with their relative distances from the outermost sphere; and the circumstance that each of the planets is embedded in a sphere of its own, which is served by subordinate spheres, whereas the many fixed stars all share a single sphere.[58] It was an ancient opinion that the celestial spheres make a 'fearful, mighty' sound as they rotate around the earth; the 'entire school of

[50] *MN* ii. 20 (45*a*). See Aristotle, *Physics*, 2.5; 8. [51] *MN* iii. 13 (22*b*). See Aristotle, *Physics*, 2.8.

[52] *MN* iii. 13 (23*a*): they are the same 'in species'. See Aristotle, *Physics*, 2.7, 198a, 24–8, which also has 'in species'. The Arabic manuscript on which the printed edition of the Arabic translation of the *Physics* is based is defective at this point.

[53] *MN* iii. 10 (16*a*). See Aristotle, *Al-ṭabīʿa*, 841 (= *Physics*, 8.4, 255b, 25–7). [54] *MN* ii. 1 (2).

[55] *MN* ii. 14 (31*a*) (*ʿabath*); iii. 13 (23*a*) (*ʿabath*). Aristotle, *On the Heavens*, 1.4, 271a, 31–3 (*bāṭil*); 2.11, 291b, 13–14 (*ʿabath*). The statement also appears in Aristotle's zoological works (see below) and in the *Politics*, which was not available to Arabic readers in the Middle Ages.

[56] *MN* ii. 24 (52*a*). See Aristotle, *On the Heavens*, 2.3, 286a, 13–15 (*thābit*).

[57] The outermost, or diurnal, sphere is the one that revolves around the earth once every twenty-four hours and carries the stars and planets with it. It is the mirror image of what we know today as the daily rotation of the earth on its axis.

[58] *MN* ii. 19 (42*a*). See Aristotle, *On the Heavens*, 2.5, 2.10, 2.12, 292a, 10–14.

Pythagoras believes' that the sounds made by the heavens are, notwithstanding their volume, harmonious, pleasant, and musical; but 'Aristotle . . . in *On the Heavens*' rejected the notion that the heavens make any sound as they rotate.[59] 'Aristotle states' that men have always regarded the heavens as the abode of God and spiritual beings, their thinking being that the heavens are commonly acknowledged to be eternal and accordingly are the appropriate abode for the divine.[60]

The rule that nature does nothing in vain is found in *On the Heavens* as well as in other works of Aristotle. The rest of the statements can be traced directly to *On the Heavens*, with a single qualification. When Aristotle refutes the proposition that the heavens make a sound as they move, he mentions persons who held that the sound made by the heavens is melodious but does not identify them. The detail that those persons were Pythagoreans came to Maimonides from another quarter.

Finally, in order to create a framework for explaining the purpose for which certain religious commandments were instituted, Maimonides writes: 'Aristotle made clear . . . in the [*Nicomachean*] *Ethics*' that the human need for friends is evident at every stage of human life. The reference is plainly to a chapter of the *Nicomachean Ethics* that treats the subject of friendship. As Maimonides goes on, he expands on the subject of friendship in the spirit of the chapter in question, and terminological contacts can be detected between what Aristotle says there and what Maimonides reproduces.[61]

In fine, it is virtually certain that he read the *Physics*, *On the Heavens*, and *Nicomachean Ethics*.

A couple of Maimonides' later compositions reveal a familiarity with Aristotle's *On Animals*. *On Animals* is a medieval name for a zoological trilogy comprising what today are treated as three separate books: the *History of Animals*, *Parts of the Animals*, and *Generation of Animals*.

Maimonides' *Medical Aphorisms*, his most comprehensive medical composition, has twenty-five chapters, each of which comprises a number of brief paragraphs, almost all of them quotations from the medical literature. The quotations are primarily from Galen, but other medical writers appear, and in two places Maimonides cites Aristotle's *On Animals* as a source of medical information.

[59] *MN* ii. 8. Aristotle, *On the Heavens*, 2.9.

[60] *MN* ii. 14 (31*b*). See Aristotle, *On the Heavens*, 1.3, 270b, 4–8; id., *De coelo et meteorologica* (medieval Arabic trans.), 140–1. The Greek text speaks about an abode for the 'gods' and in the next line about 'God' or 'deity'. The Arabic translation renders 'gods' as 'spiritual beings'.

[61] *MN* iii. 49 (113*a*). See Aristotle, *Nicomachean Ethics*, 8.1.

In a chapter devoted to diseases, Maimonides records an observation made by 'Aristotle at the end of treatise 9 of *On Animals*' and he expresses surprise that Galen failed to take notice of it despite its being 'very useful for the practice of medicine'. The observation is that 'children are commonly subject to convulsions, especially children who are well nourished and who consume a large quantity of milk, with a high fat content, from corpulent nurses'. Maimonides' report closely mirrors a statement in the ninth treatise of the Greek original of the *History of Animals*. It differs somewhat from the preserved medieval Arabic translation of the *History of Animals*, but there is evidence that the Arabic translation existed in an alternative, or perhaps corrected, version, which has not survived.[62]

Whereas each of the first twenty-four chapters of the *Medical Aphorisms* treats a single medical topic, the twenty-fifth examines instances where statements within the voluminous Galenic corpus contradict, or are incompatible with, other statements made by Galen. One of the contradictions uncovered by Maimonides concerns the question whether the natural heat in the female body is greater or less than the natural heat in males. A certain work of Galen's took the former position, but other works by him adopted the latter. After setting forth the contradiction, Maimonides suggests that Galen may not yet have seen Aristotle's thinking on the issue when he held the natural heat in the female body to be greater. Maimonides thereupon quotes what Aristotle stated in 'treatise 18' of *On Animals*.

Aristotle, he writes, explained: the level of natural heat in a living body correlates with the amount of blood in the body, blood being a hot humour. Since women regularly have a large menstrual discharge, which would seem to imply that their bodies contain a high level of blood, some thinkers mistakenly conclude that the amount of blood in females is greater than in males and their bodies are warmer. In actuality, the menstrual discharge, although red and resembling blood, contains an admixture of various other materials and is not pure blood. The male body is the one with the higher level of pure blood, and the natural heat of the male is therefore greater than that of the female. This, Maimonides writes, is a 'verbatim statement' (*naṣṣ kalām*) of Aristotle's and 'it is the truth'. What he calls a verbatim statement is close to, although it does not exactly match, a passage in the preserved Arabic translation of Aristotle's *Generation of Animals*. Perhaps he had an alternative version of the Arabic here too.[63]

[62] Maimonides, *Medical Aphorisms*, 9.127; Aristotle, *Historia animalium* 9 (7), 588a, 3–6. Maimonides' version of the passage is compared with the preserved Arabic translation and the Greek by Zonta in 'Maimonides as Zoologist?', 93–4.

[63] Maimonides, *Medical Aphorisms*, 25.29 (for treatises where Bos's edition is not yet available, I consulted the Arabic original in Leiden MS Or. 128 = #844 in the Jong-de Goeje catalogue); Aristotle,

In a different work, the *Treatise on Resurrection*, which Maimonides wrote shortly after finishing the *Moreh nevukhim*, he cites Aristotle's *On Animals* a third time. His object here is to support a naturalistic exegesis of Isaiah's prophecy: 'And the wolf shall dwell with the lamb, and the leopard shall lie down with the kid.' Maimonides did not reject the possibility of miracles, but he maintains that the intellectual elite, in contrast to the multitude, tries to minimize rather than maximize divine intervention in the world. And he insists that when a miracle does occur, it effects only a temporary, and never a permanent, change in nature. To avoid the supposition that Isaiah envisaged a future permanent change in the nature of wolves and leopards, Maimonides cites *On Animals*, where the gentleness of wild animals in Egypt is linked to the abundance of food in the country. Isaiah, he suggests, may have envisioned, and depicted in poetic language, a future in which food would be so plentiful that the wolf and the leopard, while retaining their predatory nature, would not have to exercise it. The observation about the gentleness of wild animals in Egypt is found in Aristotle's *History of Animals*.[64]

Possible traces of the zoological trilogy can be discerned in the *Moreh nevukhim* itself: the *Moreh nevukhim* attributes to Aristotle the proposition that each of an animal's parts exists 'for the sake of' something else; each part, in other words, is designed to perform a function contributing to the organism's overall functioning.[65] That is a theme pervading Aristotle's *Parts of Animals*, the third of the works making up the zoological trilogy. As already mentioned in connection with *On the Heavens*, the *Moreh nevukhim* describes Aristotle as 'constantly' stating the rule that nature does nothing in vain. Among the Aristotelian works containing the statement are the *Generation of the Animals* and *Parts of Animals*, both of which have it twice.[66]

Maimonides further writes in the *Moreh nevukhim*: it is made clear in 'physical science' that the 'final cause' is the 'most excellent [*ashraf*] of the four causes'—in other words, of the material, formal, efficient, and final causes that play a central role in Aristotle's physics. The reference could be to a passage in *Parts of Animals* comparing efficient causes with final causes. Aristotle determines there that final causes are prior, inasmuch as they are the 'logos', the

Generation of Animals, 4.1.765b, 19–28; *Generation of Animals, the Arabic Translation*, 139, which is a very loose translation of the Greek.

[64] Maimonides, *Treatise on Resurrection*, Hebrew–Arabic section, 22–3; Aristotle, *Historia animalium*, 8 (9).1.608b, 29–35.

[65] *MN* iii. 13 (22*b*–23*a*).

[66] Aristotle, *Generation of Animals*, 2.5, 741b, 5, 2.6, 744a, 36; *Parts of Animals*, 2.13, 658a, 9, 3.1, 661b, 24.

rational principle, and hence the 'starting point' in whatever is produced by art and still more so in what is produced by nature.[67]

Perhaps also pertinent is an Arabic composition, attributed in the manuscript to Maimonides, which consists primarily of excerpts from the *History of Animals* but which contains excerpts from the other two zoological works making up the trilogy as well. The recent editor of the text has, with some justification, questioned the attribution to Maimonides.[68] If Maimonides was by chance the author, the composition would furnish solid evidence of his familiarity with all three components of Aristotle's *On Animals*.

However that may be, *On Animals* can be added to the list of Aristotelian works that Maimonides read and used.

If Aristotle ever wrote a book on the subject of plants, it has been lost, but the Arabic Middle Ages did have the translation of a work by Nicolaus of Damascus that calls itself a 'commentary' on Aristotle's *On Plants*. It was translated from Arabic into Latin in the Middle Ages, and then, in a curious twist, was translated back from Latin into Greek. Today it is commonly known as pseudo-Aristotle's *On Plants*. A page from Nicolaus' *On Plants* has been discovered that has Maimonides' signature.[69] There seems, moreover, to be an allusion to the book in the *Moreh nevukhim*.

In the context where Maimonides refers to Aristotle's statement that each of an animal's parts exists for the sake of something else, he writes: 'Aristotle stated that plants were created for the sake of [*khuliqa min ajl*] animals.'[70] The remark appears to be copied from a sentence in Nicolaus' *On Plants* that reads: 'Plants were created for the sake of [*khuliqa min ajl*] animals; animals were not created for the sake of plants.'[71] In any case, if Maimonides owned a copy of the book, he very likely read it. Pseudo-Aristotelian *On Plants* may be added to the tally of works with which he was acquainted.

Were there any others?

A number of medieval and modern scholars have thought that they see a reference to Aristotle's *Meteorology* in the *Moreh nevukhim*. Aristotle's *Meteorology* as such is not known to have been translated into Arabic in the Middle Ages, and

[67] *MN* iii. 13 (22*b*); Aristotle, *Parts of Animals*, 1.1, 639b, 15–21. *Logos* is a term for the formal cause, and Aristotle is therefore probably saying that the final-formal cause is the primary cause. See Zeller, *Die Philosophie der Griechen*, ii. 2, 328 n. 1. Ghazali, *Maqāṣid al-falāsifa*, 121, explains that the final cause is prior to the other causes.

[68] Mattock, *Tract Comprising Excerpts from Aristotle's Book of Animals*; Zonta, 'Maimonides as Zoologist?', 92–4, offers cautious support for the attribution to Maimonides.

[69] Hopkins, 'A New Autograph Fragment', 275.

[70] *MN* iii. 13 (23*a*).

[71] Pseudo-Aristotle, *On Plants*, 1.2, 817b, 25–6; Nicolaus of Damascus, *De Plantis*, 142–3.

we can safely say that Maimonides did not read it.[72] It was replaced by an Arabic composition that represents itself as Yaḥyā ibn Biṭrīq's translation of the *Meteorology*, though comparison with the original Greek quickly shows it to be something else. Yaḥyā's composition adds and omits material, mangles some, and shifts material from one place to another.[73]

Whether Yaḥyā translated a Greek or even a Syriac reworking of Aristotle's *Meteorology* or whether he perhaps pieced his version together by himself is debatable, but the way it was perceived is more important for us. Averroes believed it to be a translation of the genuine *Meteorology* and wrote two commentaries on it, a patron of the sciences persuaded Samuel Ibn Tibbon to translate it into Hebrew, and Gerard of Cremona translated most of it into Latin. A later Latin translation of the authentic *Meteorology* was made directly from Aristotle's Greek. If Maimonides was acquainted with Yaḥyā ibn Biṭrīq's *Meteorology*, he would undoubtedly have viewed it as a translation of the Aristotelian text.

The issue, when formulated correctly, is whether Maimonides refers to or uses Yaḥyā ibn Biṭrīq's reworking of the *Meteorology*, which he would have mistakenly assumed to be Yaḥyā's inept translation of the Aristotelian text. If Maimonides did use it, he did so reluctantly. He advised Ibn Tibbon a few years later that ibn Biṭrīq's 'translation' of Aristotle and Galen is 'extremely mangled' and 'the commentaries of . . . ibn Biṭrīq are worthless . . . Anyone who studies them wastes his time. No one should look at them unless absolutely necessary.'[74]

Some background is needed before a firm answer to our question can be given and it will lead us afield. The effort is not ill spent, since it contributes a few revealing brush strokes to Maimonides' intellectual portrait.

The pertinent chapter in the *Moreh nevukhim* is one that Maimonides considered pivotal, although most modern readers will be left cold. In it he analyses the creation story in Genesis 1. On his reading, the opening verses of Genesis allude to the creation of the four physical elements out of which all physical objects in the sublunar world are constituted. Earth is mentioned expressly in the opening verse: 'In the beginning God created the heaven and earth.' Maimonides takes the 'darkness' that 'was upon the face of the deep' in verse 2 to be an allusion to the element of fire. He interprets the second half of verse 2, 'the wind [*ruaḥ*] of God is moving over the face of the waters'—which is the way he understood the Hebrew—as an allusion to the elements air and water.

[72] The medieval Arabic bibliographical literature refers to a translation by Ibn Suwār, but no trace of it has been found.

[73] See Lettinck, *Aristotle's Meteorology and its Reception in the Arab World*, 7–8.

[74] Marx, 'Texts by and about Maimonides', 380; Maimonides, *Igerot harambam*, 532.

A few lines later, Scripture speaks of God's fashioning a 'firmament in the midst of the waters' and thereby dividing the waters below the firmament from the waters above it; and Scripture states that 'God called the firmament heaven'. No medieval student of the Bible who was conversant with the natural science of the day could accept the equating of the firmament with heaven literally, for water, according to the best medieval science, exists only in the sublunar world and not in or above the true heaven, the region of the celestial spheres. There were two possible exegetic strategies. One was to take the firmament and the waters above it as metaphors for celestial or super-celestial entities.[75] The other was to understand that the firmament is not the true heaven and Scripture calls it heaven only by extension; once the firmament was distinguished from heaven in the proper sense, it could be located, together with the waters above and below it, within the sublunar region.[76] Maimonides takes the second route.

The dividing of the waters was not, for him, merely a separation in place. It was, more significantly, a separation in form. He writes that a portion of the elemental water of Genesis 1: 2 received an additional natural form and became the kind of water found on earth, particularly in the sea basins. Another portion received a different natural form and became a different kind of water, a kind located 'above the air'. The firmament itself likewise 'came into existence' from water. In short, 'a certain matter' called water was divided into three by virtue of three different forms. One of the resulting products is the water found on the surface of the earth. A second, which Scripture calls the firmament, is located within the region of air. The third is located above the air.

Maimonides concludes his account of the firmament with a talmudic anecdote through which, as Salomon Munk puts it nicely, one enigma is exchanged for another. In the anecdote, Rabbi Akiva warned his colleagues: when you are in the supernal pleasure garden (*pardes*) and 'reach the stones of pure marble, do not cry "water, water"; for Scripture cautions: "He that speaketh falsehood

[75] Examples: Ibn Gabirol, *Keter malkhut*, 262: the firmament is the sphere of the moon; Ibn Gabirol does not address the waters. Nahmanides, *Commentary on the Pentateuch*, Gen. 1: 8: the firmament and the waters above it (and perhaps the waters below as well) represent the celestial spheres, whereas the heavens of Gen. 1: 1 represent an entity or entities above the spheres. In addition, the firmament and the waters symbolize a kabbalistic mystery that Nahmanides refrains from explaining. Zohar: the firmament and waters symbolize a stage in the emanation of *sefirot* that is subsequent to the stage of emanation that Scripture alludes to in the preceding verses; see Tishby, *Mishnat hazohar*, i. 407.

[76] Examples: Ibn Ezra, *Commentary on the Pentateuch*, Gen. 1: 6: the firmament is the element air. Kimhi, *Commentary on Genesis*, 1: 6, following Ibn Ezra: the firmament is the element air, and the upper waters are water vapour that is located in the region of air and turns into rain. Sforno, *Commentary on Genesis*, 1: 6: the firmament is a division within the primeval waters. It separates the layer of water that forms seas, lakes, and other bodies of water on the surface of the earth from a layer that becomes water vapour and ascends into the air.

shall not be established before mine eyes.'"[77] Maimonides reads the warning as having in view the waters above the firmament, those that he locates above the air. And he writes: 'If you consider and grasp everything demonstrated [*tabarhana*] in *meteorology* [or: in the *meteorology* (*al-āthār*)]', you will appreciate how 'the whole issue is clarified . . . and disclosed [or: 'how Rabbi Akiva clarified . . . and disclosed the whole issue']' in a single sentence.[78] Only an intrepid soul would venture an opinion as to what the talmudic anecdote intended by the stones of pure marble and what Maimonides finds to be especially significant about the water-like substance located above the air. A more modest question is the meaning of the term *al-āthār*, used here by Maimonides.

The suggestion has been made that in the present context, *al-āthār* does not mean meteorology at all but rather *tradition*.[79] Although the Arabic word can have that meaning,[80] the suggestion has two fatal flaws and can be dismissed. The first is that Maimonides would never have written 'demonstrated in tradition', since demonstration is the business of philosophy and science. The second is that a few pages later, Maimonides speaks of *al-āthār al-ʿulwiyya*.[81] *Al-āthār al-ʿulwiyya*, literally *the upper signs*, is the term chosen by Yaḥyā ibn Biṭrīq as the title of his version of Aristotle's *Meteorology*. It is the title of the meteorological works of Pseudo-Olympiodorus, Ḥunayn ibn Isḥāq, and Avicenna, and it has the sense of 'meteorological phenomena' in Arabic scientific literature,[82] phenomena that include meteors, comets, clouds, vapour, rain, other forms of precipitation, thunder and lightning, rainbows, wind, and even the Milky Way. Maimonides uses the term precisely in the sense of meteorological phenomena. When he speaks of what has been 'demonstrated in *al-āthār*', he plainly means what has been demonstrated in meteorology.

Ibn Tibbon's Hebrew translation of Maimonides' *Moreh nevukhim* prejudges matters. Although the Arabic text of the *Guide* makes no mention of a *book*, Ibn Tibbon inserts the word and has Maimonides say: 'If you consider and grasp everything demonstrated in the *Book of Meteorology*'.[83] It is by no means certain, however, that Maimonides is naming a book; he could very well be referring to the science of meteorology. On the assumption that he is talking about a book, the question would still remain whether the book is Yaḥyā's version of the *Meteorology*.

[77] BT *Ḥag.* 14*b*, and parallels. The verse is Ps. 101: 7.
[78] *MN* ii. 30 (68*b*–69*a*).
[79] *MN* (Kafah), ad loc.
[80] Blau, *Dictionary*, 2.
[81] *MN* ii. 30 (69*b*).
[82] Lettinck, *Aristotle's Meteorology and its Reception in the Arab World*, 1.
[83] The same thing occurs, although with less damage, at another juncture where Maimonides refers to what Aristotle stated 'in metaphysics' and Ibn Tibbon translates: 'in the Book of *Metapyhysics*'. Below, n. 138. The other medieval Hebrew translation of *MN*, that of Judah al-Harizi, spreads an impenetrable fog over what Maimonides writes here.

Aristotle's *Meteorology* envisages a sublunar world in the shape of a sphere. The natural regions of the elements earth and water are located at and around the centre; the element air forms a belt around the earth and water; and the element fire surrounds the air. Elemental earth is by nature cold and dry; the element water, cold and moist; air, hot and moist; and fire, hot and dry.[84] A passage in Aristotle's *On Generation and Destruction* states that what most characterizes water is the quality of being cold, and what most characterizes air is the quality of being moist, but in the *Meteorology*, Aristotle explicitly makes moistness the distinctive characteristic of water.[85] Yaḥyā's version presupposes the general scheme of Aristotle's *Meteorology*, and that scheme was common coin among the Arabic Aristotelians.

Aristotle's *Meteorology* describes two 'exhalations', or gaseous substances, that ascend from the region of earth and water into the atmosphere. One is vapour, a moist exhalation that the heat of the sun draws out of the sea and other bodies of water and that ascends into the lowest layer of air or, more precisely, becomes the lowest layer of air. The second is a dry exhalation that is drawn up from the land and ascends to where the highest layer of air borders on the region of fire. Each of the exhalations has a small admixture of the other: vapour in the belt of air contains a small admixture of the dry exhalation,[86] and the dry exhalation, a small admixture of vapour. Vapour is nonetheless basically moist, and the other exhalation basically dry. Rain, according to the theory, occurs when the heat of the sun abates, and the lowest layer of air, where vapour is found, cools. The vapour turns into clouds, the moisture in the clouds condenses, and the condensed moisture falls back to earth as rain. The circumstance that the vaporous exhalation ascends no higher than the lowest layer of the region of air explains, for Aristotle, why clouds exist only there and not in the upper atmosphere.[87]

The assertion that two exhalations ascend into the atmosphere is repeated several times in Yaḥyā's version of the *Meteorology*, but at a certain point, his version distinguishes not two but three, or, as he puts it a few pages afterwards, two exhalations that subdivide into three. They are a hot dry exhalation, which rises to the border between the region of air and the region of fire, 'burning' the air through which it ascends; a hot, somewhat moist exhalation that rises to

[84] Aristotle, *On Generation and Destruction*, 2.3.

[85] Ibid. 2.3, 331a, 3–6, but at least one other passage in the book suggests otherwise; see H. Joachim's note in his edition. Aristotle, *Meteorology*, 4.4, 382a, 3–4.

[86] The admixture of the dry exhalation, which subsequently returns to earth together with rain, gives Aristotle an explanation for the saltiness of the oceans.

[87] Aristotle, *Meteorology*, 1.3, together with the endnote in the Loeb edition, 1.4, 1.9, 2.2, 354b, 23–34, 2.3–4.

the region below the hot dry exhalation and is transformed there into air; and a cold moist exhalation, which remains close to the earth and is the stuff from which clouds and related phenomena come.[88]

For Maimonides, then, both Scripture and Rabbi Akiva recognize two water derivatives in the atmosphere: the firmament and the water-like substance located above the air.[89] Aristotle's *Meteorology* recognizes only a single moist exhalation, which rises out of water into the lower layer of air, and a single dry exhalation, which is drawn up from the land and rises to where the highest layer of air borders on the region of fire. At one point, Yaḥyā's version of the *Meteorology* speaks of three exhalations, two of which are moist, but it still places only a hot dry exhalation above the region of air.

Medieval commentators on the *Moreh nevukhim* who used Ibn Tibbon's translation took for granted that the *Book of Meteorology* referred to by Maimonides—as Ibn Tibbon misleadingly translated the Arabic—is Aristotle's *Meteorology* in the version they knew. They therefore had the task of matching the two guises of water located by Maimonides in the atmosphere with items in the Aristotelian scheme. The commentators' solution was to say in one way or another that the problematic water-like substance found above the region of air is itself a type of air, and that it lies above only a lower layer, and not above the entire region, of air.[90] The gallant exegetic efforts founder on Maimonides' express words. He locates the upper waters above *the* air and not above *some* air or *a layer* of air. That cannot be squared with either Aristotle's *Meteorology* or Yaḥyā's version. Both locate only a dry exhalation above the air.

There is an additional consideration. Maimonides interprets the sentence, 'the *ruaḥ* of God is moving over the face of the waters' in Genesis 1: 2, as stating that 'the *wind* of God is moving over the face of the waters' and by extension that '*air* is moving over the face of the waters';[91] elsewhere in *Moreh nevukhim*, he explains that the Hebrew word *ruaḥ*, which primarily means wind, can have 'air' as a secondary meaning.[92] By identifying the wind of

[88] Schoonheim, *Aristotle's Meteorology in the Arabico-Latin Tradition* 26–9, 34–5; Ibn Tibbon, *Otot hashamayim*, 40–3, 48–9.

[89] A couple of pages after his discussion of the 'firmament' verse, Maimonides refers to two vapours (*bukhārān*), which constitute the rung after the four elements in the hierarchy of physical existence. He is presumably referring to the moist and dry exhalations; see *MN* ii. 30 (69*b*). Medieval Arabic writers often use *bukhār* as the term specifically for the moist exhalation and a different term, usually *dukhān*, for the dry exhalation. But they also sometimes use *bukhār* as a general term for an exhalation, whether moist or dry, and that is what Maimonides is almost surely doing here. See the examples in Lettinck, *Aristotle's Meteorology and its Reception in the Arab World*, 46, 47, 48, 318.

[90] See the commentaries of Narboni, Efodi (Profiat Duran), and Shem Tov on *MN* ii. 30, summarized in Klein-Braslavy, *Maimonides' Interpretation of the Story of Creation* (Heb.), 165–7.

[91] *MN* ii. 30 (68*a*).

[92] *MN* i. 40. *MN* ii. 6 (16*b*) takes for granted that 'wind' means air.

Genesis 1: 2 as air, he is able, as already seen, to uncover an allusion to the element air in the scriptural account of creation.

Aristotle, however, insisted in the *Meteorology* that wind develops out of the dry exhalation arising from the earth and he branded as absurd the notion that wind is nothing but moving air.[93] Yaḥyā ibn Biṭrīq's version similarly rejected the notion that wind is moving air as 'an error' and 'reprehensible'.[94] By equating wind and air, Maimonides takes a position that Aristotle branded as absurd and his medieval Arabic surrogate rejects as a reprehensible error. The theory that wind is simply air in motion did have its proponents. It was espoused by Aristotle's student Theophrastus[95] and it appears in medieval Arabic literature, for example, in al-Kindi, the Pure Brethren (Ikhwān al-Ṣafā᾿),[96] and Ghazali's *Maqāṣid al-falāsifa*.[97] Maimonides could have encountered it in his reading or, alternatively, have arrived at it on his own as he searched Scripture for an allusion to the creation of the element air.

Too much should not perhaps be put into an allegorical interpretation of a scriptural term. Yet since Maimonides regarded Aristotle as authoritative where sublunar physics is concerned, it is hard to imagine him identifying the scriptural wind as air if he knew that Aristotle categorically rejected the identification. Moses Narboni observes in his commentary on the *Moreh nevukhim* that the view expressed by Maimonides resembles 'the erroneous position' of 'Ghazali, which construes wind as moving air'. Narboni took upon himself the task of harmonizing Maimonides' words with Aristotle's whenever possible and he accordingly struggles to show that Maimonides did not really mean to equate wind with air.[98] Today we no longer stand under such constraints.

The science of meteorology elicited a good deal of interest in the medieval Arabic world, and Yaḥyā's composition was not the sole text on the subject that could have come to Maimonides' attention. One of the additional texts he could have seen was an Arabic *Compendium of Aristotle's Book on Meteorology* ascribed to Ḥunayn ibn Isḥāq, the Arabic translator whom he deemed much more adept than Yaḥyā ibn Biṭrīq. Ḥunayn's *Compendium* is only a fifth as long as Yaḥyā's composition, it handles the Aristotelian material more freely, and it reads more smoothly.

It repeats the Aristotelian proposition that the sun causes a moist and a dry

[93] Aristotle, *Meteorology*, 2.4, 360a, 12–33.

[94] Schoonheim, *Aristotle's Meteorology in the Arabico-Latin Tradition*, 84–5; Ibn Tibbon, *Otot hashamayim*, 104–5.

[95] Theophrastus, *De ventis*, 28–9.

[96] Daiber, *Kompendium der Aristotelischen Meteorologie*, 76 n. 23; Lettinck, *Aristotle's Meteorology and its Reception in the Arab World*, 176–7.

[97] Ghazali, *Maqāṣid al-falāsifa*, 271: 'wind' is a 'term for moving air'.

[98] Narboni, *Commentary on* Moreh nevukhim (Heb.), *MN* ii. 30 (39*a*).

exhalation to rise from water and earth into the atmosphere,[99] and adds that the moist exhalation divides into two: the finer part becomes air, and the thicker part is the source of rain and dew.[100] It further follows the Aristotelian position in tracing wind to the dry exhalation, although without mentioning, let alone branding as absurd, the alternative position that wind is moving air.[101] Nothing in the *Compendium* suggests that a moist exhalation rises above the region of air.

The medieval Arabs had a commentary on Aristotle's *Meteorology* attributed to Olympiodorus but differing from the Greek commentary on the *Meteorology* that carries Olympiodorus' name; it has been dubbed Pseudo-Olympiodorus. When Pseudo-Olympiodorus discusses the moist and dry exhalations, he locates the latter above the former and states that each of them can be either thick or attenuated. In both instances, the thicker remains in the lower part of its region and the attenuated rises to the higher part.[102] Pseudo-Olympiodorus thus recognizes two guises that vapour—as well as the dry exhalation—can take. He nonetheless locates no moist vapour above the stratum of air. Regarding wind, he is unambiguous: It comes from the dry exhalation.[103]

The sections on meteorology in Avicenna's comprehensive philosophical works affirm the following. The region of air has four layers: at the bottom, a moist warm layer, then a moist cold layer, and then two dry layers.[104] As for wind, Avicenna embraced the Aristotelian position and ascribed it to the dry exhalation.[105] Ghazali's account of the views of the philosophers devotes a few pages to meteorology, and they follow Avicenna in distinguishing four layers of air: a warm moist layer, a cold moist layer, and two dry layers. Ghazali locates no water or moisture between the region of air and the region of fire.[106] As already mentioned, he espoused the non-Aristotelian position that the winds are moving air.

Ibn Bājja, whom Maimonides refers to several times in the *Moreh nevukhim*, wrote a commentary—more precisely, an epitome—based on what must have been Yaḥyā's *Meteorology*. Like others, he recognizes two moist layers within the region of air.[107] The preserved sections of his commentary say nothing that I could discover about the nature of wind.

[99] Daiber, *Kompendium der Aristotelischen Meteorologie*, 43. [100] Ibid. 35, 41. [101] Ibid. 43.

[102] Badawi, *Commentaires sur Aristote perdus en grec*, 85; Lettinck, *Aristotle's Meteorology and its Reception in the Arab World*, 47–9. [103] Badawi, *Commentaires sur Aristote perdus en grec*, 116.

[104] Avicenna, *Shifāʾ: Al-afʿāl wa-al-infiʿālāt*, 204; id., *Najāt*, 152–3; Lettinck, *Aristotle's Meteorology and its Reception in the Arab World*, 56.

[105] Avicenna, *Shifāʾ: Al-maʿādin wa-al-āthār al-ʿulwiyya*, 58; id., *Najāt*, 155; Lettinck, *Aristotle's Meteorology and Its Reception in the Arab World*, 177. [106] Ghazali, *Maqāṣid al-falāsifa*, 266.

[107] Lettinck, *Aristotle's Meteorology and its Reception in the Arab World*, 406–7. One of the moist layers gives rise to clouds and rain, the other to dew and frost.

Several medieval Arabic texts therefore distinguish two moist exhalations in the atmosphere, but none that I have been able to discover locates a moist exhalation above the region of air. Of written sources that Maimonides probably knew and might have relied on, Ghazali's account of the views of the philosophers stands apart in its explanation of the phenomenon of wind as moving air.

The upshot is that there is no way of telling where Maimonides acquired the snippets of meteorological information he presents in the *Moreh nevukhim*, no way of determining whether his reference to meteorology is to a book or to the science of meteorology, and if to a book, no way of determining what the book might be. As for Aristotle's *Meteorology*, which was not available, and Yaḥyā's inept adaptation of it, which was, Maimonides adopts two positions running counter to them, namely: a moist layer is found above the stratum of air, and wind is moving air. There are hence no grounds for supposing that he knew Aristotle's *Meteorology* even in Yaḥyā's version.

Although the firmament verses posed a challenge for every medieval student of the Bible who had a knowledge of natural science, Maimonides was much more exercised by them than others were, more pleased with the 'marvellous secrets' he uncovered in the verses,[108] and much more insistent on keeping his discovery hidden from 'the general run of mankind'. The little he does disclose seems so trivial that his characterizing it as marvellous secrets cannot help striking today's reader as outlandish. A minimally plausible rationale for his gingerly handling of the firmament verses is offered by the medieval commentator Asher Crescas (first half of fifteenth century). Although Maimonides makes no mention of rain, Crescas suggests that Maimonides hesitated to publicize the naturalistic explanation of the phenomenon of rain implied in his reading of the biblical text. Maimonides' worry, Crescas theorizes, was that his exegesis, if made public, might confound simple-minded folk who accept what Scripture and the rabbinic sources say about rain literally and who believe that God decides—constantly or once a year during the New Year season—how much should fall and exactly where.[109]

So much for Maimonides' reference to meteorology.

One more Aristotelian work that Maimonides might be thought to have known and used is the collection of compositions on psychological and biological topics that today carries the title *Parva naturalia*. Neither the ancients nor

[108] *MN* ii. 30 (68*b*).

[109] A. Crescas' commentary on *MN* ii. 30, cited by Klein-Braslavy in *Maimonides' Interpretation of the Story of Creation* (Heb.), 172.

the medieval Arabs had that title. The earliest identified use of the phrase *Parva naturalia* was by Giles of Rome at the end of the thirteenth century, and the name became the accepted title for Latin translations of the collection still later.[110]

It seems that not all of the nine compositions now making up the collection were translated into Arabic; at any rate, not all were known to the medieval Arabic bibliographers and philosophers.[111] The first composition in the series is *De sensu et sensibile* (*On Sense and the Object of Sensation*), and for the medieval Arabs, *De sensu et sensibile* (*Al-ḥiss wal-maḥsūs*) served as the title for the entire collection, to the extent that they possessed it.

In one of his medical works, Maimonides writes: 'Aristotle said in the *De sensu et sensibile*, "Most of those who die do so because of medical practice [*min al-ṭibb*], as a result of ignorance of nature among the majority of physicians."'[112] In another medical work, he quotes two versions of the statement. The first has a garbled look to it. It reads: 'Aristotle said in one of his well-known books, and the following is verbatim: "Before this [that is, before the subject about to be broached], we must examine nature, such as health and illness. For most physicians err regarding this power with the result that the cause of human death is medical practice [*al-ṭibb*] and treatment."' Maimonides continues: 'I saw in another translation that he says on the present matter [or: at the present spot]: "Most of those who die do so because of medical practice [*min al-ṭibb*]."'[113]

The quotations can be traced to a passage in *De sensu et sensible* in the proper sense, that is, to the initial composition in the *Parva naturalia*. Aristotle writes there: 'It . . . pertains to the student of physics to know the first principles of health and disease.' 'Hence most students of nature . . . come in the end to issues of medicine, while physicians who pursue their art more philosophically begin with matters of nature.'[114] Aristotle is concerned with the curriculum of students of physical science and mentions incidentally that nature is also the starting point in the curriculum of philosophically minded students of medicine. Maimonides' ostensible quotation from Aristotle, in both its versions, looks at things from a wholly different angle. It is concerned with the practice of medicine and the disastrous result of failing to ground medical practice in a knowledge of nature.

Maimonides refashions what Aristotle wrote to such a extent that the origin in the *De sensu* could easily be missed if Maimonides did not explicitly name his

[110] Aristotle, *Parva naturalia*, Ross's introd., 1.
[111] Steinschneider, 'Die *Parva Naturalia* des Aristoteles bei den Arabern'.
[112] Maimonides, *Fī tadbīr al-ṣiḥḥat*, 296; English trans.: *The Regimen of Health*, 21a.
[113] Maimonides, *On Asthma*, 91.
[114] Aristotle, *De sensu*, 1.436a, 17–436b, 1.

source. He must be quoting from a work written by someone who was distressed by the inadequacy of medical practice that lacks a grounding in natural science and who cited Aristotle's *De sensu* for support. Since Maimonides does not realize that Aristotle's statement had been wholly recast to serve a new purpose—relating not to the curriculum of students of physics but to the shortcomings of physicians—and that he is quoting the adaptation and not Aristotle himself, he did not have the *De sensu* before him when he wrote.

Nor is there the slightest evidence that he saw any of the other compositions making up the *Parva naturalia*. One of them, *On Dreams*, which was among the parts translated into Arabic, helped to inspire the Arabic Aristotelian conception of prophecy, and that conception plays a central role in Maimonides' thought. He could have studied *On Dreams* with profit. Nothing indicates that he did.

By the same token, the *Moreh nevukhim* and other late works of Maimonides disclose no trace of Aristotle's *De anima*. Most notably, the theory of intellect that Maimonides takes for granted in the *Guide* is not the theory of the *De anima* but rather that of the Arabic Aristotelian school.

We come to Aristotle's *Metaphysics*. What Maimonides adduced in the *Commentary on the Mishnah* from the science of metaphysics or from the author of the subject of metaphysics was consistently alien to Aristotle.[115] The level of his knowledge of Aristotle's *Metaphysics* when he wrote the *Moreh nevukhim* remains to be determined.

Before setting forth his full-fledged proofs of the existence of God in the *Guide*, he lists twenty-six philosophical propositions that he would employ in the proofs. The twenty-fifth proposition quotes a 'verbatim statement [*naṣṣ kalām*] of Aristotle's: "Matter [*al-mādda*] does not move itself."' The quotation seems to reflect a sentence in Aristotle's *Metaphysics*, where the Greek says: '*hulē* will not move itself'.[116] Since Aristotle's contention is that the art of carpentry is what moves *hulē*, the word is probably intended in its primary meaning of *wood* rather than its extended meaning of *matter*. Aristotle is probably saying that *wood* will not move itself, and the art of carpentry is what moves it. One of the two preserved medieval Arabic translations of the *Metaphysics*, however, understands *hulē* in the extended sense of *matter* and has Aristotle say that 'matter [*al-ʿunṣur*] does not move itself'.[117] Maimonides' quotation is not verbatim—he uses a different Arabic term for matter, a term that was more common in his day—but it is very close.

[115] Above, Ch. 3, §4.

[116] *MN* ii, introd., proposition 25; Aristotle, *Metaphysics*, 12.6.1071b, 29–30.

[117] Averroes, *Tafsīr mā baʿd al-ṭabīʿa*, 1564.

All the other passages in the *Moreh nevukhim* that purportedly cite Aristotle's *Metaphysics* or indicate they are doing so are non-Aristotelian.

(*a*) In a precursor of his four demonstrations of the existence of God, Maimonides establishes that all formal causes in the universe go back to a first formal cause.[118] He reasons as follows: when we examine 'generated and destructible natural forms' in the world, we observe that a given portion of matter receives a certain form; the matter is prepared to receive the form by the action of a prior form that already exists in a different portion of matter; that prior form is able to perform its function because its matter received it through the action of yet a prior form, which exists in yet a different portion of matter; and so on. Since causal chains cannot regress indefinitely, the series must stop at 'the ultimate form of all existence', which is 'God'. Whereupon Maimonides hastens to forestall a misunderstanding.

He warns readers against confusing the ultimate form he is talking about with 'the ultimate form of which Aristotle states in the *Metaphysics* that it is not subject to generation and destruction'. The latter is 'natural'—or 'physical' (*ṭabīʿiyya*)—whereas the form that Maimonides is talking about is 'an incorporeal intellect', a being wholly free of matter.[119] The ultimate natural, or physical, form, the one that Maimonides is not concerned with, stands at the opposite end of the ladder from the first form that is wholly free of matter and whose existence is entailed by the impossibility of an infinite regress.

Aristotle recognized four primary physical elements, each of which is constituted by the presence of a form—of fire, air, water, or earth—in sublunar matter. The presence of the form of fire in sublunar matter constitutes the element fire, the presence of the form of air in matter constitutes air, and so on. Aristotle had no concept of an ultimate physical form more basic than the forms of the elements. Nothing, in his scheme, interposes itself between the form of an element and bare matter.

The forms of the four elements are, moreover, unstable. A portion of fire can shed its form, and its matter can accept the form of air, so that the fire ceases to exist and air comes into existence in its stead; the other elements undergo similar transformations. In the genuine Aristotelian physical scheme, substances constituted by the presence in matter of the ultimate natural forms, those of the elements, are, then, subject to generation and destruction. Aristotle, it should be noted, was careful to stress that the forms themselves, although now they are present and now they are not, do not strictly undergo

118 He draws similar conclusions regarding efficient causes and final causes, the final cause being a cause of an object's existence in the sense that it is the end, or purpose, for which the object exists.

119 *MN* i. 69 (89*b*).

generation and destruction.[120] When Maimonides uses the phrase 'generated and destructible natural forms', he expresses himself poorly from the Aristotelian standpoint.

In a word, Aristotle's *Metaphysics* knows nothing of a form that interposes itself between bare matter and the forms of the four elements and that can be described as 'not subject to generation and destruction' in contrast to all other natural forms, which *are* generated-destructible.

An addition was later made, one that was adumbrated, as Wolfson shows,[121] by the Greek commentator Simplicius but came into its own in the Middle Ages with Avicenna. Analysis led to the positing of a stage, which came to be called *corporeal form*, between matter and the forms of the four physical elements. Corporeal form was understood to prepare pure matter for receiving the next level of form. What receives the form of fire, air, and so forth is now matter already joined to, and conditioned by, corporeal form.

Corporeal form, unlike the forms of the four elements, is permanently bonded to its substratum: the compound of matter and corporeal form does not undergo generation or destruction, just as the underlying matter of the world does not do so in genuine Aristotelianism. A believer in creation *ex nihilo*, which Maimonides professes to be, would insist on the qualification that although the compound of matter and corporeal form is not subject to generation, it was nevertheless brought into existence by an act of creation, which is a different process.

When Maimonides has Aristotle state in the *Metaphysics* that ultimate, natural form differs from other natural forms in being immune to generation and destruction, he plainly is talking about corporeal form. The concept, alien to Aristotle, was expounded in the metaphysical sections of Avicenna's major philosophical works and in the metaphysical section of Ghazali's account of the views of the philosophers.[122] Although Avicenna and Ghazali maintained that matter is never free of corporeal form, I have not found them employing the language used by Maimonides and describing ultimate natural form as 'not subject to generation and destruction'. Maimonides may have received Avicenna's theory through a filter or recast what he learned in his own words. What counts here is that the notion of corporeal form, which Maimonides ascribes to Aristotle's *Metaphysics*, comes from the metaphysical writings of Avicenna and his adherents.

[120] Aristotle, *Metaphysics*, 7.8, 8.5.

[121] Wolfson, *Crescas' Critique of Aristotle*, 581–2.

[122] See commentaries of Narboni and Efodi on *MN* i. 69; Wolfson, *Crescas' Critique of Aristotle*, 580–5; Avicenna, *Shifāʾ: Ilāhiyyāt*, 57; id., *Najāt*, 203; Ghazali, *Maqāṣid al-falāsifa*, 93.

(*b*) The last of the twenty-six philosophical propositions with which Maimonides prefaces his full-fledged proofs of the existence of God is a hypothesis tentatively accepted for the sake of argument. All the others, he writes, were 'demonstrated' by 'Aristotle and the peripatetics coming after him'. Again: they were 'demonstrated' either in the 'Book of the *Physics* and its commentaries' or the 'Book of the *Metaphysics* and its commentary'.

Most of the propositions come from Aristotle's *Physics*. A few originate in Aristotle's *Metaphysics* but would also have been accessible in a work such as Ghazali's account of the views of the philosophers. A few cannot be linked to anything that Aristotle expressly writes, yet are in the general spirit of his philosophy.[123]

Three propositions do not fall within any of those categories. They are propositions that explicate the concepts *possibly existent by reason of itself* and *necessarily existent by reason of itself*.

The first of the three posits that 'whatever has a cause of its existence is possibly existent by virtue of itself'. The second posits that when something is 'necessarily existent by virtue of itself, its existence has no cause whatsoever and in any respect'. The third spells out the implication of the words *whatsoever and in any respect*. Maimonides explains that when something is 'composed of two factors [*ma'nā*], the combining together [of the factors] is perforce the cause of the thing's existing in the condition in which it exists'. Such a thing 'is not necessarily existent by virtue of itself, for it exists thanks to the existence of its parts and their being combined together'.[124] What contains components of any sort depends on those components for its existence and consequently—although it sounds a little strange—does not exist by virtue of itself.

In *Metaphysics* 12, Aristotle does write that, in contrast to the celestial spheres, which are constantly in motion and hence undergo a type of change, the unmoved mover, whose existence can be inferred from the motion of the spheres, cannot in any respect be other than it is. One of several senses of *necessary* is 'what cannot be otherwise'. The unmoved mover accordingly exists 'of necessity'.[125]

The notion that the first mover of the universe 'exists of necessity' is therefore Aristotelian. But the concept *necessarily existent by virtue of itself*, its counterpart *possibly existent by virtue of itself*, and, most pertinently, the far-reaching implication of something's existing *by virtue of itself*[126] are alien to Aristotle and

[123] *MN* ii, introd. Likely sources for the principles in Aristotle, Avicenna, and Ghazali are given in *MN* (Schwarz), ad loc.

[124] *MN* ii, introd., propositions 19, 20, and 21.

[125] Aristotle, *Metaphysics*, 12.7, 4–13.

[126] It cannot be stressed too many times that what distinguishes the first cause or deity for Maimonides is not that He is *necessarily existent*. Anything eternal—for example, the spheres and intelligences

to every known work that might be called a peripatetic commentary on Aristotle's *Physics* or *Metaphysics*. The implication of something's existing wholly by virtue of itself has its roots in the Neoplatonic *De causis* and was picked up by Alfarabi, who was followed by Avicenna. The concepts *possibly existent by virtue of itself* and *necessarily existent by virtue of itself*, and the analysis of the latter, all come from Avicenna.[127]

The concepts and the analysis play a central role in Avicenna's *Metaphysics*, where they prepare the ground for his distinctive proof of the existence of God.[128] They appear as well in the metaphysical section of Ghazali's account of the views of the philosophers, although Ghazali is lax in failing to bring out that the *necessarily existent by virtue of itself* and not merely the *necessarily existent* without further qualification is what cannot have components making it what is.[129]

Maimonides should have stated that at least three of the propositions he uses in his proofs of the existence of God are not demonstrated or alluded to in Aristotle's *Physics*, Aristotle's *Metaphysics*, or peripatetic commentaries on the two books. They come from the *Metaphysics* of Avicenna.

(c) Maimonides writes in the *Moreh nevukhim*: it is 'well-known', 'clear', and 'necessary' that in the case of anything having a cause, 'existence is something accidental attaching itself to the existent being and therefore a factor added to the quiddity of the existent being'. In a similar vein: 'It has been made clear in the *Metaphysics*'—or, possibly: 'in metaphysics'—'that unity and multiplicity are accidents attaching themselves to the existent being insofar as it is one or multiple.'[130] The notion that, with the exception of uncaused being, existent objects have an accident of existence attached to them and the still odder notion that they have an accident of unity or multiplicity attached to them are again wholly foreign to Aristotle. They are peculiar to Avicenna, and Ghazali's account of the views of the philosophers follows in Avicenna's footsteps. Averroes subsequently rejected both notions on their merits and because they have no basis in Aristotle.[131]

The theses that Maimonides describes as well-known and as having been made clear in the *Metaphysics*, or in 'metaphysics', are a sharp departure from Aristotle and are innovations of Avicenna's.

if they are eternal—is *necessarily existent* for Maimonides. What is operative and distinguishes the first cause is that He exists *by reason of Himself*.

[127] H. Davidson, *Proofs for Eternity, Creation, and the Existence of God*, 289–91, 294–8.

[128] See ibid. 299–304.

[129] Ghazali, *Maqāṣid al-falāsifa*, 131–7.

[130] *MN* i. 57 (69*a*).

[131] See Avicenna, *Manṭiq al-mashriqiyyin*, 22–3, trans. in Goichon, *La Distinction de l'essence et de l'existence d'après Ibn Sīnā*, 142–3; Avicenna, *Shifā': Ilāhiyyāt*, 81, 83; Ghazali, *Maqāṣid al-falāsifa*, 101, 106, 219; Averroes, *Compendio de Metafisica*, 1, §§22, 39 (German trans.: *Die Epitome der Metaphysik des Averroes*, 8, 17); Munk's note on his translation of *MN* i. 57.

(*d*) After presenting what he characterizes as apodictic demonstrations of the existence of God, Maimonides supplements them with an argument for the existence of subordinate incorporeal beings—the incorporeal intelligences—that maintain the celestial spheres in circular motion. He introduces the subject by conceding: 'The views held by Aristotle concerning the causes of the motion of the spheres, from which [motion] he inferred the existence of incorporeal intelligences', are 'hypotheses [*daʿāwā*] not amenable to demonstration [*burhān*]'. Nevertheless, 'those views, as Alexander [of Aphrodisias] states in the *Principles of the Universe*', are subject to fewer doubts and hold together better than other attempts to explain celestial motion.[132] The thesis that the spheres are moved by incorporeal intelligences is more plausible than any other possible explanation of celestial motion.

The incorporeal intelligences are an essential constituent of Maimonides' picture of the universe, and he uncovers allusions to their existence in Scripture and midrashic literature, where they are called angels. Having conceded that he does not have an apodictic demonstration for their existence, he offers *proofs* (*dalāʾil*), which are less ironclad than demonstrations. Philosophy raised the belief in the existence of God to the level of certain knowledge, and it will now raise the belief in the existence of subordinate incorporeal—or angelic—beings to a level somewhat short of certainty. The seedbed out of which the proofs grow is indeed Aristotelian.

In *Metaphysics* 12, Aristotle writes that the motion of the 'first heaven' comes about from its having the incorporeal and unchanging first cause—God—as an object of desire (*mushtahā*) and object of intellectual thought (*maʿqūl*). Aristotle does not say in so many words that the heaven possesses a soul and intellect. but a soul would be implied by its having desire, and an intellect, by its having intellectual thought.[133] A passage in *On the Heavens* moreover affirms explicitly that the heaven 'possesses soul' (*dhāt nafs*).[134]

The rotation of the first heaven somehow comes about through an interaction between its soul and intellect, on the one side, and the incorporeal mover, which is distinct from it, on the other. The soul and intellect of the heaven perform their part by having the incorporeal mover as an object of desire and object of intellectual thought; the incorporeal mover performs its part not

[132] *MN* ii. 3. The quoted sentence might also conceivably, although much less plausibly, be read as saying: 'from which [views] he inferred'. As far as the structure of the sentence goes, it could even be read as saying: 'from which [causes] he inferred', but that would make little sense. Despite the prevalent myth to the contrary, not everything in the *MN* is written with great care.

[133] Aristotle, *Metaphysics*, 12.7, 1072a, 22–3, 26–7.

[134] Aristotle, *On the Heavens*, 2.2, 285a, 29; Arabic trans., 231.The statement here is to be harmonized with *On the Heavens*, 2.1, 284a, 27–9.

through doing anything but by being 'loved'. Aristotle does not explain how desire and intellectual thought give rise to motion.

Metaphysics 12 also recognizes that besides the first heaven, there exist other eternally rotating celestial spheres, in which the planets are embedded, and Aristotle infers that each sphere has its own eternal unmoved mover.[135]

There are gaps in Aristotle's account, and the *Moreh nevukhim* fills them. Maimonides analyses celestial motion in order to show why the heaven must possess a soul and intellect, he explains the mechanism whereby the soul and intellect of the heaven cause it to rotate, he superimposes a scheme in which the incorporeal movers of the spheres emanate from God, and he attributes the package to Aristotle.

His reasoning goes: the motion of 'the sphere' is not 'natural'. Natural motion occurs when one of the four physical elements or a physical object in which one of the elements predominates happens to be outside its natural place, moves in a straight line either up or down to its natural place, and comes to rest there. But the celestial sphere is observed to move in a circle and not in a straight line, and it never comes to rest. Since celestial motion is not natural, the 'principle' producing it must be a soul.

Beings with souls, Maimonides continues, undergo motion in one of two ways. Either they do so thanks to 'a nature' that they possess, the term nature here having a different sense from before, namely: a factor within an animal's soul that induces the animal to move towards what it judges to be congenial or away from what it judges to be unpleasant and threatening; or they do so thanks to 'a concept' (*taṣawwur*). The celestial sphere plainly does not move in order to reach something congenial or to avoid what is unpleasant. As it rotates, it repeatedly moves away from, and returns to, each point in its orbit, and if its aim were to reach or avoid something, its unceasing circular motion would be futile. Celestial motion must therefore occur 'through a concept that dictates that the sphere should move in such a fashion'.

Concepts, however, exist only in intellects; the soul of the sphere therefore possesses an intellect. Further, as 'made clear [*buyyina*] in first philosophy' and by common sense, a concept in the intellect does not by itself suffice to produce motion: a person can think endlessly about moving, without ever budging. In addition to the concept dictating motion, the sphere must have the desire (or: impulse; *ishtiyāq*) to move.[136]

The rotation of the sphere thus entails a soul possessed of intellect, a concept, and a desire.

[135] Aristotle, *Metaphysics*, 12.8, 1073a, 28–34.

[136] Similar reasoning is found in Averroes, *Tahāfut al-tahāfut*, 479–80. For the translation of *ishtiyāq* as 'impulse' see Wolfson, 'The Problem of the Souls of the Spheres', 30–1.

Maimonides hereupon posits, with no ado, that the 'object of love' (*shay' ma'shūq*) to which the sphere's desire is directed is God, whose existence he demonstrated in the immediately preceding chapters of the *Guide*. 'In this manner, he [that is, Aristotle] stated, God moves the sphere. That is to say, the sphere's desire to render itself similar [*tashabbuh*] to what it conceives'—to render itself similar to a being of 'the highest degree of simplicity, wholly immune to change . . . from whom goodness constantly emanates'—expresses itself in circular motion; for circular motion is the most simple and perfect action possible for a body. From the sphere's perfect circular motion there proceeds an 'emanation of goodness' upon the lower, sublunar region.

There is more. After the foregoing 'became clear to Aristotle', he found 'through demonstration' (*burhān*) that there exists not just one, but a number of spheres, each with its own proper motion. The exigencies of physical science led him to conclude that every sphere must have its own concept, which differs from the concepts of the others; and he deduced the existence of a corresponding number of incorporeal intelligences, each of them responsible for the motion of a sphere by serving as its object of thought and desire. The incorporeal intelligences, Maimonides remarks, are identical with the 'nigh-standing [*muqarrabūn*] angels'.[137] In a later chapter, he expressly cites metaphysics—or the *Metaphysics*—as the place where Aristotle posited the existence of multiple incorporeal intelligences.[138]

As it approaches completion, Maimonides' exposition takes a surprising turn. He had credited Aristotle with a step-by-step argument establishing that the celestial 'sphere' performs its circular motion from a desire to render itself as similar as possible to the deity. He then had Aristotle proceed to the proposition that there are multiple spheres, each with a motion, and hence a mover proper to itself. Now he informs us that the deity is not after all the object of desire and immediate mover of any of the spheres. As the subject 'developed for him', that is, for Aristotle, he realized that every mover of a sphere perforce contains a certain duality: it has the attribute of moving a sphere in common with the movers of the other spheres and, in addition, it has something that distinguishes it from the other movers. The first cause must, by contrast, be absolutely simple and free of components. God is consequently distinct from,

[137] The term comes from Qur'an 4: 171. A few other quranic expressions have been detected in *MN*, none, however, as distinctively Islamic as the one we have here. See *MN* (Schwarz), 40 n. 14 (correct 'page 221' to 'page 211'), 353 n. 19, and the references Schwarz gives. To conclude from the few quranic expressions thus far identified in Maimonides that he was acquainted with the Qur'an would be analogous to concluding from a writer's use of expressions such as 'break of dawn', 'feet of clay', 'green pastures', or 'holocaust' that he knew and was quoting the Bible.

[138] *MN* ii. 19 (42*b*). Ibn Tibbon's translation represents Maimonides as referring to 'the Book of *Metaphysics*', but the Arabic says only 'metaphysics' with no mention of a book.

and transcends, the movers of the spheres. He acts on the spheres and the rest of the universe through intermediaries.

The soul of the first sphere, it turns out, has as its object of desire, as the being to which it endeavours to render itself similar, and as its mover, not God Himself, but an incorporeal intelligence that God brings into existence. Each subsequent sphere has as its object of desire and mover a subsequent link in the series of emanated intelligences.[139]

Throughout the complex series of arguments, Maimonides insists that he is conveying not what Aristotle's statements imply or the way commentators interpreted him, but what Aristotle explicitly wrote. He sets forth Aristotle's 'views and proofs'.[140] He speaks about what 'became clear to Aristotle' concerning the cause of celestial motion; what Aristotle 'stated' about celestial motion; how Aristotle 'pondered and found' by 'demonstration' that there exist a number of celestial spheres, each requiring its own mover. He writes that he reported 'Aristotle's statements [*qawl*] and view'. In connection with one key detail, he refers to what was 'made clear in first philosophy', that is to say, in metaphysics, without naming any philosopher.[141] He summarizes: 'The upshot of his [that is, Aristotle's] discussion is thus that all the spheres are living bodies, possessing soul and intellect.' The spheres 'have a conception and cognition of God and cognition of their principles [that is, of the beings that move them]. And there exist incorporeal intelligences that emanate from God and are the intermediaries between God and the aforementioned bodies.'[142]

But Aristotle did not offer an argument showing that the motion of the heaven cannot be natural. He did not state that the heaven rotates in order to render itself as similar as possible to its mover.[143] The propositions that the movers of the spheres contain a certain duality whereas the first cause is absolutely simple, that the first cause of the universe is therefore not the mover of a celestial sphere, that the intelligences receive their existence through a process of emanation, that goodness emanates from the first cause, that goodness emanates from the circular motion of the heaven—those propositions are completely alien to Aristotle's philosophy.

Maimonides furnishes the key when he writes that Aristotle's 'proofs regarding these matters are set forth . . . in the writings of his followers'.[144] His

[139] *MN* ii. 4 (14*a*–*b*). [140] *MN* ii. 3. [141] *MN* ii. 4 (13*a*).

[142] *MN* ii. 4 (14*b*). The statement that the spheres, that is, their intellects, have a conception and cognition of God, raises a couple of questions. Does Maimonides intend what he says *au pied de la lettre*? If so, does he mean that each sphere moves from a desire to make itself similar to both God and its intelligence?

[143] Theophrastus, *Metaphysics*, 5a, 23–8, 11a, 26–7, records the theory that the celestial spheres rotate from a desire to imitate a higher being. He ascribes the theory to Plato and the Pythagoreans.

[144] *MN* ii. 4 (14*b*).

initial reference to Alexander of Aphrodisias' *Principles of the Universe* tells us where to begin to look.

The *Principles of the Universe* opens: 'Alexander says' that he was going to offer a 'discourse [*qawl*] on the principles [of the universe] in accordance with Aristotle's view'. The *Principles* contains the following statements: a strict 'demonstration' (*burhān*) is not possible when one deals with 'the first principles', for demonstrations go from what is prior and the cause to what is posterior and caused, whereas nothing is either prior to, or the cause of first principles. The subject of the book will be 'what the first cause is', the motion of the celestial spheres, and related matters. Inanimate natural bodies move to their natural places and there come to rest. The eternal divine body, that is to say, the celestial sphere, is not inanimate but ensouled, for it is the best of bodies and the best bodies have souls.[145] Inasmuch as the sphere does not have to take any action to preserve itself, its soul experiences neither 'aversion nor attraction', and its motion results from a 'desire' (or 'impulse'; *ishtiyāq*) for what is 'conceived in [its] intellect' (*al-mutaṣawwar bi-al-ʿaql*). The concept in the intellect does not suffice, and a desire (or 'impulse') must be assumed as well because, 'as has been made clear' (*tabayyana*)—where is not specified—a concept in the sphere's intellect (*al-taṣawwur bi-al-ʿaql*) does not by itself cause motion.

Furthermore, the object of the sphere's intellect and desire is 'the true good', the being that outdoes all others in goodness and beneficence (*jūd*). The sphere performs circular motion in order to render itself as similar (*tashabbuh*) as possible to the object of its love (*maʿshūq*), the supreme, truly good being. Besides the outermost celestial sphere, there are other rotating celestial spheres possessing soul and intellect, and paralleling them, a series of incorporeal intelligences, each of which is responsible for the motion of a corresponding sphere.[146]

Maimonides' focus is somewhat different from that of the *Principles of the Universe*. The *Principles* states that it is going to give Aristotle's less than demonstrative account of the principles, that is, the causes, of the universe, starting with the first cause;[147] Maimonides states that he is going to give less than demonstrative proofs for the existence of the incorporeal intelligences and he does not mention the first cause. The shift is probably due to his confidence that he had already established the existence of God through an apodictic demonstration.[148] He is now interested not in the first cause but in what comes after it.

[145] Aristotle, *Generation of Animals*, 2.1, 731b, 28–9, states that what has a soul is superior to what does not.

[146] Alexander(?), *Principles of the Universe*, §§1, 2, 5, 7, 10, 12–15, 23 and apparatus, 24–5, 50, 92, 94.

[147] Ibid., §3.

[148] In his demonstrations of the existence of God, Maimonides significantly ignores the point

There are one or two dissimilarities in the explanations of celestial motion. Maimonides' argument establishing that the celestial sphere possesses a soul—on the grounds that the motion performed by the sphere does not fit the description of natural motion—is not the argument whereby the *Principles of the Universe* establishes the same proposition. The *Principles* does not hesitate to describe the sphere as a natural body and to speak of the sphere's nature, something that Maimonides is careful to avoid; since, however, it quickly adds the qualification that the sphere's nature is nothing other than its soul,[149] the difference between it and Maimonides on this score may be merely terminological. Otherwise, Maimonides' account of celestial motion looks like a tightening of the wordy and meandering *Principles of the Universe*. His remark about its being 'made clear in first philosophy', in other words, in metaphysics, that a concept in the intellect does not suffice to cause motion sounds, moreover, like an echo of the sentence in the *Principles* stating: 'as has already been made clear', the concept in the sphere's intellect does not suffice by itself to effect motion. The remark about what is 'made clear in first philosophy' appears to refer to the *Principles of the Universe*.

Maimonides could also have had access to the analysis of celestial motion in Avicenna and very likely did have access to Ghazali's analysis. It is not hard to detect the mark of the *Principles of the Universe* on Avicenna's two major philosophical works, the *Shifā'* and *Najāt*, which are virtually identical on the present issue; and Avicenna expressly characterizes the author of the '*Epistle on the Principles of the Universe*', whom he does not name, as 'one of the more correct' successors of Aristotle. Almost everything that Maimonides says about celestial motion can be found in Avicenna, although Maimonides' straightforward presentation is not at all like Avicenna's, which is highly dialectical.[150]

Avicenna was, in turn, the springboard for Ghazali. The latter discusses the causes of celestial motion at some length in *Maqāṣid al-falāsifa*, his account of the views of the philosophers, and he outlines them in *Tahāfut al-falāsifa*, his refutation of what he calls key positions of Aristotle's as transmitted by Alfarabi and Avicenna. Almost every point that Maimonides makes can be found in the *Maqāṣid*, although Ghazali's handling of the subject, which has

made by the *Principles of the Universe* about strict demonstrations' going from what is prior to what is posterior. His proofs of the existence of God, which he repeatedly states are demonstrations, do go from what is posterior to what is prior.

149 Alexander(?), *Principles of the Universe*, §§6, 16–17.

150 Avicenna, *Shifā'*, *Ilāhiyyāt*, 307–18 (= id., *Najāt*, 258–67). The reference to the *Principles of the Universe* appears on p. 317 of the former work and p. 266 of the latter. Alexander(?), *Principles of the Universe*, §91, states that the movement of the heavens serves to exercise providence over the sublunar world.

fewer twists and turns than Avicenna's, is still different from that of Maimonides.[151] It is noteworthy that both of Ghazali's works have the philosophers equate the incorporeal intelligences with the 'nigh-standing angels', an expression we met in Maimonides.[152]

When Maimonides reaches the stage where he determines that the first cause of the universe cannot be the mover of the outermost sphere, he leaves the *Principles of the Universe* behind. The *Principles* knows nothing of the proposition that the movers of the spheres contain a certain duality, the conclusion that the first cause of the universe must therefore transcend the movers of the spheres, the emanation of the movers of the spheres from the first cause, and the emanation of goodness from the first cause and from the heavens. Those are notions that Maimonides learned from the Arabic Aristotelians—Alfarabi, Avicenna, Ghazali's account of the views of the philosophers, or conceivably some other work from the school no longer available.[153] The *Principles* nonetheless does portray the supreme being as the ultimate source of beneficence, and a different work attributed to Alexander and employed by Maimonides in the *Moreh nevukhim* speaks of 'things that proceed [*taṣdur*]' from God 'in accordance with will and choice', and, again, of 'goodness' that 'proceeds' (*ṣādir*) from the gods' choice.[154] It would therefore not have been a large leap for Maimonides to combine Arabic Aristotelian notions with the 'discourse . . . in accordance with Aristotle's view' that he borrowed from the *Principles of the Universe*.

Despite Maimonides' assurance that he is conveying what Aristotle stated, proved, and demonstrated, he did not consult Aristotle's *Metaphysics* on the issue of the movement of the spheres. He took the *Principles of the Universe* and the Arabic Aristotelians to be authoritative spokesmen for Aristotle, and as a consequence affixes Aristotle's name to positions completely foreign to him.

[151] Ghazali, *Maqāṣid al-falāsifa*, 200–17.

[152] Ibid. 171, 211, 217; Ghazali, *Tahāfut al-falāsifa*, 153; above, n. 137, where it is pointed out that the expression is quranic. The nigh-standing angels are identified with the incorporeal intelligences, which move the spheres as an object of emulation, in *Risāla al-ziyāra*, attributed to Avicenna. See Goichon, *Lexique*, s.v. *malak*; Avicenna, *Traités mystiques*, Arabic section, 45; French section, 25. The opuscule departs from the positions of the genuine Avicenna in several respects, most egregiously in reducing the number of incorporeal intelligences—which it calls 'active intellects' (or 'active intelligences')—to eight and in assigning the functions of the active intellect responsible for human thought to the intelligence of the lunar sphere rather than to an incorporeal being that emanates from the intelligence of the lunar sphere.

[153] Alfarabi, *Risala fi al-ʿaql*, 34–6, argues—differently from the way Maimonides does—that the movers of the spheres contain duality, and the first cause therefore lies beyond the movers of the spheres. The first cause of the universe, he concludes, is the 'intellect that Aristotle discusses in *Metaphysics* 12'.

[154] Alexander of Aphrodisias, *Traité de la Providence*, Arabic text, 15, 17; French trans., 113, 116.

(*e*) Aristotle, Maimonides has written, found 'through demonstration' (*burhān*) that there exist a number of spheres, each with its own proper motion, and then deduced the existence of multiple incorporeal intelligences, each responsible for the motion of a corresponding sphere. The existence of multiple incorporeal beings creates a problem that exercised medieval as well as modern interpreters of Aristotle.[155]

Physical objects are differentiated and distinguished from each other inasmuch as the portion of matter belonging to one is distinct from the portion of matter belonging to another, and the place occupied by one is different from that occupied by another. The question arises: how can incorporeal beings, which are free of matter and do not occupy space, be differentiated? If they cannot be differentiated, how might multiple incorporeal intelligences exist side by side with each other and with the incorporeal first cause?

Maimonides writes that the solution to the problem 'according to him', that is, according to Aristotle, is as follows: 'God . . . brings the first intelligence into existence, that is to say, the intelligence that moves the first [outermost] sphere[156] as we have explained', by serving as an object of desire for the soul of the sphere. 'The intelligence that moves the second sphere has the first intelligence as *its* cause and principle. And so on.' God is thus differentiated from the first intelligence by reason of being the cause of its existence, and each successive intelligence is differentiated from the next in the series by reason of being the cause of that intelligence's existence.[157]

Maimonides raises an additional problem. It is, he writes, a 'proposition agreed upon by Aristotle and all who philosophized that from a simple [non-composite] thing there can proceed in a necessary manner [*yalzam*] only one simple [non-composite] thing'. Applying 'this proposition, Aristotle stated that there proceeds, immediately, from God only a single, simple intelligence, nothing more'. How then could the universe, in all its complexity, come into existence?

Aristotle's solution here, Maimonides explains, was that the intelligence is not quite as simple in its essence as the first cause, for unlike the first cause, it has two objects of thought: 'itself and something else'. Its thought of itself produces the first celestial sphere, the sphere that it maintains in motion, and its other thought produces the next link in the series of intelligences. The second intelligence similarly has two objects of thought, and they give rise to the existence of the second sphere, the one that the second intelligence maintains in motion, and the existence of a third intelligence. As the process keeps

[155] See Wolfson, 'The Plurality of Immovable Movers in Aristotle, Averroes, and St. Thomas', 9–19.

[156] Regarding the outermost sphere, see above, n. 57.

[157] *MN* ii. 4.

replicating itself, the full complement of spheres and intelligences emerges. To avoid any misunderstanding, Maimonides warns readers that when Aristotle spoke of the procession of the first intelligence from God, the procession of the second from the first, and so on, 'he clearly did not mean' thereby that the intelligences came into existence after not existing. Aristotle was describing an eternal causal nexus. God and each succeeding intelligence is the cause of the existence of the next in the series eternally and constantly.[158]

The scheme Maimonides has ascribed to Aristotle grows out of the grafting of Neoplatonic conceptions on to Aristotle's picture of the universe, and the primary thinkers who spell out the hybrid scheme are Alfarabi, Avicenna, and Ghazali in his account of the views of the philosophers. As for the precise channel through which Maimonides learned it, we have clues, namely: the proposition that from a simple thing only one simple thing can proceed necessarily; the statement that each intelligence has two objects of thought; and the ascription of the theory to Aristotle.

Avicenna is the first philosopher known to have articulated the proposition that from a simple thing only one simple thing can proceed in a necessary manner.[159] Ghazali follows in Avicenna's wake and records the proposition in both the *Maqāṣid al-falāsifa* and *Tahāfut al-falāsifa*.[160]

Regarding the thoughts possessed by each of the intelligences, Alfarabi and Avicenna differ. Alfarabi writes in his *Risāla fī al-ʿaql*—a work referred to by name in the *Guide*—that the first intelligence's objects of thought are 'itself and the essence of the thing that is the principle [in other words, the cause] of its existence'. From the two thoughts, the first intelligence's thought of itself and its thought of its cause, two things emanate—the outermost sphere and the second intelligence. Alfarabi does not explain whether, as the pattern replicates itself, each intelligence has itself and the intelligence that is its immediate cause, or itself and the ultimate cause of the universe, as its two objects of thought.[161]

Avicenna's main Arabic works add a nuance by distinguishing not two, but three thoughts in each intelligence, namely, the intelligence's thought of the first cause; the intelligence's thought of its own self insofar as it is necessarily existent by reason of its cause; and its thought of its own self insofar as it is possibly existent by reason of itself. From the intelligence's three thoughts, there

[158] *MN* ii. 21 (47*b*), ii. 22.

[159] Avicenna, *Shifāʾ*: *Ilāhiyyāt*, 330 (= id., *Najāt*, 276): 'From the one, insofar as it is one, only one can come into existence [*yūjad*].'

[160] Ghazali, *Maqāṣid al-falāsifa*, 218 (*yūjad*); id., *Tahāfut al-falāsifa*, 65 (*yaṣdur*). Shahrastani ascribes the rule to Aristotle himself. See Shahrastānī, *Al-milal wa-al-niḥal* (Cureton), 315; French trans.: *Livre des religions et des sectes*, 292 (*yaṣdur*).

[161] Alfarabi, *Risala fi al-ʿaql*, 35.

emanate, respectively, the next intelligence in the series, the soul of the sphere co-ordinated with the given intelligence, and the body of the sphere. The process then repeats itself.[162]

Ghazali's *Tahāfut al-falāsifa* similarly has the philosophers ascribe three objects of thought to each intelligence, and the three thoughts give rise to a threefold emanation. But his *Maqāṣid al-falāsifa* states, in language similar to Alfarabi's, that the first intelligence 'knows itself and knows its principle', that is, the cause of its existence, and from the two acts of knowledge, there emanate the outermost sphere and the second intelligence. The *Maqāṣid* continues: 'From the second intelligence there proceed a third intelligence and the sphere of the constellations', which is the sphere moved by the second intelligence. And so forth.[163] Like Alfarabi, Ghazali does not say whether the two objects of thought, or knowledge, in the second and each subsequent intelligence are itself and the intelligence that is its immediate cause or itself and the first cause.[164]

In short, from the multiple thoughts in each intelligence, there emanate the celestial sphere paralleling the intelligence and the next intelligence in the series. Alfarabi distinguishes two thoughts in each intelligence. Avicenna's main philosophical works distinguish three, the first being the source of the body of the sphere moved by the intelligence, the second, the source of the sphere's soul, and the third, the source of the next intelligence in the series. Ghazali's account of the views of the philosophers ascribes two thoughts to each intelligence, and his critique of what he calls Aristotle's views ascribes three.

Maimonides could have learned the proposition that from a simple thing only one simple thing can emanate necessarily from either Avicenna or Ghazali. He could have learned that each intelligence has two—rather than three—objects of thoughts from Alfarabi or from Ghazali's account of the views of the philosophers. He could have noticed that Alfarabi, after setting

[162] Avicenna, *Shifā': Ilāhiyyāt*, 331 (= id., *Najāt*, 277). Avicenna's *Ishārāt* distinguishes only two objects of thought in the intelligence—apparently in each intelligence—namely, the first cause and itself, whereupon Avicenna adds: 'It may be' that the second of the two thoughts is subdivided into two as well. See Avicenna, *Al-ishārāt wa-al-tanbīhāt*, 174.

[163] Ghazali, *Maqāṣid al-falāsifa*, 219–20. See the comment concerning Avicenna's *Ishārāt* in the previous note.

[164] Shahrastani, who lived and was active about half a century before Maimonides, also writes that Aristotle distinguished two aspects in the first intelligence, but he identifies the first intelligence as the 'active intellect'. See *Al-milal wa-al-niḥal*, 316; French trans.: *Livre des religions et des sectes*, 292–3. If the statement came to Maimonides' attention, he would have given it little credence, since any philosopher worth his salt would know that the active intellect is the *last* stage in the hierarchy of incorporeal intelligences, the stage that emanates from the intelligence associated with the sphere of the moon.

forth his theory of emanation in the *Risāla fī al-ʿaql*, writes that he had been expounding the sense of the term *intellect* in Aristotle's *Metaphysics* 12. Alternatively, Maimonides could have understood that when Ghazali writes in the *Maqāṣid al-falāsifa* that he was reporting the views of the philosophers, he meant the views of Aristotle and his school. The failure of both Alfarabi and Ghazali to specify what the second and subsequent intelligences have as their objects of thought—whether themselves and their ultimate cause or themselves and the intelligence immediately above them in the hierarchy—could be reflected in Maimonides' leaving the matter open and having Aristotle maintain that each intelligence has 'itself and something else' as objects of thought. Of the possible sources that could have misled Maimonides into thinking he was conveying the authentic position of Aristotle, Ghazali's account of the views of the philosophers would seem to be the best match.

Such are the possibilities, but this much is sure: neither the 'proposition agreed upon by Aristotle and all those who philosophized that from a simple [non-composite] thing there can proceed in a necessary manner only one simple [non-composite] thing' nor the explanation of the way complexity evolves out of the non-composite first cause is remotely Aristotelian.

The winding path through which Maimonides' references to metaphysics have led us has a clear-cut outcome: Maimonides names Aristotle and his *Metaphysics* as the source, or implies that they are the source, of a full complement of propositions wholly alien to Aristotle. He attributes to Aristotle the concept of corporeal form. His list of propositions supposedly found in the books of *Physics* and *Metaphysics* and demonstrated by Aristotle and the peripatetics includes definitions of the *possibly existent by virtue of itself* and the *necessarily existent by virtue of itself*, together with an analysis of what *necessarily existent by virtue of itself* entails. He asserts: it is 'well-known', 'clear', and 'necessary' that existence is an accident attached to existent objects that have a cause, and 'it has been made clear in the *Metaphysics*'—although, possibly: 'in metaphysics'—that when an object is one or objects are many, an accident of unity or of multiplicity is attached to them. He ascribes to Aristotle the theses that the first cause transcends the movers of the spheres; that the first cause brings the incorporeal intelligences into existence from all eternity through a process of emanation; that goodness emanates from the first cause; that the celestial spheres rotate from a desire to render themselves as similar as possible to their incorporeal causes; that goodness emanates from celestial motion. He has Aristotle address the question of what differentiates the incorporeal intelligences from the first cause and from one another. He burdens Aristotle with the proposition that only one non-composite being can proceed in a necessary manner from another non-composite being and then has him address the riddle of the emergence of multiplicity out of absolute simplicity. He attributes to Aristotle the solution that multiple thoughts in the intelligences give rise to multiple products. None of it is authentically Aristotelian.

As far as the factors responsible for celestial motion are concerned, Maimonides draws to a large extent from the *Principles of the Universe*. Otherwise, it is metaphysical theories of Alfarabi and Avicenna that he takes as genuinely Aristotelian. There is more than one indication that he learned at least some of those theories through Ghazali.

Just where he encountered the 'verbatim statement of Aristotle's' to the effect that 'matter does not move itself'[165] is uncertain. Wherever he got it, it is an isolated detail, far outweighed by the un-Aristotelian metaphysical propositions that he attributes to Aristotle. The contrast with Avicenna, Averroes, and Thomas Aquinas, Maimonides' Muslim and Christian peers, is instructive. Each of the three grappled with Aristotle's *Metaphysics* line by line. Maimonides chooses short cuts, as we saw him do in his discussion of philosophical ethics during his rabbinic period. He relies on secondary works rather than on Aristotle's *Metaphysics* itself and unwittingly substitutes the metaphysics of the Arabic Aristotelians for that of Aristotle.

When our findings concerning Maimonides' references to Aristotle's *Metaphysics* are added to what we found regarding his familiarity with other works of Aristotle, the result is as follows: there is solid evidence that when he wrote the *Moreh nevukhim*, he was acquainted with Aristotle's *Physics*, *On the Heavens*, *Nicomachean Ethics*, and the trilogy of biological works making up *On Animals*. He refers to a statement made by Aristotle in the *Rhetoric*, and what he represents Aristotle as saying there is similar to, although not identical with, a statement found in the Aristotelian work. He may therefore have read the *Rhetoric*. He apparently owned, and he once appears to quote from, *On Plants*, a work carrying Aristotle's name but actually composed by Nicolaus of Damascus; if Aristotle ever wrote a work on the subject of plants, it has been lost. At an earlier stage of his career, in his *Commentary on the Mishnah*, he demonstrated a familiarity with the Arabic recension of *Problemata physica*, a Greek work erroneously attributed to Aristotle.

He quotes a passage from Aristotle's *Topics* and in the same breath repeats observations on the passage from Alfarabi's commentary on the *Topics*; in the context where Alfarabi made those observations, the Aristotelian passage is

[165] Above, §2.

reproduced in full. Maimonides may well be quoting through the medium of Alfarabi and not directly from Aristotle.

He once refers to what is 'demonstrated in *meteorology*' or 'in the *meteorology*'. If he is referring to a book, and not the science, the book was not Aristotle's *Meteorology*, since that work is not known to have been translated into Arabic. Its place was taken by a composition that represents itself as a translation of the *Meteorology* by Yaḥyā ibn Biṭrīq but is actually Yaḥyā's translation of a reworking of the Aristotelian work or perhaps his own reworking of it. In the chapter of the *Moreh nevukhim* where the reference to meteorology occurs, Maimonides embraces positions that run counter both to the genuine Aristotelian *Meteorology* and to Yaḥyā's version. There are consequently no grounds for thinking that he ever saw Yaḥyā's text and good grounds for thinking that he did not. Meteorology was a subject of considerable interest in medieval Arabic circles, and a number of treatments of the subject that were more readable than Ibn Biṭrīq's circulated. An examination of them fails to suggest a link between any of them and the *Moreh nevukhim*.

No sign of Aristotle's *On Generation and Destruction* or *De anima* is detectable in the *Moreh nevukhim*. The absence of the *De anima* is telling, since there are places where it offered much that should have been of interest to Maimonides. When Maimonides ostensibly quotes from the *De sensu* in his medical writings, the purported quotations come from somewhere other than the *De sensu* itself. He must unwittingly be quoting the remark of a medical writer who wanted to make a point about proper medical training and adduced the *De sensu* for support. Nothing else in Maimonides' writings suggests a familiarity with any of the opuscula making up the *Parva naturalia*.

Especially eye-opening is the full complement of metaphysical propositions that he attributes to Aristotle but that are wholly un-Aristotelian.

In his rabbinic period, Maimonides exhibited no evidence of having read a single authentic line of Aristotle's. In his later period, he did study a fair number of Aristotle's works. But if credence is given solely to actual evidence and not to a priori conjectures, the conclusion must be that his reading extended to only part of the available Aristotelian corpus and did not include key works. Maimonides eked out the genuine Aristotelian works that he read with material from the Arabic Aristotelians, the *Principles of the Universe*, and other, unidentifiable, sources.

3. The Commentators on Aristotle

Aristotle makes difficult reading, and, for good measure, the medieval Arabic translations overlay the difficulty with their own patina of obscurity. About a decade after Maimonides completed the *Moreh nevukhim*, he accordingly advised Samuel Ibn Tibbon to 'read the books of Aristotle only in their interpretations, namely, the interpretation of Alexander [of Aphrodisias], the interpretation of Themistius, or the commentary of Averroes'.[166] The original Arabic letter to Ibn Tibbon is lost, and we are thrown back on medieval Hebrew translations. As a consequence, it is uncertain what lies behind the Hebrew terms rendered here as 'interpretation' (*perush*) and 'commentary' (*be'ur*) and what Maimonides wants to bring out by differentiating between them. It is equally unclear what he means by saying '*only* in their interpretations'. By the interpretations of Alexander and Themistius he could mean compositions in which the two rework Aristotelian texts rather than strictly commenting on them; he could be recommending commentaries and reworkings of the Aristotelian texts as legitimate substitutes for the difficult texts themselves.

However that may be, Maimonides' insistence that Aristotle should be read in conjunction with the three named commentators is unambiguous. The importance of commentaries on Aristotle is also underlined in the *Moreh nevukhim* when Maimonides lists the philosophical propositions that he planned to use in his proofs of the existence of God. Twenty-five of the propositions, he writes, are demonstrated by 'Aristotle and the peripatetics coming after him'. Again: they are demonstrated either in the 'book of the *Physics* and its commentaries' or in the 'book of the *Metaphysics* and its commentary'.[167]

The efforts of a half-dozen or so Greek commentators on Aristotle were translated into Arabic in the Middle Ages,[168] and the most prominent of the commentators were Alexander of Aphrodisias and Themistius, the two whom Maimonides recommends to Ibn Tibbon. Given Maimonides' approbation, one might easily take for granted that Alexander and Themistius were the peripatetics coming after Aristotle—or the chief among them—who helped demonstrate the twenty-five propositions and whom Maimonides had in mind when speaking of commentaries on the *Physics* and a commentary on the *Metaphysics*. The two men are, in fact, the sole ancient commentators on Aristotle named in the *Moreh nevukhim*. A fair number of aids for understanding Aristotle from the pens of both were available in Arabic.

166 Marx, 'Texts by and about Maimonides', 378.

167 *MN* ii, introd. (4*b*).

168 See Steinschneider, *Die arabischen Uebersetzungen aus dem Griechischen*, index, entries on Alexander, Themistius, Syrianus, Ammonius, Philoponus, Simplicius, Olympiodorus.

Translations had been made of Alexander's reworking of Aristotle's *De anima* and of a piece on intellect—known as *De intellectu*—written more or less in an Aristotelian spirit and ascribed to Alexander, although it may not be an authentic composition of his.[169] Much of Alexander's commentary on Aristotle's *Physics* was translated into Arabic and was used by Averroes, a contemporary of Maimonides and a fellow Cordovan;[170] no copy of the translation has been preserved. Averroes further reports in his *Long Commentary on Aristotle's Metaphysics* that he consulted several commentaries on the *Metaphysics*, that they all restricted themselves to Book 12 (*lamda*), that Alexander's was among them, and that his copy of Alexander's commentary broke off about two-thirds of the way through Book 12.[171] He provides a number of quotations from what he knew as Alexander's commentary.

There also exists a commentary in Greek covering the entire *Metaphysics* and attributed to Alexander, but none of it is known to have been translated into Arabic. The scholarly consensus recognizes only the first five books of the Greek text as Alexander's work. Book 12 of the Greek does not match Averroes' quotations from what he cites as Alexander's commentary on *Metaphysics* 12, and the text Averroes had may very well be the authentic one.[172]

Maimonides could, then, have had access to Alexander's *De anima*, the *De intellectu* attributed to Alexander, most of Alexander's commentary on the *Physics*, and what may well be the authentic commentary of Alexander on *Metaphysics* 12.

Two additional compositions preserved solely in Arabic and attributed to Alexander deserve special attention: the *Principles of the Universe*, which we have already encountered, and a treatise entitled *On Providence* (*Fī al-ʿināya*). Both revolve around Aristotle, but neither is a commentary. Each instead undertakes to clarify Aristotle's position on a particular issue—the factors producing the motions of the celestial spheres in the former, and divine providence in the latter.

The *Principles of the Universe* is extant in two medieval Arabic translations, and a manuscript of one of them informs us that it was made from a Syriac version, which would probably go back to a lost Greek original. As noted earlier,

169 Arabic translation of Alexander's reworking of the *De anima*: Steinschneider, *Die hebräischen Uebersetzungen des Mittelalters*, 151–2. Arabic translation of *De intellectu*: Alexander(?), *Texte arabe du peri nou*, and Badawi, *Commentaires sur Aristote perdus en grec*, 31–42.

170 Peters, *Aristoteles Arabus*, 30, 34; J. Freudenthal, *Die durch Averroes erhaltenen Fragmente*, 9 n. 1.

171 Averroes, *Tafsīr mā baʿd al-ṭabīʿa*, 1393.

172 J. Freudenthal, *Die durch Averroes erhaltenen Fragmente*, 4–8; Alexander of Aphrodisias, *On Aristotle Metaphysics 1*, introd., 3. J. Freudenthal (ibid. 41–52) presents reasons for recognizing the commentary used by Averroes as the authentic commentary of Alexander.

the book is cited by Avicenna. It is cited a few times by Averroes, and one of the passages he quotes is not, as far as I could see, found in the printed edition of either of the two translations;[173] that would suggest that the book may have existed not just in different translations but in different recensions as well. The *Principles of the Universe*, as preserved, is repetitive and, though by no means profound, occasionally impenetrable and incoherent. Even when allowance is made for inept translators and scribes, it can hardly be considered a product of one of Alexander's better days—if he is indeed the author. If Alexander did indeed write both the *Principles*, which draws heavily upon *Metaphysics* 12, and the Arabic commentary on *Metaphysics* 12 carrying his name and known through Averroes, they are different modes in which he treated the same Aristotelian text.

On Providence, the other composition, is extant in two Arabic manuscripts and is attributed to Alexander in both; it was recently published with an annotated French translation. Evidence that it originally circulated in Greek is furnished by a few passages quoted in that language by Cyril of Alexandria, who states that he extracted them from Alexander's *On Providence* (*Peri pronoías*).[174]

As for Themistius, his paraphrases of Aristotle's *Physics*, *On the Heavens*, *De anima*, and *Metaphysics* 12 were translated into Arabic. Averroes used the paraphrase of the *Physics*, the Arabic translation of which has been lost.[175] When he refers to Alexander's commentary (*tafsīr*) on *Metaphysics* 12, he also mentions Themistius' paraphrase (*talkhīṣ*) of Book 12.

The question that poses itself is what the evidence, when weighed without preconceptions, tells us about Maimonides' knowledge of Alexander and Themistius.

Maimonides refers to Themistius once in the *Moreh nevukhim* and merely credits him with the platitude that 'what exists does not conform to [men's] opinions; rather correct opinions conform to what exists'.[176] Alexander is cited nine times, and Maimonides names a pair of compositions written, or purportedly written, by him. They are: the *Principles of the Universe*, which he, like other writers of his day and the consensus of scholars today, accepts as an authentic work of Alexander's; and a work that he calls 'Alexander of Aphrodisias' treatise *On Governance* [*Fī al-tadbīr*]', in other words, on the governance of the sublunar world by higher beings.

173 Averroes, *Tahāfut al-tahāfut*, 495.

174 Alexander, *Traité de la providence*. The fragments in Cyril of Alexandria are given on pp. 54–61.

175 Themistius, 'Paraphrase of the *Physics*'; id., 'Paraphrase of *On the Heavens*' (since Maimonides' quotations from Aristotle's *De caelo* betray no echoes of Themistius' paraphrase, it is highly unlikely that he used it as a substitution for the Aristotelian text itself); id., *An Arabic Translation of Themistius, Commentary on Aristoteles 'De anima'*; id., 'Paraphrase of *Metaphysics*', 12.

176 *MN* i. 71 (95*b*).

On Governance is named twice in Maimonides' discussion of divine providence. In both instances, what Maimonides adduces from *On Governance* corresponds to statements in the Arabic treatise known as *On Providence*, and *On Providence* is also the source of statements that he adduces in Alexander's name without mentioning the book from which he is borrowing.

The picture is augmented and complicated by a medieval Arabic composition that is entitled, literally, 'Alexander of Aphrodisias' treatise *On Spherical Governances* [*Fī tadbīrāt al-falakiyya*]', or, put less awkwardly: *On the Spheres' Governance* [*of the Lower World*].[177] *On the Spheres' Governance* parallels much of *On Providence*, although with different wording. It opens with a sentence that generates little confidence in the attribution to Alexander; the sentence reads: 'He [that is, Alexander] said: the philosopher [*ḥakīm*; presumably Aristotle] stated in his book entitled the *Book of Governance* [*al-tadbīr*]' that the celestial bodies are the cause of what occurs in the lower world.[178] No such composition of Aristotle's, of course, exists.

The book that Maimonides cites as *On Governance* is either the treatise *On Providence* as it has been published or an alternative version; the existence of an alternative recension is corroborated by the circumstance that not all of Cyril of Alexandria's Greek citations from *On Providence* appear in the preserved Arabic text.[179] What Maimonides calls *On Governance* is plainly not the same as *On the Spheres' Governance*, despite the similarity in titles. The latter contains neither the statements quoted by him from *On Governance* nor the other statements that he adduces from Alexander without naming a book and that are found in *On Providence*.

Every time that Maimonides cites Alexander he draws from either the *Principles of the Universe* or *On Providence*.

He refers to the *Principles of the Universe* by name only once, in the sentence introducing Aristotle's supposed proofs for the existence of the incorporeal movers of the spheres. But additional instances where he cites Alexander can be traced to the *Principles*.

After the *Principles* opens by conceding that there can be no strict demonstration concerning the first principles of the universe and celestial motion, it submits that what it would say about the first principles is consistent with, and accounts for, recognized facts about the universe. Later, as the book approaches its conclusion, it shows how the eternal celestial spheres endow the sublunar world of generation and destruction with permanence and eternal existence. It

177 Ruland, *Die arabischen Fassungen von zwei Schriften des Alexander von Aphrodisias*.

178 Ibid. 33–4. The philosopher's book entitled the *Book of Governance* is mentioned again on pp. 51–2.

179 Alexander, *Traité de la providence*, editor's introd., 55, 59.

then recommends its findings: the governance (*siyāsa*) of the universe has been explained 'in accordance with what we extracted from the divine Aristotle'. Aristotle's 'view' is superior to all other views concerning God and the heavens and it alone accounts adequately for 'the continuity and order [*niẓām*] of things brought into existence by' them. What Aristotle writes may contain a 'slight difficulty' and 'slight doubts' (*shukūk yasīra*), and further study may be warranted. But 'to find any theoretical view free of doubts is difficult'. Aristotle's treatment of the subject is therefore the very best that can be hoped for.

In an aside, the *Principles* comments on the 'cause of the difference [*ikhtilāf*] and opposition [*taḍādd*] of views' among thinkers. There are several factors, namely: 'love of being on top and prevailing, which hinders [one from] discerning the truth'; 'the difficulty of the matters treated, their subtlety, and their abstruseness'; and 'the weakness of our nature, and our inability to know the true character of things'.[180]

Returning to the *Moreh nevukhim*, we find Maimonides observing in an early chapter: 'Alexander of Aphrodisias stated that the causes of difference [of opinion; *ikhtilāf*] concerning matters are three: one, love of being on top and of prevailing, which hinders man from knowing the truth . . . the second, the subtlety of the matter known . . . its abstruseness, and the difficulty of knowing it; and the third, the ignorance of him who seeks to know.' Maimonides makes the same observation in the same words in one of his medical works.[181] He has lightly paraphrased the *Principles of the Universe*.

When introducing Aristotle's 'views' regarding the causes of the motion of the spheres, Maimonides expresses himself as follows: although Aristotle's views on the subject are hypotheses for which demonstration is not possible, they contain 'fewer doubts' (*aqall . . . shukūkan*) than other views on the subject and they best form a consistent 'order [*niẓām*], as Alexander states in *The Principles of the Universe*'.[182] The notion that a strict demonstration of the existence of the incorporeal movers of the spheres is impossible is clearly adapted from the statement in the *Principles of the Universe* about the impossibility of demonstrations concerning 'first principles'. The assertion that Aristotle's views contain 'fewer doubts' than the views of other thinkers does not reproduce the exact language of the preserved version of the *Principles*, which acknowledges rather that Aristotle's view may contain 'slight doubts'. Nevertheless, the expression 'fewer doubts' is not of Maimonides' making. That is corroborated by Averroes' *Long Commentary on the Metaphysics*.

In the course of commenting on *Metaphysics* 12, Averroes takes up a certain

180 Alexander(?), *Principles of the Universe*, §§1–2 (pp. 143–51).

181 *MN* i. 31 (34*b*); Maimonides, *On Asthma*, 110; see apparatus.

182 *MN* ii. 3.

knotty philosophical problem unrelated to the issue occupying Maimonides. After analysing several proposed solutions, he writes that his own solution would rest on premisses and principles drawn from Aristotle. For he 'had found Aristotle's system [*madhhab*] to be, as Alexander states, the one with fewer doubts [*aqall . . . shukūkan*], the one that most strongly reflects reality . . . and the one that best avoids self-contradiction [*tanāquḍ*]'.[183] Averroes does not name the work of Alexander's to which he refers, and since he quotes Alexander's commentary on *Metaphysics* 12 a number of times in his *Long Commentary*, it would be natural to assume that he is drawing from Alexander's commentary here too. Yet the assertion that Alexander characterized Aristotle's *system* as the one with *fewer doubts* uncannily echoes Maimonides' assertion that the *Principles of the Universe* characterized Aristotle's *views* as those containing *fewer doubts*. And the notion that Aristotle's system most strongly reflects reality is fully in the spirit of the *Principles*. Averroes, like Maimonides, appears to be citing the *Principles of the Universe* in a version that had the expression *fewer doubts*.

The rule that where demonstration is not possible, philosophical questions can be settled by ascertaining which position involves fewer doubts is brought to bear by Maimonides when he takes up a pivotal issue in the *Moreh nevukhim*. The rule supplies the underpinning for his proofs of the creation of the world.

As we saw, he marshals passages from Aristotle's *Physics*, *De caelo*, and *Topics* to establish for himself and his readers that Aristotle, the greatest of all philosophers, not only did not demonstrate the eternity of the world but also acknowledged the impossibility of doing so. Maimonides writes that Aristotle offered 'arguments and proofs' for eternity which he—Aristotle—considered to be plausible and well adapted to 'sway the soul'. Those arguments and proofs, 'so Alexander contends, contain fewer doubts [*aqall shukūkan*]';[184] Maimonides could here be alluding to the section of the *Principles* that describes the eternal celestial spheres as endowing the sublunar world with eternal existence and that endorses Aristotle's views even though they may involve a 'slight difficulty' and 'slight doubts'.

If Aristotle based his advocacy of the eternity of the world on arguments and proofs, as distinct from demonstrations, and indeed acknowledged as much, the tables can be turned. Aristotle's position can be countered and outweighed should it be shown that the arguments and proofs for the contrary position are the ones subject to fewer doubts.

Maimonides' own proofs for creation play on what he contends are insurmountable difficulties in the hypothesis of the world's eternity. As he nears his

[183] Averroes, *Tafsīr mā baʿd al-ṭabīʿa*, 1497.

[184] *MN* ii. 15 (32*a*).

conclusion, he acknowledges that he might be criticized for dwelling on doubts besetting the opposing view rather than directly proving creation. In answer to potential critics, he cites Alexander: 'Alexander has explained that when philosophical issues do not lend themselves to demonstration', the doubts affecting the alternatives have to be weighed, and the thesis 'with fewer doubts [*aqalluhā shukūkan*] believed'.[185] Such, Maimonides avers, was his procedure, and the arguments he developed establish that the doubts affecting the thesis of eternity substantially outweigh those affecting the thesis of creation. By Alexander's rule, creation prevails.

Maimonides, in sum, cites the *Principles of the Universe* by name when establishing a rationale for proofs of the existence of the incorporeal intelligences, which move the celestial spheres. Although he does not expressly say so, the *Principles* is the source not only for the rationale, but also for most of the content of what he describes as Aristotle's proofs for the existence of the intelligences. It is his source when he cites Alexander on the causes of disagreements among thinkers. And the critical rule about fewer doubts, which Maimonides like Averroes ascribes to Alexander and which he adduces to validate his proofs for the creation of the world, derives from the *Principles*.

The other work attributed to Alexander and used by Maimonides is the composition that he calls *On Governance*. As already noted, it is identical with, or a recension of, Alexander's *On Providence*.

On Providence has as its main subject Aristotle's 'view' on providence, or, to be more precise, since Aristotle never treats providence formally, the position implied in his writings. Before getting to Aristotle, Alexander—if he is accepted as the author—sets the stage by outlining and refuting two unacceptable extremes. At one end of the spectrum, 'Leucippus and Democritus' as well as 'Epicurus and those who philosophized in accordance with his view' maintained that 'God is outside' the universe, and 'everything . . . generated naturally comes about spontaneously and by chance' (*'an al-ittifāq*; *bi-ḥasab mā yattafiq*) through the combining (*ijtimā'*; *ta'līf*) of atoms. At the other end stand thinkers who maintain that nothing in the world escapes divine providence, nothing falls outside of God's knowledge and will, and the gods govern (*mudabbir*) everything. 'Some assert that Plato was of this opinion. . . . Zeno of Citium and the Stoics clearly were.'[186]

On Providence presents a number of considerations for and against the two extremes and it has a liking for a certain style of argumentation. It first puts the argumentation in the mouth of the party maintaining that the gods exercise

[185] *MN* ii. 22 (50*a*). *MN* i. 71 (96*a*) does not seem wholly consistent with what Maimonides writes here.

[186] Alexander, *Traité de la providence*, Arabic text, 1–3; French trans., 85–90.

providence over everything in the universe. Here the thinking is: if the gods did not exercise providence over the world, the reason would be that they are unable to do so, do not want to, or both. To say that the gods are unable to care for the world would be to depict them as weak, and to say that they are unwilling would be to depict them as envious (Arab.: *ḥāsid*), evil, and corrupt. Inasmuch as both alternatives are untenable, the conclusion drawn by the party in question was that the gods exercise thoroughgoing providence.[187]

In a refutation of that very thesis, *On Providence* inverts the argument. It exclaims: on the assumption that divine providence embraces the human species, 'Would that I knew! Are the gods incapable and unwilling to make men good? Or are they capable and unwilling? Or are they willing and incapable?' None of the alternatives is tenable. Yet if the gods were concerned with mankind, able to make men good, and willing to do so, no one would be evil, which is scarcely the case. The assumption that the gods exercise providence over mankind—that it is a fitting and proper activity for them—must therefore be rejected as foolish and baseless.[188] The same style of argumentation is employed at yet another spot with another twist,[189] but that instance is not relevant for us.

After setting forth and rejecting the two extremes—the complete absence of providence and thoroughgoing providence—*On Providence* brings Aristotle on to the stage. The section where Aristotle's position is initially spelled out is difficult to follow; either the writing or the translation is poor. The details, however, are not important. Stated broadly, Aristotle is represented as having held that God or the gods exercise providence, but that their providence extends to individual beings in the sublunar world only incidentally: Aristotle held that 'by first intention' providence operates down 'to [*ilā naḥw*] the sphere of the moon'; and the 'divine body', where providence is focused, is 'the entire body that terminates at [*yantahī ʿinda*] the sphere of the moon'. Yet, although focused on the celestial region, providence does, in Aristotle's view, reach 'things below the sphere of the moon as well; for it is he who asserts that man is generated by man and the sun'. By according the sun a role in the generation of human beings, Aristotle in effect recognized a degree of providence within the sublunar region.[190]

On Providence rambles a little and then completes the theme that a modicum

187 Ibid., Arabic text, 2–3; trans., 88–9.

188 Ibid., Arabic text, 9; trans., 101. The argument is not entirely clear and there are other ways of reading it, but the conclusion the author wishes to draw is clear.

189 Ibid., Arabic text, 8; trans., 99–100.

190 Ibid., Arabic text, 15; trans., 113–14. For the proposition that man is generated by man and the sun, see Aristotle, *Physics*, 2.2, 194b, 13.

of providence reaches the sublunar world: The celestial spheres exercise providence in the sublunar world by participating in the generation of living beings and by doing something more 'through the mediacy of nature'. Just as a parent provides his offspring with what is necessary (*ḍarūrī*) for life, nature provides living beings with what is necessary for their nourishment (*ghidhā'*).[191]

Maimonides opens his discussion of eternity and creation in the *Moreh nevukhim* by listing the positions that had been taken on the issue. He gives one position short shrift. Since he demonstrated the existence of God conclusively, nothing would be gained by taking into account those 'who do not recognize the existence of God', who 'suppose that things come into existence and are destroyed by the chance [*bi-ḥasab al-ittifāq*] combination [*ijtimāʿ*] and separation' of material particles, and who deny that anything 'governs [*mudabbir*] and regulates [*nāẓim*] existence'. The proponents of the position in question are 'Epicurus, his school, and their like, as Alexander reports'.[192]

When Maimonides turns to the subject of divine providence, he again has something to say about Epicurus. He writes: the first view on providence is that it does not exist anywhere in the universe, that everything in the universe occurs by chance (*bi-al-ittifāq*), and that 'nothing regulates [*nāẓim*], governs [*mudabbir*], or exercises providence'. 'Such is Epicurus' view', and Epicurus 'further affirms [the existence of] atoms and maintains that they mix together by chance'. 'Aristotle demonstrated the falsity of this view and [showed] that things do not come into existence by chance but have an agent who regulates and governs [them].'[193]

Maimonides is obviously borrowing the language of *On Providence* both when he cites Alexander in giving Epicurus' position on the creation-eternity issue and when he reports Epicurus' position on providence without mentioning Alexander. His identifying of 'Epicurus, his school, and their like' as advocates of the position that everything occurs by chance clearly reflects *On Providence*'s attribution of that position to Leucippus, Democritus, Epicurus, and 'those who philosophized in accordance with his view'. Leucippus and Democritus, whom Maimonides does not mention, would have been mere names for him.

Before actually entering into his discussion of divine providence, Maimonides takes up an 'outrage' perpetrated by philosophers in connection with divine knowledge. They reasoned that God either knows what happens to

[191] Alexander, *Traité de la providence*, Arabic text, 22; trans., 126.

[192] *MN* ii. 13 (29*a*). At *MN* ii. 32, Maimonides omits Epicurus from his discussion of prophecy as well on the same grounds.

[193] *MN* iii. 17 (31*b*). Aristotle rejects atomism in the *Physics*, *On the Heavens*, and *On Generation and Destruction*. See Zeller, *Die Philosophie der Griechen*, ii. 2, 410–11.

individual human beings or does not. On the assumption that He knows what happens, there are three possibilities. God either institutes order (*niẓām*) and governance (*tadbīr*) over events, so that justice reigns and men receive their just deserts; He is powerless to do so; or He is unwilling to. Instances where the wicked thrive and the good suffer exclude the first possibility. To suppose that God is powerless is out of the question. To suppose that He is able to regulate events but is unwilling to, would impute to Him disdain or envy (*ḥasad*) towards His creatures, qualities that are incompatible with the divine. Since the philosophers in question rejected all the alternatives growing out of the thesis that God knows what happens to individuals, they drew the deplorable conclusion that God does not have such knowledge. The argument and the error into which the philosophers fell are, Maimonides writes, spelled out 'in Alexander of Aphrodisias' treatise *On Governance*'.

He adds that not all philosophers followed suit: 'Some philosophers believe what we believe, namely that God knows everything, and nothing is in any way hidden from Him. These were great personages prior to Aristotle, whom Alexander refers to in his aforementioned treatise.' Alexander 'rejects their view . . . particularly . . . because of the evils that affect good men and the good that accrues to evil men'.[194]

The style of reasoning ascribed here to Alexander's treatise *On Governance* —God either knows or does not know; if He knows, and so on—follows the form of the argument deployed by the treatise *On Providence* against the thesis of thoroughgoing providence. God's knowledge is, however, now brought into the mix; what cannot be squared with God's knowledge of human affairs is the thriving of the wicked and suffering of the just, and the conclusion purportedly drawn by the philosophers is that God does not have *knowledge* of events in the world. Maimonides has either extrapolated from what *On Providence* says or once again used a slightly different recension. His reference to pre-Aristotelian personages who affirmed divine omniscience reflects the statement in *On Providence* concerning Zeno, the Stoics, and, 'some assert', Plato. Zeno would, like Leucippus and Democritus, have been a mere name for Maimonides, and he appears to date him prior to Aristotle.

Maimonides also cites Alexander, now without naming the book from which he is borrowing, when delineating Aristotle's position on providence. He writes: 'Alexander stated verbatim: Aristotle's view is that God's providence terminates at [*intahat 'inda*] the sphere of the moon', yet a degree of providence extends to the sublunar region inasmuch as each species of animals is furnished with the faculties it needs in order to survive.[195] Although

194 *MN* iii. 16.

195 *MN* iii. 17 (32*a*).

On Providence does not express itself in just those words, the expression 'terminates at the sphere of the moon' is too distinctive to be accidental: Maimonides' report weaves together statements in *On Providence* to the effect that *providence* operates down 'to the sphere of the moon' and that the *divine body* 'terminates at the sphere of the moon'.[196]

A few pages later, Maimonides writes that Aristotle recognized providence in the supplying of 'necessary nourishment' (*ghidhā' ḍarūrī*) to each species, and that Alexander conveyed as much 'in the name of ['*an*] Aristotle'.[197] The terminology of *On Providence* is again unmistakable.

Whenever Maimonides names Alexander in the *Moreh nevukhim*, his source is thus either *The Principles of the Universe* or *On Providence*. Both works serve him at critical junctures: the former provides a proof of the existence of the incorporeal intelligences and supplies the rule of *fewer doubts* that underpins his proofs of creation. The latter provides an overview of positions on providence, with Epicurus at one end of the spectrum, Plato and the Stoics at the other, and Aristotle in the middle. Neither work is a commentary on Aristotle. Hence neither properly qualifies as one of the commentaries on the *Physics* or the commentary on the *Metaphysics* that, Maimonides said, help demonstrate the philosophical propositions he employed in his proofs of the existence of God.

There is a single item in the *Moreh nevukhim* that suggests a possible acquaintance with a true commentary of Alexander on Aristotle or one of Themistius' paraphrases of Aristotle. It is a demonstration of the existence of God that Maimonides describes as a proof of 'theirs', in other words, of the philosophers. Gomperz, in his history of Greek philosophy, dubbed it the argument from logical symmetry.[198]

'Aristotle', Maimonides writes, prefaced the proof with a premiss: 'when something exists that is composed of two things and one of the two things exists by itself [*'alā infirādihi*] apart from the composite, then the existence of the other apart from the composite follows necessarily'; for if the existence of the components were such 'that it requires them to exist only together, like matter and natural form', that is to say, corporeal form,[199] 'neither of the two would ever exist without the other'. An illustration is oxymel (*sakanjabīn*), vinegar mixed with honey. 'Since oxymel exists, and honey moreover exists by itself [*waḥdahu*], the existence of vinegar by itself follows necessarily.'

196 I did not find either expression in the version entitled *On the Spheres' Governance*.

197 *MN* iii. 17 (37*a*).

198 Gomperz, *Greek Thinkers*, iv. 218–19.

199 See above, §2.

Maimonides continues: after establishing the premiss, 'he', that is, Aristotle, 'stated: "We find many objects compounded of mover and moved, in other words, that move other objects and are moved by something other than themselves when they do so, as is clear in regard to the intermediate links in [the phenomenon of] motion. . . . We also find objects that are moved without moving anything else. . . . It follows necessarily [*ḍarūratan*]"' that the other component likewise exists by itself, that '"a mover exists which is absolutely unmoved. That is the first mover."'[200]

The argument ultimately goes back to a consideration advanced by Aristotle in Book 8 of the *Physics* not as a proof in its own right but as one of several steps forming one of several stages in the demonstration of the existence of a first unmoved mover. Aristotle states that 'there are three things' in the phenomenon of motion: what is moved, the mover, and that by which the mover causes what is moved to move; and this last is something that both is itself moved and moves another. Inasmuch as we actually observe the existence of what is moved without moving anything else as well as what both is moved and moves something else, the existence of what moves another without being moved 'stands to reason' (*awlā*).[201] A sentence in *Metaphysics* 12 intimates the same. After determining that the first heaven rotates eternally and something moves it, Aristotle writes: 'Since that which is moved and moves [another] is intermediate, there is something that moves and is not moved, being eternal, substance, and actuality.'[202]

Aristotle could be presupposing the general proposition about composites that Maimonides attributes to him but he reveals no hint of doing so. The illustrations offered by Maimonides—matter and corporeal form constituting a compound that cannot be dissolved, and oxymel, a compound that can be—are not taken from Aristotle; corporeal form is not even an Aristotelian concept. The principal occurrence of the argument, in the *Physics*, serves as just one step in a preliminary stage of the demonstration of an unmoved mover and makes no claim to being a demonstration in its own right. There, the argument only 'stands to reason'. Maimonides plainly has credited Aristotle with a good deal more than what he said.

The argument from logical symmetry is elevated into an explicit and formal demonstration of the existence of God in the *Principles of the Universe* attributed to Alexander, in Alexander's commentary on *Metaphysics* 12, and in Themistius' paraphrases of the *Physics* and *Metaphysics*. The formulations vary.

200 *MN* ii. 1 (2).

201 Aristotle, *Al-ṭabīʿa*, 848–9 (= id., *Physics*, 8.5, 256b, 14–24).

202 Aristotle, *Metaphysics*, 12.7, 1072a, 24–6, following Ross's Greek text.

The *Principles of the Universe* reasons: what is both moved and moves other things has two components: *being moved* and *moving another*. The component *being moved* is seen to exist apart from the component *moving another* in the case of objects that are moved without moving anything else. Hence the second component, *moving another*, must also sometimes exist apart. 'We must therefore posit first beings that move things without being moved.' It has thus been 'proved' that 'the first mover does not undergo motion'.[203] Themistius' paraphrase of *Metaphysics* 12 lays down the general proposition about composites: when something is 'composed of two things such that one of them can exist as self-subsistent and by itself [*mufrad*], then the other can likewise exist as self-subsistent and by itself'. Applying the rule to things that are moved and move others, Themistius arrives at the expected conclusion: there exists a 'mover that is not moved', that is free of matter, the 'substance [of which] is actuality', and that moves as an 'object of desire [*maʿshūq*]'.[204]

The formulations in Alexander's commentary on *Metaphysics* 12 and Themistius' paraphrase of the *Physics* are more pertinent. The Arabic translation of Alexander's commentary is, as already noted, preserved in part through quotations in Averroes' *Long Commentary on the Metaphysics*. Themistius' paraphrase of the *Physics* is reported to have been translated into Arabic in the Middle Ages, but the translation has not survived, and we have to go back to the Greek original.

Alexander's commentary on *Metaphysics* 12 explicates the sentence in the *Metaphysics* stating: 'Since that which is moved and moves [another] is intermediate, there is something that moves and is not moved.' The rationale, Alexander explains, is the general proposition that whenever something is 'composed of two things and one of the two can exist by itself [*mufrad*], then the other can also exist by itself—on the condition that one of the two things is not an accident and the other a substance'.[205] An example is 'honey drink', which is composed of honey and water. Since honey exists apart (*mufrad*) from water, water necessarily exists apart from honey. 'Once the premiss has been established for us and we find something that moves and is moved' and is hence an intermediate, as well as something that is moved without moving anything else, there plainly must (*wājib*) exist something that moves without being moved. 'This mover is free of potentiality and does not, in any respect, exist in matter.'[206]

[203] Alexander, *Principles of the Universe*, §§29–31.

[204] Themistius, 'Paraphrase of *Metaphysics* 12', 14–15.

[205] The exception forestalls a counter-example such as compounds of physical substance and colour. Physical substance—for instance, air—can exist without colour. Colour nevertheless cannot exist apart from physical substance.

[206] Averroes, *Tafsīr mā baʿd al-ṭabīʿa*, 1588–9.

Themistius' paraphrase of the *Physics* again lays down the proposition that whenever something is composed of two things and one of the two can exist by itself, the other can exist by itself as well. He illustrates with honey-wine: 'Since honey-wine is made of wine and honey, and honey can exist apart from wine, wine too exists apart from honey.' Applying the rule to moving objects and their movers, Themistius concludes: 'It is necessary . . . that the first mover is unmoved.'[207]

Maimonides' presentation of the argument obviously comes close to these last two formulations, which state the general rule about components and illustrate it with a honey compound. Although he ascribes the argument to Aristotle, we can picture him reading it in Alexander or Themistius, assuming that it derives from Aristotle, quoting it in Aristotle's name, and even expanding on it a little. Yet the example of oxymel, whereby he illustrates the rule, differs, albeit slightly, from the examples offered by Alexander and Themistius.

The only place outside the *Moreh nevukhim* where I have discovered the oxymel illustration is a short composition carrying Avicenna's name and entitled *On the Affirmation of* [*the Reality of*] *Prophecies*. It is concerned solely with prophecy, and the existence of God does not come up.

Whoever the author was, he prefaces his discussion of prophecy with a brief account of the stages through which the human intellect progresses and he prefaces that account with the familiar premiss: when something is composed of two factors and one of the two exists separately (*mufāriq*) from the other, then the second exists separately from the first. 'An example is oxymel [*sakanjabīn*], which is composed of vinegar and honey. Since vinegar exists without honey, honey exists without vinegar.' Another example is 'a statue that is composed of brass and the form [*ṣūra*] of a man. Since brass exists without the form of a man, the form exists without brass.'[208] After the author lays down the rule about compounds, he lets it dangle. He must have come upon it, liked it, thought that it in some way added to what he was going to say, and then neglected to explain how.

Oxymel as an illustration of divisible compounds is precisely the illustration that Maimonides offers. The second illustration of a divisible compound, a statue composed of brass and the form of a man, is an odd inversion of Maimonides' illustration of *indivisible* compounds by matter and natural—that is to say, corporeal—form. Unfortunately, the author of *On the Affirmation of Prophecies*, scarcely someone of Avicenna's stature, has blundered. For what is

207 Themistius, 'Paraphrase of *Physics*', 223.

208 Avicenna (misattributed), *Fī ithbāt al-nubuwwāt*, 42; English trans.: *Medieval Political Philosophy*, 113.

present in brass is not the human form in either a Platonic or an Aristotelian sense but rather the human *shape*, and shapes plainly do not exist apart from the matter in which they are impressed.

The similarity between the illustration of matter and natural form in Maimonides and that of a statue composed of brass and the human form is probably just a coincidence. It is conceivable, though, that behind Maimonides and the author of *On the Affirmation of Prophecies* there was a common Arabic source containing the illustration of oxymel and some sort of illustration involving matter and form, and that Maimonides and the author of *On the Affirmation of Prophecies* read the matter-form illustration differently. Wherever the truth lies, *On the Affirmation of Prophecies* testifies that the underlying premiss of the argument from logical symmetry circulated in Arabic together with the illustration of oxymel.

The demonstration of the existence of God from logical symmetry, which Maimonides attributes to Aristotle, came to him from a writer other than Aristotle. It could be an adaptation of the argument in Alexander's commentary on *Metaphysics* 12 or the one in Themistius' paraphrase of the *Physics*, but there is insufficient evidence to conclude that it is either. There is accordingly a possibility that Maimonides borrowed an item from Alexander's commentary on the *Metaphysics* or from Themistius. In an earlier chapter we saw that an important detail in Maimonides' *Commentary on the Mishnah* concerning the immortality of the human intellect could possibly come from one of Alexander's compositions that rework Aristotle's *De anima*.[209] The only works carrying Alexander's name that Maimonides definitely did read and use are the *Principles of the Universe* and *On Providence*, neither of which is properly a commentary on Aristotle.

The scholar who stated, without offering evidence, that 'there is no reason to doubt that Maimonides was acquainted with all the writings of Aristotle known in Moslem Spain'[210] also averred: 'It may be taken as certain that Maimonides made extensive use' of Alexander's commentaries.[211] On the contrary, there is no certainty that Maimonides ever looked at a true commentary of Alexander's—or of any other ancient commentator—on Aristotle.

[209] See above, Ch. 3, §4.

[210] See above, Ch. 3, §4.

[211] *MN* (Pines), translator's introd., p. lxiv. Pines offers no actual evidence for his certainty but relies on Maimonides' letter to Ibn Tibbon and the general high regard in which Alexander was held in Arabic philosophical circles.

4. Other Greek Philosophers

Maimonides mentions a few additional ancient philosophers but shows no familiarity with the writings of any of them.

In the letter to Samuel Ibn Tibbon, he informs him that Plato's works are 'obscure', express themselves in 'metaphors', and can be 'dispensed with', since Aristotle superseded all his predecessors.[212] Plato's name does come up occasionally in the *Moreh nevukhim*, but he only plays a significant role in connection with a single issue.

In the *Moreh nevukhim*'s discussion of the eternity or creation of the world, he serves as the foremost advocate of one of the positions that Maimonides rejects, namely, the proposition that the world was created from a pre-existent, eternal matter.[213] When delineating exactly what Plato held, Maimonides writes: 'Aristotle relates in the *Physics* that Plato believes the heavens to be generated-destructible. You can also find his position [affirmed] expressly in his Book for [or: to] Timaeus.'[214] Nothing in Aristotle's *Physics* matches Maimonides' report. Closest is a statement there that we met earlier in another connection and that says: 'Plato alone takes it [time] to be generated. For he asserts that it came into existence together with the heavens and that the heavens are generated.'[215]

Although Aristotle undoubtedly had Plato's *Timaeus* in view,[216] he does not mention it in the *Physics* passage. Since the *Timaeus* was translated into Arabic, Maimonides could be conveying what he himself found. But he misrepresents Plato's position, for while the *Timaeus* describes the world as generated, it maintains that the world will not be destroyed—which, Maimonides does not realize, would coincide with the stand he himself would adopt in the *Moreh nevukhim*.[217] That he had direct knowledge of the *Timaeus* is therefore unlikely.

He could have seen the title *Timaeus* and its connection with Plato's position on creation in Aristotle's *On the Heavens*, a work that he read: *On the Heavens*

212 Marx, 'Texts by and about Maimonides', 380.

213 Discrepancies and contradictions can be detected in Maimonides' discussion of creation. As I have pointed out on an earlier occasion, if one assumes in a Straussian vein that Maimonides planted them intentionally in order to hint at an esoteric position on creation, the logic of the contradictions would lead to the conclusion that his esoteric position is creation from a pre-existent matter, as opposed to creation *ex nihilo*. In my opinion, as I made clear, the contradictions are most probably not intentional, Maimonides most probably did not have an esoteric position on creation, and he did not secretly endorse creation from a pre-existent matter. See H. Davidson, 'Maimonides' Secret Position on Creation', 21–2, 25–7, 31–2, 35–6.

214 *MN* ii. 13 (2).

215 Aristotle, *Al-ṭabīʿa*, 810 (= *Physics*, 8.1.251b, 16–19).

216 See Plato, *Timaeus*, 28 and 38.

217 *MN* ii. 27.

identifies the *Timaeus* as the place where Plato taught that the heavens are generated and that the world was created from a pre-existent matter.[218] Both pieces of information appear in Galen's compendium of the *Timaeus*, a book that was translated into Arabic and that Maimonides should have come across as he worked his way through the Galenic corpus during his medical studies.[219] But no matter what his source, Maimonides was careless in having Aristotle state that Plato believes the heavens 'to be generated-destructible': Aristotle's *Physics* says only that Plato took the heavens to be generated, and *On the Heavens* and Galen's compendium of the *Timaeus* report correctly that Plato believed the heavens, although generated, to be indestructible and to exist forever.

Besides citing Plato on the creation-eternity issue, the *Moreh nevukhim* records a few occasional remarks in his name. At one point Maimonides writes: 'Plato and his predecessors called matter the female [*al-unthā*], and form, the male [*al-dhakar*].'[220] A passage in the *Timaeus* does state: The 'receptacle', that is, the space in which physical objects are generated, is as it were the 'nurse of all becoming' and analogous to the 'mother'. The model in whose likeness objects are generated, in other words, the separately existing Form of each object that comes into existence, is, as it were, the 'father'.[221] The terms *female* and *male* attributed by Maimonides to Plato are absent; Maimonides is consequently not quoting directly.

A likely source for the female-male imagery has recently been identified. Alfarabi's epitome of the *Sophistical Refutations* criticizes the use of metaphorical language in philosophy and illustrates such language by what it describes as Plato's use of the metaphors 'female' (*al-unthā*), 'mother', and 'nurse' for matter, and 'male' (*al-dhakar*), for form.[222] A comment of Aristotle's in the *Physics* may have contributed. Speaking in his own name, Aristotle asserts that matter desires form as the female desires the male.[223] The portrayal of matter as female in character caught Maimonides' fancy, and he employs it elsewhere in the *Moreh nevukhim*.[224]

A further reference to Plato in the *Moreh nevukhim* ascribes to him the proposition that 'God looks [*yanẓur*] at the world of the intelligences, and existence thereupon emanates from Him.' Maimonides assures readers that the expression 'looks at' is a verbatim quotation (*naṣṣ*); the words caught his atten-

[218] Aristotle, *On the Heavens*, 1.10, 280a, 29–32; 3.2, 300b, 16–18; Arabic trans., 201–2, 317.
[219] Galen, *Compendium Timaei Platonis*, 5, 6, 13, 22.
[220] *MN* i. 17 (23*a*).
[221] Plato, *Timaeus*, 49–51; Cornford, *Plato's Cosmology*, 177–88.
[222] Robinson, 'Some Remarks', 55.
[223] Aristotle, *Al-ṭabīʿa* (= *Physics*, 1.9, 192a, 20–3). Pointed out by Robinson in 'Some Remarks', 54.
[224] *MN*, introd. (8*a*); iii. 8 (11*b*).

tion and appealed to him because he knew of a remark in rabbinic literature to the effect that 'the Holy One does nothing, so to speak, until He looks at the supernal host'.[225] Plato, of course, never wrote anything of the sort, and the purported quotation is not authentic. Nor, despite its Neoplatonic tone, does the quotation come from the Arabic paraphrases of Plotinus' *Enneads*. The *Theology of Aristotle*, the *Enneads* paraphrase that circulated most widely, states: 'The first agent' or 'Creator . . . looks at [*yanẓur*] *Himself* [or: at His essence] and at once produces what He produces.' He does not look at 'anything outside Him; for there exists nothing outside Him that is higher than He'. The cosmic Intellect, by contrast, does 'look at what is above it and produces what it produces'.[226] Where Maimonides came upon the 'verbatim quotation' is uncertain.

In a final reference to Plato, Maimonides cites Alfarabi's introduction to his lost commentary on the *Nicomachean Ethics*. Alfarabi, Maimonides reports, wrote there: Plato said that divine providence is evidenced most fully in persons who possess the power to elevate themselves from one ethical quality to another.[227]

The pattern is one of reliance not on Plato's works themselves but on what others conveyed about his views.

We met several references to Epicurus in the *Moreh nevukhim* that are copied directly from Alexander's *On Providence*. The only additional reference to Epicurus informs us that he considered the inventory of atoms in the universe to be fixed, in contrast to Kalam thinkers, who held that God continually creates new atoms as He pleases.[228] Maimonides may be extrapolating from what he read in *On Providence*. Whatever the case, he could not have had direct knowledge of Epicurus' writings, since they were not translated into Arabic in the Middle Ages.

The remaining ancient philosopher named in the *Moreh nevukhim* is John Philoponus. Some of Philoponus' commentaries on Aristotle were translated into Arabic, but Maimonides reveals no acquaintance with them. He depicts Philoponus merely as a link in the history of the Kalam mode of thought.

He offers the following sketch, which was touched upon in an earlier chapter: After the 'Christian community' (*milla*) incorporated the Greek and Syriac communities (*milal*) into itself, Greek and Syriac scholars undertook to serve their rulers by defending their new faith against the challenge of philosophy. They adopted premisses not because the premisses were true but because they

[225] *MN* ii (16*b*–17*a*). The source of the rabbinic statement quoted by Maimonides has not been identified.

[226] *Theologie des Aristoteles*, 39; Plotinus, *Opera*, ii. 207.

[227] *MN* iii. 18.

[228] *MN* i. 73 (1).

could be used to ward off the philosophical threat, and that was the origin of 'the science of Kalam'. When the 'community [*milla*] of Islam' came on the scene and, in its turn, faced the challenge of philosophy, the 'Kalam of John Philoponus' was one source from which it drew.[229] Although Philoponus would hardly have been flattered by his transformation into a Kalam thinker, Maimonides' account contains a kernel of truth, since Philoponus' arguments for the creation of the world were adopted by the Islamic Kalam.

Maimonides would seem to have obtained his information from a composition of Alfarabi's entitled *On Changeable Beings*, which had as a main subject the refutation of arguments for creation. *On Changeable Beings* has been lost but it was known to Maimonides and Averroes.[230]

Averroes writes in his *Long Commentary on the Metaphysics*: creation *ex nihilo* was espoused by 'Kalam thinkers among members of our community [*milla*] and members of the community [*milla*] of Christians. The Christian John Philoponus went as far as to maintain that the only sense in which one may speak of the possibility [of the existence of the world prior to its coming into existence] is in reference to the agent' who brought the world into existence. In other words, although the possibility of a thing's coming into existence ordinarily resides in the matter from which it emerges, Philoponus maintained that the possibility of the existence of the world was not located in a pre-existing matter. The world had the possibility of coming into existence before it existed only in the sense that the agent who brought it into existence had the ability to do so. The foregoing, Averroes goes on, is 'according to what Alfarabi reports in his [that is, Philoponus'] name in *On Changeable Beings*'.[231]

As the passage is written, Alfarabi's *On Changeable Beings* is expressly credited only with what Averroes reports regarding Philoponus and not with what he writes about the Kalam in general. Yet the linking of Kalam thinkers in the Christian *community*, Kalam thinkers in the Islamic *community*, and John Philoponus mirrors Maimonides' sketch of the movement's history. The threads—Christian Kalam, the Islamic Kalam school, and Philoponus as a bridge between them—form a single web, and Averroes' remarks indicate that Alfarabi's *On Changeable Beings* was the venue in which he and hence Maimonides encountered the web in its entirety. *On Changeable Beings* is thus the probable source for Maimonides' characterizing Philoponus as an impetus in the development of Islamic Kalam.

The *Moreh nevukhim* does furnish evidence of a direct acquaintance with

[229] *MN* i. 71 (94*b*).

[230] See the references to *On Changeable Beings* culled from Maimonides and Averroes by Steinschneider in *Al-Farabi*, 119–22.

[231] Averroes, *Tafsīr mā baʿda al-ṭabīʿa*, 1498.

the works of a few more ancient writers. None of them, however, were philosophers.

Maimonides had a good knowledge of mathematics and employs it in his critique of Kalam atomism. When he considers the proposition that space consists of infinitesimal, discrete, atomic intervals—which he takes to be the view of the generality of Kalam thinkers—one of his objections is mathematical: to construe space as a conglomeration of atomic intervals would undermine much of geometry, which postulates continuous and infinitely divisible lines and planes. Specifically, mathematical demonstrations concerning the commensurability or incommensurability of lines and planes, rational and irrational lines, and all else 'contained in Euclid [Book] 10', would be rendered invalid.[232] At another stage of his critique of the Kalam, Maimonides makes the point that the human imagination often rejects what human reason judges to be true. To illustrate the tension between imagination and reason, he writes: 'It has been demonstrated in the second book of Conic Sections' that two lines, one straight and one curved, can be extended indefinitely, continually approach one another, and yet never meet. Although the human imagination cannot countenance such a possibility, reason demonstrates its truth. Maimonides is referring to the demonstration of the possibility of asymptotes in Book 2 of the *Conic Sections* by the Greek mathematician Apollonius of Perga.[233]

Maimonides studied Ptolemy's *Almagest* with Joseph ben Judah, to whom he dedicates the *Moreh nevukhim*, and the *Moreh nevukhim* has several references to Ptolemy. They relate in particular to a pair of issues growing out of the geocentric picture of the universe to which reputable ancient and medieval astronomers subscribed. The first is the question whether the spheres of the planets Mercury and Venus are located between the earth and the sphere of the sun or lie beyond the solar sphere. Maimonides reports that Ptolemy

232 *MN* ii. 73 (3). Maimonides' commentary on *The Aphorisms of Hippocrates* displays a knowledge of the commentary on Euclid written by the Muslim mathematician al-Nayrīzī. See G. Freudenthal, 'Maimonides' *Guide of the Perplexed* and the Transmission of the Mathematical Tract "On Two Asymptotic Lines"', 115 n.

233 *MN* i. 73 (10, excursus). See Apollonius of Perga, *Treatise on Conic Sections*, 53. The explicit reference to Book 2 of the *Conic Sections* would seem to show that Maimonides was familiar with the work. G. Freudenthal, 'Maimonides' *Guide of the Perplexed* and the Transmission of the Mathematical Tract "On Two Asymptotic Lines"', 113–20, suggests, however, that Maimonides' wording reflects not the *Conic Sections* itself but one of the minor works dependent on it. A manuscript containing a series of glosses on Apollonius' *Conic Sections* identifies Maimonides as the author, but attributions of the sort cannot be accepted at face value, since dozens of compositions carrying Maimonides' name in the manuscripts are clearly not his. Langermann, 'Mathematical Writings of Maimonides', 57–9, accepts the attribution to Maimonides, and G. Freudenthal, ibid. 115 n., gives specific reasons for doubting it.

located Mercury and Venus within the sphere of the sun. He himself leans towards placing them beyond the sun, partly because that configuration accords with his understanding of biblical and rabbinic texts; he grants Scripture and rabbinic literature an unexpected voice in a scientific debate.[234]

Ptolemy comes up again when Maimonides discusses the issue of epicycles and eccentric spheres. The epicyclical hypothesis locates a given planet in a subordinate sphere that rotates around a spot on the surface of a primary sphere, which in turn rotates around the earth. The eccentric hypothesis locates a given planet on the surface of a sphere that rotates around a mathematical point that, in turn, travels in a circle around the earth. Maimonides shows that both hypotheses are incompatible with basic laws of Aristotelian physics and he supports his contention with astronomical data drawn from Ptolemy.[235]

Galen was regarded by Maimonides as the greatest medical authority ever to have lived, and Maimonides' *Medical Aphorisms* consists in the main of excerpts from no fewer than ninety of Galen's works.[236] He observes there that Galen had philosophical pretensions and he joins the Arabic Aristotelians in belittling those pretensions. Galen, he writes, is the perfect example of a man whose expertise in one area beguiled him into laying claim to expertise in areas beyond his competence. The man's unequalled mastery of medicine led him to fantasize that he had a gift for philosophy as well.[237]

The *Moreh nevukhim* cites Galen half a dozen times[238] and refers to two of his works by name: *The Usefulness of the Parts of the Body* (*De usu partium*) and *On the Natural Faculties* (*De naturalibus facultatibus*). From the former, Maimonides adduces, approvingly, observations on the ingenious design of the human muscular system[239] and he quotes, again with approval, the thought that living beings generated from semen and menstrual blood cannot expect to live forever or without pain.[240] The other work, *On the Natural Faculties*, is cited by him in his critique of the Islamic Kalam. He attributes to the generality of Kalam thinkers the proposition that human sense perception is fallible

[234] *MN* ii. 9–10. [235] *MN* ii. 24. On epicycles and eccentric spheres, see below, Ch. 7, §1.

[236] See H. Davidson, *Moses Maimonides*, 443–4.

[237] Maimonides, *Medical Aphorisms*, Arabic text and English trans. in Schacht and Meyerhof, 'Maimonides against Galen', 66, 79; medieval Hebrew trans. in Mutner (ed.), *Pirkei mosheh*, 365–6.

[238] *MN* i. 73 (3): the true nature of time cannot be understood; *MN* i. 73 (end): Galen's *On the Natural Faculties* reported that the Sophists branded the five senses as mendacious; *MN* ii. 13 (27*b*): repeats the comment on time; *MN* ii. 15 (33*b*): Alfarabi looked down on Galen because Galen held the issue of creation and eternity to be beyond demonstration; *MN* iii. 12 (19*a*), 32 (69*a*), which cite Galen's *De usu partium*; see immediately below.

[239] *MN* iii. 32. Pines' translation provides the reference in Galen.

[240] *MN* iii. 12. See Galen, *De usu partium*, 3.10; English trans., 189.

and he notes: 'As Galen states in *On the Natural Faculties*', the fallibility of sense perception was a doctrine of the ancient Sophists.[241]

Plato, Epicurus, and John Philoponus, whom Maimonides refers to but whose works he did not read, were philosophers. Euclid, Apollonius, Ptolemy, and Galen, whose works he did read, were natural scientists.

It is conceivable of course that Maimonides was acquainted with additional Greek philosophical texts that he does not name; Proclus' *De aeternitate* could, for instance, be the source of some of the arguments for the eternity of the world from the nature of God that Maimonides examines and refutes in the *Moreh nevukhim*. But if we restrict ourselves to actual evidence, the sole permissible conclusion is that the ancient philosophers of whom he discloses direct knowledge in his later period are a truncated Aristotle, two Arabic works attributed to Alexander of Aphrodisias, and possibly the argument for the existence of God from logical symmetry in the version of either Alexander or Themistius.

5. The Arabic Philosophers

Maimonides' letter to Ibn Tibbon offers a thumbnail assessment of a number of Arabic philosophers. He advises Ibn Tibbon to ignore Abū Zakariyya Rāzī's *Theology*, since Rāzī was only a physician, and his book is 'useless'. 'The commentaries of al-Ṭayyib, Yaḥyā ibn ʿAdī, and Biṭrīq are worthless books, and anyone who studies them wastes his time.'[242] In the *Moreh nevukhim*, Maimonides brackets Ibn ʿAdī with John Philoponus as a practitioner of the Christian Kalam[243] and he dismisses Razi's *Theology* for its 'enormous inanities and stupidities', one of which is the pernicious notion that evil is more prevalent in the universe than good.[244] It is unclear whether his judgement is based on his own reading.

His opinion of the Arabic Aristotelians is very different. In the letter to Ibn Tibbon, he recommends Alfarabi as an 'exceptional scholar', submits that where logic is concerned Alfarabi alone should be consulted, extols Alfarabi's works as 'pure fine flour', and singles out his *Principles of Existent Beings* for praise. The *Principles of Existent Beings* is better known under the title *Al-siyāsa al-madaniyya*, that is, *Political Government*, and each title captures an aspect of the book: in the first half, Alfarabi outlines the structure of existence descend-

241 *MN* i. 73 (end). See Galen, *On the Natural Faculties*, 1.2.

242 Marx, 'Texts by and about Maimonides', 378, 380.

243 *MN* i. 71 (94*b*).

244 *MN* iii. 12 (18*a*). In his *Treatise on Resurrection* Maimonides mentions, but shows no familiarity with, the *Kitāb al-muʿtabar*, a philosophical work by the 12th-cent. Abū al-Barakāt. See Davidson, *Moses Maimonides*, 528 n. 194.

ing from the first cause, through the intelligences, celestial spheres, and active intellect, to the sublunar region. The second half is a discourse on political regimes.

Maimonides rates Avicenna's writings as inferior to Alfarabi's, but as having 'value' and as worthy of study; Averroes, Maimonides' contemporary and fellow Cordovan, similarly ranked Avicenna below Alfarabi. Ibn Bājja, in Maimonides' words, was 'a great philosopher' whose compositions are 'correct'. Averroes' name comes up when Maimonides advises Ibn Tibbon to 'read the books of Aristotle only in their interpretations' and sets the 'commentary of Averroes' side by side with the 'interpretation[s]' of Alexander and Themistius.

Maimonides also mentions Averroes in a letter that he sent to Joseph ben Judah when he was well along in composing the *Moreh nevukhim* or had completed it. He informs Joseph that he recently received 'everything that Averroes wrote on Aristotle's works, with the exception of the *Parva naturalia*'. He 'saw that Averroes nicely hits the mark', but he had 'not yet had the leisure to peruse it all'.[245] Averroes composed his commentaries in three formats, known today as Epitomes, Middle Commentaries, and Long Commentaries, and the phrase 'everything that Averroes wrote' might suggest that Maimonides had received all three. It is no less possible, however, that he had either the Epitomes or the Middle Commentaries and thought that he had everything; he must be talking about more than just the Long Commentaries, since Averroes' commentaries in that format cover only five of Aristotle's works, and the *Parva naturalia* is not among them. If it was the Epitomes that Maimonides received and examined, he should have felt on familiar ground. In that cycle, Averroes barely begins his campaign of cutting away the foreign growths that his Arabic Aristotelian predecessors grafted on the authentic Aristotle.[246]

Alfarabi is the Arabic philosopher cited and quoted most frequently in Maimonides' writings, and as far as Maimonides was conscious of his sources, Alfarabi was the Arabic philosopher who had the strongest impact on him. As seen in an earlier chapter, the *Commentary on the Mishnah* incorporates extensive passages from Alfarabi's ethical and political *Fuṣūl muntazaʿa*, without mentioning the author's name or the book's title; it was from the *Fuṣūl* and not from Aristotle that Maimonides learned the theory of the middle way in ethics. In his *Sefer hamitsvot*, Maimonides quotes a sentence from 'the students of the art of logic' regarding a peculiarity of the Arabic language, and the sentence comes from Alfarabi's epitome of Aristotle's *De interpretatione*.[247]

[245] Maimonides, *Epistulae*, 70.

[246] In a number of instances, Averroes later went back and annotated the Epitomes, explaining that he had changed his opinion.

[247] See above, Ch. 3, §4.

The *Moreh nevukhim* refers to Alfarabi a half-dozen times and in four instances names the work of Alfarabi from which it draws. The four works are: *On Changeable Beings*, the *Risāla fī al-ʿaql*, glosses on the *Physics*, and the introduction to Alfarabi's commentary on the *Nicomachean Ethics*. What Maimonides reports in one of the two remaining instances comes from Alfarabi's *Risāla fī al-ʿaql*, and what he reports in the other, from Alfarabi's commentary on the *Topics*.[248] Traces of Alfarabi's logic were detected by Munk in a chapter of the *Moreh nevukhim* where Alfarabi is not named.[249] And we saw an instance where Maimonides very likely borrows from Alfarabi's epitome of Aristotle's *Sophistical Refutations*.[250]

Two compositions of Alfarabi's are quoted by title in the final chapter of Maimonides' *Medical Aphorisms*, a chapter that he completed a decade and a half after he finished the *Moreh nevukhim*. They are Alfarabi's *Book of Particles* (or: *Letters*; *Ḥurūf*), a work conceived somewhat along the lines of the lexicographic parts of Aristotle's *Metaphysics* while also treating the relationship between philosophy, language, and society;[251] and Alfarabi's *Long Commentary on Aristotle's Prior Analytics*.[252] There is thus good evidence that at various times Maimonides used eleven of Alfarabi's philosophical works. If we add the *Principles of Existent Beings*, which Maimonides praises to Ibn Tibbon but about which he says nothing, the number rises to a dozen. In subject matter, the works of Alfarabi that he uses fall under three broad rubrics: logic; physics, cosmology, and metaphysics; ethics and politics. Alfarabi served Maimonides across the philosophical spectrum.

Maimonides refers to Ibn Bājja five times in the *Moreh nevukhim*. In one

248 *MN* i. 73 (10): *Risāla fī al-ʿaql*, without naming the book (see Pines' note in his translation); *MN* i. 74 (7): *On Changeable Beings*; *MN* ii. 15 (33*b*): commentary on the *Topics*, without naming the book; *MN* ii. 18 (37*b*): *Risāla fī al-ʿaql*, from which Maimonides quotes 'verbatim'; *MN* ii. 19 (43*b*): glosses on the *Physics*, from which Maimonides again quotes 'verbatim'; *MN* iii. 18 (38*b*–39*a*): introd. to *Commentary on Aristotle's Nicomachean Ethics*.

249 *MN* (trans. Munk), i. 193 n. and i. 197 n.

250 See above, §4.

251 Maimonides, *Medical Aphorisms*, 25, §58, citing *Kitāb al-ḥurūf*: languages of peoples who live in the moderate latitudes are superior to those of peoples living in a hot or cold latitude. Nothing in Alfarabi's work fits Maimonides' citation. Mahdi, in his introduction to the text (p. 39), conjectures that Maimonides' quotation is from Galen and not Alfarabi. Vajda, 'Langage, philosophie, politique et religion', 248, suggests that Maimonides may have had a better text than the one that has been preserved.

252 Maimonides, *Medical Aphorisms*, 25, §§59–60 quotes two passages from Alfarabi's *Long Commentary on the Prior Analytics*, both of which sign off with the words: 'end of quotation from Alfarabi'. The point Alfarabi makes is that Galen's work on syllogisms focused on assertoric and necessary syllogisms and ignored syllogisms having possible premisses and leading to possible conclusions; but as a physician Galen should have focused on possible syllogisms, since they are the ones that are useful in practical pursuits such as medicine. I was not able to identify the source of either quotation in the available text of Alfarabi's *Commentary on the Prior Analytics*.

instance he writes that he is citing Ibn Bājja's commentary on the *Physics* and, in another, a discourse of his on astronomy.[253] Besides the explicit citations, the distinction between four levels of human perfection—physical possessions, bodily strength, ethical attainments, and intellectual attainments—around which the final chapter of *Moreh nevukhim* is constructed, has been traced to Ibn Bājja.[254] In addition, statements of Maimonides on human intellectual perfection echo Ibn Bājja's views.[255]

Avicenna is never mentioned in *Moreh nevukhim*.[256] Despite the absence of his name and despite Maimonides' judging him inferior to Alfarabi, what Maimonides assumes to be Aristotle's metaphysics is largely Avicenna's, and Maimonides' picture of the universe and theory of prophecy, which are indebted to both Alfarabi and Avicenna, owe more to the latter than to the former.[257] The absence of Avicenna's name from the *Moreh nevukhim* and the confusion of Avicenna's metaphysics with Aristotle's suggest that Maimonides drew from the writings of Avicenna's followers rather than from those of Avicenna himself.

Maimonides' encounter with Averroes' commentaries occurred too late for them to leave a mark in the *Moreh nevukhim*. He makes no mention of Averroes in the *Guide*, he never quotes Aristotle through the medium of Averroes' commentaries, as later medieval Jewish philosophers would do, and nothing in the *Moreh nevukhim* or in any other of Maimonides' writings, whether earlier or later than the *Moreh nevukhim*, can be traced to Averroes.

Two Muslim thinkers affiliated with the Arabic Aristotelian school also had an impact, either direct or indirect, on the *Moreh nevukhim*, although they are not named by Maimonides. One is Ghazali, whose protean career arrayed him in ever-changing plumage: now he was a Kalam thinker, now a mystic, now a philosopher in the Arabic Aristotelian mould, now, *en revanche*, a critic of philosophy on its own terms. The straightforward account of the philosophers' theories in Ghazali's *Maqāṣid al-falāsifa* and the sketch of the views of 'Aristotle' that Ghazali refutes in the *Tahāfut al-falāsifa* are, I have suggested, among the places where Maimonides likely learned Avicenna's version of the

[253] *MN* i. 74 (7): immortality of the intellect; *MN* ii. 9: the location of the spheres of Venus and Mercury *vis-à-vis* the sphere of the sun; *MN* ii. 24 (51*b*): the position taken on epicycles in a discourse of Ibn Bājja's on astronomy; *MN* ii. 24 (53*b*): another astronomical matter; *MN* iii. 29 (62*b*): Ibn Bājja's *Commentary on the Physics* (also referred to in a letter of Maimonides' to Ibn Tibbon; see Maimonides, *Igerot harambam*, 546).

[254] Altmann, 'Maimonides' "Four Perfections"', 15–23.

[255] See below, Ch. 6, §5.

[256] For Maimonides' use of Avicenna's *Canon of Medicine*, see Bos, 'Maimonides' Medical Works', 250, to which add Maimonides, *On the Causes of Symptoms*, 145ʳ–146ʳ (a cardiac medicine). In the *Treatise on Resurrection* Maimonides refers to a work of Avicenna's on the hereafter, but what he says about it indicates that he did not himself see it; see H. Davidson, *Moses Maimonides*, 528 n. 194.

[257] See H. Davidson, *Alfarabi, Avicenna, and Averroes on Intellect*, 197–207.

Arabic Aristotelian system. Ghazali, moreover, plays a specific and unmistakable role at a critical juncture in the *Moreh nevukhim*. The dialectic give-and-take of the *Tahāfut al-falāsifa* leads Ghazali to frame arguments on the creation-eternity issue that Maimonides transforms into full-fledged proofs of creation.[258] Unless there was an unknown intermediary, Maimonides read the arguments in the *Tahāfut*.

A passage in the *Moreh nevukhim*—again from the section on eternity and creation—echoes a motif in Ibn Ṭufayl's philosophical novel.[259] The novel is constructed on the premiss that a highly intelligent boy is brought up by a doe on a desert island without seeing human beings. Maimonides adapts the motif for his own purpose.

When answering Aristotelian arguments for eternity from the nature of the world—for example, the argument that since everything generated comes from matter, matter, if generated, would have to be generated from a prior matter, whence it would follow that matter already existed—Maimonides counters that the laws obtaining before and during the creation of the world would differ from those obtaining after the world already existed. To make his point, he asks us to imagine a highly intelligent boy who is brought up by his father on an island without ever seeing a woman or a female animal. When the boy is told that human beings initially spend a gestation period of nine months completely enclosed within the womb of a member of the species who is of female gender and that the infant then emerges through a passageway that opens spontaneously in the female's body, he is of course incredulous; he does not realize that laws of nature obtaining after the infant's birth need not have obtained in the prenatal state.[260] By the same token, the laws obtaining before the world came into existence would not be those obtaining at later stages. Maimonides undoubtedly has reworked Ibn Ṭufayl's premiss, cleansed of its fabulous colouring. Since the notion of a child growing up alone on a desert island is appealing and could have been taken up by others, it is not certain that Maimonides got it directly from Ibn Ṭufayl.

6. Medieval Jewish Thinkers

The medieval Jewish writers before Maimonides who are commonly honoured with chapters in histories of Jewish philosophy barely deserve to be called *philosophers*, and Maimonides exhibits little interest in them. He dismisses the

[258] H. Davidson, 'Maimonides' Secret Position on Creation', 28–34. In *MN* i. 74 (5) and ii. 19 (40*a*), Maimonides openly acknowledges that some of his arguments for creation refine Kalam motifs by raising them to a salubrious philosophical level.

[259] Ibn Ṭufayl, *Ḥayy ben Yaqdhân*.

[260] *MN* ii. 17 (34*b*–35*b*).

philosophical efforts of Isaac Israeli as 'inanities, wind, and vanities'.[261] A manuscript of Sa'adiah's theological work *Emunot vede'ot* has been discovered with a faint signature on the title page that a scholar who examined the fragment identified as being in Maimonides' hand.[262] If the identification is correct and the copy of *Emunot vede'ot* belonged to Maimonides, he presumably read it. At a certain juncture in the *Moreh nevukhim*, he speaks disparagingly of arguments for the existence and unity of God that were borrowed from the Kalam by 'one [or: some] of the *ge'onim*'.[263] One of the *ge'onim* whom he has in view could be Sa'adiah Gaon and others could be Samuel ben Hofni and Hefets ben Yatsliah, both of whom dabbled in philosophy and with whose works Maimonides was familiar;[264] all three offer arguments for the existence of God that are redolent of the Kalam. Maimonides also refers to Sa'adiah by name in contexts where philosophy is not involved.[265]

Scholars have called attention to passages in Maimonides that might disclose traces of Judah Halevi, Abraham Ibn Ezra, or Abraham ibn Daud.[266] I suggested in an earlier chapter that the mark of Bahya ibn Pakuda can perhaps be detected in Maimonides' conceptualization of the first two positive religious commandments. None of the evidence comes close to being conclusive, and remarks that Maimonides makes about Joseph Ibn Tsadik—or Hatsadik—raise a warning flag.

Ibn Tsadik is reported to have been a rabbinic judge in Cordova during Maimonides' father's time. He tried his hand at philosophy in a work entitled *Microcosm*, and Maimonides writes to Ibn Tibbon that he had heard of the book, had never seen it, yet knew the quality of the man. The Arabic original of Maimonides' letter is lost, and at this juncture the two preserved Hebrew translations diverge. One renders the Arabic as saying that Ibn Tsadik 'without doubt followed the fashion of those who endorse [divine] attributes', and the other, as saying that Ibn Tsadik 'without doubt followed the fashion of the Pure Brethren [*Ikhwān al-Ṣafā'*]', whose writings 'are prolix'.[267] Whether Maimonides was

261 Marx, 'Texts by and about Maimonides', 378.

262 Scheiber, 'Autograph Manuscripts of Maimonides', 188.

263 *MN* i. 71 (94*a*).

264 See above, Ch. 2, §2.

265 See Maimonides, *Responsa*, index, s.v. Sa'adiah; id., *Epistle to Yemen*, 64–5; English trans., [xii].

266 Regarding all of these philosophers see Kaufmann, *Geschichte der Attributenlehre*, index, s.v. Maimûni. Regarding Halevi, see Pines, introd. to his translation of *MN*, p. cxxxiii, and Kreisel, 'Judah Halevi's Influence on Maimonides', 108–21. Regarding Abraham ibn Ezra, see Bacher, *Die Bibelexegese Moses Maimûni's*, 172; Perla, *Sefer hamitsvot*, i. 15–16 (an overstatement of Ibn Ezra's influence on Maimonides' *SM*); and Twersky, 'Did R. Abraham Ibn Ezra Influence Maimonides?' (Heb.), 25–40.

267 Marx, 'Texts by and about Maimonides', 379. Kaufmann, *Geschichte der Attributenlehre*, 336–7, reads Maimonides' evaluation as approbation. Stroumsa, 'Note on Maimonides' Attitude to Joseph Ibn Tsadik' (Heb.), 37–8, makes what appears to me to be an incontrovertible case for the opposite interpretation.

bracketing Joseph with thinkers who affirm divine attributes or with the Pure Brethren—a real or fictitious Muslim circle that was the ostensible author of a large, sprawling composition infused with Neoplatonic concepts and treating all the sciences at no great depth—his opinion of the distinguished judge's philosophical efforts was not high. What is more noteworthy, either because no copy of the *Microcosm* was accessible or because Maimonides did not consider it worth spending time on, he never read it. If he was unfamiliar with a book having philosophical pretensions that was written a generation earlier by a scholar in his own city, conjectures about books by Jewish authors who were more distant in place and whom he never mentions face a considerable hurdle.

At all events, even if we accept every conjecture about traces in the *Moreh nevukhim* of Jewish writers whom Maimonides does not mention, those writers had far less to offer him than the medieval Arabic Aristotelians did.

7. Summary

In the period of Maimonides' activity examined in the present chapter, he discloses no consciousness of a Neoplatonic school of philosophy and reveals no familiarity with the paraphrases of Plotinus and Proclus that were available in Arabic, or of medieval writings that might be characterized as Neoplatonic. Key Neoplatonic motifs, notably, the conception of a cause of the existence and not just the motion of the universe, the unknowability of the divine essence, and the concept of emanation, do play a significant role in his thought. He knew them, however, through the medium of the Arabic Aristotelian school, which appropriated them and wove them into its picture of the universe, and he mistakenly took them to be Aristotelian.

He had some familiarity with the Kalam school, knew its proofs for creation and the existence of God, and points out differences between its two main branches, the Asharites and Muʿtazilites. But despite his assurance that he had studied the 'books of the Kalam thinkers as far as was feasible', the information that he imparts with confidence concerning the Kalam picture of the universe is badly flawed.

He used Aristotle's *Physics*, *On the Heavens*, *Nicomachean Ethics*, and the trilogy of biological works making up *On Animals*. He may have read the *Rhetoric*. He owned, and once appears to quote from *On Plants*, a work actually composed by Nicolaus of Damascus. He quotes a passage from Aristotle's *Topics* but may be doing so through the medium of Alfarabi and not directly from the *Topics* itself.

There is no reliable evidence that an Arabic translation of the authentic

Aristotelian *Meteorology* ever existed. Maimonides could have read the reworking of the *Meteorology* that was translated, or perhaps composed, by Yaḥyā ibn Biṭrīq, but positions he takes on meteorological matters indicate that he did not do so. The single occasion on which he says that he is quoting from the *De sensu* shows that he did not have the work in front of him, and there is no reason to suppose that he was acquainted with any of the other compositions making up the *Parva naturalia*. He shows no acquaintance with Aristotle's *On Generation and Destruction* and *De anima*. Most strikingly, what he cites from Aristotle's *Metaphysics* and the propositions of a metaphysical character that he cites from Aristotle without mentioning the *Metaphysics* by name are consistently non-Aristotelian.

He thus knew only part of the available Aristotelian corpus, which he eked out with what he learned from the Arabic Aristotelians and other sources.

He read and made considerable use of *The Principles of the Universe* and *On Providence*, two works attributed to Alexander of Aphrodisias and known only in Arabic. His *Commentary on the Mishnah* explained the immortality of the human intellect in a way that might derive from one or the other of Alexander's two compositions on Aristotle's *De anima*; and he could have learned one of the proofs of the existence of God that he sets forth in the *Moreh nevukhim* from Alexander's commentary on *Metaphysics* 12, or Themistius' paraphrase of the same book. Otherwise there is nothing to suggest that he ever looked at a commentary of Alexander's—or of any other ancient commentator—on Aristotle.

He read Euclid, Apollonius of Perga, Galen, and Ptolemy, but they were natural scientists, not philosophers.

He knew and used a number of Alfarabi's writings and he knew a few of Ibn Bājja's. He does not mention Avicenna in the *Moreh nevukhim* and hardly mentions him elsewhere, although key philosophical theses that he adduces, especially those of a metaphysical character, come from Avicenna. There are echoes of Ghazali and Ibn Ṭufayl in the *Moreh nevukhim*, but no trace of Averroes' commentaries on Aristotle.

The precise extent of his knowledge of medieval Jewish philosophy cannot be determined. Whatever it may have been, the Jewish philosophers had little to offer him and they have left little or no mark on the *Moreh nevukhim*.

Maimonides constantly expressed his commitment to the philosophical ideal and philosophical life, yet sought the knowledge necessary for such a life in an economical manner that would not usurp the time demanded by his rabbinic studies in his earlier, and medical activity in his later, period.

SIX

Maimonides on Metaphysical Knowledge

> It would surely appear the better, indeed the obligatory, course to controvert even what touches us closely for the sake of upholding the truth, especially since we are lovers of wisdom. For while both [Plato and the truth] are dear, it is a sacred duty to give preference to the truth.
>
> ARISTOTLE
> *Nicomachean Ethics*, 1.6

1. Introduction

MAIMONIDES CONSIDERED apodictic demonstration (*burhān*) to be the surest tool the human intellect has for acquiring knowledge, since no one but the ignorant would think of rejecting a demonstration. At the same time, he acknowledges that some issues are not amenable to demonstration and consequently remain in dispute; issues of the sort, in his view, are absent from mathematics, present to a small extent in physics, and numerous in metaphysics.[1] Metaphysics here has the sense that Aristotle gives it in effect when he writes: knowledge of what is 'eternal, immovable, and separate [from matter], if there is such a thing', belongs to the science that is prior to mathematics and physics; the subject of metaphysics is what is eternal and incorporeal.[2]

Maimonides nonetheless recognizes a role for demonstration even in metaphysics. He never tires of stating that the existence, unity, and incorporeality of a first cause of the universe, and hence the existence of God, can be demonstrated.[3] He stresses that a number of negative propositions about God have likewise been demonstrated, among them: God is free of potentiality;[4] God's essence is not composite; God possesses no characteristic distinct from His essence; His essence is unknowable, and no descriptive term can therefore be predicated of Him.[5] The more demonstrations a person masters of what God *is not*, the more the person narrows down what He is, and the greater his

[1] *MN* i. 31 (34*a*–*b*).

[2] Aristotle, *Metaphysics*, 6.1, 1026a, 10–13; Wolfson, 'Classification of Sciences', 518, where it is pointed out that Aristotle describes metaphysics in two additional ways as well.

[3] *MN* i. 70 (end), 71 (97*a*), 76 (end), ii. 1–2.

[4] *MN* i. 68 (87*b*), ii. 1 (4).

[5] *MN* i. 58.

knowledge of God.[6] It is further 'demonstrable' that in God, *intellect*, the *intelligizing* subject, and the *intelligible* object of thought are identical with one another.[7] 'It has been demonstrated' that God acts in the universe through intermediaries.[8]

Knowledge of the supernal realm outside God is possible too, with the proviso that to some extent, recourse must be had there to *proofs*, which are less probative than *demonstrations*. We have seen Maimonides affirm the following: it has been established through 'demonstration' (*burhān*) that there exist a number of celestial spheres, each with its own motion; it is 'clear' (*bayyin*) that the spheres possess souls and proven (*tabayyana*) that the soul of each sphere maintains its sphere in motion through its desire to imitate an incorporeal being. The existence of the transcendent active intellect, which is the source of the forms of the four elements, of the forms of natural beings composed of the elements, and of actual human thought has been 'proved [*dalla ʿalayhi*] . . . without doubt'.[9]

Although the body of demonstrable knowledge in metaphysics is smaller than the body of such knowledge in physics, what exists is of utmost significance. Maimonides, like other medieval rationalists, maintains that authentic religion must be grounded in demonstrative knowledge of the existence of God. The first two positive commandments from among the 613 given to Moses at Sinai are, he holds, dictates to *know* through rational demonstration that God exists and is one. The religious obligation and divine commandment to love God is contingent on rational knowledge not only of God's existence, but also of the other propositions about Him that can be known. The highest form of worship consists in focusing one's thoughts exclusively on God after having acquired 'scientific knowledge' (*ʿilm*) of Him; the greater one's knowledge, the higher the quality of one's worship.[10] Religion aside, science, for Maimonides, has knowledge of God as its end.[11] Philosophers and prophets have established that the goal of human life is knowledge of God, which is 'true science'.[12] Man's 'final goal' lies in 'conceiving intelligible thoughts that give rise to true opinions in matters of *metaphysics* [*ilāhiyyāt*]'.[13]

It is hard to imagine anything less ambiguous, yet not every scholar was convinced. Strauss sowed hints for years that Maimonides' deep secret was nothing more nor less than the dubiousness of the existence of God[14] and he allowed those hints to emerge a little more clearly in his introduction to

[6] *MN* i. 59. [7] *MN* i. 68 (86*b*). [8] *MN* ii. 4 (14*a*). [9] *MN* ii. 4.
[10] See above, Chs. 1 and 2. [11] *MN* iii. 54 (132*a*).
[12] *MN* iii. 54 (133*b*–134*a*). [13] *MN* iii. 54 (133*b*).
[14] Strauss, *Persecution and the Art of Writing*, 19, 43, 83, 124–6; see *MN* (Pines), introd., pp. xxi–xxii, xli, xlviii, liii. Everything must be read with a consciousness of Strauss's heavy irony.

Pines' translation of the *Moreh nevukhim*. He concludes his introduction by conveying, in his typically allusive style, that Maimonides considered 'the only genuine science of beings' to be 'natural science or a part of it', whence it would follow that the existence of God—and of other incorporeal beings—cannot be known philosophically and scientifically.[15] Articles that Pines published in his later years make Strauss's intimations explicit and argue the case in detail, although without referring to his predecessor.

Despite Maimonides' insistence on the possibility of demonstrative knowledge of God, on the possibility of demonstrative knowledge and knowledge of less probative force concerning the supernal beings subordinate to God, and on metaphysical knowledge as the goal of human life, Pines represents him as rejecting all possibility of non-empirical knowledge and specifically of metaphysics, taken in the sense of 'knowledge of God and the incorporeal entities'.[16] On Pines' reading, Maimonides harboured a 'critical (in the Kantian sense) attitude' and was a full-fledged sceptic in matters of religion to boot. 'Both Kant and Maimonides, the first outspokenly and the second partly by implication, have tried to show that because of the limitations of his mind man is incapable of intellecting some of the main objects of the traditional metaphysics'. After having been viewed in the decades after his death as a crypto-Averroist and in recent decades as a crypto-Aristotelian, Maimonides is now decked out in a new guise, that of a crypto-Kantian agnostic.[17]

In working out his thesis, Pines quotes reports regarding Alfarabi's lost commentary on the *Nicomachean Ethics*, particularly a report that he found in a brief, previously ignored composition attributed to Ibn Bājja. In addition, he adduces a statement that Ibn Bājja—assuming the attribution to him to be correct—made in his own name in the same composition. Alfarabi's commentary on the *Nicomachean Ethics* and Ibn Bājja's statement, Pines proposes, were the factors leading Maimonides to a critical stance on non-empirical knowledge.[18] Pines then expounds passages in the *Moreh nevukhim* where he finds that the possibility of non-empirical knowledge was indeed rejected by Maimonides.

The following three sections will examine what is known about Alfarabi's lost commentary on the *Nicomachean Ethics*, Ibn Bājja's views on metaphysical knowledge, and the passages cited by Pines from the *Moreh nevukhim* to support

15 *MN* (Pines), introd., pp. lv–lvi.

16 Pines, 'Les Limites de la métaphysique', 213.

17 Pines states his thesis in 'The Limitations of Human Knowledge' and in 'Les Limites de la métaphysique'. He summarizes the thesis in 'The Philosophical Purport of Maimonides' Halachic Works'. The connection with Kant is made in 'The Limitations of Human Knowledge', 94 and 100. The notion that Maimonides had a sceptical opinion of organized religion pervades that article and is spelled out in an appendix. Pines may have backed away a little in the third of the articles.

18 Pines, 'The Limitations of Human Knowledge', 82, 94–5, 99, 100.

his thesis. Then I shall offer evidence for Maimonides' assertion that the human intellect can have the active intellect as a direct object of thought and conjoin with it. The final section in the chapter will attempt to reconstruct the process whereby man can, in Maimonides' view, acquire knowledge of incorporeal substances.

2. Alfarabi's Lost Commentary on the *Nicomachean Ethics*

Alfarabi's preserved works recognize a first cause consisting in pure thought, from which there emanate: the incorporeal intelligences, the active intellect, which is the last link in the incorporeal hierarchy, the celestial spheres, and the sublunar world. The active intellect constantly radiates a power that enables the inborn human potentiality for thought to pass to actuality. Should a human intellect master all, or almost all, scientific and philosophical knowledge, it reaches a level at which it 'conjoins' (*ittaṣala*) with the active intellect, is 'free of matter', and 'remains in that state perpetually', its 'eudaemonia [*saʿāda*] complete'. Virtuous political regimes create the conditions that human intellects require in order to fulfil their potential.[19] Although Alfarabi's preserved works differ on details, none of them diverges from the general scheme, but his lost commentary on the *Nicomachean Ethics* reportedly repudiated the scheme wholly or in large part.

Only a single reference to the commentary is found in the *Moreh nevukhim*. To buttress his theory that the degree of providence a person enjoys is proportional to the person's perfection, Maimonides quotes a number of proof texts from Scripture and thereupon states that the position he documented from Scripture is also that of 'the philosophers'. For 'in the introduction to his commentary on Aristotle's *Nicomachean Ethics*, Alfarabi states: "Those who are able to elevate themselves [or: their souls] from one moral quality to another, are those of whom Plato said that God's providence is with them in a pre-eminent degree."'[20] The sole reference to the lost commentary in the *Moreh nevukhim* is thus a bland comment about morality and divine providence that Maimonides ascribes to the 'philosophers'; and the philosophers turn out to be Alfarabi's citation of Plato in the introduction to his commentary on the *Nicomachean Ethics*. There is not a soupçon of anything out of the ordinary.

Reports of the radical character of the commentary on the *Nicomachean*

[19] Alfarabi, *Al-madīna al-fāḍila*, 100–5, 198–201, 242–5, 262–3; id., *Al-siyāsa al-madaniyya*, 31–5, 42, 52–3, 55, 79. Alfarabi, *Risāla fi al-ʿaql*, 20–2, 24–7, 31, 34–5; English trans., 217–21. The *Risāla* differs somewhat from the other two works, but the differences are not significant for the present purpose.

[20] *MN* iii. 18 (38*b*–39*a*).

Ethics come from the newly discovered composition ascribed to Ibn Bājja as well as from Ibn Ṭufayl and Averroes.

Pines discovered the composition in a collection of then unpublished writings carrying Ibn Bājja's name; the collection was subsequently published by J. Alaoui.[21] Ibn Bājja is always difficult to comprehend, and, as both Pines and Alaoui observe, the composition we are concerned with was not copied with care. As a consequence, it is problematic in a number of places. Alaoui even raises doubts about the attribution to Ibn Bājja.[22]

The opening paragraph reads, in my translation from the Arabic:

As to what is supposed [or: might be supposed (*yuẓann*)] regarding Alfarabi's statements in his commentary on the *Nicomachean Ethics* to the effect that there is no survival after death, there is no eudaemonia except civic [or: political] eudaemonia [*al-saʿāda al-madaniyya*], there is no existence apart from what is perceived by the senses, and talk of another existence apart from existence perceived by the senses is an old wives' tale—all of that is false and a fabrication against Alfarabi. Alfarabi stated the above at a first reading [*awwal qirā'atihi*] of it [that is, of his commentary], and what he says here does not resemble statements of his [elsewhere] that are demonstrable conclusions. Most of his statements in this book [that is, in the commentary] are attributed, and his aim was to advance a censorious refutation of them.[23]

Pines' translation of the passage differs in a number of particulars, but most are matters of style and just two differences deserve attention. The pertinent sentences in his translation read as follows (the brackets are his):

[I am of the opinion that] all this [that which is believed about al-Farabi] is false, [that those are lies used to attack] Abū Naṣr [al-Farabi]. For Abū Naṣr [al-Farabi] has made these remarks at his first reading [of the *Ethics*].

Where Ibn Bājja writes: 'all of that is false and a fabrication against Alfarabi', Pines' translation has: '[I am of the opinion that] all this . . . is false.' The bracketed addition, which is unsupported by the Arabic text, waters down what Ibn Bājja writes. Rather than asserting categorically that the supposition about Alfarabi is false, Ibn Bājja, with the addition, merely says that the supposition is in his opinion false.

More importantly, in place of the words 'Alfarabi stated the above at a first reading of it', that is, on a first reading of the commentary on the *Nicomachean Ethics*, Pines' translation has Ibn Bājja say that Alfarabi 'has made these remarks at his first reading [of the *Ethics*]'. The words '[of the *Ethics*]', which again have nothing in the Arabic text to support them, change the meaning

[21] Ibn Bājja, *Rasā'il falsafiyya*, 197–202. The collection of texts is found in Bodleian MS Pococke 206, and I have consulted the manuscript.

[22] Ibn Bājja, *Rasā'il falsafiyya*, 19, 62–4.

[23] Ibid. 197.

substantially. Ibn Bājja no longer attributes the perception of Alfarabi's commentary as rejecting survival after death and so on to a first, incorrect reading of the commentary. Ibn Bājja is made to say instead that the perception is correct but only reflects what Alfarabi held on *his* first reading of the *Nicomachean Ethics*. In a footnote, Pines acknowledges that the clause may also be translated: Alfarabi 'has in effect made these remarks according to what one understands at a first reading'.[24]

Ibn Bājja can, then, be taken as reporting that, upon a first reading of the commentary on the *Nicomachean Ethics*, Alfarabi might be supposed to have rejected the afterlife and so on, whereas in fact he did not and the false allegations grew out of a misunderstanding of what he wrote. Alternatively, Ibn Bājja can be taken as reporting that Alfarabi did take the positions in question upon his first reading of Aristotle's *Nicomachean Ethics*—or on the occasion of his first reading in philosophy—and subsequently changed his mind. By construing the clause in the latter fashion and adding the words in brackets, Pines allows himself to state flatly: 'Ibn Bājja does not deny al-Farabi's having made the remarks which were used to denigrate him'.[25]

In defence of Pines' reading of the Ibn Bājja passage, one might cite the words 'what he says here does not resemble statements of his [elsewhere] that are demonstrative conclusions'. as well as an observation of Ibn Bājja's later in the composition—if the preserved text is not corrupt—conceding that 'the beginning [*awwal*] of the commentary' has 'caused much damage'.[26] Those sentences might be taken as accepting the unconventional statements in the commentary as Alfarabi's own. It is no less possible, however, to take them as merely noting that Alfarabi's unfortunate manner of expressing himself lent itself to misinterpretation on a first, casual reading of what he wrote.

Several considerations tip the scales against Pines' reading. Ibn Bājja's stressing that the allegations concerning the commentary on the *Nicomachean Ethics* are 'false and a fabrication' can hardly be understood as anything other than a denial of Alfarabi's having endorsed the radical positions. What Ibn Bājja meant by saying that most of Alfarabi's statements in the commentary are 'attributed' is uncertain. But when he proceeds to write that Alfarabi's aim was to offer a 'censorious refutation' of statements quoted from others, he undoubtedly means that the problematic statements were among those

[24] Pines, 'The Limitations of Human Knowledge', 82–3 and n. 9.

[25] Ibid. 83. In his introduction to his translation of *MN*, p. lxxx, Pines reads the phrase in the second of the two senses.

[26] Ibn Bājja, *Rasā'il falsafiyya*, 201. The reason why I add the qualification 'if the text is not corrupt' is that the 'beginning [*awwal*] of the Commentary' sounds suspiciously like 'at a first [*awwal*] reading' of the Commentary. Could *qirā'a*, 'reading of', have fallen out?

Alfarabi quoted in order to refute them.[27] Later in the text Ibn Bājja remarks: if one examines the last part of Alfarabi's commentary on the *Nicomachean Ethics*, one will 'find that he states something' to the effect that the true purpose of society is to create conditions enabling citizens to develop their 'intellect'.[28] Ibn Bājja therefore did not understand that the commentary made civic and political eudaemonia the be-all and end-all of human life. Averroes settles the matter.

He characterizes the commentary on the *Nicomachean Ethics* as a work conveying Alfarabi's final thinking regarding conjunction with the active intellect and human immortality.[29] If the commentary contains Alfarabi's final position, Pines' rendering of the words 'at a first reading' as 'at his', that is Alfarabi's, 'first reading [of the *Ethics*]' is ruled out. Averroes further testifies that Ibn Bājja—incorrectly, in his judgement—read Alfarabi's commentary as concurring with the 'Peripatetics' and maintaining that 'conjunction [with the active intellect] is possible and does constitute the end [for man]'.[30] As far as Averroes knew, Ibn Bājja did not concede that the commentary on the *Nicomachean Ethics* rejected the possibility of conjunction with the active intellect and recognized no eudaemonia except civic or political eudaemonia.

Once Pines takes the statements recorded by Ibn Bājja to be Alfarabi's own and not a misreading of Alfarabi, he puts a good deal of weight on the clause: 'There is no eudaemonia except civic [or: political] eudaemonia'. He theorizes: 'In the framework of the Aristotelian system this means that intellectual perfection is not the final end of man. This view seems to be due to the fact that, according to al-Farabi, metaphysics, regarded as cognition of the immaterial entities, is a science that transcends human capacity.' The 'reference to political happiness [the term I translate as *eudaemonia* (H.D.)] provides a clue for this interpretation. They [Alfarabi's statements (H.D.)] negate traditional philosophy'.[31] Pines goes on, cautiously but unmistakably, to propose that Alfarabi's comments on intellectual perfection, the cognition of immaterial entities, and political happiness played a key role in leading Maimonides to a critical stance towards metaphysical knowledge.[32]

In sum, the newly discovered Ibn Bājja text reports that Alfarabi's commentary on the *Nicomachean Ethics* had been, or might be, thought to maintain that

[27] Averroes, *Long Commentary on the De anima*, 433, writes that the lost commentary on the *Nicomachean Ethics* cited Alexander of Aphrodisias as a philosopher who rejected the possibility of conjunction with the active intellect. Averroes' opinion, unlike Ibn Bājja's, is that Alfarabi 'apparently' agreed with what he took to be Alexander's position.

[28] Ibn Bājja, *Rasā'il falsafiyya*, 199–200.

[29] Averroes, *Long Commentary on the De anima*, 485; id., *Drei Abhandlungen über die Conjunction*, Hebrew section, 9; German trans., 46.

[30] Averroes, *Long Commentary on the De anima*, 433.

[31] Pines, 'The Limitations of Human Knowledge', 83.

[32] Ibid. 99, 100.

there is no existence apart from what is perceived by the senses;[33] that there is no afterlife; that talk of existence apart from what is perceived by the senses is an old wives' tale; and that the only human eudaemonia is political or civic in character. Pines construes the text as characterizing those as Alfarabi's early positions. On what I have contended must be the correct construction, Ibn Bājja branded the attribution of the radical propositions to Alfarabi as false and a fabrication and rejected it. Averroes knew whereof he spoke when he described the commentary on the *Nicomachean Ethics* as a late work and reported that Ibn Bājja took this commentary—like Alfarabi's other works—to affirm the possibility of the conjunction of the human intellect with the active intellect.

In the accounts of Ibn Ṭufayl and Averroes, what Ibn Bājja labels as false allegations are in large measure presented as positions that Alfarabi did endorse in his commentary on the *Nicomachean Ethics*. Ibn Ṭufayl provides only a couple of sentences. He reports that the 'commentary on the *Ethics*', unlike other works of Alfarabi, took the impious position that 'human eudaemonia' is 'restricted to this life'. Alfarabi then followed with a statement the 'sense of which' is that 'anything else asserted' about human eudaemonia is 'raving and old wives' tales'.[34]

Averroes refers to the commentary on the *Nicomachean Ethics* in several works, belonging to different stages of his career. Some of what he writes could be his own fleshing-out of what he found in the commentary, since he sometimes recreated the reasoning of philosophers whom he discusses and may have done so in the present instance.

He reports that even in the commentary on the *Nicomachean Ethics*, Alfarabi recognized a transcendent active intellect, which is the agent enabling the human intellect to pass from potentiality to actuality.[35] Alfarabi hence continued to recognize the existence of at least one being that cannot be perceived by the senses. He nevertheless branded talk of human immortality as an old wives' tale,[36] and Averroes explains how he arrived at that conclusion.

Alfarabi's *Risāla fi al-ʿaql* describes the human potentiality for thought as having the power to 'abstract lucidities and forms of objects from their

[33] The meaning is probably that there is no *human* existence apart from what is perceived by the senses, since the rest of Ibn Bājja's report concerns human existence and human eudaemonia.

[34] Ibn Ṭufayl, *Ḥayy ben Yaqdhân*, Arabic section, 13–14; French trans., 12.

[35] Averroes, *Long Commentary on the De Anima*, 485, 502; id., *Drei Abhandlungen über die Conjunction*, Hebrew section, 11; German trans., 51.

[36] Averroes, *Drei Abhandlungen über die Conjunction*, Hebrew section, 10, 13; German trans., 46, 54; id., *Epistle on the Possibility of Conjunction*, §14, Hebrew text, 108; English trans., 85.

matter', to take the form abstracted from matter as its own form, and to unite with it. That is what happens when man has a concept of a physical object. Alfarabi further maintained that the human intellect can reach a stage where it 'encounters' incorporeal beings—and specifically the active intellect—whose forms do not have to be abstracted. When this occurs, the human intellect takes the incorporeal form as its own form and unites with it, just as it does with forms abstracted from matter.[37] Maimonides, in his *Commentary on the Mishnah*, likewise wrote that the human intellect can have both kinds of form as objects of its thought.[38]

But, Averroes informs us, Alfarabi reconsidered the subject in his commentary on the *Nicomachean Ethics* because of a rule to the effect that a single 'disposition' has the potentiality for receiving only a single sort of thing. The human disposition for thought is plainly able to receive 'intelligible forms' abstracted from material objects. If it were also capable of receiving the very forms of incorporeal intelligences and fuse with them—and not merely have thoughts *about* incorporeal beings—it would receive two very different kinds of intelligible forms, those abstracted from physical objects and those that are immaterial in their own right and do not have to be abstracted. Since, Alfarabi now was convinced, such a situation is impossible, he concluded that the human disposition for thought cannot have an incorporeal being as a direct object of its thought. 'This is what led Alfarabi . . . to aver that man has no perfection other than perfection in the theoretical sciences.' Alfarabi therefore still held that human perfection consists in the acquisition of scientific knowledge. He only rejected the possibility of man's ever reaching a stage where he encounters an incorporeal form and takes the incorporeal form as the very thought he thinks.

Averroes immediately supplements the foregoing with an additional comment: 'Alfarabi stated that the proposition according to which man can become an incorporeal substance is an old wives' tale, for what is generated-destructible cannot become eternal.'[39] The point is expanded in another of Averroes' works.

There he writes that in the commentary on the *Nicomachean Ethics*, Alfarabi reasoned as follows: the human intellect comes into existence. 'If it should receive the form of an incorporeal intellect' and have the incorporeal intellect as the concept it thinks, 'it would unite with it, become identical with it', and

[37] Alfarabi, *Risāla fī al-ʿaql*, 12–13, 21–4.

[38] See above, Ch. 3, §4.

[39] Averroes, *Epistle on the Possibility of Conjunction*, §14; Hebrew text, 108. Averroes' *Long Commentary on the De anima*, 433, similarly states that in his commentary on the *Nicomachean Ethics* Alfarabi 'apparently rejects conjunction with the incorporeal intelligences' and maintains instead that 'the human goal' is not 'anything besides theoretical perfection'.

thereby be rendered indestructible. 'Something generated would become eternal.' That, however, is impossible because—by a well-known Aristotelian principle[40]—whatever is generated is perforce destructible. The human intellect consequently cannot have the active intellect as a concept that it thinks and unites with.[41]

In short, since a disposition can receive only one sort of thing, the human intellect cannot receive two very different kinds of intelligible forms, those of physical objects and those of incorporeal beings. Furthermore, if it did receive an incorporeal intelligence as the thought it thinks, it would become indestructible. Something generated would be rendered eternal, which is impossible.

On yet another occasion, Averroes ascribes Alfarabi's revisionism to a personal factor. Alfarabi, he writes, became disillusioned by his own failure to get the active intellect as a direct object of his thought and to conjoin with the active intellect, despite, so he believed, having achieved intellectual 'perfection at the end of his life'. As a consequence, he dismissed the possibility of conjunction with the active intellect and the possibility of human immortality.[42]

When the reports of Ibn Ṭufayl and Averroes are combined with that of Ibn Bājja, we find: the commentary on the *Nicomachean Ethics* belongs to the end of Alfarabi's life. The commentary could be read as labelling human immortality as an old wives' tale, locating human eudaemonia in the civic or political framework, and rejecting the existence of what cannot be perceived by the senses. Ibn Bājja rejects the supposition that Alfarabi held those positions as a false allegation resulting from a superficial first reading of the commentary. Ibn Ṭufayl and Averroes, by contrast, validate the part about Alfarabi's calling immortality an old wives' tale, and Averroes attributes to Alfarabi arguments to the effect that the human intellect cannot have any incorporeal being as a direct object of thought.

From Ibn Bājja and Averroes, we learn that the commentary on the *Nicomachean Ethics*, like Alfarabi's earlier works, still affirmed the existence of the active intellect, understood it to be the agent that brings the human intellect to actuality, and viewed human perfection as mastery of the theoretical sciences. The theoretical sciences would ordinarily include metaphysics.

[40] Aristotle, *De caelo*, 1.12.

[41] Averroes, *Drei Abhandlungen über die Conjunction*, Hebrew section, 13; German trans., 54; id., *Long Commentary on the De anima*, 481.

[42] Averroes, *Drei Abhandlungen über die Conjunction*, Hebrew section, 9; German trans., 46.

3. Ibn Bājja's Position on Metaphysical Knowledge

Pines pins a good deal on another passage in the newly discovered Ibn Bājja composition. Here Ibn Bājja speaks in his own name.

In works apart from the one we are concerned with, Ibn Bājja pictures the universe and the human intellectual process much as Alfarabi's preserved works do. He recognizes an incorporeal first cause, incorporeal intelligences, and a transcendent, incorporeal active intellect, which enables the human potentiality for thought to pass to actuality.[43]

He distinguishes 'three levels' of human intellectual accomplishment. In the first, the 'multitude' (*al-jumhūr*) abstract 'universals' from sense perceptions of objects in the physical world in such a manner that the universals continue to refer back to objects outside the soul; Ibn Bājja calls universals of this sort 'material intelligible thoughts'. At a second level, 'theoretical thinkers' (*nuẓẓār*) consider things from a higher standpoint: they focus not on objects in the physical world but on 'spiritual forms' in the soul, that is to say, on images and impressions present in the imaginative faculty, and they abstract their intelligible thoughts from them. At the third level, the human intellect frees itself completely from its ties to sense perception and images, and thinks intelligible thoughts 'insofar as the intelligible thoughts are existent beings in the universe'. The successive degrees of abstraction cannot run to infinity but must culminate in 'a concept that has no further concept'. Human intellects then 'see the thing in itself', a single encompassing thought common to all who reach the apex. Since intellect is identical with the thought it thinks, an intellect at the culminating degree becomes one with the all-encompassing thought it thinks and hence one with all other intellects that think the same thought. 'Aristotle and other fortunate persons' become 'one in number, with no distinction whatsoever between them'.

The all-encompassing, common intelligible thought is the thought possessed by the active intellect and consequently nothing other than the active intellect itself. Human intellects accordingly become 'conjoined . . . with the last intelligence', the active intellect. They attain 'final life', the 'ultimate eudaemonia for united humanity', and immortality; intellects at the two lower levels perish with the body.[44] The thesis that human intellects at a certain level

[43] Ibn Bājja, *Tadbīr al-mutawaḥḥid*, Arabic section, 85; Spanish section, 123; id., *Al-wuqūf ʿalā al-ʿaql al-faʿʿāl*, 107, 109; French trans.: 'Le Traité d'Avempace', 75, 77; id., *Ittiṣāl al-ʿaql bi-al-insān*, Arabic section, 19; Spanish section, 40; id., *Risālat al-wadāʿ*, Arabic text, 35; Spanish trans., 79; Altmann, 'Ibn Bājja on Man's Ultimate Felicity', 85.

[44] Ibn Bājja, *Ittiṣāl al-ʿaql bi-al-insān*, Arabic text, 13–21; Spanish trans., 30–45. See also Ibn Bājja, *Risālat al-wadāʿ*, Arabic text, 38–9; Spanish trans., 84–5,id., *Tadbīr al-mutawaḥḥid*, Arabic section,

coalesce upon the death of their bodies is cited by Maimonides in Ibn Bājja's name.[45]

In one of several analogies, Ibn Bājja compares the highest of the three levels to viewing the sun itself, the second to viewing the reflection of the sun in a body of water, and the lowest to viewing the reflection in the water as it is re-reflected in a mirror.[46] The Platonic overtones are obvious.

Pines finds a very different theory in the newly discovered Ibn Bājja text. The pivotal sentences for him occur in a description of the process whereby the human intellect acquires intelligible thoughts. Pines analyses the sentences in both the English article from which I have quoted thus far and in an article written in French; but he translates the sentences only in the latter. I shall start by giving his French translation of the key passage, followed by my English translation of his French. From that point on, I quote from both articles and when quoting from the French, immediately translate into English.

In the new text, Ibn Bājja maintains that should a man rise to a certain level with the aid of the divine power emanated by the active intellect, his intellect no longer stands in need of matter and is rendered incorruptible and immortal. So far, the new composition is in complete harmony with what Ibn Bājja writes elsewhere. But Pines discerns a critical difference between the level bringing about immortality according to the new text and the level doing so according to Ibn Bājja's other writings. As an example of thoughts rendering the human intellect immortal, Ibn Bājja, as translated by Pines, writes:

(Citons), à titre d'exemple, ce que nous imaginons [*takhayyalanā*] relativement aux mouvements célestes. En effet, à partir de la connaissance de la quiddité de ces mouvements s'actualisent [*ḥaṣala*] en nous (les objets de) connaissance les plus nobles [*ashraf al-maʿlūmāt*] et les plus sublimes.[47]

[Let us take], for example, what is present in our imaginative faculty concerning the motions of the celestial bodies. From knowledge of the quiddity of those motions, there are actualized in us the most noble and sublime [objects of] knowledge.

As Pines goes on to interpret the sentences, they say that the most noble and sublime objects of thought, which are 'actualized in us' from knowledge of the quiddities of the motions of the celestial bodies, are those quiddities themselves. He writes: 'The quiddities of the celestial movements are regarded as the noblest objects of intellection.'[48] 'These objects of knowledge, which are

61–2; Spanish trans., 100–1; id., *Qawl yatlū risālat al-wadāʿ*, 152; Maʿṣūmī, 'Ibn Bājjah on the Human Intellect', 128, 132; Altmann, 'Ibn Bājja on Man's Ultimate Felicity', 79–84, 86, 93.

[45] *MN* i. 74 (7). [46] Ibn Bājja, *Ittiṣāl al-ʿaql bi-al-insān*, Arabic text, 18–19; Spanish trans., 39.

[47] Pines, 'Les Limites de la métaphysique', 219, translating Ibn Bājja, *Rasāʾil falsafiyya*, 201.

[48] Pines, 'The Limitations of Human Knowledge', 86.

the most noble, fall exclusively within the purview of physics. . . . They do not belong to "divine science" in the strict sense of the word, that is to say, to metaphysics insofar as it is the science of God and immaterial substances.'[49] 'There is . . . no reference to objects of intellection that were not prior to their transmutation percepts of the imagination (and before that percepts of the senses).'[50] 'In the work we are considering, Ibn Bājja furnishes no argument that might lead one to believe that knowledge of these substances [that is, immaterial substances—H.D.] is possible for us. It seems that he tacitly accepts Alfarabi's reasoning, which concludes with the impossibility of knowledge of the sort.' 'It follows that study of the natural sciences suffices to attain immortality.' 'The doctrine of the unity of the intellect is not mentioned.' 'No need for divine science [that is, metaphysics—H.D.], the essential parts of which exceed human understanding.'[51]

On Pines' interpretation, Ibn Bājja thus rejects scientific knowledge of anything beyond the quiddities of the motions of the celestial bodies; and he does so because he tacitly accepts 'Alfarabi's reasoning' in the commentary on the *Nicomachean Ethics* which—on Pines' reading—ruled out metaphysical knowledge. At the same time, Ibn Bājja departs from the commentary on the *Nicomachean Ethics* and also abandons what he himself insisted on elsewhere. In opposition to Alfarabi, he affirms the possibility of human immortality. In opposition to what he writes elsewhere, it is intellect having knowledge of physical science, a level of intellect that perishes according to his other works, that now achieves immortality,

A few comments are in order before we proceed. What the text means by the quiddities of the motions of the celestial bodies is hard to fathom, but Ibn Bājja is often far from transparent. The verb Pines translates as 'are actualized' is more accurately rendered as 'come about' or 'result'; Ibn Bājja states that from knowledge of the quiddities of the spheres' motions, there *result* the most noble and sublime objects of knowledge. By construing Ibn Bājja as maintaining that the most noble and sublime objects of knowledge resulting from knowledge of the quiddities of celestial motions are nothing other than those same quiddities, Pines represents him as committing an odd tautology or circularity. He has him say that what comes about and results from knowledge of X is knowledge of X.

It may be a platitude that everything must be seen in context, but platitudes are often apposite. The passage in the Ibn Bājja text we are considering has to be read in its context.

[49] Pines, 'Les Limites de la métaphysique', 220.
[50] Pines, 'The Limitations of Human Knowledge', 86.
[51] Pines, 'Les Limites de la métaphysique', 220–1; 'The Limitations of Human Knowledge', 86.

After insisting that Alfarabi's commentary on the *Nicomachean Ethics* does not endorse the subversive propositions that it might be thought to endorse at a first reading, Ibn Bājja examines two of the propositions on their merits, namely: there is no eudaemonia except civic [or: political] eudaemonia; and the human intellect cannot attain immortality.

In general, he writes, a 'political regime' is an 'enormous help for the existence of the human intellect' and that is especially true of a 'virtuous regime'; for a virtuous regime has as its 'final end the existence of the intellect through multiple items of knowledge'. The 'first' item of knowledge inculcated by such a regime is 'God', and others are God's 'angels, His Scriptures, His apostles, and all His creatures'. Ibn Bājja therefore does affirm that knowledge of non-physical beings is possible. Pines takes notice of the statement but does not regard it as pertinent because he assumes that Ibn Bājja speaks here as 'a theologian, and not as a philosopher'.[52]

On the previous page, however, Ibn Bājja states that the human intellect 'approaches the First'—the deity—by acquiring 'non-visible intelligible thoughts' and thereby enters a state in which 'it does not need matter for its existence'. The discipline through which the intellect acquires the intelligible thoughts allowing it to exist without matter is 'metaphysical theorizing' (*naẓar mā baʿd al-ṭabīʿa*). 'Physical theorizing', by contrast, links man to the material world.[53] The statements sound strikingly similar to what Ibn Bājja writes in his other works.

And he continues: 'It is clear from what Aristotle says in his treatise * * * ' that 'substances . . . are three [in kind]'. The name of the Aristotelian treatise is illegible in the manuscript, but as Alaoui, the editor, observes, the reference must be to Book 12 of the *Metaphysics*, since what Ibn Bājja reports in Aristotle's name fits that work perfectly.

The three classes of substance distinguished by Aristotle, Ibn Bājja explains, are substances subject to 'generation and destruction', the 'celestial substances', and 'substance that is intellect and does not require matter for its existence'.[54] At the head of the last-mentioned class stands the 'most exalted' being, which has 'itself as an object of knowledge' and by knowing itself, knows everything 'that emanates from It'. At the bottom of the same class stands 'man's intellect'.[55] It is not, then, as a theologian but as a student of metaphysical philosophy that Ibn Bājja recognizes the existence of incorporeal substances, including the most exalted, the incorporeal cause of the exis-

[52] Ibn Bājja, *Rasāʾil falsafiyya*, 199; Pines, 'Les Limites de la métaphysique', 220 n. 23.
[53] Ibn Bājja, *Rasāʾil falsafiyya*, 198. [54] Ibid. 199, reflecting Aristotle, *Metaphysics*, 12.6.
[55] Ibn Bājja, *Rasāʾil falsafiyya*, 199.

tence of the universe. As support, he cites Aristotle's *Metaphysics* 12, a strange work to lean on if one is arguing for the impossibility of metaphysical knowledge.

Let us return to the sentences that Pines interprets as ruling out human knowledge of 'objects of intellection that were not prior to their transmutation percepts of the imagination (and before that percepts of the senses)'. Ibn Bājja prefaces the sentences with the proposition that every being in possession of cognition (*idrāk*) is to be described as 'alive', even if its cognition is at the level of sense perception, which is the lowest cognitive level. *A fortiori*, something is alive if it possesses the 'more noble' cognition of the 'quiddities . . . of images in the imagination faculty', and a being is even more alive if it has the 'certain science' that is 'from what comes about from those quiddities taken from the imaginative faculty'.[56] A bit more transparency would not have hurt, but Ibn Bājja plainly envisages successive levels of thought, including cognition at the level of sense perception, cognition at the level of the imaginative faculty, and the certain science that goes a step further.

The passage on which Pines focuses follows. Translating it more exactly and more fully than before, we get:

> [Take,] for example, what is present in our imaginative faculty concerning the motions of the spheres. From knowledge of the quiddities of the motions of the spheres there come about [or: result] in us the most noble and sublime pieces of knowledge [*al-ma'lūmāt*;]. He who has cognition [*al-mudrik*] of those intelligible thoughts is most deserving of the description *alive*.

If the sentences are read within their context and not made to clash with it, Ibn Bājja does not say that the quiddities of the motions of the celestial bodies are themselves the most noble and sublime objects of knowledge. He states that *from* knowledge of the quiddities of the motions of the celestial bodies, in other words, through abstraction from impressions in the imaginative faculty that relate to motions of the spheres, there results a further level, consisting in intelligible thoughts of the most noble and sublime sort. Ibn Bājja clinches things a few lines later, writing: when the foregoing occurs, a man, that is to say, a human intellect, 'thinks itself . . . and no longer needs matter or anything other than itself. . . . It no longer has to give heed to [images of] individuals in the imaginative faculty' of the soul.'[57]

The newly discovered text therefore aligns itself with what Ibn Bājja maintains elsewhere. It does not say that 'the quiddities of the celestial movements' are the 'noblest objects of intellection', that metaphysical knowledge is

[56] Ibid. 201. [57] Ibid. 201–2.

beyond man's power, and that 'study of the natural sciences suffices to attain immortality'. As in his previously known writings, Ibn Bājja posits successive levels of abstraction and a culminating stage in which, through 'metaphysical theorizing', the human intellect transcends its ties both to physical objects and to images in the imaginative faculty. At the highest level of abstraction, the intellect possesses knowledge of non-physical beings, including the 'most exalted' incorporeal substance from which everything else emanates. In its supreme state, it attains immortality. A virtuous civic or political regime creates conditions conducive to that goal.

Pines submits: 'It may be assumed with a certain degree of likelihood that he [that is, Maimonides—H.D.] was acquainted with' the views expressed in the Ibn Bājja text. 'Maimonides, probably under the influence of al-Farabi and the . . . theory . . . of Ibn Bājja, appears to hold' that 'because of the nature of his cognitive faculty' man is unable to pursue a life of theory.[58]

In fact, the matter stands as follows: Averroes tells us that Alfarabi's commentary on the *Nicomachean Ethics* was a late work. When Ibn Bājja speaks of the radical views that Alfarabi might be supposed to have held 'at a first reading', he therefore cannot mean Alfarabi's first reading of the *Nicomachean Ethics*. He must be talking about a first, imprecise reading of Alfarabi's commentary and insisting that the attribution of the sceptical statements to Alfarabi is a false allegation, growing out of the imprecise reading. Ibn Bājja and Averroes agree that the commentary on the *Nicomachean Ethics* continued to recognize the existence of the active intellect, still construed it as the agent that leads the human intellect to actuality, and viewed the acquisition of theoretical knowledge as the goal of human life. None of the reports concerning the commentary says anything about metaphysics.

The contention that Ibn Bājja rules out the possibility of metaphysical knowledge when he speaks in his own name in the newly discovered text requires tearing a few sentences out of context and reading them unnaturally. When what precedes and follows them is taken into consideration, his statements are wholly in harmony with the position he takes elsewhere. He maintains that acquiring metaphysical knowledge is the goal of human life.

Although Maimonides records an anodyne sentence from the introduction to the commentary on the *Nicomachean Ethics*, there is no evidence that he read the entire commentary. There is no reason to suppose that if he read it, he would have understood it as Pines, and not as Ibn Bājja, did. There is nothing to suggest that Maimonides ever saw the newly discovered Ibn Bājja text.

[58] Pines, 'The Limitations of Human Knowledge', 94, 100.

There is no reason to suppose that if he did, he would have dismissed what it plainly says in favour of Pines' forced interpretation.

If Maimonides rejected the possibility of metaphysical knowledge, he must have done so on his own.

4. The *Moreh nevukhim* on Metaphysical Knowledge

Pines adduces six or seven passages from the *Moreh nevukhim*[59] to support his contention that Maimonides rejected the possibility of man's attaining non-empirical, metaphysical knowledge. I have extracted them from the framework in which Pines discusses them and taken them up in an order that best serves my exposition.

(*a*) In *Moreh nevukhim*, iii. 9, Maimonides writes that 'matter is a powerful veil [*ḥijāb*] preventing cognition [Arab.: *idrāk* = Heb.: *hasagah*] of the incorporeal as it truly is'. Even the 'most noble and pure matter . . . the matter of the celestial spheres', places limits on the intelligible thought of the souls of the spheres; '*a fortiori*, this dark, turbid matter' of which man is made. 'Hence when our intellect aspires to cognition of God or one of the [incorporeal] intelligences, the powerful veil interposes itself.'[60]

Pines comments:

> This passage entails at least two conclusions: man cannot cognize God because the human intellect is tied up with the body. For the same reason man cannot cognize the separate intellects [that is, the incorporeal intelligences]. The second conclusion . . . appears to mean that man can only know material objects or objects connected with matter.[61]

Throughout his writing career, Maimonides kept before him the distinction between knowledge of God's existence and knowledge of God's essence. He stresses repeatedly that the existence of a single, first, incorporeal cause of the universe, hence the existence of God, can be demonstrated conclusively, whereas knowledge of the essence of God lies beyond man's capacity.[62]

[59] In the original version of the present chapter, I also included Pines' comments on *MN* i. 68; see Pines, 'The Limitations of Human Knowledge', 91, 93–4. On a rereading, those comments seem to be Pines' interpretation of *MN* i. 68, which he bases on his thesis, rather than a citation of *MN* i. 68, to support the thesis.

[60] See the text in Badawi, *Arisṭū ʿind al-ʿArab*, 246, and translated by Gutas, *Avicenna and the Aristotelian Tradition*, 59. Avicenna writes there that he reveals what he can, either straightforwardly or 'from behind a veil' (*ḥijāb*) , and he acknowledges—as Gutas translates—that 'what is known to mankind is limited'.

[61] Pines, 'The Limitations of Human Knowledge', 92.

[62] For example, *MN* i. 59 (72*a*). It is not wholly clear how Maimonides and others would harmonize the proposition that God's essence is unknowable yet His existence can be known with the proposition that in God, existence is identical with essence. They would presumably distinguish different senses of 'existence'.

The statement that a material being cannot have cognition of the incorporeal as 'it truly is' plainly relates to knowledge of the essence of God and other incorporeal beings. Maimonides very likely also has in view the corollary that man cannot have God and the incorporeal movers of the spheres as the very forms he thinks and unites with. He does indicate in the *Moreh nevukhim* that one incorporeal being, the active intellect, which is the lowest rung in the hierarchy, can become a direct object of human thought; I take the point up later in the chapter.

The impossibility of the human intellect's grasping God's essence and having God as a direct object of thought has no bearing on the demonstrability of the existence of God or the demonstrability of other propositions about Him. It consequently does not exclude the possibility of metaphysical knowledge. Far from being out of the ordinary, what Maimonides expresses in the passage Pines cites was a topos among the Arabic Aristotelians.

(*b*) Part II of the *Moreh nevukhim* opens with what Maimonides considers to be a watertight demonstration of the existence of God, and then turns to the existence of incorporeal beings subordinate to God. The following statement, discussed earlier in another context, is Maimonides' introduction to the subject:

Although the views held by Aristotle concerning the causes [*asbāb*] of the motion of the spheres, from which [motion] he inferred the existence of incorporeal intelligences . . . are hypotheses [*da'āwā*] not amenable to demonstration [*burhān*], those views, as Alexander [of Aphrodisias] states in the *Principles of the Universe*, are subject to fewer doubts than other views and hold together better.[63]

Whence Pines concludes:

This view clearly entails the consequence that the existence of the separate intellects [that is, the incorporeal intelligences] is merely probable and that no way has been found to attain certainty with regard to this matter. This being so, there is no point in setting oneself the aim to intellect or achieve a conjunction with a separate intellect.[64]

In the passage under consideration, Maimonides' position is that the existence of the incorporeal intelligences can be supported by proofs, although not by demonstrations, and is therefore more than 'merely probable'. He takes the existence of the intelligences for granted throughout the *Moreh nevukhim*, and as the book progresses, at one spot even drops the reservations he expressed on the authority of the *Principles of the Universe*; he states that the existence of incorporeal intelligences—although perhaps not their exact number—can be 'known through demonstration'.[65] Regarding God and the incorporeal active intellect, the last rung in the incorporeal hierarchy, he harbours

[63] *MN* ii. 3. [64] Pines, 'The Limitations of Human Knowledge', 94. [65] *MN* iii. 45 (99*a*).

no reservations: the existence of the former can be demonstrated apodictically, and the existence of the latter has been 'proved . . . without doubt'.

Even if Maimonides rejected the possibility of man's being able to 'intellect or achieve a conjunction with a separate intellect', that would in no way be tantamount to a rejection of knowledge of God's existence, knowledge of other propositions about God, knowledge of the existence of the active intellect, as well as other non-empirical, metaphysical knowledge. Everything Maimonides writes here is again in harmony with the views of the Arabic Aristotelians.

(*c*) The metaphor of light has long been used in descriptions of intellectual activity—the metaphor survives today in the word *enlighten* and its derivatives—and in one ancient and medieval version, knowledge is pictured as coming to man in flashes.[66] The Introduction to the *Moreh nevukhim* plays on the image of flashes of light, and Pines finds support for his thesis in the way Maimonides develops the imagery.

The passage at issue begins with Maimonides' opinion that what the ancient rabbis called the *account of creation* (*ma'aseh vereshit*) was equivalent to the philosophical science of physics, and what they called the *account of the chariot* (*ma'aseh merkavah*) was equivalent to 'divine science', that is to say, metaphysics. The rabbis insisted that only a tiny number of highly qualified persons be given access to the account of the chariot, and they restricted access to the account of creation almost as narrowly.[67] The reason for the latter restriction, Maimonides explains, is that a number of propositions belonging to physics are closely linked to the secrets of metaphysics and therefore 'they too are among the secrets of metaphysics'.

The introduction to the *Moreh nevukhim* continues: 'These immense secrets', in other words, the secrets of metaphysics together with secrets of physics that are closely linked to metaphysics, cannot be fully known to man. 'The truth at times shines for us so that we consider it to be day, but then material circumstances and habits conceal it [that is, the truth], and we return into an obscure night' 'We are like a person in a very dark night, upon whom lightning repeatedly flashes.' (i) 'One of us was such that the lightning flashed upon him constantly, with the result that he was almost always in light. . . . Such was the level of the greatest of the prophets', that is to say, Moses. (ii) 'There are some for whom the lightning flashes once in the night;

[66] Plato, *Seventh Letter*, 341C–D, employs the metaphor of the lightning flash in portraying human intellectual activity. Pines, 'The Limitations of Human Knowledge', 89–90, notes that the image of lightning flashes' illuminating the human soul appears in Avicenna, *Al-ishārāt wa-al-tanbīhāt*, 202, and in Ibn Bājja. The image is also found in Suhrawardī, *Ḥikmat al-ishrāq*, 4 (*al-bāriq al-ilāhī*).

[67] Mishnah *Ḥag.* 2: 1.

this is the level of those of whom it is said that "they prophesied but they did so no more".'[68] (iii) 'There are others for whom the flashes of lightning are separated by greater or lesser intervals.' (iv) Still others 'do not reach the level where their darkness is illuminated by lightning', yet they enjoy illumination 'by a polished body or something similar, such as certain stones and the like, which gleam in the darkness . . . and even the lesser light shining on us is not constant'. The foregoing are classes of 'perfect men'. (v) Finally, 'the truth, despite its intense clarity, is entirely hidden' from some, and they spend their entire lives in darkness.[69]

Pines hypothesizes that not just the first, but also the second and third classes, that is, persons for whom the lightning flashes only once and those for whom it flashes at greater or lesser intervals, are prophets. Maimonides accordingly intimates that 'only the prophets appear to see the lightning flashes', whereas the 'common run of people as well as the philosophers' have their darkness lit up through a lesser source of light, through polished surfaces. Pines further hypothesizes that the two broad types of illumination, through lightning flashes and through polished surfaces, stand for knowledge going beyond the empirical and knowledge limited to the empirical, respectively. Maimonides consequently tells us that 'only prophets' can 'cognize incorporeal entities', whereas philosophers, of whom Maimonides presumably is one, cannot.[70] Since Maimonides, in Pines' view, only pretended to believe that prophecy is a genuine source of knowledge,[71] no human being is able to have cognition of incorporeal entities.

Each step in the interpretation is questionable. The second class of men in the analogy, those who prophesied but 'did so no more' are, in Maimonides' theory of prophecy, not full-fledged prophets: when he enumerates the levels of prophecy in the *Moreh nevukhim*, he places the elders of whom the book of Numbers relates they prophesied and then did so no more, in a category that he characterizes as pre-prophetic and not covered by the definition of prophecy.[72] There is no reason to assume that the third class, those who are vouchsafed repeated lightning flashes, but whose flashes are separated by intervals, comprises only prophets.

Even on the supposition that the first three classes distinguished in the passage are prophets, there is no reason to suppose that illumination through flashes of light and illumination through polished surfaces represent non-empirical and empirical knowledge. Maimonides tells us that the imagery as a

[68] Num. 11: 25.

[69] *MN*, introd. (4*a*–*b*).

[70] Pines, 'The Limitations of Human Knowledge', 89–90.

[71] See ibid. 92–3; id., 'Les Limites de la métaphysique', 221 and n.

[72] *MN* ii. 45.

whole is designed to illustrate different levels in comprehending a single body of knowledge, which comprises the 'immense secrets' of metaphysics together with certain associated propositions of physics.

Maimonides devotes a number of chapters to the subject of prophecy, and at the centre of his discussion is an explanation of the way prophecy furnishes knowledge; that it does furnish genuine knowledge is taken for granted throughout the *Moreh nevukhim*. The supposition that he nonetheless secretly rejected prophecy as a genuine source of knowledge is in the spirit of a style of exegesis that has come into vogue in recent decades, but it is a bizarre sort of exegesis. It posits that Maimonides consistently intends the opposite of what he says, and the more frequently he affirms a proposition, the less likely it is that he accepts it.[73] It requires assuming that he delivered his former student Joseph ben Judah and others of a similar background from their perplexity by hoodwinking them into believing the opposite of what he himself secretly held.

The straightforward sense of the imagery of light in the Introduction to the *Moreh nevukhim* is not that metaphysics lies completely beyond man's grasp, but that because of the circumstances of human life and differing aptitudes, some relatively perfect men attain to a greater amount and do so more constantly, some attain to a lesser amount and less constantly, and some attain to no metaphysical knowledge at all. One should be wary of seeing too much in a metaphor. But if Maimonides perchance did have something more specific in mind, illumination through lightning flashes may signify knowledge of metaphysics through the good offices of the active intellect without the aid of a human teacher, and illumination through polished surfaces may signify knowledge of metaphysics with the aid of a teacher.

Maimonides, Pines' contention goes, indicates that 'only prophets' and not philosophers can 'cognize incorporeal entities' while he actually believed that prophets cannot do so either. If by the phrase 'cognize incorporeal entities', Pines means knowing that incorporeal beings exist, he construes Maimonides as intending the opposite of what he writes. Maimonides expressly and repeatedly states that the existence of God can be demonstrated apodictically, he maintains that the existence of the active intellect can be proved beyond doubt, and he contends that the existence of the incorporeal intelligences can be supported with highly plausible proofs. If Pines means that the human intellect cannot have incorporeal entities as the very forms it thinks, Maimonides—I shall presently try to show—held that man can have such cognition of a single incorporeal being, the active intellect.

[73] Strauss, *Persecution and the Art of Writing*, 73–4.

His statements are here too in harmony with standard positions of the Arabic Aristotelians.

(*d*) In the opening pages of the Introduction to the *Moreh nevukhim*, Maimonides describes the perplexed for whom the book is intended and to whom he refers in the title. They are, in the first instance, persons who do not know how to reconcile scriptural anthropomorphisms with philosophical demonstrations of the incorporeality of God. In the second instance, they are those who are troubled by scriptural imagery and by passages in Scripture that Maimonides reads as allegories.[74]

Much of Part I of the *Moreh nevukhim* is a glossary of terms that the Bible uses to describe God, and Maimonides shows how each term can be construed in a manner that removes anything untoward concerning the deity. Some biblical anthropomorphisms are more tractable than others. When, for instance, Scripture speaks of God's eyes, ears, and hearing, the words can easily be understood as metaphors for knowledge, and rationalist thinkers before Maimonides had long read them in that way. One of the more difficult challenges is the incident in Scripture in which Moses asks to be shown God's 'glory' and receives the reply: 'Thou shalt see My back, but My face shall not be seen.' Moses seems to have been accorded sight of God's back.[75]

Maimonides addresses the challenge by construing Moses' petition to be shown God's glory as a request for knowledge of God's essence; and he purges God's reply of anthropomorphism by taking the two kinds of sight of God—sight of His face that Moses is denied and sight of His back that Moses is granted—as levels of knowledge. The tactic is put to use, somewhat differently, in the *Mishneh torah* and the *Moreh nevukhim*.

The *Mishneh torah* explains that Moses requested knowledge of 'the true nature of God's being [Heb.: *amitat himatsao*] . . . as it is' in order to know God much as one knows a person by viewing his face. God's answer was that knowledge of the sort is beyond the power of human beings, who are composed of body and soul, but Moses would be granted a level of knowledge that was higher than any ever attained by any other human. Moses received cognition (Heb.: *hisig*) of 'something of the true nature of God's being' that was sufficient to set God apart from every other existent thing, much as viewing a person from the back suffices to set the person apart from everyone else.[76] God's face and back represent two modes of knowing God, one impossible for man, and the other possible for an extraordinary man such as Moses.

74 *MN*, introd. (2*b*–3*a*).
75 Exod. 33: 18, 23.
76 *MT*, 'Hilkhot yesodei hatorah', 1: 10.

In the *Moreh nevukhim*, Maimonides offers two variations of the tactic. In his own name he writes: the term *face* signifies, among other things, 'presence', and *back* signifies 'following and imitating . . . the conduct of someone'. Given those allegorical senses, he construes the clause 'My face shall not be seen' as saying that 'the true nature of My being' (Arab.: *ḥaqīqat wujūdī* = Heb.: *amitat metsiuti*), as it truly is, cannot become an object of human cognition (Arab.: *tudrak* = Heb.: *tusag*). He construes the clause 'thou shalt see My back' as assuring Moses that 'You will have cognition of what follows Me, is similar to Me, and proceeds from My will, namely, all My creatures.' God's face has the meaning it had in the *Mishneh torah*, but His back is no longer a lesser knowledge of God's being. It is now knowledge of everything outside God.

Maimonides further notes that Targum Onkelos, the Aramaic translation of the Pentateuch, places a different allegorical sense on the terms *face* and *back*. The Onkelos translation takes *face* in the sense of what is in front, and *back* in the sense of what is behind. It renders the words 'My face shall not be seen' as 'those in front of Me shall not be seen', thereby 'indicating', as Maimonides understands Onkelos, that besides God, 'there also are mighty created beings', namely 'the incorporeal intelligences', of which 'man cannot have cognition as they truly are'. Onkelos renders the words 'thou shalt see My back' as 'you shall see what is behind Me', thereby indicating, on Maimonides' reading, that human beings can know 'existent things' standing at a 'distance from God's being'. God's face now represents what is close to God, namely, the incorporeal intelligences, and His back represents what is further away, namely, corporeal beings. The class of beings that mankind, including Moses, can 'have cognition of in accordance with its true nature is, for Onkelos, things below [the incorporeal intelligences] in the hierarchy of existence, that is to say, what possesses matter and form'.[77]

Speaking in his own voice in the *Moreh nevukhim*, Maimonides thus interprets Scripture as stating that the true nature of God's being cannot be known to man, which carries the corollary that man's intellect cannot have God as the form it thinks and unites with; Moses was nevertheless vouchsafed cognition of 'all' God's creatures. Maimonides understands Targum Onkelos to place additional limits on Moses' knowledge. Not even Moses was able to grasp the true nature of either God or the incorporeal intelligences, with the corollary that he could not take them as forms his intellect thought and with which it united.

Pines writes that the explanation of the words 'thou shalt see My back', which Maimonides gives in his own name

[77] *MN* i. 37–8.

clearly implies that as a result of God's response to Moses' request, the latter was given the capacity to know even such transcendent beings as the separate intellects [that is, the incorporeal intelligences].

Maimonides had no need to give . . . Onkelos' translation or to put on it an interpretation that runs counter to the explanation which is put forward as his own. This way of proceeding may possibly be accounted for by the supposition that he wished to hint that the natural limitations of the knowledge of a corporeal being made it probable that 'Onkelos' interpretation' was correct and that Maimonides' own interpretation was propounded for theological reasons, a doctrine emphasizing the uniqueness of Moses being needed for the defense of religion.[78]

Maimonides certainly takes pains, here and elsewhere, to portray Moses as a superior member of the human species. Moses' superiority in the present depiction is purely intellectual, and to characterize such a depiction as 'needed for the defense of religion' is passing strange; what raises Moses above other men in mainstream Jewish religious thinking is scarcely his intellectual, not to speak of his philosophical, accomplishments. As for the significance of Maimonides' citing another interpretation of the biblical verses side by side with his own, that depends upon one's view of him. Conscientious authors commonly inform readers of opinions other than their own, and Maimonides states several times in the *Moreh nevukhim* that he is open to alternative interpretations of Scripture, as long as they do not ascribe physical qualities to God.[79]

However that may be, the topos that knowledge of God's essence and a direct thought of God are beyond man's power, and the proposition that knowledge of the essence of the incorporeal intelligences and having them as a direct object of thought was perhaps beyond the power even of Moses, do not, as already said, constitute a rejection of all metaphysical knowledge.

(*e*) Maimonides' philosophical case for creation turns largely on the inability of human reason to formulate a set of natural laws that can explain the structure of the heavens. His reasoning is that since the heavens are known by demonstration to have a cause and the structure of the heavens cannot be explained naturally, the cause must be a voluntary agent who wanted things to be as they are; a voluntary agent acts after not having acted; the voluntary agent who is responsible for the existence of the heavens must therefore have brought them into existence after they did not exist. In an aside, Maimonides

[78] Pines, 'The Limitations of Human Knowledge', 92.

[79] *MN* i. 21 (26*b*) and 28 (31*a*), iii, introd. (2*b*) and 4 (8*a*). Samuel Ibn Tibbon, who did not consciously differ from Maimonides on substantive matters, had no hesitation about differing in his interpretation of Scripture, presumably because Maimonides gave a green light for alternative scriptural interpretations.

remarks that 'everything Aristotle says about the sublunar region is in accordance with syllogistic method . . . but of what is in the heavens, man can comprehend merely a small amount, mathematical in character'. In other words, man can ascertain measurements of the celestial bodies and accurately predict most of the movements of the heavens. 'God alone' has 'complete' knowledge of 'the truth [Arab.: *ḥaqīqa*], nature, substance, form, motions, and causes, of the heavens'. And a few lines later: 'Let us then stop at the point where we are still competent and cede what cannot be known [Arab.: *yudrak* = Heb.: *yusag*] syllogistically to him who received the immense divine emanation [that is, to Moses].'[80]

Pines writes:

Moses is the only human being that may be assumed to have had this knowledge. In this context too the exception made in favor of Moses is in all probability connected with Maimonides' interpretation [of God's promise to let Moses see his back] . . . and may also be supposed to have been formulated for theological reasons. . . . Maimonides . . . considers that man can have scientific knowledge (which involves intellection) only of the phenomena of the sublunar world. . . . Maimonides is of the opinion that no scientific certainty can be achieved with regard to objects that are outside the sublunar world.[81]

Maimonides' proofs of creation are adapted from Ghazali's acerbic critique of philosophical attempts to explain the structure of the heavens, and his comments about man's limited knowledge of the celestial region are a coda to those proofs.[82] The comments are more in the spirit of the fideist scepticism of Ghazali than the radical epistemological scepticism of Kant. Maimonides, moreover, does not maintain that man can attain no scientific knowledge whatsoever regarding the celestial region. In addition to mathematical information, we have seen him state that Aristotle found by 'demonstration' that there exist multiple celestial spheres, each with a motion proper to itself; it followed necessarily by 'natural theory' that Aristotle should 'believe' that the concept possessed by each given sphere, which inspires it to perform its motion, differs from the concepts inspiring the other spheres; a number of additional propositions about celestial motion became 'clear' to, or were proved by, Aristotle.[83]

Most pertinently, man's inability to know everything about the heavens does not entail that man can have no scientific knowledge about incorporeal beings beyond the heavens.

80 *MN* ii. 24 (54*a*).

81 Pines, 'The Limitations of Human Knowledge', 93 (Pines' reference to *MN* iii. 24 should read ii. 24).

82 H. Davidson, 'Maimonides' Secret Position on Creation', 28–31.

83 See above, Ch. 5, §3.

(*f*) Scripture relates that side by side with the request to be shown God's glory, Moses made another. He asked: 'Let me now know Thy ways, that I may know Thee, to the end that I may find grace in Thy sight.' Maimonides prefaces his discussion of the request by observing, 'The sentence "Let me now know Thy ways, that I may know Thee" shows that God is known through His attributes, for when he [that is, Moses] knew God's ways [that is to say, His attributes], he knew God.' 'The sentence "to the end that I may find grace in Thine sight" shows that the person who knows God is the one who finds grace in His sight, not the person who merely fasts and recites the liturgy.' By contrast, 'the person who does not know God is the object of His wrath and is alienated from Him.'

Maimonides goes on to say that God does not have actual attributes. God's ways or attributes are 'the actions that proceed from Him', and Moses' request was consequently for knowledge of those actions, in other words, knowledge of what God produces. It is from the universe, God's handiwork, that the existence of God can be demonstrated and everything else knowable about Him can be known.[84]

The answer to Moses' request to know God's ways—as Maimonides reads the sequence of verses—was 'I will make all My goodness pass before thee'. God's goodness is His ways, or actions, and the passing of His goodness before Moses was the 'presenting of all existent beings to him . . . so that he could comprehend their nature and interconnections with one another'. As a result, Moses 'would understand God's governance of the universe as a whole and in its parts'.

Scripture further relates that Moses experienced a theophany soon afterwards in which he heard the pronouncement of what Jewish literature knows as the thirteen divine attributes (*midot*): 'The Lord, the Lord, merciful and gracious, long-suffering, and abundant in kindness and truth, keeping mercy unto the thousandth generation, forgiving iniquity and transgression and sin; and that will by no means clear the guilty; visiting the iniquity of the fathers upon the children.' The thirteen attributes, Maimonides writes, are merely a part of the full gamut of divine attributes of action, and the entire gamut, as just seen, was presented to Moses. God, or Scripture, calls attention to these thirteen because they are the attributes of action that a political leader needs to know and copy. A political leader should be merciful, gracious, long-suffering, and so on; he should by no means clear the guilty; and when the occasion requires, he should visit the iniquity of the fathers upon the children. Men

[84] See above, Ch. 1.

who, like Moses, have the dual role of political leader and prophet must take those attributes in particular to heart.[85]

Maimonides concludes the chapter in the *Moreh nevukhim* from which the foregoing statements are taken by acknowledging that he had 'digressed from the subject'; he wanted to explain why Scripture selected the thirteen attributes for particular attention. The reason, again, is that they 'are necessary in the governing of states, for[86] man's ultimate virtue is making himself similar to God to the extent of human ability'. 'The general point is that the attributes ascribed to God are attributes of His actions, not that He possesses any quality.'[87]

In brief, the person who finds favour in God's eyes is he who knows God, and one knows God through His ways. God's ways are attributes of actions, and hence everything God produces. Although God imparted the full gamut of divine attributes to Moses, Scripture calls attention in particular to thirteen divine attributes, because they are indispensable for someone who combines the role of political leader with that of prophet.

Pines gives the gist of what Maimonides writes, but with the significant omission of the observation that the person who knows God, not he who merely fasts and recites the liturgy, is the one who finds grace in God's sight. And he places considerable weight on the words that I translate as 'man's ultimate virtue is making himself similar to God to the extent of human ability'. According to Pines's reading of Maimonides:

> To become similar to God in respect of the attributes of action constitutes the highest perfection of man: 'For the utmost virtue of man is to become like unto Him . . . as far as he is able, which means that we should make our actions like His.'

The denouement is that:

> The only positive knowledge of God of which man is capable is knowledge of the attributes of action, and this leads and ought to lead to a sort of political activity which is the highest perfection of man. The practical way of life, the *bios praktikos*, is superior to the theoretical.[88]

Pines has taken the sentence that he translates 'the utmost virtue of man is to become like unto Him' as asserting in effect: 'to become similar to God in respect of the attributes of action constitutes the highest perfection of man'. The inference is not valid.

Like everyone standing in the Aristotelian tradition, Maimonides recognized two kinds of virtue, intellectual and moral. Since making one's actions

[85] *MN* i. 54 (64*a*–65*b*). The verses are Exod. 33: 13, 19, 34: 6–7.

[86] I did not understand the point of the word 'for'.

[87] *MN* i. 54 (66*b*).

[88] Pines, 'The Limitations of Human Knowledge', 100.

similar to God's is obviously not the ultimate intellectual virtue, Maimonides must be talking about moral virtue. And moral virtue, as he stresses over and over again, is subordinate to intellectual virtue.

In the chapter we are considering, he has told us that the person who finds grace in God's sight is the person who *knows* God, and he does not tire of returning to the theme throughout the *Moreh nevukhim*. Man's 'final perfection', he later writes, consists in becoming 'an actual intellect' and 'knowing everything in man's power to know concerning the totality of what exists'; it 'clearly . . . does not contain actions or moral qualities'.[89] 'Man's goal, insofar as he is a man, is nothing other than conceiving intelligible thoughts to the extent possible, the most certain and noblest of them being cognition of God, the angels, and God's other handiwork.'[90] 'True human perfection' and man's 'final goal' is acquisition of 'the rational virtues', which consist in conceiving 'intelligible thoughts that give rise to correct opinions in matters of metaphysics [*ilāhiyyāt*]'.[91] A man achieves the highest human level when he exercises his intellect, reaches 'perfection' in 'metaphysics' (*ilāhiyyāt*), and contemplates God's governance of the universe. The ideal man is he who masters 'the demonstration for whatever can be demonstrated, who possesses certainty concerning metaphysical [*ilāhī*] matters where certainty is possible while approaching certainty where only approaching it is possible'.[92]

Human perfection thus lies in intellectual or rational virtue, not moral virtue, and intellectual virtue consists in acquiring metaphysical knowledge.

Pines also quotes a few sentences from the concluding paragraph of the *Moreh nevukhim* that—despite Maimonides' repeated and unambiguous insistence to the contrary—he and others have read as making the acquisition of ethical virtue, and not intellectual accomplishments, the final goal of human life. I discuss those sentences in Chapter 8.

The six passages in the *Moreh nevukhim* cited by Pines to make his case do show that human knowledge has limitations for Maimonides, but the line does not run between empirical and metaphysical knowledge. Maimonides' position is as follows:

Man is capable of acquiring scientific knowledge of the sublunar world; he is capable of demonstrating the existence of multiple celestial spheres, each with its own proper motion, although complete knowledge of the nature, substance, and form of the celestial spheres is beyond human grasp; man can demonstrate the existence of God and other propositions about God, but

89 *MN* iii. 27 (60*a*).
90 *MN* iii. 8 (12*b*).
91 *MN* iii. 54 (133*b*).
92 *MN* iii. 51 (124*a*).

knowledge of God's essence and having God as a direct object of thought are again beyond the power of the human intellect.

The unknowability of God's essence has a history going back to Philo and Plotinus and it was a commonplace among medieval thinkers. If denying that a human being can attain knowledge of God's essence and the essences of other incorporeal beings were tantamount to denying the possibility of metaphysical knowledge, not only Maimonides, but the entire Arabic Aristotelian school and most or all scholastic writers would have to be classified as empiricists who renounced metaphysics.[93]

It is, in Maimonides' view, also possible to formulate plausible proofs, although not demonstrations, of the factors involved in the celestial spheres' motion—the number of incorporeal intelligences that maintain the spheres in motion, the love the spheres experience for their respective incorporeal movers, their desire to render themselves as similar as possible to their movers, and the expression of their desire in circular motion. If we take Maimonides at his word, he believed that the greatest of the prophets was vouchsafed a cognition of the incorporeal intelligences and a knowledge of the celestial spheres which are beyond the powers of the philosophers. Finally, Maimonides writes that the existence of a transcendent, incorporeal active intellect, which is the source of actual human thought and of actual natural forms in the sublunar world, has been established beyond doubt. The next section will undertake to show that he affirmed the possibility of the human intellect's reaching a level where it has the active intellect as a direct object of thought.

There is a good deal of metaphysical knowledge here, and Maimonides states unequivocally that acquiring such knowledge is 'true human perfection' and man's 'final goal'. As for the supposition that he set the practical life and political activity above a life of theoretical thought, it flies in the face of what he insists on throughout the *Moreh nevukhim*, including the chapter Pines cites to clinch his argument.

5. The Active Intellect as the Form that the Human Intellect Thinks; Conjunction with the Active Intellect

As was seen in an earlier chapter, Maimonides' *Commentary on the Mishnah* speaks of man's being able to take hold both of forms abstracted from physical objects and of incorporeal beings, which already are pure form and do not

[93] In the case of Aquinas, the impossibility of man's knowing the essence of God appears to be limited to the period during which his soul is attached to a body. See *Summa Theologiae*, 1.12, articles 4 and 11.

need to undergo abstraction from matter. The human intellect in a state of actuality becomes one with whatever thought it thinks and has 'cognition' (*idrāk*) of, whether it be a form abstracted from a physical object or the form of an incorporeal being.

The *Commentary on the Mishnah* further states that 'the ultimate end and eudaemonia' for man and highest conceivable human pleasure consists in attaining the intellectual level at which the soul has 'unending . . . permanence by reason of the permanence of the Creator, who is the cause of the soul's permanence thanks to the soul's having cognition [*idrāk*] of Him, as explained in first philosophy'. By having God, who is incorporeal, unchanging, and immortal, as a direct object of its cognition—not by thinking *about* something to which it attaches the name God, but by having the very form, or essence, of God as the thought it takes hold of—the human intellect becomes one with God and hence immortal as well.[94]

Maimonides has to be speaking loosely, however, because he also insists that man cannot know God's essence; if man cannot know the divine essence, he can hardly have it as the thought he thinks. For any sense to be made out of what Maimonides is saying, the incorporeal being that can become the direct object of thought of the human intellect must be not God Himself but one of the incorporeal beings subordinate to Him.

Those incorporeal beings are the intelligences that move the celestial spheres and the final rung in the incorporeal hierarchy, which is not the mover of a sphere but instead performs certain functions *vis-à-vis* the sublunar world. The Arabic Aristotelians identified the final rung in the hierarchy with the active intellect of Aristotle's *De anima*.[95]

When we jump ahead from the *Commentary on the Mishnah* to the *Moreh nevukhim*, we find Maimonides basing the existence of the active intellect on the premiss that whatever comes into existence is brought into existence by an agent of similar nature. It follows 'without doubt', that 'what gives form is an incorporeal form, and what brings intellect into existence is an intellect'. In other words, when the form of a natural object appears in the world where such a form did not exist before and a new natural object comes into existence, the source must be an entity that is actual form; and when a man thinks an intellectual thought, the source must be an intellect in which the thought is already actual. Without further ado, Maimonides posits a transcendent, incorporeal being, the active intellect, which is emanated from the incorporeal intelligence responsible for the motion of the last of the celestial spheres and

[94] See above, Ch. 3, §4. [95] Aristotle, *De anima*, 3.5.

which performs the two functions. It is the source of natural forms in the sublunar world and the source of human intelligible thought.[96]

Maimonides' rabbinic works do not say very much about the active intellect, but he does write in the *Commentary on the Mishnah* that the intellect of prophets 'conjoins [*yattaṣil*] . . . with the active intellect, whereupon a noble emanation from the active intellect emanates upon them'—upon the prophets.[97] The proposition that a highly developed human intellect may, either in this life or the next, *conjoin* with the active intellect was common among the Arabic Aristotelians, and it is almost surely the active intellect that, Maimonides assumes in the *Commentary on the Mishnah*, may become an object of human thought, thereby rendering the human actual intellect immortal.

Our question here is whether Maimonides takes the same stand in the *Moreh nevukhim*. He has been seen to state in the *Moreh nevukhim* that when the human 'intellect aspires to cognition of God or one of the [incorporeal] intelligences'—which apparently means when man wants to have their form and essence as the thought his intellect thinks—man's material side interposes itself and frustrates the effort.[98] The human intellect—at least during the lifetime of the human body—cannot take hold of the form of God or of one of the incorporeal intelligences. There are good grounds for not reading the statement as excluding the possibility of the human intellect's having the active intellect as the form it thinks.

Maimonides draws a parallel in the *Moreh nevukhim* between man, man's actual intellect, and the active intellect, on the one hand, and a celestial sphere, the intellect belonging to the soul of the sphere, and the incorporeal intelligence existing apart from the sphere and responsible for its motion, on the other. 'Actual human intellect', which comes from the 'emanation of the active intellect' and through which man has 'cognition of the active intellect', parallels the celestial sphere's intellect, 'which comes from the emanation' of the accompanying incorporeal intelligence and enables the celestial sphere 'to have cognition of the incorporeal [intelligence], conceive it, and desire to be similar to it'.[99]

Cognition (*idrāk*) was the term Maimonides used in the *Commentary on the Mishnah* for having an abstract form as the thought one thinks. That would suggest that the words 'cognition of the active intellect' and 'cognition of the incorporeal' intelligence mean man's having the essence and form of the active

[96] *MN* ii. 4 (14*a*), ii. 6 (17*a*), ii. 12 (25*a*–*b*).

[97] Maimonides, *Commentary on the Mishnah*, *San*. 10, introd., p. 212; similarly, *MT*, 'Hilkhot yesodei hatorah', 7: 1.

[98] See above, §4 (a).

[99] *MN* ii. 4 (14*a*).

intellect, and the sphere's having the essence and form of the accompanying incorporeal intelligence, as the thoughts they think and fuse with. But Maimonides was not meticulous in his terminology, and the term *cognition* does not by itself settle matters, since he regularly uses it more broadly. To take just a couple of examples, he speaks in the *Moreh nevukhim* of man's having cognition (*idrāk*) of God only 'to the extent of our ability' and again of man's approaching 'cognition [*idrāk*] of God's true nature' through discovering what God is not.[100] He plainly is not talking in either instance about a human intellect's having God as the form it thinks and unites with. God's essence, Maimonides insists, is unknowable. Besides, there could not be degrees of man's having God and His essence as the form he thinks, inasmuch as God's essence is simple and indivisible; and it would make no sense to say that the human intellect unites with a negative.

The statement about having 'cognition of the active intellect' nevertheless very likely does mean having the active intellect as the very form being thought. Maimonides writes in the *Moreh nevukhim*: 'It has been proved [*tabayyana*] in the books composed on metaphysical science [*ʿilm ilāhī*], that this science is not susceptible to being forgotten [*nisyān*]; that is to say, cognition [*idrāk*] of the active intellect [cannot be forgotten].'[101] Maimonides does not explain the move from the science of metaphysics to cognition of the active intellect or why cognition of the active intellect is not susceptible to being forgotten. A passage in Ibn Bājja, which Shem Tov Falaquera, Moses Narboni, and Munk all cited as the probable source of his remark,[102] fills in the gaps.

Ibn Bājja takes up the question whether man can ever have permanent continuous pleasure. He observes that although the pleasure arising from knowledge of the 'sciences' is superior to physical pleasure, man can forget ordinary scientific knowledge, and consciousness of it disappears completely when the human subject dies. Such knowledge is therefore not permanent. But 'it has been proved [*tabayyana*] that the ultimate science [*ʿilm*], which is the conception [by man] of the [incorporeal] intellect . . . is not susceptible to being forgotten [*nisyān*]'.[103] From what we saw of Ibn Bājja earlier, we know that his 'ultimate science' is the apex of metaphysics, and all who reach it share a single, common thought, identical with the thought content of the active intellect and hence with the active intellect itself.[104] That stage, for Ibn Bājja, cannot be forgotten; once attained it remains forever, and it is what constitutes human

[100] *MN*, introd. (5*a*). [101] *MN* i. 62 (80*b*). [102] See *MN* (trans. Munk), i. 278.

[103] Ibn Bājja, *Risālat al-wadāʿ*, §15. I have corrected a misprint in the Arabic text.

[104] See above, §3.

immortality. Read against the background of Ibn Bājja, Maimonides would likewise appear to be saying that mastery of metaphysics, as distinct from lesser degrees of human knowledge, leads to direct cognition of the active intellect, and when man achieves such cognition, he does not forget it.

Near the end and climax of the *Moreh nevukhim*, Maimonides writes: when Moses and the three patriarchs of the Israelite nation—Abraham, Isaac, and Jacob—attained the ultimate level of intellectual perfection and had their minds constantly focused on God, their 'intellects' were in 'union [*ittiḥād*] . . . with cognition of Him'. They enjoyed 'union with God, that is, cognition and love of Him'. The passage recognizes a crowning union—a conjunction—with the incorporeal realm in the present life, although the intent, once again, cannot be that the patriarchs had God's essence itself as the concept and form they thought, for God's essence is beyond human comprehension.[105]

Maimonides elaborates with the aid of a midrashic conceit according to which Moses and his two siblings experienced death through God's 'kiss'.[106] The *kiss* is viewed by Maimonides as an apt image for intimate intellectual contact with the incorporeal realm, and he explains death through the kiss as a metaphor for the death of a perfect person, whose 'cognition', 'love for the object of cognition', and intellectual 'joy' are at the supreme level. The 'soul then departs the body in that state of pleasure' and 'remains [permanently] in immense pleasure . . . as I have explained in my compositions and as another has explained [or: as others have explained] before me'.[107] The echoes of Ibn Bājja point to him as the other author whom Maimonides has in mind. Ibn Bājja's statements on the permanent pleasure and immortality of the human intellect when it has the active intellect as the thought it thinks would therefore lie behind Maimonides' notion of death through the divine kiss as the permanent immense pleasure enjoyed by a man who attains intellectual perfection. The supreme 'object of cognition' to which Maimonides refers would be the active intellect.[108]

The 'compositions' of his own that Maimonides mentions must, in the first instance, be the *Commentary on the Mishnah*, where he talks about having the Creator as the form one thinks, fusing with the form of the Creator, and thereby achieving immortality. A passage in his *Mishneh torah* makes an

[105] *MN* iii. 51 (126*b*).

[106] For the image, see BT *BB* 17*a*, and parallels. The scriptural basis is Num. 33: 38 and Deut. 34: 5, which say, literally, that Moses and Aaron met their death 'by the mouth of the Lord'. The midrashist explains that Scripture does not make the same explicit in the case of Miriam because of the impropriety of applying the expression 'by the mouth of the Lord' to a woman.

[107] *MN* iii. 51 (129*a*–*b*). Maimonides' interpretation of the kiss was picked up by the Zohar. See *Zohar* i. 168*a*: death by the divine kiss is 'the conjunction of the soul with its root'.

[108] As suggested by Munk in his translation of *MN* i. 278.

oblique allusion to the same doctrine, and that could be why he speaks of 'my compositions', in the plural.[109]

None of Maimonides' works offers a systematic discussion of the human intellect and immortality, partly, without doubt, because the positions towards which he gravitated were radically different from popular conceptions. We are thrown back on extrapolations and conjectures. The evidence nonetheless indicates that in his early period he almost surely, and in his later period very likely, recognized the possibility—in this life and at death—of the human intellect's not merely thinking *about* the incorporeal active intellect but having it as the very form and thought it thinks. When such occurs, the human intellect enters a state of permanent, immortal, intensely pleasurable union, or conjunction, with the active intellect.[110]

6. The Manner Whereby Metaphysical Knowledge Can Be Acquired

Certain statements of Aristotle are most plausibly read as saying that human knowledge begins with concepts and that after man possesses concepts, he combines them into propositions.[111] That reading has, however, been challenged, and Aristotle has been interpreted as maintaining instead that the simplest mode in which man has knowledge is propositional, concepts being known to man through the propositions containing them.[112] The Arabic Aristotelians relate to the issue in their explanations of the way the active intellect brings about the passage of the human intellect from potentiality to actuality. There were two basic models.

Alfarabi's model, which reappears with variations in Ghazali's account of the views of the philosophers, in Ibn Bājja, and in Averroes, pictures the active intellect as emitting a kind of light that enables the human intellect to see, as it were. Alfarabi himself offers different versions of the way the light from the active intellect works. His *Al-madīna al-fāḍila* and *Al-siyāsa al-madaniyya* describe it as entering the potential human intellect and producing there the 'first intelligible thoughts', that is to say, the general laws of thought—propositions such as: the whole is greater than the part, and things equal to the same

[109] *MT*, 'Hilkhot teshuvah', 8: 2.

[110] Altmann, *Von der mittelalterlichen zur modernen Aufklärung*, 81–2, 84, 118, disputes the reading of Maimonides as having envisioned a conjunction of the human intellect with the active intellect.

[111] Aristotle, *De interpretatione*, 1; *De anima*, 3.6, 430a, 26–8, read together with 3.3, 428b, 18–22. Averroes, *Long Commentary on the De anima*, 455, understands Aristotle as suggested here.

[112] Sorabji, *Time, Creation and the Continuum*, 139–42. Aristotle, *Metaphysics*, 12.7, 1072b, 18–20, to be read with Ross's commentary, makes it reasonably clear that God's thought consists in a concept—the concept of itself.

thing are equal to each other—and certain principles of science; man then constructs a body of knowledge employing the propositions with which he has been provided. Alfarabi's *Risāla fī al-ʿaql* describes the light emitted by the active intellect as illuminating both potential objects of thought and the human potentiality for thought, thereby enabling the latter to abstract 'quiddities' and 'forms' from their material substratum. Here it is concepts that the active intellect enables the human intellect to see.[113]

In the other basic model, that of Avicenna, human intelligible thoughts are emanated directly from the active intellect. The human soul, in Avicenna's system, prepares itself for thinking intelligible thoughts by contemplating images in its imaginative faculty. When the soul is properly attuned for receiving a given thought, it enters into 'conjunction' with the active intellect—which is to say that it makes contact with the undifferentiated emanation constantly transmitted by the active intellect—and it differentiates the appropriate thought out of the emanation. The active intellect broadcasts a range of radio signals, as it were, and the human intellect receives the signal for which it is attuned.

The intelligible thoughts acquired by man directly from the active intellect include, according to Avicenna, the first principles of thought, such as the law that the whole is greater than the part and that things equal to the same thing are equal to each other. Those plainly are propositions. The active intellect's emanation also furnishes concepts. With the aid of the first principles of thought, man can combine the concepts into propositions and the propositions into syllogisms. Avicenna identified the cogitative faculty (*mufakkira*, *fikra*) of the human soul as the faculty that differentiates concepts out of the active intellect's emanation, and combines the concepts into propositions and the propositions into syllogisms.[114]

The active intellect was thus credited by both Alfarabi and Avicenna with furnishing the human intellect with both propositions and concepts.

Maimonides does not say very much on the subject, but a couple of statements in the *Moreh nevukhim* indicate that, despite never mentioning Avicenna's name in the *Moreh nevukhim* and despite ranking Alfarabi as a more accomplished philosopher than Avicenna, he knew the Avicennan model and subscribes to it. He writes that human actual intellect is 'from the emanation of the active intellect'.[115] At another spot, he praises the superior man who

[113] H. Davidson, *Alfarabi, Avicenna, and Averroes on Intellect*, 49–53, 68–9 (Alfarabi); 145 (Ibn Bājja); 316 (Averroes); Ghazali, *Maqāṣid al-falāsifa*, 303.

[114] H. Davidson, *Alfarabi, Avicenna, and Averroes on Intellect*, 84–5, 87–94 (esp. 93), 96–8. For precedents in Plotinus, Kindi, and an Arabic text incorrectly ascribed to Porphyry, see ibid. 24–8.

[115] *MN* ii. 4 (14*a*).

occupies himself solely in 'conceiving intelligible thought' and establishing 'conjunction [Arab.: *ittiṣāl;* Heb.: *hidabek*] with the divine [active] intellect, which emanates upon him and from which the aforementioned form comes into existence'. The 'aforementioned form' is what Maimonides a few lines earlier calls the 'noble human form' and 'God's image and likeness', and what he says about it shows it to be an actualized human intellect.[116] The two passages tell us that actual human intellect, which is the same as actual human thought, comes *from* the emanation of the active intellect.[117]

He understands, then, that the active intellect's role in human thought is to continually broadcast an emanation, and it is from the ever-present emanation that man acquires actual thoughts. If Maimonides accepted the entire Avicennan scheme—which is by no means certain—man begins with the first principles of thought, receives concepts from the emanation of the active intellect, and combines the concepts into propositions and syllogisms.

Maimonides has insisted that the existence of God and various propositions concerning God can be demonstrated. Since nothing in human experience can prepare a human intellect to receive the concept *God* from the emanation of the active intellect, one may ask how man can demonstrate the existence of something of which he does not have a concept. The question does not merely arise in connection with Maimonides; it affects any thinker who embraces the epistemological model of either Alfarabi or Avicenna and who maintains that God's existence can be demonstrated.

We can only speculate about how Maimonides would envisage the construction of a body of demonstrated knowledge concerning God without one's possessing a direct concept of God. The following is a possible scenario.

The human imaginative faculty, which is a part of the soul, presents images to the soul as a whole or to one of the higher faculties of the soul such as the cogitative faculty; Maimonides does not indicate which. By contemplating the images, the soul prepares itself to differentiate the first principles of thought as well as forms, or concepts, out of the active intellect's emanation. As it continues to acquire thoughts from that emanation, the human intellect expands its corpus of concepts. I did not see that Avicenna, who analyses the role of the active intellect in the human intellectual process with considerable subtlety,

[116] *MN* iii. 8 (12*a*). *MN* i. 1, 2 makes clear that man is in 'God's image' when he possesses an actualized intellect.

[117] Altmann, *Von der mittelalterlichen zur modernen Aufklärung*, 80–1, 83, takes note of Maimonides' statements yet does not accept what they expressly say, in order to avoid reading Maimonides as tracing actual human thought to an emanation from the active intellect. Following Pines' translation of *MN*, Altmann renders the term *faiḍ* as 'overflowing' rather than as 'emanation', and that helps cloud matters.

explains whether the soul receives higher-level abstractions directly from the active intellect or whether it advances by its own efforts from one rung to another—whether it receives abstractions such as *corporeality* and *necessity* from the emanation or fashions them out of simpler concepts that it does receive. Nor is there a way of telling how Avicenna understood that the human intellect obtains negative concepts. For example, even if he be assumed to have understood that a concept such as *corporeal* is emanated from the active intellect, it remains unclear how he viewed the negative concept incorporeal—whether he took it to be emanated or supposed that the human soul receives the concept *corporeal*, adds the negative sign on its own initiative, and coins the concept *incorporeal*. Maimonides betrays no hint of how he might have handled instances of the sort.

At all events, by contemplating images refined out of sense perceptions, by receiving concepts from the active intellect, perhaps by building on already obtained concepts to coin new ones on its own, the human intellect can develop an inventory of concepts such as *first*, *one*, *corporeal*, *incorporeal*, *motion*, *time*, *finite*, *infinite*, *existent*, *possible*, and *necessary*.

The soul of a man with a philosophical bent would combine concepts into propositions and propositions into syllogisms, draw conclusions, and construct a science. As long as the thinker works in physical science, the concepts would primarily be those he received from the emanation of the active intellect, although he might also need concepts that he himself coined by coupling concepts from the active intellect with one another.

When a thinker would graduate to the subject of supernal incorporeal beings, he would have no access to such concepts as *God*. Nothing in human sense perception could be refined into an image that might prepare the soul for receiving the concept *God* from the active intellect's emanation, even assuming that the active intellect itself has the concept. Still, the thinker would have the concepts *one*, *first*, *cause*, *incorporeal*, *motion*, *necessary*, *existence*. By combining them, he would be able to formulate such propositions as: 'every moving object has a cause of its motion' and then go on to frame a demonstration of the existence of a single, first, incorporeal cause of the motion of the universe. He could similarly frame a demonstration of a single, first, incorporeal cause of the very existence of the universe. Without knowledge of God's essence and without an adequate concept of *God*, a philosopher could frame demonstrations of the existence of the being represented by descriptive phrases that refer, in effect, to God.

Although lacking a prior adequate concept of the *active intellect*, the philosopher could demonstrate the existence of a being represented by the descriptive phrases *cause of sublunar natural forms* and *incorporeal cause of human thought*. To the degree that the philosopher could formulate propositions about the individual incorporeal movers of the spheres, he would do so using descriptive phrases rather than an adequate concept of *incorporeal intelligence*. He could, moreover, demonstrate additional propositions about the first cause of the universe and the active intellect, all without grasping the essence of either—although, as we have seen, Maimonides may have believed that Moses, the prince of prophets, was granted knowledge of the essence of beings in the incorporeal realm, and although Maimonides very likely affirms the possibility of the human intellect's ultimately having the active intellect as a direct object of thought.

Propositions and demonstrations concerning incorporeal beings would thus be possible, without knowledge of those beings' essence.

7. Summary

The newly discovered Ibn Bājja text does not, on the most plausible reading, concede that Alfarabi endorsed any of the subversive positions appearing in the lost commentary on the *Nicomachean Ethics* and that Ibn Ṭufayl and Averroes ascribe to Alfarabi. When Ibn Bājja speaks in his own name in the newly discovered text, he explicitly states that philosophy can establish the existence of incorporeal beings and that life in the truest sense consists in reaching the apex of metaphysical knowledge.

Maimonides' only reference to Alfarabi's commentary on the *Nicomachean Ethics* is a conventional remark on morality, and there is no evidence that he read the entire commentary and not merely the introduction. There is no evidence that he ever saw the newly discovered Ibn Bājja text. On the assumption that he did, there is no reason to suppose that he would understand Ibn Bājja to have said anything other than what he plainly does say about Alfarabi and about his own position. In fine, there are no grounds for supposing that Alfarabi and Ibn Bājja led Maimonides to the notion that metaphysical knowledge is impossible for man.

The passages adduced by Pines from the *Moreh nevukhim* show that Maimonides set certain limitations on what man can know. But they in no way affect Maimonides' insistence that the existence of God and other propositions about God can be demonstrated, that the existence of the active intellect can be established beyond doubt, that the existence of the celestial spheres, although not their nature, can be demonstrated, that proofs, albeit not demonstrations, can be framed for the existence of a hierarchy of incorporeal intelligences, and that man's ultimate perfection consists in developing his intellect, acquiring as much metaphysical knowledge as is possible for man, acquiring as much knowledge about God as is humanly possible, and contemplating what he knows of God and His governance of the universe.

There is, moreover, textual evidence that the human intellect can, in Maimonides' judgement, have the active intellect itself as a direct object of thought at the culmination of its development and thereby enter into a permanent state of conjunction with the active intellect.

Kant remains the first Kantian.

SEVEN

A Problematic Sentence in Moreh nevukhim, *ii. 24*

Eliminate all other factors, and the one which remains must be the truth.

ARTHUR CONAN DOYLE
The Sign of Four

1. The Setting

A SENTENCE IN *Moreh nevukhim*, ii. 24, could, if read in a certain way, serve to support Pines' thesis that Maimonides rejected the possibility of man's acquiring metaphysical knowledge. The sentence comes at the culmination of a series of carefully reasoned arguments that are the backbone of the philosophical strand in the *Moreh nevukhim*.

Part II of the *Moreh nevukhim* opens with Maimonides demonstrating the existence of God. In order to have the most fundamental tenet of religion and philosophy stand on its own feet, no matter what position is taken on the issue of the creation or eternity of the world, Maimonides proceeds on parallel tracks.[1] On the hypothesis of creation, he writes, the existence of a cause that brought the world into existence follows immediately; it went virtually without saying for him, as for other ancient and medieval thinkers, that whatever comes into existence has a cause bringing it into existence. The hypothesis of eternity was a bigger challenge and it receives most of Maimonides' attention: he offers four philosophical 'demonstrations', that is to say, apodictic and conclusive proofs, for the existence of a first cause of the universe on the hypothesis that the world is eternal. A full demonstration of the existence of God requires that the ultimate cause of the universe be shown to be one and incorporeal, and Maimonides furnishes the requisite proofs of the unity and incorporeality of the first cause on both tracks.[2]

The first of his four demonstrations on the eternity hypothesis reasons from the eternal motion of the celestial spheres to an incorporeal mover that

[1] *MN* i. 71 (97*a*). [2] *MN* ii. 1–2.

constantly maintains them in motion. The second reasons from the existence of beings that are in motion and move something else and of beings that are in motion without moving anything else to the existence of a being that moves other things without undergoing motion itself.[3] The third looks at things that are subject to generation and destruction. It argues that if whatever exists were of that sort, everything would eventually cease to exist and the universe would revert to nothingness; there must therefore be something that is not subject to generation and destruction but exists necessarily, in other words, eternally. A necessarily existent, or eternal, being could have a cause, and the latter could have a cause as well, but a chain of necessarily existent beings, each the cause of another, cannot regress without end. We must consequently arrive at a being necessarily existent *by virtue of itself*, in other words, not dependent on anything whatsoever for its eternal existence.[4] The fourth demonstration turns again on the impossibility of an infinite regress of causes. It reasons from things that pass from potentiality to actuality and accordingly have a cause rendering them actual to the existence of a being that is the ultimate cause of whatever passes from potentiality to actuality and hence is itself free of potentiality.[5]

The third and fourth demonstrations would seem to have advantages over the first.[6] They do not tie the existence of God to a particular cosmology, whereas the first is tied to Ptolemy's geocentric system. They moreover go farther with less, for they outdo the proof from the motion of the spheres by concluding with a first cause of the existence, and not just the motion, of the universe. The first proof, which derives from Aristotle, is nonetheless the one that Maimonides marks as the demonstration of the existence of God *par excellence*.[7]

It is also the proof that he calls on to represent the eternity alternative when he combines the two tracks into a complete demonstration of the existence of God. The complete demonstration runs: the celestial region and its motion either have a beginning or are eternal. On the former hypothesis, there must exist a cause that brought the celestial region into existence, set it in motion, and continues to maintain it in motion. On the latter hypothesis, the proof from the motion of the celestial spheres establishes the existence of a first cause that keeps the spheres constantly in motion.[8] On each, the first cause—

[3] See above, Ch. 5, §3.

[4] For a fuller exposition, see H. Davidson, *Proofs for Eternity, Creation and the Existence of God*, 381.

[5] *MN* ii. 1.

[6] The second demonstration is embarrassingly weak and is best left aside.

[7] *MN* i. 70 (93*a*), ii. 18 (39*b*).

[8] Aristotle and the medieval thinkers, lacking Newton's first law, needed a cause to maintain moving objects in motion.

whether of the existence or the motion of the spheres—can be shown to be incorporeal and one. The existence of a single incorporeal first mover of the spheres is thus assured, whether the world is assumed to be created or eternal.[9]

After Maimonides is satisfied that the existence of God rests on an unshakeable foundation, he turns to the issue that he left in abeyance, the question whether the universe came into existence after not existing or is eternal. A voluntary God, he posits, goes hand in hand with creation, and a God who acts out of necessity and inalterably, hand in hand with eternity. Positions taken on the question of creation and eternity therefore divide those who maintain that God can intervene in the world from those who maintain that God's relation to the universe is governed by necessary and ineluctable laws—the theists, if you will, from the deists. Maimonides makes clear that the implications for the nature of God are of far greater significance than the question whether the universe did or did not have a beginning.

Although he concedes that his proofs for creation, unlike his proofs for the existence of God, are not apodictic demonstrations, they do, in his judgement, 'approach demonstration'.[10] They operate by showing that the thesis of eternity is open to much weightier doubts than the thesis of creation; and by the rule laid down in Alexander's *Principles of the Universe*, when an issue is not amenable to apodictic demonstration, the proper philosophical procedure is to weigh the doubts on each side and embrace the alternative affected by fewer doubts.[11] The proofs that are pertinent for our purpose are formulated within the same picture of the universe that lent itself to the demonstration of the existence of God from the motion of the spheres. They bring out aspects of the celestial region that are inexplicable on the hypothesis of a necessary and unchanging nexus between the world and its cause, that are therefore affected by more weighty doubts than the alternative.

To account for the complicated motions of the planets and stars around the sublunar region, medieval astronomers posited eight or nine primary celestial spheres and as many as forty-odd secondary spheres—spheres that interact with the primary spheres like interlocking cogs in a machine. The circumstance that all the spheres perform circular motion would indicate that they are made of a common matter. If they were governed by a necessary law, their motions should fall into a logical pattern. But astronomical observations indicate that some spheres rotate from east to west and others from west to east, that in some instances more rapidly moving spheres are located above less rapidly moving spheres, and in other instances, the opposite is the case. No order or pattern can be detected.

[9] *MN* ii. 2. [10] *MN* ii. 19 (40*a*). [11] See above, Ch. 5, §3.

Maimonides adds to those long-recognized difficulties in astronomical theory the contention that the matter of the planets and stars must be different from the matter of the spheres in which they are embedded, since they are stationary whereas the spheres rotate. Yet nothing can explain how objects made of different matters could be permanently welded to one another or how the fixed stars could come to be distributed in an entirely random fashion over the sphere in which they are all embedded.

He points out another, related anomaly: the nature of matter is such that it continually sheds one form and receives another. Should events take their natural course, the matter of the celestial spheres and the matter of the stars and planets would act as the matter of the sublunar region does. Each sphere and each star and planet would repeatedly shed its form and receive another; the changes would manifest themselves through constant changes in the direction and velocity of the spheres' motion and constant changes in the colour and brilliance of the stars. Nothing of the sort can be observed.[12]

Maimonides thereupon reasons: since Aristotle believed that the universe issues necessarily from God, he could not, try as he might, account for the anomalies.[13] But on the hypothesis that God, for reasons determined by His infinite wisdom,[14] willed and chose how the heavens should be constructed, everything falls into place, all the anomalies are resolved.[15] Inasmuch as the exercise of choice implies action after non-action, the heavens together with everything subordinate to them must have been created.

In the chapter containing the passage of interest to us, Maimonides adds a final and culminating anomaly. It grows out of a pair of related astronomical theories, that of epicycles and that of eccentric spheres.

On the epicyclical assumption, a planet is embedded in the surface of a secondary celestial sphere that rotates around a fixed point on the surface of a primary sphere, which, in turn, rotates around the earth. On the eccentric assumption, a planet is embedded in the surface of a sphere that rotates around a point that is not stationary but travels around the earth. The interaction of the rotations of the secondary and primary spheres, in the one instance, and of

[12] The central thought goes back to John Philoponus, who contended that the matter of the celestial region should behave as the matter of the sublunar region does. See Simplicius, commentary on the *Physics*, 1329. Philoponus advanced the contention in the course of a proof of creation, but his proof is completely different from that of Maimonides. Cf. H. Davidson, 'John Philoponus as a Source of Medieval Islamic and Jewish Proofs of Creation', 364. The argument that Maimonides makes may have been suggested by Ghazali, *Maqāṣid al-falāsifa*, 247, who explains that the matter of each sphere must be unique, for otherwise the spheres would continually change their forms. I could not find Ghazali's contention in Avicenna's Arabic works, but Avicenna's Persian *Dānesh nāmeh* seems to state it. See Avicenna, *Dānesh nāmeh*, 193.

[13] *MN* ii. 19 (39*b*).

[14] *MN* ii. 19 (43*a*).

[15] *MN* ii. 22 (49*b*).

the spheres and moving points, in the other, gives rise to the apparent routes taken by the planets as they travel around the earth. Epicycles, eccentric spheres, or a combination of the two had to be posited in order to construe as circular movements around the earth what we today know to be elliptical orbits around the sun.

Looked at mathematically, the two assumptions come to the same thing and, on the mathematical level, they work. They enabled astronomers to calculate the orbits described by the heavenly bodies and the positions of the heavenly bodies at every moment in the present, past, and future. They do not, however, work as physical theories. By entering into the most technical astronomical discussion in the *Moreh nevukhim*, Maimonides shows that both assumptions are incompatible with basic laws of physics—that is to say, Aristotelian physics.

The incompatibility of the epicyclical and eccentric hypotheses with the laws of physics means that 'enormous doubts' beset anyone 'who thinks that man can give a scientific account of the order of the motions of the sphere and construe them as natural, following a necessary law, and exhibiting a clear arrangement and order'.[16] When Alexander's rule about weighing doubts is applied, the scales tip decisively against the hypothesis that the world is the product of a cause acting by necessity. The world must consequently be the product of a voluntary cause who exercised choice; and what is produced by choice comes into existence after not existing. Maimonides was not the first to point out the incompatibility of the epicyclical and eccentric hypotheses with the laws of Aristotelian physics.[17] He moreover acknowledges that his proofs for creation from the heavens resemble a certain Kalam argument for creation. Some of his reasoning comes from Ghazali.[18] Nevertheless, although the raw material is borrowed from others, the resulting proofs of creation are original with him, and he uncovers intimations of similar thinking in Scripture.

When the biblical Abraham spoke of 'the Lord, God of the heavens', and Moses of Him 'who rideth upon the heavens', when the prophet Isaiah exclaimed 'Lift up your eyes on high and see who hath *created* these' and when Jeremiah declared that God '*made* the heavens', Maimonides understands them to have taught, in the first instance, that the existence of God can be inferred from the heavens. They were alluding to the demonstration of the existence of God from the motion of the celestial spheres. But he submits that in adducing the heavens as evidence of God's existence, they likewise called

[16] *MN* ii. 23 (51*a*), referring ahead to ii. 24.

[17] See Sabra, 'The Andalusian Revolt against Ptolemaic Astronomy', 133–53; Langermann, 'The True Perplexity', 160–2.

[18] *MN* i. 71 (97*b*). See H. Davidson, *Proofs for Eternity, Creation and the Existence of God*, 195–9.

attention to the signs of will in the structure of the heavens and motions of the spheres. Abraham and the prophets knew and alluded to proofs of creation from the structure and motion of the heavens along the lines of the proofs for creation that Maimonides offers.[19]

2. The Problematic Sentence

After expounding the incompatibility of the epicyclical and eccentric theses with the laws of Aristotelian physics Maimonides comments: all that man can know regarding the heavens is the aforementioned 'small amount of mathematical information', that is to say, the calculations made by mathematicians of the position of each of the heavenly bodies at any given moment in the past, present, and future, and of the route whereby the heavenly bodies get there. God alone has perfect knowledge of the true nature, substance, and form of the heavens, and of the factors that cause them to rotate; man, by contrast, has been vouchsafed adequate knowledge only of the sublunar region. 'The above is the truth, for . . .'.

Whereupon the passage we are concerned with follows. The Arabic reads:[20]

וד̇לך הו אלחק̈ לאן אסבאב אלאסתדלאל עלי אלסמא ממתנעה̈ ענדנא קד בעד ענא
ועלא באלמוצ̇ע ואלמרתבה̈ ואלאסתדלאל אלעאם̈ מנה אנה ד̇לנא עלי מחר̈כה לאמר
לא תצל עקול אלאנסאן אלי מערפתה.

Since every translator of the *Moreh nevukhim* has felt the need to add a few words to supplement what Maimonides writes and some have felt a need to ignore a word or two as well, it would be helpful to have a wholly literal translation before us as a baseline. Unfortunately, such a translation is not feasible. First, Arabic, like Hebrew, leaves the copula—the present tense of the verb *to be*—unstated, and a translator into a Western language has to supply it. Our passage has at least three spots in which the word *is* has to be supplied, and while placing it is easy in the first two, determining the proper location in the third is the very pith of the puzzle. By putting the third *is* in one place rather than another, a translation immediately takes a stand on the correct interpretation of the passage. Secondly, the term *istidlāl* appears twice, and its meaning is another bone of contention.

In order to have something to start with, I shall provide a translation that is as close to literal as possible, with the disputed *is* placed within angle brackets where Munk, the dean of modern translators of the *Moreh nevukhim*, puts it

[19] *MN* ii. 19 (44*a–b*). The verses are Gen. 24: 7, Deut. 33: 26, Isa. 40: 26, and Jer. 32: 17 (not quoted exactly).

[20] *MN* ii. 24 (54*a*).

and with *istidlāl* translated into English as he translated it into French. It will be observed that he rendered *istidlāl* in two different ways in the space of a couple of lines. The quasi-literal translation goes:

> The above is the truth. For the causes of reasoning [*istidlāl*] regarding the heaven are inaccessible to us. It [the heaven] is distant from us and elevated in place and rank, and the general proof [*istidlāl*] from it, that it has shown us its mover, <is> indeed a matter to the knowledge of which human intellects cannot attain.

The term *causes* is plainly used here in the logical sense that it has in Aristotle's *Posterior Analytics*.[21] By the causes of *istidlāl*, Maimonides means premisses that produce the conclusion of a demonstration and particularly of a syllogism. He is saying that man does not have access to premisses whereby a conclusive proof regarding the nature, substance, and form of the heavens might be framed.

We are concerned with the end of the passage. As tentatively translated, it asserts, albeit in an intolerably clumsy fashion, that human intellects are unable to know the general proof of the existence of a first mover of the heavens. The clumsiness is as follows.

By speaking of 'the general proof' through which the heaven 'has shown us' its mover, the passage apparently recognizes that there is such a proof and, thanks to it, at least some among us have been *shown* the mover of the heaven. At the same time, the passage says that the proof is beyond the reach of the human intellect. The existence of a mover of the heavens has been shown to us through a proof that is at the same time beyond our grasp. Had Maimonides wanted to deny that a proof of the sort is possible, he should have said so straightforwardly: 'There can be no general proof from the heavens that shows us its mover.'

Something still more basic is wrong. Maimonides stressed earlier in the *Moreh nevukhim* that his arguments for the existence of God are not merely proofs; they are apodictic demonstrations. In the *Mishneh torah*, he interpreted the first two commandments given by God at Sinai as obligations to know the existence and the unity of God, the first cause, by mastering a demonstration; and the demonstration that he supplied for both tenets was a bare-bones version of the proof from the motion of the celestial spheres. The *Moreh nevukhim* has four demonstrations of the existence of God on the hypothesis of eternity, but when Maimonides offers the full demonstration on parallel tracks, it is the proof from motion that he calls on to represent the eternity track. His discussion of the proper way to construe descriptions of God, an

[21] Aristotle, *Posterior Analytics*, 1.2.

issue of paramount importance for him, makes extensive use of the findings of the proof from motion. Much of his exegesis of Scripture rests on a conception of God as the mover of the spheres. Subsequently in the *Moreh nevukhim*, he would ground his treatment of prophecy, providence, and human immortality on demonstrative knowledge about God and particularly about God as the first mover.

He would state that worship of God worthy of the name consists in contemplating demonstrations of the existence of God and what can be known about Him.[22] Demonstrating the existence of God and comprehending what can be known about Him is also the end at which the study of science aims.[23] And the proof from the motions of the spheres is the best of the best, the demonstration of the existence of God *par excellence*.

The chapters immediately prior to the one containing the passage at issue advance proofs for creation resting on the presupposition that God is the cause of the celestial spheres. The present chapter, which sets forth the culminating proof—from the incompatibility of the eccentric and epicyclical hypotheses with the laws of Aristotelian physics—rests on the same presupposition. Maimonides' conclusion is that God, who is known by demonstration to be the cause of the celestial region, must have created it—and the rest of the universe—after they did not exist and, in the act of creation, implanted the irregularities.

If the problematic passage is taken as tentatively translated, Maimonides thereupon drops a casual remark that announces in effect: by the way, the general proof from the heavens, which has shown us that they have a mover, is something to which the human intellect cannot attain. I accordingly hereby repudiate what I wrote about the initial commandments of the Law in my *Mishneh torah*, my two-track demonstration of the existence of God, my proofs for creation, most of the rest of what I have said thus far in the *Guide*, and most of what I shall say in the coming chapters. The *Moreh nevukhim* becomes a unique literary artefact, a weighty tome in which a busy, gifted author invested thousands of his precious hours, only to plant a bomb plumb in the middle that blows the book to smithereens.

Pines does not cite the problematic passage to support his thesis that Maimonides rejected the possibility of metaphysical knowledge, although he adduces sentences in the immediate context. The passage did, however, find a mill for which it was grist.

22 *MN* iii. 51(124*a*).

23 *MN* iii. 54 (132*a*). The important point that natural science is not an end in itself for Maimonides is made in G. Freudenthal, 'Science in the Medieval Jewish Culture of Southern France', 33–4.

Leo Strauss allows hints that he had been sowing for decades to emerge a little more clearly in his introduction to Pines' translation of the *Moreh nevukhim*,[24] and the meditation with which he brings his introduction to a close alludes obliquely, yet unmistakably, to our passage. Maimonides' stated position, he reminds us, is that 'knowledge of heaven' supplies 'the best proof, not to say the only proof, of the being of God'. Maimonides' 'strange remarks' in *Moreh nevukhim*, ii. 24—that is to say, in the problematic passage—do seem 'to suggest that the only genuine science of beings is natural science or a part of it'. But if natural science is the only genuine science, 'the proof of the First Mover of heaven, i.e., the philosophic proof of God's being, unity, and incorporeality . . . becomes a subject of perplexity'. Strauss hastens to reassure us in his inimitable manner: 'It is obvious that one cannot leave it at this apparent suggestion.'

It is obvious. The words are a red flag, signalling to the cognoscenti that they are being transported into the land of irony, where what is obviously the case is not the case at all and where what is obviously not the case is precisely the case. Sure enough, Strauss makes no effort to correct the 'apparent suggestion' that Maimonides disavows his proof of the existence of God from the motion of the celestial spheres. Instead, he calls attention to Maimonides' assertion that 'the hypotheses on which astronomy rests cannot be true and yet they alone enable one to give an account of the heavenly phenomena'. And in the next sentence: 'Astronomy shows the necessity of recurring for the purpose of calculation . . . to what is possible in a philosophically inadmissible sense.'[25] Perceptive readers are expected to ask themselves whether Maimonides' strange remarks do not lift the veil and lay bare the stark truth that natural science is indeed 'the only genuine science', that not just astronomy, but 'the best proof, not to say the only proof' of the existence of God is possible solely in a philosophically inadmissible sense—which is to say that it is not possible at all. And if the proof collapses, belief in the existence of God collapses with it, for, as Strauss already carefully observed: 'Fundamental verities regarding God are genuinely believed in by nonprophetic men only when they are believed in on the basis of demonstration.' 'The being of God is doubtful as long as it is not established by demonstration.'[26]

Few students of Jewish philosophy have exhibited a desire to join Strauss in reading Maimonides' remarks as the self-disclosure of an agnostic or atheist.[27]

[24] See *MN* (trans. Pines), translator's introd., pp. xxi–xxii, xli–xlviii, li–liv.

[25] *MN* (trans. Pines), translator's introd., pp. lv–lvi.

[26] *MN* (trans. Pines), translator's introd., pp. xli, li.

[27] Scholem saw an explicit profession of atheism in the early pages of Strauss's *Philosophie und Gesetz*. See Scholem, *Walter Benjamin/Gershom Scholem: Briefwechsel*, 192–3.

Unless one goes that route, something must be done about the puzzling passage in the *Moreh nevukhim*.

3. Ibn Tibbon's Emendation

Some of the manuscripts of Samuel Ibn Tibbon's Hebrew translation of the *Moreh nevukhim* have a note in the margin that reads:[28]

> אמר שב"ת: נראה לי כאן חסרון מה שיהיה עניינו "אבל שאר עניינם הוא עניין", שאין לחשוב שאמ' על הראייה הלקוחה מתנועתם על מניעם שהוא עניין לא יושג, שהוא לקחו אם למופת או לראייה חזקה וזה במקומות רבים.

Samuel ibn Tibbon states: it appears to me that there is a lacuna here, the sense of which [that is, of the missing words] would be 'but whatever else concerns them [*aval she'ar inyanam*] is something that.' One can scarcely think that Maimonides said of the proof from their [that is, the heavens'] motion to their mover that it is a matter to which we cannot attain. For in a number of places, he regarded it [the proof from motion] as a demonstration or strong proof.

Ibn Tibbon's solution is thus to conjecture that a few words have fallen out of the Arabic text but he merely suggests what the sense of the words would have been and not necessarily what they were. It will appear in a moment how his suggestion would rescue the passage.

Ibn Tibbon left other marginal notes regarding the text of the *Moreh nevukhim*, and Carlos Fraenkel drew up an inventory of all such notes that are found in manuscripts of the Hebrew translation of the *Moreh nevukhim*. Over 150 manuscripts of Ibn Tibbon's translation are extant, and Fraenkel looked at the 145 that have been photographed for the Institute of Microfilmed Hebrew Manuscripts in Jerusalem. On his estimate, about half have notes in the margin authored by Ibn Tibbon. He recorded the marginal notes from twenty manuscripts and reports that the note we are interested in appears in seven of the twenty.[29] I examined a manuscript of Ibn Tibbon's translation of the *Moreh nevukhim* reproduced on the website of the Jewish National Library and six manuscripts of the translation from the library of the Jewish Theological Seminary, which are available on microfilm. One of the latter is among Fraenkel's twenty, and it has the marginal note. I did not find the note in the margin of any of the others. The sample thus indicates that only a fraction of the manuscripts of Ibn Tibbon's translation have it.

A smaller number of manuscripts of Ibn Tibbon's translation of the *Moreh nevukhim* go further and emend the Hebrew text itself by incorporating the

[28] As quoted in Fraenkel, *From Maimonides to Samuel Ibn Tibbon* (2007), 339.

[29] Ibid. 231–2; Fraenkel, 'From Maimonides to Samuel Ibn Tibbon' (Heb.) (2000), 242, col. 3.

three words that the marginal note conjectures convey the sense of what Maimonides wanted to say. With the emendation, Ibn Tibbon's translation reads:[30]

> זהו האמת כי סבות הראיה על השמים נמנעות אצלנו, כבר רחקו ממנו ונעלו במקום ובמעלה, והראיה הכוללת מהם—שהם הורונו על מניעם, אבל שאר ענינם הוא ענין לא יגיעו שכלי האדם לידיעתו.

The above is the truth. For the causes of proof regarding the heavens are inaccessible to us. They [the heavens] are distant from us and elevated in place and in rank, and the general proof from them <is> that they have shown us their mover. *But whatever else concerns them* [*aval she'ar inyanam*] <is> a matter to the knowledge of which human intellects cannot attain.

In our baseline translation, the pivotal clause read: 'the general proof from it [the heaven], that it has shown us its mover, <is> indeed a matter to the knowledge of which human intellects cannot attain'. The addition of the three Hebrew words breaks the clause in two. We now have one sentence reading: 'The general proof from them [the heavens] <is> that they have shown us their mover', and a second sentence reading: 'But whatever else concerns them <is> a matter to the knowledge of which human intellects cannot attain.' Maimonides is made to say that the existence of a mover of the heavens has been proved and there is something else of which human intellects cannot attain knowledge.

Joel Kraemer has come forward as the staunchest defender of the emendation. He points out that Ibn Tibbon judged the Arabic manuscript of the *Moreh nevukhim* furnished him to be faulty and sent it back to Maimonides for corrections. In his accompanying letter, Ibn Tibbon informed Maimonides that he had already corrected Part III of the *Moreh nevukhim* with the aid of a superior Arabic manuscript and that he marked other suspect passages in the margin of the copy he was returning. Kraemer understands Ibn Tibbon to be saying that he submitted possible corrections in the margin, but the letter is read more naturally as saying merely that he marked the manuscript where he was uncertain about the text. Maimonides replied: 'Wherever you surmised that a word or more had fallen out, such was the case.' Corrections of the Arabic text that Maimonides sent back to Ibn Tibbon have been preserved. The emendation suggested by Ibn Tibbon's marginal note is not among them.[31]

Kraemer speculates: 'Ibn Tibbon's marginal notes were probably related to questions' that he addressed to Maimonides. 'When the translator received confirmation from the master that his emendation was correct, he would then

[30] Many of the Hebrew manuscripts omit the words *shehem horunu*. The translation that follows is my own.

[31] Maimonides, *Kovets teshuvot*, 2: 27*a*; id., *Igerot harambam*, 531, 533–49.

insert it into the body of his translation, and this is what I propose happened here.'[32] His supposition is that the emendation suggested by the marginal note and incorporated into some of the manuscripts of the Hebrew translation reflects what Maimonides originally wrote or meant and that Maimonides so informed Ibn Tibbon.

Zev Harvey reports that he examined twenty manuscripts of Ibn Tibbon's Hebrew translation of the *Moreh nevukhim* and found the added words *aval she'ar inyanam* incorporated into the text of two; only two of twenty emend the Hebrew text in accordance with the marginal note.[33] Of the seven manuscripts of the translation that I examined, two have the emendation in the text and a third has the three words in the margin, where they are written in a hand different from that responsible for the text itself. Another witness is a learned annotator who lived before 1382. He knew of the conjectural emendation but warns readers that it is not part of the text of the Hebrew translation of the *Moreh nevukhim* and should be kept in the margin.[34] Harizi's medieval Hebrew translation of the *Moreh nevukhim* does not have the emendation. The emendation is thus not well documented in the Hebrew tradition of the *Moreh nevukhim*.

By chance, the publishers of the first printed edition of Ibn Tibbon's translation of the *Moreh nevukhim*—Rome, prior to 1480—selected a Hebrew manuscript that does incorporate the emendation and included the emendation in the text they published. Subsequent printed editions (I have examined nine, including Venice 1551, Sabbioneta 1553, and Yesnits 1742), which appear simply to have copied from one another, have it. Even-Shemuel, in his semi-critical edition of Ibn Tibbon's translation, prints the emended text, while noting that the emendation is Ibn Tibbon's addition.

As for the Arabic original, Sirat's inventory of manuscripts of the *Moreh nevukhim* has forty-four entries, but just fifteen are complete, or virtually complete, copies of the book. As I read her descriptions, only four of the fragmentary manuscripts include Part II, chapter 24.[35] Langermann identified four additional complete, or virtually complete, manuscripts of the Arabic text as well as three dozen additional fragments, none with ii. 24.[36]

Munk appears to have based his edition of the Arabic text of the *Moreh nevukhim* on six manuscripts that contain the entire book and other manuscripts that contain parts; none of the latter includes ii. 24. Issachar Joel, who

32 Kraemer, 'How (Not) to Read *The Guide of the Perplexed*', 369.
33 W. Harvey, 'Maimonides' First Commandment', 156 n. 10.
34 Langermann, 'New Source' (Heb.), 53, 62.
35 Sirat, 'Une liste de manuscrits: Préliminaire à une nouvelle édition du *Dalālat al-Hāyryn*', 19–27.
36 Langermann, 'Supplementary List of Manuscripts and Fragments of *Dalālat al-ḥā'irīn*', 33–6.

reissued Munk's Arabic text, made an addition to the manuscript information: he lists variants recorded by Hirschfeld from an Arabic manuscript that Munk did not consult.[37] Kafah writes in the introduction to his edition of the Arabic text that he collated three manuscripts of Yemenite provenance, and adduces a bit of evidence indicating that the Yemenite manuscripts represent a somewhat different recension of the book from the recension known in Europe.[38] I was able to examine two complete manuscripts of the Arabic text, one from the library of the Jewish Theological Seminary and the other a manuscript belonging to the Jewish National Library and reproduced on its website. Langermann was kind enough to check the passage in the handsome, and relatively early, manuscript that once belonged to the India Office and is now in the British Library. In one form or another, the passage has been collated or checked in at least thirteen manuscripts of the Arabic text of the *Moreh nevukhim*, about half of the manuscripts that are known. None has the emendation based on Ibn Tibbon's marginal note.

That is not all. Most of the manuscripts recording Ibn Tibbon's marginal note give *aval she'ar inyanam* as the words conveying the gist of what may have fallen out of the text. When those words are added to the text, Maimonides is made to say that *whatever else concerns them*, that is, the heavens, apart from their having shown us the existence of their mover, is beyond human grasp. In one or two manuscripts, the marginal note gives *aval she'ar inyanim* as the words conveying the gist of what is missing. The insertion of these words into the text would make Maimonides say only that certain *other matters concerning them*, apart from having shown us their mover, are beyond our grasp. As far as I could determine, every manuscript of the Hebrew translation that emends the text in accordance with the marginal note has the former reading. Such is also the reading of the printed editions. All have Maimonides state: *whatever else* concerns the heavens is beyond man's grasp.

Maimonides could not have made the statement or validated it.

In an earlier chapter of the *Moreh nevukhim* that reverberates back and forth with our passage, he describes Aristotle as having 'pondered and found' by 'demonstration' that not just one, but a number of celestial spheres exist, each requiring its own mover. He offers a proof establishing that the spheres 'without doubt' possess souls and he expounds other aspects of the spheres' motions that were 'proved' by Aristotle.[39] He writes that certain astronomical matters have been 'demonstrated'.[40] Immediately before the problematic passage, he refers to the 'small amount of mathematical information' regarding the heavens—that is

[37] *MN* (Joel), 8, 474.
[38] *MN* (Kafah), i, introd., pp. 14–15.
[39] *MN* ii. 4 (12*b*–14*b*).
[40] *MN* ii. 11 (22*b*).

to say, mathematical calculations of the routes travelled by the heavenly bodies and the position of the heavenly bodies at any given moment—that man can 'know'. Since Maimonides was sure that scientists and philosophers had in fact produced a body of knowledge concerning the heavens, he could hardly have written that 'whatever else concerns' the heavens apart from showing us their mover is beyond the grasp of the human intellect.[41]

To summarize the evidence: Ibn Tibbon's marginal note suggests merely the sense of what he thought had fallen out of the Arabic text and not an actual emendation. There is no evidence that he and Maimonides ever discussed the passage. No known manuscript of the Arabic text of the *Moreh nevukhim* takes cognizance of Ibn Tibbon's conjecture. Although the printed editions of Ibn Tibbon's translation leave the impression that the emendation is an integral part of the text, only a small proportion of manuscripts of the Hebrew translation have it; the emendation must therefore have entered the text after the translation left Ibn Tibbon's hands and multiple copies were in circulation. To cap it all, the text as emended in accordance with Ibn Tibbon's marginal note could not have come from Maimonides' pen or been validated by him.

Kraemer, who contends that the emendation reflects Maimonides' intent and was confirmed by him, addresses one consideration. To account for the absence of the emendation from every known copy of the Arabic original, he raises the possibility that the Arabic manuscripts may not preserve Maimonides' exact words.[42] It is conceivable, of course, that Maimonides wrote something different from what has been preserved in the manuscripts. But there is nothing to support the supposition that he did. There are no grounds whatsoever for imagining that if he did write something different in our passage from what has been preserved in all known Arabic manuscripts, Ibn Tibbon's lame guess somehow hits the mark.

A phalanx of evidence is therefore arrayed against the gratuitous emendation based on Ibn Tibbon's marginal note, and not a scrap of evidence can be marshalled to support it. The emendation is so unfounded that to belabour the point any further would be otiose. The solution to the puzzle must be sought elsewhere.

[41] When quoting Ibn Tibbon's marginal note and again when quoting the printed version of Ibn Tibbon's Hebrew translation, Kraemer too writes *she'ar inyanam*, 'whatever else concerns them'. He nevertheless renders the words as if they were *she'ar inyanim* both in his English translation of the passage in the printed edition of Ibn Tibbon's translation and in his English translation of what he calls the Arabic text of the passage as restored and reconstructed with the aid of 'Ibn Tibbon's version'. He translates what he calls his restoration of the Arabic text thus: 'And the general inference from it is that it indicates for us its Mover, but *other matters concerning it* are indeed something which human intellects cannot know' (italics added), See Kraemer, 'How (Not) to Read *The Guide of the Perplexed*', 355.

[42] Ibid. 374.

4. Other Proposed Solutions

Joseph Kafah, in his recent Hebrew translation of the *Moreh nevukhim*, dismisses the emendation of the Hebrew text as a 'bungle' resulting from Ibn Tibbon's misguided notion that 'Maimonides' words required correction'. Kafah's opinion of Ibn Tibbon was not high.

The pivotal clause in our baseline translation reads: 'the general proof from it, that it has shown us its mover, <is> indeed a matter [*la-amr*] to the knowledge of which human intellects cannot attain'.[43] Kafah leaves the unvocalized Arabic text untouched but rearranges the syntax by repositioning the elusive unexpressed copula *is* and by vocalizing a critical word in an ingenious fashion. In place of the obvious vocalization *la-amr*, '<is> indeed a matter that', he reads: *li-amr*, 'to a matter'. His Hebrew translation of the Arabic goes:

> וזהו האמת, כי סבות הלמידות על השמים נמנעים אצלינו, וכבר רחקו ממנו ונעלו במקום ובמעלה, והלמידות הכללית ממנו היא שהוא הורנו על מניעו, לדבר שלא יגיע שכל האדם לידיעתו.

The above is the truth. For the causes of drawing an inference regarding the heaven are inaccessible to us. They are distant from us and elevated in place and rank, and the general drawing of an inference from it [the heaven] <is> that it has shown us [or: proved to us] its mover, *to a matter* [*li-amr*], to the knowledge of which the human intellects cannot attain.

For some reason, Kafah takes the 'causes of drawing an inference' to be the thing that Maimonides describes as distant and elevated in place and rank. That is a patent misunderstanding of what Maimonides wants to say, but it has little bearing on the problem we are dealing with. The following clause is the pertinent one.

Kafah has Maimonides state that the heaven has shown us its mover, 'to a matter to the knowledge of which the human intellect cannot attain'. Maimonides is represented as maintaining that the proof from the unceasing motion of the spheres establishes a first mover, who is something whose essence is beyond the power of man to comprehend.

But there are flaws. The words 'has shown us [or: proved to us] its mover, to a matter' are unacceptably awkward in Arabic, as they are in my English translation of Kafah's Hebrew translation. 'To' is the wrong preposition in all three languages.[44] Furthermore, the term *amr* in Arabic means a matter or subject for consideration or discussion, not a being in any substantial sense. Kafah

[43] See above, §2.

[44] For the tactic to have a chance of succeeding, the Arabic should have said *ʿalā muḥarrikihi*, *ʿalā amr*, or *ʿalā muḥarrikihi*, *amr*.

requires us to suppose that Maimonides made the virtually incomprehensible statement: the drawing of an inference from the heaven is that it has shown us its mover, *to a matter [for discussion]*, to the knowledge of which the human intellect cannot attain.

His tactic therefore does not succeed.

Harvey takes a different tack. He reads the problematic sentence as doing what it appears at first sight to do—as disavowing the demonstration of a first mover of the heavens. Efforts to understand the passage in any other way spring, in Harvey's judgement, from the mistaken 'assumption that Maimonides is a confident rationalist'.[45] He sees Maimonides as a man whose faith was 'constantly wrestling with doubt',[46] although he refrains from going the final mile with Strauss and transforming Maimonides into an agnostic or atheist.

Harvey addresses the difficulty attendant on supposing that Maimonides included the proof from the motion of the spheres among his apodictic demonstrations for the existence of God on the eternity track and then turned around and dismissed it out of hand. Specifically, he supplies an explanation for Maimonides' offering the proof from the motion of the spheres side by side with the third of his four demonstrations, which Harvey characterizes as a proof of the existence of God 'as Necessary Existence'.

The explanation goes as follows: the proof of the existence of God 'as Necessary Existence' is identical with what Harvey calls 'the Avicennian proof from contingent existence to Necessary Existence'. Avicenna deemed his proof from contingent existence to be superior to the proof from the motion of the heavens on the grounds that it is a metaphysical proof, whereas the other is a physical proof. Avicenna's metaphysical proof is 'vacuous unless one understands contingent existence'. The proof from the motion of the spheres, even if fallacious, serves an important function because it is 'a summons to study physics'. 'The more one studies physics, the more one understands contingent existence, and the more one is able to apprehend the Avicennian proof'. Despite the impossibility of a human being's ever entirely grasping contingent existence, and hence the impossibility that Avicenna's proof will ever become 'thoroughly comprehensible', the pair of proofs, working in tandem, summon readers to acquire scientific knowledge. The proof from motion, despite its fallacious character, is offered by Maimonides because it is 'pedagogically (if not epistemologically) preparatory to the metaphysical proof based on the distinction between necessity and contingency'.[47]

45 W. Harvey, 'Maimonides' First Commandment', 159

46 Ibid. 161–2.

47 Ibid. 160–1. Harvey also sees a connection, which I could not understand, between the problematic passage and Maimonides' procedure of demonstrating the existence of God on parallel tracks.

The scenario is marred by inaccuracies.

Although Maimonides employs terminology that ultimately derives from Avicenna, he employs the terminology differently. In Avicenna, necessary existence is tantamount to actual existence; whatever actually exists, whether transient or eternal, 'contingent' or not 'contingent', is necessarily existent.[48] The object of Avicenna's proof is to establish the existence of something that is not merely necessarily existent—everything existing is—but necessarily existent *by virtue of itself*. Avicenna accomplishes the task with the aid of certain abstract propositions that he develops combined with just a single fact, the fact that something—it can be anything whatsoever—exists.[49] The proof is therefore neither an argument from 'contingent existence' nor an argument concluding with 'Necessary Existence'.

In Maimonides' usage, *necessarily existent* is tantamount to *eternal*, as it is in Aristotle, and his proof of the existence of a being necessarily existent by virtue of itself is a version of the venerable proof from the impossibility of an infinite regress of causes. It reasons from beings that are generated-destructible to a being that is necessarily, that is to say, eternally, existent. A necessarily existent being could have a cause, and the latter too could have a cause. Since, however, a chain of causes cannot regress indefinitely, we must sooner or later reach a being that is not merely necessarily existent but is necessarily existent *by virtue of itself*, in other words, not dependent on anything whatsoever for its eternal existence.[50]

Inasmuch as (1) Maimonides' proof is different from Avicenna's, there are no grounds for assuming that he ever saw Avicenna's proof. He was more likely inspired by a work such as Ghazali's account of the views of the philosophers, which records reasoning similar to his.[51] (2) Maimonides writes that his four proofs for the existence of God on the eternity track draw from both metaphysics and physics.[52] He never mentions or alludes to a contrast between a metaphysical and a physical proof of the existence of God, and there is no reason to think that the contrast ever crossed his mind. (3) Avicenna's proof requires no knowledge of physical science and, far from being 'vacuous unless one understands contingent existence', requires no understanding of 'contingent existence'. It merely requires that something exists, and that was part of

[48] Avicenna, *Shifā'*: *Ilāhiyyāt*, 28: '*Necessary* signifies firmness of existence'; 37–9; id., *Najāt*, 226: 'When the possibly existent by virtue of itself comes into existence, it is necessarily existent by virtue of another.' As long as 'the existence of something is not rendered necessary, it remains possibly existent' and hence non-existent.

[49] See H. Davidson, *Proofs for Eternity, Creation and the Existence of God*, 290–3, 298–304.

[50] *MN* ii. 1 (3). See H. Davidson, *Proofs for Eternity, Creation and the Existence of God*, 380–1.

[51] Ghazali, *Maqāṣid al-falāsifa*, 146–8.

[52] *MN* i. 55 (67*b*), 71 (97*b*), ii, introd. (4*b*).

its technical elegance. (4) Maimonides' proof, which arrives at the existence of a being necessarily existent by virtue of itself through a more conventional route, likewise requires no understanding of 'contingent existence'.

Harvey's attempt to make sense of the problematic passage—as a call to the study of contingent being and thereby as a preparation for understanding Avicenna's proof—thus stumbles at every step. Even if Harvey's scenario were accepted, we would, moreover, still be faced with the clumsiness of Maimonides' maintaining that a proof in which the heavens have 'shown us' their mover is at the same time beyond the grasp of the human intellect, and the grotesqueness of a book in the middle of which a sentence is planted that blows the book to bits.[53]

Josef Stern proposes yet another solution. It goes back to a distinction, drawn by Aristotle in the *Posterior Analytics*, between two kinds of *scientific knowledge* (Greek: *epistēmē*, Arab.: *ʿilm*).

There are, Aristotle writes, syllogisms that establish a proposition and in addition explain *why* the proposition is so, and syllogisms that establish *that* a proposition is true without explaining why. He illustrates with the following two arguments: (1) The planets do not twinkle; what does not twinkle is near; the planets are therefore near (that is to say, near relative to the fixed stars). (2) The planets are near; what is near does not twinkle; therefore the planets do not twinkle. The first syllogism provides scientific knowledge of its conclusion, the truth that the planets are nearer than the stars. It does not, however, explain why the conclusion is so, since the non-twinkling of the planets is not the cause of their being near. The second syllogism not only establishes a true proposition but also conveys the reason behind it: the nearness of the planets is the cause of their not twinkling.[54]

Ghazali, probably borrowing from Avicenna, who in turn was elaborating on Aristotle,[55] distinguishes two kinds of 'demonstrative syllogism': a 'demonstration [*burhān*] of why', which conveys the 'cause [*ʿilla*] of the existence of the conclusion', and a 'demonstration that', which provides the 'cause [*ʿilla*] for affirming the truth [*taṣdīq*]' of the conclusion but not the cause why the conclusion is so. An example of the former is the argument: there is smoke; for there is fire, and wherever there is fire, there is smoke. An example of the latter is: there is fire; for there is smoke, and wherever there is smoke, there is fire. The presence of smoke demonstrates the presence of fire in the manner in

53 See above, §2.

54 Aristotle, *Posterior Analytics*, 1.13, 78a, 22–78b, 3. For a more complete picture, see *Posterior Analytics*, 1.2, 9–33.

55 See n. 57.

which an effect establishes the existence of its cause, not in the manner in which a cause establishes the existence of its effect.[56]

Neither Aristotle nor Ghazali applies the distinction to the existence of God,[57] but Thomas Aquinas subsequently does. When preparing the ground for his proofs of the existence of God, Aquinas distinguishes between a *demonstratio propter quid*, that is, a *demonstration why*, which reasons 'through the cause', and a *demonstratio quia*, that is, a *demonstration that*, which reasons 'through the effect'.[58] In the case of the existence of God, only the second sort of demonstration is possible. Inasmuch as God has no cause and nothing is prior to Him, the only way to demonstrate His existence is by reasoning from the effect, the universe, to God as its cause.

Stern undertakes to make sense of our problematic passage with the aid of the distinction between the two kinds of demonstration.

Just prior to the passage at issue, Maimonides writes: God alone has perfect knowledge of the true nature, substance, and form of the heavens, and of the factors that cause them to rotate, whereas man has been vouchsafed adequate knowledge only of the sublunar region. Maimonides continues, in our tentative translation:

> The above is the truth. For the causes of reasoning [*istidlāl*] regarding the heaven are inaccessible to us. It [the heaven] is distant from us and elevated in place and rank, and the general proof [*istidlāl*] from it, that it has shown us its mover, <is> indeed a matter to the knowledge [*maʿrifa*] of which human intellects cannot attain.

The true nature, substance, and form of the heavens are, Stern understands, what Maimonides is referring to when he speaks of the 'causes of reasoning regarding the heaven', which are inaccessible to us; and the inaccessibility of the nature, substance, and form of the heavens is what frustrates human efforts to frame a *demonstration of why* for the existence of God. In Stern's words: 'In order to *explain* the conclusion that the deity exists, the premisses of the inference would have to contain "the true reality, the nature, the substance, the form, the motions, and the causes of the heavens"' (his emphasis). If the true nature, substance, and form of the heavens were known, a demonstration showing not only that a mover, God, exists but also explaining *why* He exists, would accordingly be feasible.

56 Ghazali, *Maqāṣid al-falāsifa*, 64–5.

57 Avicenna, from whom Ghazali apparently is borrowing, distinguishes between *demonstrations of why* and *demonstrations that*, stresses that both produce true results, and points out that a proof of the existence of God must be of the latter sort, since there is no cause (*sabab*) of God's existence. See Avicenna, *Shifāʾ*: *Manṭiq*: *Burhān*, 134 (called to my attention by Ch. Manekin).

58 Aquinas, *Summa Theologiae*, 1.2.2, resp.

Stern proceeds to solve our problem by putting a new twist on the clause 'the general proof [*istidlāl*] from it, that it has shown us its mover, <is> indeed a matter to the knowledge of which human intellects cannot attain'. On his reading, Maimonides does not mean that the proof from motion is beyond man's grasp. He means only that the proof from motion is not a *demonstratio propter quid*, and no *demonstratio propter quid*, no *demonstration of why*, has thus far been formulated for the existence of God. Stern further calls attention to Maimonides' recognition, immediately after our passage, of the possibility that someone would one day discover 'the true reality of what is obscure' at the present time. Maimonides thereby 'leaves open the possibility "that someone else may find a demonstration by means of which the true reality of what is obscure for me [for Maimonides] will become clear to him," i.e., a demonstration *propter quid*.'[59] Although a demonstration *propter quid* for the existence of God has not yet been formulated, it is not completely beyond man's grasp and may eventually be achieved.

Once again, there are flaws.

As regards the nature and substance of the heavens, on the one hand, and the 'causes of reasoning', that is to say, the premisses, on the other, Stern has got things backwards. Maimonides does not mark the nature and substance of the heavens as the causes of reasoning that are inaccessible to man and he does not say that since they are inaccessible, no *demonstration of why* has been framed for the existence of God. He says, on the contrary, that the nature, substance, and form of the heavens and the factors that cause them to rotate are unknown to us, '*for* the causes of reasoning' whereby we might know them are inaccessible. *Because* man does not have the requisite premisses regarding the heavens, he cannot frame a cogent proof of the heavens' nature and substance.

As for the possibility of a *demonstration of why* for the existence of God, Stern has committed an even more serious slip. If Maimonides gave thought to the distinction between the two kinds of demonstration—something that by no means can be taken for granted—he would scarcely have held that by comprehending the nature and substance of the heavens, a person might frame a *demonstration of why* for the existence of God, and that, moreover, such a demonstration may someday actually be achieved. To produce a *demonstration of why* for God's existence, one would need premisses conveying the cause or causes of His existence, and God's existence has no cause. A *demonstration of why* for the existence of God is impossible in principle, and the substance and nature of the heavens have nothing to do with it.

Furthermore, if Maimonides had wanted to tell us that only a *demonstration*

59 Stern, 'The Knot That Never Was', 333–9. The quotations are from p. 338.

that and not a *demonstration of why* has been achieved in the case of the existence of God, he should have said so and not written something else. What he does say, in the tentative translation of the passage, is that the proof from the motion of the heavens is, without qualification, 'a matter to the knowledge [*maʿrifa*] of which human intellects cannot attain'. (It will be noted that Maimonides uses the term *maʿrifa*, *knowledge*, and not *ʿilm*, which means *scientific knowledge*.) If Maimonides wanted to make the point that a *demonstration of why* is impossible in the case of the existence of God, the proper place for him to do so would not be the present context, where he treats anomalies in the movements of the celestial spheres. He should have done so in the earlier chapters of the *Moreh nevukhim* where he offered his demonstrations for the existence of God that argue from the effect to the cause.

5. The Solution

To repeat our tentative translation of the passage one final time:

> The above is the truth. For the causes of reasoning [*istidlāl*] regarding the heaven are inaccessible to us. It [the heaven] is distant from us and elevated in place and rank, and [*wa-*] the general proof [*istidlāl*] from it, that it has shown us its mover, <is> indeed a matter to the knowledge of which human intellects cannot attain.

The key clause begins with the Arabic conjunction *wa-*, and the tentative translation follows the consensus of translators of the *Moreh nevukhim* in taking *wa-* as the co-ordinate conjunction 'and'. I accordingly translated: '*and* the general proof from it, that it has shown us its mover'. Arabic *wa-* can, however, also function as a subordinate conjunction with the meaning 'while', 'whereas', or the like. That occurs in what are known as circumstantial clauses. Wright's *Arabic Grammar* illustrates such clauses by the sentences: *dhahaba Zayd wa-ʿAmr bāqin* = 'Zaid went away *while* Amr remained' and *dhahaba Zayd wa-ʿAmr yashtaghil* = 'Zaid went away *while* Amr was busy.'[60]

The solution to our problem lies in construing the words tentatively translated: 'and the general proof from it, that it has shown us its mover' (*wa-al-istidlāl alʿāmm … muḥarrikihi*) as a parenthetical clause introduced by the *wa-* that has the force of a subordinate conjunction. An elusive copula 'is' again has to be supplied, and the corrected translation of the parenthetical clause will then read: 'while the general proof [*istidlāl*] from it <is> that it has shown us its mover'. Once the problematic clause is bracketed as parenthetical, the previously mentioned 'heaven' becomes 'the matter to the knowledge of which

[60] Wright, *Grammar of the Arabic Language*, ii. 330–1.

human minds cannot attain'. Before I fully spell out the proposed translation, a comment should be made about the term *istidlāl.*

Istidlāl, which appears twice in the passage, is a verbal noun, or gerund. Verbal nouns in Arabic—much like those in Hebrew—can designate either an activity and process or the result of the activity or process. Wehr's Arabic dictionary thus includes among its definitions of *istidlāl*: 'reasoning' and 'argumentation', which are activities, and 'inference' and 'proof', which are the results. The double possibility should be familiar to English-speaking readers. The verbal noun *writing*, for instance, denotes an activity in sentences such as: 'He is engaged in writing the great American novel.' It denotes the result of the activity in expressions such as 'Maimonides' writings'.

Translations of the passage in the *Moreh nevukhim* exemplify the two possible ways of construing *istidlāl.* Munk's French translation renders the first occurrence of the term as 'raisonner', that is to say, the activity of reasoning, and the second occurrence as 'preuve', 'proof', which is what reasoning produces. Pines paraphrases the words 'the causes of reasoning [*istidlāl*] regarding the heaven' in our tentative translation as: 'the points starting from which conclusions may be drawn about the heavens'; it is unclear whether he takes *istidlāl* as the activity or the result. He translates the second occurrence as 'conclusion', the result. In Hebrew translations of the *Moreh nevukhim*, we find the following: Ibn Tibbon's translation renders both instances of the term as *re'ayah*, that is, 'proof', the result. Harizi anticipates Munk by rendering the first occurrence as *lekiḥat hare'ayah*, which means adducing or formulating a proof, and the second as *re'ayah*, 'proof'; the first is the process or activity, and the second, the result. Kafah translates both occurrences as *lemidut*, by which he appears to mean: the drawing of an inference, the activity. Schwarz's Hebrew translation renders the first occurrence as *hasakat masekanot*, 'drawing of conclusions', which would mean the process and activity. He renders the second as *masekanah*, 'conclusion', the result.

The term *istidlāl* appears a number of times in the *Moreh nevukhim* and Maimonides' other Arabic writings.[61] In most instances, it clearly denotes the activity of framing an argument or proof, and the translators generally recognize as much; in a few instances, it can be read as denoting either the activity or the result. Maimonides' usage in the *Moreh nevukhim* and elsewhere makes it probable that both instances of the term in our passage denote an activity and that he is in both instances talking about framing proofs.

[61] See H. Davidson, 'Further on a Problematic Passage', 8–12. Without searching systematically, I know of over a dozen occurrences in *MN*, some of which were pointed out to me by Josef Stern, and eight occurrences in other Arabic works of Maimonides.

When the pivotal clause is taken as parenthetical and introduced by a subordinate conjunction and when *istidlāl* is understood in the sense of *framing a proof*, a more or less literal translation of the passage will be:

The above is the truth. For the causes of the framing of a proof regarding the heaven are inaccessible to us. It [the heaven] is distant from us and elevated in place and rank—while the general framing of a proof from it <is> that it has shown us its mover—indeed a matter to the knowledge of which human minds cannot attain.

Turning that into more acceptable English, we get:

The above is the truth. For the causes [that is, the premisses] whereby proofs might be framed regarding the heavens are beyond our grasp. They [that is, the heavens] are distant from us and elevated in place and rank—the general framing of a proof from them coming to this, that they have shown us [or: proven to us] their mover. Indeed [they are] a matter to the knowledge of which human minds cannot attain.

I realize that there are colleagues who have not felt wholly comfortable with my reading. They should remember Sherlock Holmes's rule: 'Eliminate all other factors, and the one which remains must be the truth.' I was gratified that Schwarz accepted the reading in his exemplary Hebrew translation of the *Moreh nevukhim*.

Determining whether or not Maimonides was a *confident* rationalist, to use Harvey's expression, is probably impossible. But Maimonides definitely saw himself as a rationalist.

EIGHT

Maimonides' Ethical Systems

God is not an enemy of the body, who wants its destruction.

MAIMONIDES
Shemonah perakim, chapter 4

When the claims of matter beckon him [who chooses to be truly a man and not a beast in man's shape and figure] to its dirt and . . . shame, he is pained at being immersed in it. He is embarrassed and ashamed . . . and tries to . . . safeguard himself from it at all costs, like someone whom the sovereign became angry with and commanded to carry manure from one place to another in order to humiliate him.

MAIMONIDES
Moreh nevukhim, iii. 8

1. *Commentary on the Mishnah*; *Shemonah perakim*

THE ETHICAL THEORY OF Maimonides' earlier period rests on a pair of interrelationships—between a person's actions and the characteristics in his soul, and between moral virtue and the intellectual life.

Actions and characteristics in the soul form a tight circle. Repeatedly performing an action creates a habit (Arab.: *hay'a*) in the conative, or appetitive, (Arab.: *nuzūʿiyya*; Heb.: *mitorer*) faculty of the soul. Once the characteristic takes root, it manifests itself in the performance of additional actions of the sort that created it.[1] The cycle is not hermetically closed, for, Maimonides insists, human beings never lose freedom of choice. By an exercise of will, a person can break free and initiate actions in opposition to the characteristics in his soul, no matter how firmly they are ingrained. Those actions will then feed back and alter the characteristics.[2]

Despite the close link between actions and psychological characteristics, the latter alone are the locus of virtue and vice. Actions may be good or bad, but they are not properly described as virtuous or vicious; only characteristics in

[1] *ShP*, ch. 1, p. 375, ch. 2, p. 377, ch. 4, pp. 379, 381; see also above, Ch. 4. For a description of the conative faculty of the soul, see Peck's edition of Aristotle's *Generation of Animals*, 576.

[2] *ShP*, ch. 8, p. 400: 'Every [human] situation can be changed from good to bad and from bad to good, for a man retains the power to choose' even though he may have sunk into vice. Maimonides may be expanding here on Alfarabi, *Fuṣūl muntazaʿa*, §17.

the soul are. Alfarabi, from whom Maimonides borrowed most of his ethical theory at this stage of his career, made a similar point although he did not place as much weight on it as Maimonides.[3] The ultimate source is Aristotle's *Nicomachean Ethics*,[4] but there is no reliable evidence that Maimonides saw that work at the present stage of his career.

As for the other interrelationship, between moral virtue and the intellectual life, Maimonides maintains in the *Commentary on the Mishnah* that philosophers and prophets concur in taking the 'goal of the human species' to be the 'conceiving of intelligible thoughts'. More specifically, the goal of human life is 'cognition [*idrāk*] of God to the extent of man's ability', it is attained by those who are 'students of science and philosophize', and every aspect of human life should be enlisted in the enterprise. When 'eating, drinking, sleeping, having sexual intercourse, awakening, moving, and resting', a man's sole object should be to mould his body into an 'instrument' that will permit his soul to devote itself to 'the sciences and the acquisition of the moral and rational virtues'. Moral virtue makes its contribution by enabling a person to marshal all the faculties of his soul to serve his intellect. The subordinate sciences make theirs by preparing the intellect for the ascent to science (*ʿilm*) at the highest level, to knowledge of 'the true nature of God's being'.[5]

Moral virtue, although not the goal, is a *sine qua non*. It is, Maimonides writes, a proposition agreed upon by the philosophers as well as the rabbis that when someone acquires moral virtue before starting on the road to science (Heb.: *ḥokhmah*, Arab.: *ʿilm*), his desire for science, love for it, and motivation are all enhanced. When, on the contrary, a person first acquires evil qualities, those qualities make the pursuit of science burdensome for him, and he abandons the pursuit.[6] Moral shortcomings are even more harmful than ignorance. A 'man who is God-fearing and abstinent, who rejects pleasures except for those necessary to sustain the body, who behaves . . . in accordance with moderation, and who possesses all the ethical virtues', yet lacks scientific knowledge, falls 'short of perfection'. He nonetheless is more nearly perfect than the man who is ostensibly knowledgeable but a slave to physical desires, the reason being that the second man 'is not in truth knowledgeable'.[7] Similar statements are found in Alfarabi,[8] and in this instance, the *Nicomachean Ethics* is

[3] Alfarabi, *Fuṣūl muntazaʿa*, §§9, 16, 18, 28.

[4] Aristotle, *Nicomachean Ethics*, 2.4–6.

[5] Maimonides, *Commentary on the Mishnah*, introd., 42–3; *ShP*, ch. 8, pp. 387–9. A similar motif appears in Ibn Ezra; see his commentary on Hos. 6: 3.

[6] Maimonides, *Commentary on the Mishnah*, *Avot* 3: 11. The tacit proviso is presumably that a person who has evil qualities always retains the power to reverse the course of his life.

[7] Maimonides, *Commentary on the Mishnah*, introd., 42–3.

[8] Alfarabi, *Fuṣūl muntazaʿa*, §98; id., *Philosophische Abhandlungen* (Arabic), 52; German trans., 87–8. Ibn al-Ṭayyib, who lived a century after Alfarabi, records virtually the same opinion in the name of Theophrastus; see Gutas, 'The Starting Point of Philosophical Studies', 121.

not the ultimate source. Aristotle's conclusion in the *Nicomachean Ethics* is that the contemplative and theoretical life *tout court*, not a theoretical life grounded in moral goodness, constitutes eudaemonia, man's true felicity.[9]

Most of what Maimonides says about moral virtue in the *Commentary on the Mishnah* is concentrated in *Shemonah perakim*, the introduction to his commentary on Mishnah *Avot*. In every area where men are said to have a virtue or vice, he envisages a full gamut of possible psychological characteristics, ranging from the excessive extreme at one end to the defective at the other. For instance, in the area of facing danger, the psychological characteristic of utter foolhardiness stands at the excessive extreme, the characteristic of utter cowardice at the defective, and various degrees of foolhardiness and cowardice can be marked off between the two.

Shemonah perakim posits that in each band of psychological characteristics, the virtuous characteristic is the intermediate one. Maimonides offers a number of examples, virtually all copied from Alfarabi's *Fuṣūl muntaza'a*: midway between utter 'cowardice' and utter 'foolhardiness' lies a characteristic judged to be the virtue in the area of facing danger, and it receives the honorific label of 'bravery'. In the area of enjoying physical pleasure, 'lechery' stands at one extreme, 'insensibility' at the other, and midway between them is the virtuous characteristic of 'temperance'. In the area of self-esteem, 'pride' is at one extreme and utter 'meekness', at the other; midway between them is the virtue of 'modesty'. In reacting to affronts, 'irascibility' and 'impassivity' are the extremes, and midway between them lies the virtue of 'patience'. Similarly, generosity, geniality, dignity, moderation in ambition, unpretentiousness, and other virtues are all intermediate characteristics.[10] Some of the virtues, for example, temperance, would seem to be exclusively the affair of the individual who cultivates them, and some, such as generosity, would seem to concern others, but Maimonides is unambiguous. He stresses the benefit that moral virtue brings the person who possesses it and he makes no mention of any benefit redounding to others.[11]

He makes no effort to prove the theory that ethical virtues are intermediate psychological characteristics; he just posits it. The problem of measurement, moreover, cries out. How can the distance between lechery and insensibility, between pride and utter meekness, be measured in order to determine the precise mean? Aristotle and Alfarabi touch on the problem of measurement,[12] but Maimonides is silent, leaving the matter on an intuitive footing.

9 Aristotle, *Nicomachean Ethics*, 10.7; similarly in Fowler, 'Manuscript Admont 608', 247–9.

10 *ShP*, ch. 4, pp. 379–80.

11 See above, Ch. 4.

12 Aristotle, *Nicomachean Ethics* 2.6; Alfarabi, *Fuṣūl muntaza'a*, §§20, 29.

Maimonides liked the hoary metaphor of sickness and health of the soul, which he again found in Alfarabi's *Fuṣūl*. Sickness of the soul is nothing other than deviant psychological characteristics; it harms the victim at least as much as sickness of his body does and, if untreated, will 'without doubt' destroy him.[13] Therapy consists in performing actions that depart from the mean in the opposite direction from the one in which the diseased psychological characteristic deviates. If a person's psychological characteristic in the area of facing danger deviates from the mean in the direction of cowardice, actions should be prescribed that depart from the mean in the direction of foolhardiness. By performing actions more foolhardy than the mean, the patient moves his psychological characteristic along the spectrum and relocates it at the midpoint.[14] The notion is that of the bent twig. When a twig leans towards the left, one straightens it by bending it to the right.[15]

The regimen for curing vice is not an exception to the theory of the ethical middle way. Corrective therapy prescribes only actions that depart from the mean, and actions are not the locus of virtue and vice. Characteristics in the soul are, and the person undergoing psychological and moral therapy does not aim at deviating from the mean in respect to them. On the contrary, his object is to reposition his psychological characteristics at the midpoint.

Shemonah perakim nevertheless does sanction psychological characteristics that depart from the mean and are therefore an exception to the theory. The sanctioned deviations are prophylactic.

The two extremes in each gamut of psychological characteristics are both vices, but one of the two, sometimes the excessive and sometimes the defective, is worse than the other. In the area of facing danger, cowardice, the defective extreme, is worse than foolhardiness, the excessive. In the area of self-esteem, pride, which happens to be the excessive extreme, is worse than meekness, the defective. Determining the more vicious of the two extremes is ultimately left to intuition.

Now, Maimonides writes, 'virtuous' (Arab.: *fāḍil*), or 'pious' (Heb.: *ḥasid*),[16] persons take especial precautions in order to avoid falling into the worse of the two vices. They determine which of the two extremes, the excessive or the defective, is more harmful and depart slightly from the mean in the direction of the less harmful, thereby securing themselves against erring in the more dangerous direction. They, for instance, intentionally cultivate a psychological characteristic slightly more foolhardy than the mean in order to avoid ever

[13] *ShP*, ch. 3.

[14] *ShP*, ch. 4, pp. 381–2.

[15] Cf. Aristotle, *Nicomachean Ethics*, 2.9, 1109b, 5–7.

[16] *ShP*, ch. 4, p. 382, calls the man who goes slightly beyond the mean prophylactically a *fāḍil*, a virtuous man. In *Commentary on the Mishnah*, *Avot* 5: 6, 13, he calls such a man a *ḥasid*, a pious man.

falling into the greater vice of cowardice, and a psychological characteristic slightly more meek than the mean in order to avoid falling into the greater vice of pride. Precautionary departure from the mean is what the rabbis had in mind when they spoke of going 'beyond the line of duty' (*lifnim mishurat hadin*).[17]

Shemonah perakim unequivocally opposes any departure from the mean apart from the temporary departure in action for the purpose of corrective therapy and the slight departure in psychological characteristics having prophylaxis as its object. The ascetic who exceeds those guidelines resembles the fool who observed a physician administering purgatives and other harsh medications to heal a disease, whereupon he, the fool, 'began to take the [medications] constantly'. Medicine designed for a diseased body will, when administered to a healthy body, result in its 'undoubtedly becoming sick'. By the same token, therapy designed for the diseased, unvirtuous soul will, when administered to a soul that is not diseased, inculcate extreme characteristics, which are the sickness of the soul.[18]

Maimonides goes as far as to assert that 'most of the religious commandments' have no other aim than moral prophylaxis. 'The Law forbids what it forbids and commands what it commands solely . . . for the purpose of training' men and women in psychological characteristics that depart slightly from the mean in the direction of the less evil of the two extremes. Thus dietary and sexual restrictions train a person to 'leave the mean slightly in the direction of insensibility to pleasure'. Commandments such as 'thou shalt not take vengeance nor bear any grudge' are designed to 'weaken' the characteristic of anger. As for the cultivation of extreme characteristics of the soul, 'the Torah of the Lord' which 'is perfect' and designed to 'perfect us . . . does not propose anything of the sort'. God is not 'an enemy of the body, who wants its destruction'.[19]

In support of his opposition to extreme behaviour and extreme psychological characteristics, Maimonides quotes scriptural verses that frown upon fasting.[20] He quotes a rabbinic 'censure of those who obligate themselves with oaths and vows of abstinence until they remain like prisoners. . . . Rabbi Idi in the name of Rabbi Isaac [said]: Is what the Torah prohibited for you insufficient, that you prohibit additional things for yourself?'[21] And he cites a midrashic comment regarding the nazirite, the person who undertakes not to

17 *ShP*, ch. 4, p. 382.

18 *ShP*, ch. 4, p. 383.

19 *ShP*, ch. 4, pp. 383–5. Kellner, *Maimonides' Confrontation with Mysticism*, 36 *et passim*, brings out the gulf between Maimonides' pragmatic view of the commandments and Judah Halevi's view, in which the commandments have mysterious intrinsic powers.

20 Zech. 7: 3–9.

21 JT *Ned.* 9: 1. Our texts of the passage have 'Rabbi Dimi' instead of 'Rabbi Idi', and differ in other small details.

cut his hair, drink wine, or come into contact with dead bodies, for a specified period of time.

By biblical injunction, if a nazirite becomes ritually impure through contact with a dead body, he must bring a sin offering to the priest, who sacrifices it to make 'atonement for him, for that he sinned regarding the soul [*nefesh*]'.[22] The obvious sense of the verse is that the nazirite atones for inadvertently coming into contact with a dead soul, a corpse. But although the term *soul* can designate a corpse in biblical Hebrew, it is not the ordinary term. The scriptural verse therefore invites a midrashic reading according to which the nazirite brings the sin offering not as atonement for coming into contact with a dead soul. It is atonement for his having sinned against his *own* soul.

The midrashic comment is found in a number of the classic rabbinic works, but the best known version is that of the Babylonian Talmud. Although the Talmud reports it as the position of a certain individual scholar and records contrary views, Maimonides treats it as the consensus of the Sages. His quotation does not exactly match any of the preserved versions exactly, but he often quotes from memory. He writes: 'They [that is, the Sages] said: "Against what soul did this man sin?! It was because he refrained from wine! . . . Now, if one who inflicts pain on himself [only by refraining] from wine needs atonement, he who inflicts pain on himself [by refraining] from everything will *a fortiori* [need atonement]."' The nazirite's abstinence from wine does not redound to his credit. It is a sin against his soul that he must atone for; *a fortiori*, the person who abstains 'from everything'.[23]

When Maimonides' *Commentary on the Mishnah* turns to tractate *Avot* itself, he reverses himself on a significant detail. He had cited modesty and the extremes that bracket it as one among the spectra of characteristics in which the virtuous or pious depart slightly from the mean by way of precaution. *Avot* contains the precept: 'Be very, very lowly in spirit',[24] and Maimonides understands *lowliness in spirit* to mean *meekness*. In his comment on the precept, he writes: 'We have explained in chapter 4 [of *Shemonah perakim*] that a man should incline [slightly] towards one of the extremes by way of precaution. . . . Nevertheless, exclusively in the present quality from among all the others, namely in pride', the 'enormity of the defect . . . and the harm' it brings are such that the ultra-virtuous 'flee from it to the opposite extreme and incline

[22] Num. 6: 11.

[23] *ShP*, ch. 4, pp. 383–4. The midrashic comment appears in BT *Ta'an.* 11*a–b*, and parallels, in the name of a certain rabbi; in JT *Ned.* 1: 1, 36*d*, in the name of a different rabbi; in *Sifrei Numbers*, ad loc., with some but not all versions attributing the saying to the rabbi to whom it is credited in the Babylonian Talmud; in the late compilation *Numbers Rabbah* 10: 15, with the same attribution.

[24] Mishnah *Avot* 4: 4.

completely to utter meekness in order to leave not even a trace of pride in their soul'.[25] Whereas *Shemonah perakim* sanctioned nothing but the precautionary slight departure from the mean as a general prophylactic exception to the rule of the middle way, the *Commentary* on *Avot* itself endorses extreme meekness as a single, total exception to the rule.

Tractate *Avot* gives Maimonides another opportunity to endorse a radical exception to the rule of the middle way, but he does not take it. 'Vows', *Avot* declares, 'are a fence surrounding *perishut*', the intimation being that *perishut* and the vows protecting it are commendable qualities. The term *perishut* is easily understood as 'abstinence', complete avoidance of physical gratification and eradication of desire.[26] Yet Maimonides has branded insensibility, the eradication of physical desire, as a vice and has further quoted a rabbinic 'censure of those who obligate themselves with oaths and vows of abstinence'. He sidesteps conflict between the aphorism and what he previously said by construing *perishut* in a narrow, ritual sense. He writes: 'When a man makes vows and keeps them . . . *perishut* is rendered easy for him. . . . *Perishut* is vigilance regarding ritual impurity, in accordance with the usage [of the term] in tractate *Ḥagigah*' where men scrupulous about ritual impurity are called *perushim*.[27] The narrow construction he places on *perishut* avoids an endorsement of the extreme of insensibility and restricts approbation of vows to those connected exclusively with ritual impurity.

One more statement in *Avot* is pertinent. *Avot* praises the man who both 'becomes angry [only] with difficulty' and also 'is easy to placate' as a 'pious man [Heb.: *ḥasid*]'. Maimonides comments: 'Observe that the man who is exceedingly mild [Arab.: *ḥalīm*] so as to approach impassiveness' is called 'pious'.[28] Piety mandates becoming angry with difficulty and approaching impassiveness. It does not mandate going to the extreme of impassiveness and not becoming angry at all.

In sum, Maimonides locates moral virtue in characteristics of the soul; actions may be good or bad, but they are neither virtuous nor vicious. Virtuous characteristics lie midway between two extremes, and the extremes are vices and sickness of the soul. The ancient rabbis taught as much by their condemnation of abstinence vows and naziritism. Maimonides does recommend one kind of departure from the mean—the cultivation of characteristics in the soul that depart slightly in the direction of what is in each instance the less damaging

[25] Maimonides, *Commentary on the Mishnah*, *Avot* 4: 4.

[26] Cf. Rabbi Jonah's commentary on Mishnah *Avot* 3: 13 (16), which explains the term *perishut* in the passage as *asceticism*.

[27] Maimonides, *Commentary on the Mishnah*, *Avot* 3: 16. Cf. Mishnah *Ḥag.* 2: 7.

[28] Maimonides, *Commentary on the Mishnah*, *Avot* 5: 10.

extreme as a cautionary and prophylactic tactic for avoiding the more damaging extreme. 'Most of the religious commandments', he submits, were imposed for that purpose, to train men and women in psychological characteristics that depart slightly from the mean in the direction of the less evil of the two extremes. In connection with the rabbinic precept 'Be very, very lowly in spirit', he further sanctions a single, total exception to the rule. The extreme of pride is so destructive a defect that the ultra-virtuous are not satisfied with moving slightly away from the mean in the direction of meekness. They go all the way to the extreme of meekness in order not to leave a trace of pride in their souls. Moral virtue is not an end in itself. Its purpose is to prepare man for intellectual perfection, which is the true goal of human life.

2. The *Mishneh torah*

The essential features of Maimonides' treatment of ethics seen thus far reappear in the section of his *Mishneh torah* entitled 'Hilkhot de'ot' ('Laws of Psychological Characteristics').[29] The format is, however, different, the dependence on Alfarabi is no longer obvious, and, most significantly, Maimonides' position undergoes a small shift.

The skeleton around which the *Mishneh torah*, a code of Jewish law, is constructed is the list of 613 commandments that Maimonides believed were given to Moses at Sinai. Eleven divine commandments form the scriptural basis for the regulations codified in 'Hilkhot de'ot', but Maimonides marks just one commandment as specifically dictating the cultivation of the 'intermediate psychological characteristics' that constitute moral virtue. It is the religious commandment embodied in the verse: 'Walk in His [God's] ways', a verse Maimonides glosses as dictating that man walk in 'intermediate ways'. The rabbis, he elaborates, 'taught in elucidation of this commandment [to walk in God's ways]: What is He called? Gracious. You too be gracious. What is He called? Merciful. You too be merciful. What is He called? Holy. You too be Holy.' Although God does not actually possess qualities such as graciousness and mercy, those and similar terms are applied to Him by the prophets 'in order to make known that they are good, correct ways, and man has the obligation to acquire them to the extent of his ability'.[30] Man walks in God's ways by acquiring the moral virtues.

[29] Maimonides' choice of the Hebrew term *de'ah* for *psychological characteristic* is presumably due to Mishnah *Avot* 5: 10: 'There are four types of characteristic: [a] easily angered but easily appeased . . .'.

[30] *MT*, 'Hilkhot de'ot', 1: 4–6. The biblical verse is Deut. 28: 9. The rabbinic comment is from *Sifrei Deuteronomy*, §49, where it is hung on a different scriptural verse.

As before, Maimonides locates virtue and vice in characteristics of the soul; he outlines the process whereby repeated actions inculcate psychological characteristics; he envisages gradations of characteristics running from defective extremes at one end of the spectrum to excessive extremes at the other; he judges both extremes to be vice, and the mean to be moral virtue; he depicts vice as a sickness of the soul requiring treatment no less than sickness of the body; he prescribes a corrective therapy wherein psychological characteristics deviating from the mean in one direction are healed through the performance of actions that depart from the mean in the opposite direction.[31]

And he rejects the thought of fleeing to the extreme. That is 'an evil way', 'one is forbidden to take it', and the person who cultivates an extreme characteristic in his soul 'is called a sinner'. Maimonides again cites the rabbinic censure of vows of abstinence: 'The sages commanded that a man should only refrain from things the Torah disallowed and not prohibit for himself what is permissible, through vows and oaths. They asked: "Is what the Torah prohibited for you insufficient, that you prohibit additional things for yourself?"' He repeats the midrashic comment regarding the nazirite: the Bible directs the priest to 'make atonement for him, for that he sinned regarding the soul', and, on the midrashic reading, it was the nazirite's own soul that was sinned against. 'The sages said: If the nazirite who abstained solely from wine needs atonement' for sinning against his soul, 'he who refrains from everything will *a fortiori* need atonement'.[32]

In *Shemonah perakim*, Maimonides recommended a slight departure from the mean in the direction of the less evil of the two extremes prophylactically, as a tactic to protect oneself from deviating in the direction of the greater evil. The slight departure, he wrote, is what the rabbis had in mind when they spoke of going 'beyond the line of duty', and he called the person who undertakes it 'pious'. In 'Hilkhot de'ot' of the *Mishneh torah*, he recommends the slight departure from the mean with a barely detectable difference in nuance: he represents it not as protection against deviating in the direction of the worse extreme but as a desideratum in itself. Someone who is 'particularly scrupulous and departs slightly from the intermediate characteristic in one direction or another'—towards the excessive extreme when the defective extreme is worse and towards the latter when the former is worse—is 'styled pious'. 'This is [what is meant by going] beyond the line of duty.'[33]

Among the examples that 'Hilkhot de'ot' gives of virtuous characteristics

[31] *MT*, 'Hilkhot de'ot', 1: 1–4, 7; 2: 1–2.

[32] *MT*, 'Hilkhot de'ot', 3: 1.

[33] *MT*, 'Hilkhot de'ot', 1: 5. Twersky, *Introduction to the Code of Maimonides*, 462–3, points out—and, I think, somewhat overstates—the difference in nuance.

'equidistant from the two extremes' is the 'correct way' in responding to affronts. It consists in being neither 'an irascible person, who becomes angry with ease', nor 'like a dead man, who is impassive'. The correct characteristic is the 'mean, becoming angry only about something grave that warrants anger, [and] for the purpose of preventing similar incidents in the future'. When illustrating what is meant by 'departing slightly from the intermediate characteristic in one direction or another', Maimonides adduces the range of psychological characteristics in the area of self-esteem: he who 'flees [pride] only as far as the midpoint and is modest' is a person who satisfies the ordinary standard of virtue (a *ḥakham*). 'He who flees pride in the direction of the extreme and is particularly meek is called pious' (*ḥasid*).[34] Modesty meets the standard for virtue; inclining from the mean in the direction of meekness is better.

A few paragraphs after laying down the rule of the ethical mean and the supererogatory slight departure from it, 'Hilkhot de'ot' takes a strange turn. 'There are', Maimonides now writes, 'psychological characteristics in which man is forbidden to follow the middle way and must flee instead to the opposite extreme.' One is pride. 'For the good way is not that a man be merely modest, but that he be meek. . . . The Rabbis consequently enjoined: "Be very, very lowly in spirit."' The other is anger. 'Anger is an extremely evil characteristic, and a man should flee from it to the opposite extreme. He should teach himself not to become angry, even about something that does warrant anger.' When circumstances require a person of authority to deter unacceptable conduct by demonstrating anger, he should merely 'simulate' anger 'without [in actuality] becoming angry'. In his *Commentary on the Mishnah*, Maimonides found support for moving towards impassiveness without going to the extreme in *Avot*'s instruction to 'become angry [only] with difficulty'. Now he finds other rabbinic maxims to support his rejection of anger even about things that warrant it. For example: 'If a wise man gets angry, he forfeits his wisdom, if a prophet gets angry, he forfeits his prophecy.'[35]

The contradiction is flagrant. On one page, Maimonides adduces anger 'about something grave that warrants anger' as an illustration of the virtuous middle way; on the next he asserts that 'man is forbidden to follow the middle way' in anger and 'should teach himself not to become angry even about something that does warrant anger'. On one page, he adduces being 'modest' as an example of the virtuous middle way, and inclining from modesty in the direction of meekness as an example of the supererogatory slight departure from the mean; on the next, he asserts that man is 'forbidden to follow the middle

[34] *MT*, 'Hilkhot de'ot', 1: 4–5. A similar distinction between *ḥakham* and *ḥasid* is drawn in Maimonides' *Commentary on the Mishnah*, *Avot* 5: 6.

[35] *MT*, 'Hilkhot de'ot', 2: 3; BT *Pes.* 66*b*.

way' in pride and must instead cultivate extreme meekness. Not only do the exceptions contradict the examples he had chosen to illustrate the middle way and the pious slight departure from it. The new assertion regarding anger also does not sit well with the interrelationship he posited between actions and psychological characteristics. Persons of authority will hardly be able to 'simulate' anger 'without [in actuality] being angry', if actions perforce inculcate corresponding characteristics.

A somewhat similar instance came to light earlier. In *Shemonah perakim*, Maimonides gave departing from modesty in the direction of meekness as an illustration of the slight prophylactic departure from the mean. Then in his commentary on Mishnah *Avot*, to which the *Shemonah perakim* is an introduction, he made the conflicting statement that the ultra-virtuous 'flee' from pride 'to the opposite extreme and go completely to utter meekness in order to leave not even a trace of pride in their soul'.[36] The dissonance was milder there because Maimonides did not declare that every characteristic on the spectrum short of utter meekness is forbidden but merely recommended total meekness as ultra-piety. In the *Mishneh torah*, by contrast, he flatly contradicts himself by first sanctioning moderate anger and self-esteem and then prohibiting them outright.

It might be tempting to regard Maimonides' insistence on extreme meekness and on extreme impassiveness as emendations made after he had written the passages on the virtuous middle way and the pious small departure from it. On that scenario, Maimonides experienced a change of heart, and his insistence on meekness and impassiveness reflects the change. What is hard to imagine is that Maimonides would have introduced extreme meekness and extreme impassiveness into the text without noticing, and correcting, his own approval, a page earlier, of intermediate characteristics precisely in the areas of anger and self-esteem. Attempts have been made to solve the contradiction, but they are unconvincing.[37] I know of no satisfactory solution.

As just seen, 'Hilkhot de'ot', like *Shemonah perakim*, quotes the midrashic comment that condemns the nazirite for abstaining from wine and the rabbinic censure of vows of abstinence. 'Hilkhot de'ot', where the condemnation of the nazirite occurs, is part of Book 1 of the *Mishneh torah*, and when Maimonides turns to 'Hilkhot nezirut' ('Laws of Naziritism') in Book 6, he portrays the nazirite in a different light.

36 Maimonides, *Commentary on the Mishnah*, *Avot* 4: 4, cited above, §1.

37 For attempts to explain the contradiction see the commentaries of Abraham de Boton (*c*.1560–*c*.1606), *Leḥem mishneh* on *MT*, 'Hilkhot de'ot', 1: 4–5, and Krakovski, *Avodat hamelekh* on *MT*, 'Hilkhot de'ot', 2: 3; Rosin, *Die Ethik des Maimonides*, 86–7; Rawidowicz, *Studies in Jewish Philosophy* (Heb.), i. 441.

The concluding sentences of 'Hilkhot nezirut' still affirm that making nazirite vows frivolously is 'wicked'. But, Maimonides adds, should someone 'make the vow to God in sanctity, what he does is fine and praiseworthy. Scripture says of such a person that "his consecration [*nezer*] unto the Lord is upon his head; he is holy unto the Lord". Scripture even equates him with a prophet; for it is written: "I raised up of your sons for prophets and of your young men for nazirites".'[38] Unlike 'Hilkhot de'ot', which condemned the nazirite as a sinner without qualification because of his abstention from wine, 'Hilkhot nezirut' recognizes a holy, praiseworthy abstention from wine and brackets the person undertaking it together with the prophets.

'Hilkhot nedarim' ('Laws of Vows'), found as well in Book 6 of the *Mishneh torah*, likewise reveals a departure, if not of substance, at least in tone and emphasis. In 'Hilkhot nedarim', Maimonides again quotes harsh rabbinic criticism of 'vows of abstinence'.[39] Yet side by side with the criticism, he applauds vows of abstinence made for the purpose of corrective therapy. Although 'a man should not multiply vows of abstinence nor accustom himself to them', he who does make a vow 'in order to correct his psychological characteristics and improve his acts is diligent and praiseworthy'. Vows of the sort are 'divine worship'.[40]

As a proof text, Maimonides quotes the rabbinic aphorism: 'Vows are a fence surrounding *perishut*.' In his *Commentary on the Mishnah* he narrowed the aphorism in order to avoid detracting from his censure of vows; he construed *perishut* as vigilance solely concerning ritual impurity.[41] 'Hilkhot nedarim' in the *Mishneh torah* construes the aphorism differently. When the rabbis of the Mishnah declared that 'vows are a fence surrounding *perishut*', Maimonides writes, they had in view the class of vows that are undertaken to correct a person's psychological characteristics and actions.[42] *Perishut* is no longer vigilance regarding ritual impurity; it is now abstinence for the wider purpose of corrective therapy.

Movement is thus discernible in the *Mishneh torah* over against *Shemonah perakim* and, moreover, within the work itself. The *Mishneh torah* rejects the middle way in two areas, those of anger and pride, and enjoins extreme impassivity and meekness instead; and it does so in a manner that creates a self-contradiction within the space of a couple of pages. Further, whereas *Shemonah*

[38] *MT*, 'Hilkhot nezirut', 10: 14, quoting Num. 6: 7–8 and Amos 2: 11. As far as I could find, neither verse is employed in rabbinic sources as a proof text for good naziritism. Bahya ibn Pakuda, *Ḥovot halevavot*, 9: 6, does cite Num. 6: 8, to prove that the nazirite is 'holy'.

[39] *MT*, 'Hilkhot nedarim', 13: 25, quoting BT *Ned.* 22*a*: 'He who makes a vow constructs, as it were, an idolatrous altar.'

[40] *MT*, 'Hilkhot nedarim', 13: 23–5.

[41] See above, §1.

[42] *MT*, 'Hilkhot nedarim', 13: 23.

perakim condemned the nazirite's abstention from wine absolutely, and 'Hilkhot de'ot' in the *Mishneh torah* reiterated the sentiment, 'Hilkhot nezirut' restricts the condemnation to the frivolous and withdraws it from those who become nazirites 'in sanctity'. The condemnation of vows cited in the *Shemonah perakim* and reiterated in 'Hilkhot de'ot' is similarly softened in 'Hilkhot nedarim'.

The goal of human life is defined in the *Mishneh torah* as it was in *Shemonah perakim*. 'A man must direct all his actions'—eating, drinking, speaking, work, sexual relations, even sleep—'solely towards [the goal of] knowing God.'[43] Although Maimonides does not expressly state that moral virtue also should be mobilized in pursuit of knowledge of God, the contribution of moral virtue to that goal is almost certainly taken for granted. Nevertheless, the faint possibility does remain that Maimonides had some inscrutable reason for failing to make the point.

3. *Moreh nevukhim*

Maimonides' *Moreh nevukhim* takes a new tack.

In Deuteronomy 4: 8, Moses asks rhetorically: 'What great nation is there that hath statutes and ordinances so righteous as all this law . . . ?' Maimonides interprets the term 'righteous' as meaning 'balanced' and he explains that the statutes and ordinances of the Torah are balanced inasmuch as they prescribe 'forms of worship containing neither . . . excess . . . nor deficiency'. They do not demand excessive, burdensome behaviour, such as a monastic life or lengthy pilgrimages; nor, unlike law codes of nations of old, do they sanction deficient behaviour, such as gluttony and self-indulgence, which would be detrimental to 'man's perfection in respect to his moral qualities [*akhlāq*] and theoretical activity [*naẓar*]'.[44] In a different context but in connection with the same verse, Maimonides writes: the commandments of the Torah aim at a 'balance' in sexual intercourse so that 'there will be neither an overdoing of intercourse . . . nor a complete avoiding of it'.[45] In yet another context, he comments on scriptural instructions to treat slaves kindly but to refuse asylum to a criminal no matter what his status: 'These are undoubtedly balanced moral qualities [*akhlāq*] belonging to the category of righteous statutes and ordinances.' They stand in contrast to the 'moral qualities' of the ancient Arabs, who regarded extending hospitality to both the criminal and the victim of crime as equal 'virtues' (*faḍā'il*).[46]

[43] *MT*, 'Hilkhot de'ot', 3: 2.
[44] *MN* ii. 39 (84*b*).
[45] *MN* iii. 49 (118*b*).
[46] *MN* iii. 39 (86*b*).

Each of the passages focuses on actions: scriptural statutes and ordinances, Maimonides writes, do not mandate *living* like a monk, *going* on arduous pilgrimages, and *refraining* completely from sexual intercourse, nor do they sanction self-indulgent behaviour and unlimited sexual intercourse. They do dictate acting towards all classes of men fairly and justly. The first passage states that behaviour lacking balance would be detrimental to a person's moral qualities; it fails, however, to explain what moral qualities consist of. The third states that Scripture commands 'balanced moral qualities' but still looks at what are in fact actions. Although *balanced* sounds much like *intermediate*, Maimonides does not come out and say that the moral virtues are intermediate characteristics in the soul.

Elsewhere in the *Moreh nevukhim* he expresses himself in a very different spirit. When discussing the qualifications for prophecy he writes that prophecy is attainable exclusively by persons whose 'thought and desire for bestial things have been eliminated', who refrain from 'choosing the pleasure of food, drink, sexual intercourse, and in general [the pleasures of] the sense of touch, which . . . Aristotle showed in the [*Nicomachean*] *Ethics* . . . is shameful for us'.[47] Freeing oneself of physical desire is not just a qualification for prophecy. The 'first step' for 'men of science, not to speak of prophets', Maimonides writes a few chapters later, is to 'relinquish bodily pleasures and foster contempt for them'. 'The sense that, as Aristotle stated, is shameful for us'—the sense of touch—must 'in particular' be suppressed, and 'most especially, the dirt of sexual intercourse'.[48] Nor is it only the prophet and man of science who are to free themselves of physical desire. Maimonides eventually instructs everyone conscious of his humanity to do so. He writes: the determination by 'divine wisdom' that forms must manifest themselves in matter has forced the 'most noble, human form, which is the image of God and His likeness', to join with 'this tellurian, turbid, tenebrose matter, which calls down every defect and corruption upon man'. All human infirmity, sin, and evil quality arise from matter, and the man who wishes to devote himself to his higher side and the intellectual life is 'pained' by his inescapable association with matter and its 'dirt'.

[47] *MN* ii. 36 (79*a*). See Aristotle, *Nicomachean Ethics*, 3: 10, 1118b, 2–4. In the same context, Maimonides writes that the prophet must have *kh-l-q insāniyya ṭāhira muʿtadil*. The term *kh-l-q* is here almost certainly the plural of *khilqa*, 'constitutional characteristic', and not of *khulq*, 'moral quality', for which Maimonides ordinarily uses the standard plural *akhlāq*. Maimonides is saying that the prophet must have 'pure, balanced human constitutional characteristics', i.e. a perfectly tempered physical constitution (Arab.: *mizāj*; Heb.: *mezeg*) and especially a brain, the matter of which is perfectly tempered. See *MN* iii. 49 (117*b*), in connection with circumcision, where *khilqa*, a constitutional characteristic, is contrasted with *khulq*, a moral quality. In *MN* iii. 8 (13*a*), *kh-l-q* does appear to be a plural of *khulq*, 'moral quality'.

[48] *MN* ii. 40 (86*b*–87*a*).

The predicament of the human form in its material frame resembles that of a subject who incurs his sovereign's wrath and whom the sovereign requires to 'carry manure from one place to another in order to humiliate him'. A slave in such a situation 'would throw himself into the manure and filth with his entire body, dirtying his face and hands; he would carry it publicly, laughing, rejoicing, clapping his hands'. A refined person, by contrast, 'might perhaps carry a little for just a short distance, so that his hands and clothes are not soiled and no one sees him'. By the same token, men not enslaved to their material side, men who aspire to what is 'most noble', regard 'the claims of matter . . . as shameful and ugly, as defects imposed by necessity'. In particular, they shrink from the demands of 'the sense of touch, which, as Aristotle observed, is shameful for us, and by reason of which we desire food, drink, and sex'. A person should limit such activities 'as far as possible and conduct them in secret, grieving all the while that they have to be done, avoiding reference to them in speech . . . never joining together in company to do them'. As for drinking parties, they are more shameful than gatherings in which 'men come together naked in broad daylight and defecate'.

Eating, drinking, and sex, likened to a filthy job imposed by a sovereign as an expression of his displeasure, should be conducted with the fastidiousness and embarrassment that the refined subject of the irate sovereign would exhibit when performing the distasteful task. 'Hence, he who chooses to be truly a man, and not a beast in man's shape and figure, must make every effort to suppress the claims of matter in respect to eating, drinking, sexual intercourse, anger, as well as all the qualities attendant upon physical desire [*shahwa*] and anger.' It goes without saying that he will not emulate the 'ignorant, corrupt gentiles' and misuse the greatest gift God gave him, his reason, by composing poetry that celebrates drinking parties and sex.[49]

Maimonides wrote in *Shemonah perakim*: 'The Law forbids what it forbids and commands what it commands' solely in order to ingrain psychological characteristics that depart slightly from the mean in the direction of the less evil of the two extremes. We just saw him state in the *Moreh nevukhim* that the commandments of the Torah aim at a 'balance' in sexual intercourse. In one of the contexts where he disparages 'wretched' souls who 'abandon themselves to food, drink, and sex', he lets his rhetoric run in the new direction. He writes that 'the commandments and prohibitions of the Law' are intended 'only to suppress

[49] *MN* iii. 8 (11*b*–13*b*). The chapter refers back to a motif in *MN*, introd. (7*b*–8*a*), where the harlot and her blandishments, depicted in Prov. 7, are taken as an allegory for matter and its temptations. Things are not, however, completely bleak, for Maimonides writes (13*a*) that someone who 'happens' to be blessed with 'a good, suitable matter' has received a 'divine gift', which is symbolized by the 'woman of valour' of Prov. 31.

all the various claims of matter'.[50] When his enthusiasm cools, he narrows that down somewhat and makes the extirpation of physical desire not the sole purpose of the ritual commandments but one of several. 'Among the purposes of the perfect Law is doing away with physical desires, fostering contempt for them, restricting them as far as possible.' In particular, the religious commandments help man free himself from 'the craving for eating, drinking, and sex'.[51]

Maimonides' *Commentary on the Mishnah* recommended total deviation from the mean in a single instance, in the case of extreme meekness, and the *Mishneh torah* rejected the mean in two instances when it mandated extreme meekness and the refraining from anger in the face of affronts.[52] The statements quoted in the preceding paragraphs do not restrict themselves to a couple of exceptions. Men who totally reject the claims of matter will suppress all physical desires and the qualities attendant upon them.

Consistency would require a re-evaluation of the nazirite and of abstinence vows. Both—despite having a place in God's Law—were condemned in *Shemonah perakim* and in 'Hilkhot de'ot' of the *Mishneh torah* because they are incompatible with the theory of the ethical mean. In a small shift, they are granted carefully circumscribed acceptance in later sections of the *Mishneh torah*.

The *Moreh nevukhim* devotes a series of chapters to the reasons for which, Maimonides believes, the divine Law institutes various commandments, and he prefaces those chapters with a list of fourteen classes of commandment. Fourteen happens to be the number of books in Maimonides' *Mishneh torah*, but he divides the commandments differently in the *Moreh nevukhim* from the way he did there.

The thirteenth class in the introductory list comprises prohibitions against eating certain foods, and, Maimonides tells us, 'vows and naziritism belong to this class'; the *Mishneh torah* put vows and naziritism under another rubric. The commandments in the present class have as their 'object' the 'extirpation of craving, of self-abandonment to the pleasurable, and of treating desire for food and drink as an end'. Such, Maimonides adds, was what 'I explained in my *Commentary on the Mishnah*, in the introduction to *Avot*', that is, in *Shemonah perakim*.[53]

After the preliminary list, he devotes a chapter to each class of commandments and in the chapter dealing with the thirteenth class, he writes: 'By the

[50] *MN* iii. 8 (13*a*).

[51] *MN* iii. 33 (73*a*). At *MN* iii. 54 (133*b*) Maimonides makes yet another statement about the commandments: 'Most of the religious commandments are [intended] only to bring about' the perfection of moral virtues that he belittles as serving others and as having no intrinsic value for the person who possesses it.

[52] See above, §§1–2.

[53] *MN* iii. 35 (13).

side of the prohibition of forbidden food', the divine Law 'has commanded vows of abstinence'. Their purpose is to 'train us . . . in satisfaction with our lot [*qanāʿa*] and in curbing our desire for food and drink. The Rabbis [accordingly] stated: "Vows are a fence surrounding *perishut*."'[54] Vows now serve a laudable end; *perishut*, which *Shemonah perakim* construed narrowly as vigilance in ritual purity, and the *Mishneh torah* as temporary abstinence within a regimen of corrective therapy, has expanded into permanent abstinence from pleasures of the flesh. Maimonides also finds the 'reason for naziritism' to be 'very clear'. Its purpose is to bring about 'abstinence from drinking wine, which has destroyed both ancients and moderns'. Mankind should learn to take no more wine than is 'necessary, for he who refrains from it is called holy and is ranked in sanctity together with the high priest . . . All this distinction is due to his having abstained from wine'.[55] The nazirite's abstention from wine has become a manifestation of sanctity.

In saying that what he now writes about abstinence vows and the nazirite is what he explained in the *Commentary on the Mishnah*, Maimonides is simply disingenuous. Of abstinence vows, the rabbinic work asked with the rabbis: 'Is what the Torah prohibited for you insufficient, that you prohibit additional things for yourself?' Far from representing the nazirite's abstention from wine as a form of sanctity, Maimonides branded it as a sin requiring atonement.[56]

No less pertinent is the class of divine commandments that are 'related to the improvement of moral qualities [*akhlāq*]'. In the preliminary list, Maimonides describes them as 'the commandments that I enumerated in "Hilkhot de'ot"' in the *Mishneh torah*. Regarding their object, he writes: 'Through good moral quality, as is well known, human society is perfected, something that is necessary for bringing order to human affairs.'[57]

Some of the chapters in the *Moreh nevukhim* that are dedicated to the fourteen classes of commandments run for pages and are crammed with detail. The chapter treating the class we are now considering merely restates in a perfunctory fashion what Maimonides already said in the preliminary list: the commandments falling under the present rubric 'are those I enumerated in "Hilkhot de'ot". The utility of all of them is clear and plain; for they are all moral qualities [*akhlāq*] furthering . . . social dealings among men. The matter is so obvious that I have no need to expatiate.' Maimonides concludes by reiterating: 'The commandments I enumerated in "Hilkhot de'ot" all openly have . . . noble moral qualities . . . as their aim.'[58]

[54] *MN* iii. 48 (112*b*). In *ShP*, ch. 4, p. 380, *qanāʿa* is an intermediate characteristic of the soul.

[55] *MN* iii. 48 (112*b*–113*a*). Naziritism and the high priesthood have certain laws in common.

[56] See above, §1.

[57] *MN* iii. 35 (3).

[58] *MN* iii. 38.

There is no mention of the scriptural verse that the *Mishneh torah* cited as embodying a formal divine commandment to acquire moral virtue or of any other verse containing such a divine commandment. All Maimonides does is accord 'noble moral qualities' the faint praise of serving a social function and intimates that he took the same position in the *Mishneh torah*. In fact, the *Mishneh torah* said nothing about a contribution that moral virtue makes to society. The *Commentary on the Mishnah* stressed the benefit that moral virtue brings the person who possesses it and methodically avoided mention of any effect that moral virtue might have on others.

If good moral qualities have as their purpose 'furthering . . . social dealings among men', the implication is inescapable: a person who lives in isolation, outside a social context, should be able to dispense with them. Maimonides does not shrink from the implication.

In the final chapter of the *Moreh nevukhim*, he follows 'the earlier and later philosophers' in delineating and ranking four human 'perfections'. The four perfections and much of what Maimonides says about them have been shown to be borrowed from a composition of Ibn Bājja's.[59]

The first of the four is perfection of 'possessions'. Even though men spend their lives in acquiring possessions, these are the least of the human perfections, since they are not part of a man at all. They amount to nothing more than a relationship between the man and something outside him—a relationship that is transient and may be gone in the blink of an eye. Second is 'bodily perfection', that is, the perfection of the body's 'constitution and figure'. Maimonides makes short work of it as well. A man's body belongs to him 'not . . . insofar as he is a man, but insofar as he is an animal'. Moreover, a human body, even when well-developed, is nothing to be proud of; it is a weakling in comparison to the body of a mule, not to speak of that of a lion or an elephant. Neither of the first two supposed perfections can be deemed genuine human perfection.

The third belongs to the person who possesses it to a greater extent than the first two. It is 'perfection of the moral virtues', that is to say, having one's 'qualities . . . at the height of virtue'. Although it is to a greater extent a 'perfection in the being of the individual', it is not 'an end in itself', but rather 'a preparation for someone [or: something] else'. The *Commentary on the Mishnah* also depicted moral virtue as a preparation; there it was an indispensable preparatory stage in man's ascent to the ultimate goal of human existence, knowledge of God. The same, although not explicit in the *Mishneh torah*, was almost

[59] Schreiner, *Igeret hapetirah*, 37; Altmann, 'Maimonides' "Four Perfections"', which shows in detail that Maimonides' language echoes Ibn Bājja's.

surely taken for granted there. Now in the *Moreh nevukhim*, Maimonides writes: ethical perfection is a preparation solely for someone, or something, else, 'inasmuch as moral matters all concern the relation between one man and another. It is as if through perfection in moral matters, an individual disposes himself for the utility of mankind and becomes an instrument to serve others.' Should a human being be assumed to exist 'alone and not have dealings with anyone else, all his moral virtues would be idle, in vain, and useless. They would not perfect a person in anything. . . . Their utility touches him [solely] in respect to others.' Moral virtue, which was an indispensable precondition for attaining the ultimate goal of human life in Maimonides' rabbinic works, has no intrinsic value for the man who cultivates it according to the *Moreh nevukhim*.

The fourth and 'true human perfection' is, as is to be expected, intellectual. It consists in 'rational virtues, that is, in the conceiving of intelligible thoughts that give rise to correct views regarding metaphysical [or: divine] subjects'. Again: true human perfection is 'cognition of God'. 'This is the ultimate end, which truly perfects the individual; it belongs to him alone, and it gives man eternal existence.' 'You should therefore strive to attain that [perfection] which is permanent for you, and not weary yourself and toil for others.'[60]

A distinction drawn at another spot in the *Moreh nevukhim* between the welfare of the soul and the welfare of the body sheds additional light. The welfare of the body is dependent on social conditions that enable citizens to work together smoothly and safely. Those conditions are promoted in two ways: through measures preventing violence; and through the inculcating of 'actions and moral qualities' that 'supplement what is deficient [in human behaviour] and moderate what is excessive', thereby 'covering over the natural difference' between men. The welfare of the human soul, which is 'unquestionably superior', consists in 'having the ordinary run of mankind provided with true opinions in accordance with their capacity' and in man's ultimately becoming 'an actual intellect' and 'knowing everything in man's power to know concerning the totality of what exists'. It presupposes the welfare of the body, since no one can devote himself to intellectual pursuits when in a state of 'pain, acute hunger, thirst, severe heat or cold'. In contrast to the welfare of the body, the perfection of the soul 'does not contain actions or moral qualities'.[61]

Maimonides is repeating, from a different perspective, that the function of good moral qualities is to create a smoothly operating society.

[60] *MN* iii. 54 (132*b*–134*a*).

[61] *MN* iii. 27, supplemented by ii. 40 (85*b*). See also iii. 33 (73*a*), where Maimonides excludes human social relationships from man's final perfection, which is intellectual.

There is no escaping the conclusion that he recognizes two different ethical standards in the *Moreh nevukhim*. The lower standard prescribes behaviour that is neither excessive nor defective, but balanced. It aims, for example, at a 'balance' in sexual intercourse so that 'there will be neither an overdoing of intercourse . . . nor a complete avoiding of it'. The behaviour and moral qualities that it prescribes are designed to serve society by creating salutary social conditions and they therefore have value. But they make only an indirect contribution to the welfare of the soul, and to invest time in them is to toil for the sake of others. If a person lived in isolation, the behaviour and moral qualities of the lower standard would be idle, in vain, and useless.

The higher ethical standard rests on the proposition that man's material side is the source of every human infirmity and evil, that the sense of touch and claims of matter are shameful and ugly. The higher standard requires rooting out even a balanced and moderate desire for physical pleasure. Men should do their best to minimize contact with the manure of bodily pleasure, foster contempt for the bestial enjoyment of food and drink, and in particular relinquish the 'dirt' of sexual intercourse. In confusing switches back and forth, Maimonides sometimes writes that the religious commandments have as their object what is in effect the lower standard, and sometimes that they have as their object what is in effect the higher.

The *moral qualities* and *moral virtues* of the lower ethical standard resemble the intermediate characteristics of the soul that *Shemonah perakim* and *Mishneh torah* construed as moral virtue. At first glance it might seem as if Maimonides has transformed the ethics of the rabbinic works into the inferior standard of the *Moreh nevukhim*. That is not, however, what he has done. Although he chooses to disguise the fact by references to *Shemonah perakim* and the *Mishneh torah*, he has turned his back on the earlier theory.

It is true that balanced actions and 'balanced moral qualities' are a concern of the *Moreh nevukhim*'s lower ethical standard, but *Moreh nevukhim* makes no mention of the heart of the earlier theory, according to which characteristics of the soul are the locus of moral virtue and vice, intermediate characteristics are the virtues, and extreme characteristics are the vices. If we go back and look again at Maimonides' explication of the third human perfection, we see clearly what he has been about.

Ibn Bājja, from whom he is borrowing, marked 'the virtues of the soul' (*al-faḍā'il al-nafsāniyya*) as one of the human perfections.[62] Maimonides for his part has told us that moral qualities serve the welfare of the human body, and perfection of the soul contains no moral qualities. When choosing a label for

[62] Ibn Bājja, *Risālat al-wadā'*, 32. The Spanish translation is not helpful.

the third perfection, he accordingly avoids mention of the soul; he calls it merely 'perfection of the moral virtues' (*kamāl al-faḍā'il al-khulqiyya*). The definition that he then offers is eye-opening. 'Perfection of the moral virtues', he writes, is having one's 'qualities . . . at the height of virtue'. Instead of taking advantage of the opportunity to repeat his old definition of moral virtues as intermediate characteristics of the soul, Maimonides gives us a meaningless tautology. He never explains anywhere else in the *Moreh nevukhim* what he means by moral virtues or moral qualities, and the notion of intermediate characteristics of the soul is never mentioned in the book.

The rabbinic works disparaged extreme characteristics as an evil way and a sickness that destroy a man and they portrayed the man who cultivates extreme characteristics as a sinner and fool. Maimonides says nothing of the sort in the *Moreh nevukhim*, even when considering things from the point of view of the lower ethical standard. Nor could he. He could hardly write that asceticism is sickness and sin according to the lower ethical standard yet devoutly to be wished according to the higher, that the ascetic is a fool by the lower standard yet he alone is not a beast in human shape, and indeed the companion of prophets and priests, according to the higher.

The lower ethical standard of the *Moreh nevukhim* preserves the shell of the ethical theory of the rabbinic works, a set of rules for sensible, socially desirable behaviour. The core is discarded.

On one matter, Maimonides is consistent and unequivocal throughout his writings: the ultimate human goal is intellectual perfection and, specifically, knowledge of God. In the ethics of his earlier period, intermediate moral virtues are an indispensable preparation for the development of the human intellect.[63] In the lower ethical standard of the *Moreh nevukhim* balanced behaviour serves society, which in turn creates conditions allowing men to pursue the welfare of their souls and the intellectual life. The extirpation of desire dictated by the higher ethical standard is a condition for intellectual perfection.

4. Possible Explanations

It is natural to wonder why Maimonides replaced the ethical theory of his rabbinic period with an ascetic regimen. A possible suggestion might be that the position of one of the periods is non-philosophical and that of the other, philosophical. The suggestion does not work.

The *Moreh nevukhim*, Maimonides' philosophical opus, would presumably

[63] See above, §1.

represent the philosophical position, and his rabbinic writings, which are intended for a non-philosophical readership, the non-philosophical. But it is *Shemonah perakim* and the *Mishneh torah* that espouse the theory of the ethical middle way, and Maimonides learned the theory from Alfarabi, the Islamic philosopher whom he held in highest esteem. Relying on Alfarabi's references to the ancients, he too attributed the theory to the 'ancients', by which he undoubtedly understood the ancient philosophers and, in particular, the greatest of them, Aristotle.

Furthermore, whereas Maimonides' rabbinic works show no familiarity with the theory of the middle way in Aristotle's *Nicomachean Ethics*, by the time he wrote the *Moreh nevukhim*, he had read the *Nicomachean Ethics* and could see that the doctrine of the ethical mean is indeed Aristotelian. If one of his ethical stances is to be labelled philosophical and the other non-philosophical, the paradoxical upshot will be that his non-philosophical writings, which he composed before reading Aristotle's primary ethical treatise, advocated the theory of ethics of the greatest of the philosophers. His philosophical opus, written after he finally read the *Nicomachean Ethics* and assured himself that the theory of the middle way is genuinely Aristotelian, rejects Aristotelian ethics.

The fashionable dichotomy of *exoteric* and *esoteric* also does not help. Maimonides' earlier works maintain openly that intermediate psychological characteristics are virtues, and total lack of desire, a vice; the *Moreh nevukhim* maintains just as openly that 'perfection of the moral virtues' does not serve the man who possesses it and that the development of man's truly human side requires the extirpation of desire. And Maimonides could have no plausible reason for hiding either position.[64] If the welfare of the soul demands elimination of physical desire, what political, social, or religious motive could have led him to conceal the truth in the earlier works? What could have led him to vilify those who deviate from the mean as fools who 'imitate [other] religions'?[65] If the health of the soul consists in intermediate psychological characteristics, what political, social, or religious motive could have led him to insist on the extirpation of physical desire in the *Moreh nevukhim*? Neither the earlier nor the later ethical position qualifies as esoteric.

The move from the ethical position of the earlier works to that of the *Moreh nevukhim* reflects a change of heart, a change that was adumbrated in the *Mishneh torah* and becomes a radical break in the *Moreh nevukhim*. Another pair of labels might suggest itself. The theory of the middle way is distinctively *Aristotelian*, and the *Moreh nevukhim*'s denigration of physical desire might be

[64] J. Levinger, 'On the Reason for Naziritism' (Heb.), does his utmost to find a reason.
[65] *ShP*, ch. 4, p. 384.

viewed as *Neoplatonic*, since Plotinus and medieval thinkers who are classified as Neoplatonists evince a strong ascetic streak. In a notable passage, Plotinus writes: 'The soul is evil when it is wholly mixed with the body, shares the body's qualities, and is entirely of the same opinion' as the body; it will 'be good and possess virtue if it should not have the same opinions . . . and not share the same qualities'. The 'condition of the soul in which it thinks intellectual thoughts and is free of qualities' may aptly be described as 'similarity to God'.[66] Perhaps Maimonides abandoned the ethics of Aristotle because he became convinced of the correctness of Neoplatonic ethics.

The suggestion is again flawed. The sentences just quoted from Plotinus do not appear in the Arabic paraphrases of the *Enneads* and are not known to have been translated into Arabic. The only philosophical source that Maimonides cites in support of his higher ethical standard is the remark that the sense of touch is shameful, a remark that he found in Aristotle's *Nicomachean Ethics* and does not tire of quoting in Aristotle's name. Moreover, even on the supposition that in his reading he happened upon one or more ascetic texts of Neoplatonic inspiration,[67] we would still want to know why he preferred such texts to the Aristotelian theory of the ethical mean.

His change of heart was rooted in developments within his personality and outlook on the world that are virtually impossible to plumb; there is little possibility of penetrating the mind of a thinker as distant and reticent about himself as Maimonides. I am nevertheless going to propose that a dialectical consideration paralleled, and perhaps gave impulse to, the new tack in his thinking. The starting point is *Sifrei*, the ancient compilation of midrashic comments on the books of Numbers and Deuteronomy.

Walking in God's ways is a recurring motif in Deuteronomy, and *Sifrei* takes up a passage there that assures the Children of Israel: 'If ye shall diligently keep all this commandment, which I command you . . . to love the Lord your God, to walk in all His ways. . . . Then will the Lord drive out all these nations.' To explain how it is possible for man to walk in God's ways, *Sifrei* harks back to the numinous incident in which Moses asked God to show him

[66] Plotinus, *Enneads*, 1.2.3; Zeller, *Die Philosophie der Griechen*, iii. 2, pp. 653–6; Trouillard, *La Purification plotienne*.

[67] For evidence of asceticism in medieval Islam, see *Encyclopedia of Islam*, article *zuhd*; Ikhwān al-Ṣafā', *Rasā'il*, iv, §46, p. 81; Yahuda's introduction to his edition of Bahya ibn Pakuda, *Al-hidāya* (the Arabic original of *Ḥovot halevavot*), 104–8 (parallels and sources of Bahya's chapter on asceticism). For evidence in medieval Jewish thought, see Bahya ibn Pakuda, *Ḥovot halevavot*, 9: 1–2; anon., *Kitāb ma'ānī al-nafs*, 60; Ibn Ezra, *Commentary on Ecclesiastes*, introd.; Vajda, *La Théologie ascétique de Bahya ibn Paquda*, 121–2. Maimonides' wife's family stood in a Jewish Sufi tradition, which his son continued. See Goitein, 'Abraham Maimonides and his Pietist Circle', 152–3; id., 'Documents on Abraham Maimonides' (Heb.), 181–97; Abraham Maimonides, *The High Ways to Perfection*, ch. 20.

His ways and soon afterwards heard: 'The Lord, the Lord, God, merciful and gracious, long-suffering, abundant in kindness and truth, keeping mercy unto the thousandth generation . . . and that will by no means clear the guilty.' *Sifrei* asks rhetorically and answers: 'What is God called? Merciful and gracious. You too be merciful and gracious. . . .What is God called? Righteous. . . . You too be righteous. . . . God is called kind. . . . You too be kind.'[68] Man walks in God's ways by imitating God's mercy, graciousness, righteousness, and kindness.

The obligation 'to walk in His ways' is recognized as a formal commandment in the list of divine commandments drawn up by *Halakhot gedolot*. *Halakhot gedolot* records its commandments tersely, it does not cite scriptural proof texts for them, and it does not disclose its criteria for deciding what to recognize as a divine commandment. In the present instance, it nonetheless says enough to show that it had in view not the verse from Deuteronomy addressed by *Sifrei* but a similar verse, which reads: 'After the Lord your God shall ye walk.'[69] Although Maimonides criticizes *Halakhot gedolot* on a number of scores, the notion that walking in God's ways is one of the 613 divine commandments struck a chord with him.

In his *Sefer hamitsvot*, he records a positive commandment to 'imitate [or: make oneself similar to (*tashabbuh*)] God in accordance with our ability'. The theme of imitating God has its own long history in both the rabbinic and the philosophical traditions and deserves a few words. We just encountered it in Plotinus, and here I add three more examples, which are remarkable in their resemblance to one another despite their diverse provenances. Maimonides knew and very likely is echoing the first. He did not know the second. He could have known the third, and it may have contributed to his formulation of the commandment to imitate God.

The Babylonian Talmud offers several midrashic interpretations of a biblical verse commonly translated as 'This is my God, and I will glorify Him.' In

[68] *Sifrei Deuteronomy*, §49; see critical notes. The text is preserved in a number of versions, and I have quoted the one closest to Maimonides' reading. The scriptural verses are Deut. 11: 22–3, and Exod. 33: 13 and 34: 6.

[69] *Halakhot gedolot* (N. Hildesheimer), iii, appendix, p. 72, includes the following in its list of commandments: 'To walk in His ways. To clothe the naked. To bury the dead. To comfort mourners. To visit the sick.' The author obviously is thinking of BT *Sot.* 14*a*, which reads: '"After the Lord your God shall ye walk." [Deut. 13: 5]. Is it possible for man to walk after the divine presence? . . . Rather walk after God's attributes [*midot*]: What is God? He clothes the naked . . . You too clothe the naked. God visited the sick . . . You too visit the sick. God comforted mourners . . . You too comfort mourners. God buried the dead . . . You too bury the dead.'

SM (Kafah), rule 1, p. 11 and rule 2, p. 14, criticizes *Halakhot gedolot* for making clothing the naked, visiting the sick, burying the dead, and the like into separate commandments. Nahmanides, *Hasagot*, rule 1, p. 44, reads *Halakhot gedolot* as listing only a single commandment, 'to walk in His ways', and then spelling out what the commandment involves.

one of the interpretations, the midrashist twists the Hebrew a little with the result that the clause ordinarily translated as 'I will glorify Him' turns into: 'Make yourself similar to Him.' The midrashist goes on to explain how man can make himself similar to God: 'What is He? Gracious and merciful. You too be gracious and merciful.'[70] A person imitates, and makes himself similar to, God by being gracious and merciful, as God is.

In an unrelated and very different literary tradition, Plato has Socrates encourage his interlocutor to 'become like God as far as this is possible' and, Socrates explains, one does so by 'becoming just and holy, with the accompaniment of wisdom'.[71] In the same spirit, a brief introduction to philosophy attributed to Alfarabi states: 'The end towards which one should aim in studying philosophy is knowledge of the creator. . . . The actions that a philosopher should perform are imitation of the creator to the extent of man's ability.'[72]

The theme of imitating, or making oneself similar to, God was thus well established by Maimonides' time.

Returning to his *Sefer hamitsvot*, we find that it derives the religious commandment to imitate God from a third verse in Deuteronomy that talks of walking in God's ways, namely: 'Thou shalt walk in His ways.' Maimonides continues: Scripture 'reiterated' the commandment in a different verse, which instructs man 'to walk in all His ways'; that is the verse around which the *Sifrei* passage turned. And, he observes, the rabbis' 'interpretation' of this latter verse explains how walking in God's ways is possible: '"What is the Holy One called? Merciful. You too be merciful. The Holy One is called gracious. You too be gracious. The Holy One is called righteous. You too be righteous. The Holy One is called pious [*ḥasid*]. You too be pious." Such is the language of *Sifrei*.'

Scripture, Maimonides goes on, repeated the command yet one more time when it instructed us: 'After the Lord your God shall ye walk.' As the rabbis explained that verse, 'its purport is imitation [*tashabbuh*] of the good actions and noble moral qualities [*akhlāq*] whereby God is described metaphorically', although in actuality He has no qualities.[73] 'After the Lord your God shall ye walk' is the very verse that *Halakhot gedolot* alluded to when it recorded 'to walk in His ways' as a divine commandment.[74]

In short, Maimonides' *Sefer hamitsvot* recognizes a divine commandment to

[70] BT *Shab.* 133*b*, with reference to Exod. 15: 2. A fuller version is given in *Mekhilta*, 'Beshalaḥ', §3, 127, and there are additional parallels.

[71] Plato, *Theaetetus*, 176B. Philo quotes the passage; see Wolfson, *Philo*, ii. 194–5.

[72] Alfarabi, *Philosophische Abhandlungen* (Arabic), 53; *Alfarabi's philosophische Abhandlungen* (German trans.), 88–9 (pointed out in Altmann and Stern, *Isaac Israeli*, 197). Berman, 'Political Interpretation', 54–6, assembles additional valuable material on the motif.

[73] *SM*, positive commandment 8. The scriptural verses are, respectively, Deut. 28: 9, 11: 22, 13: 5.

[74] See above, n. 69.

imitate God in accordance with our ability. The commandment is embodied in the instruction, expressed three times in the book of Deuteronomy, to walk in God's ways and it is fulfilled by performing the good actions and cultivating the moral qualities whereby God is described metaphorically. The qualities in question, *Sifrei* tells us, are mercy, graciousness, righteousness, and the like.

There is something unsatisfactory in the reasoning. A person who is merciful and gracious may act as God acts and may cultivate qualities by which God is described metaphorically. But if God does not actually have qualities, the person who cultivates qualities in his soul does not in truth imitate God.

The themes of walking in God's ways and making oneself similar to God recur in Maimonides' *Mishneh torah*. Everything in the *Mishneh torah* is woven around one or another of the 613 formal scriptural commandments that Maimonides identified, and he sought an appropriate niche for his theory of ethics. Scripture, he recalls, commands: 'Thou shalt walk in His ways.' 'In interpreting the commandment, the rabbis taught: "What is He called? Gracious. You too be gracious. What is He called? Merciful. You too be merciful. What is He called? Holy. You too be holy."' God is of course called *gracious* and *merciful* not because he possesses the attributes of graciousness and mercy but 'in order to make known that they are good, correct ways, and man has the obligation to acquire them and render himself similar, to the extent of his power'. And Maimonides writes, one walks in God's ways and renders oneself similar—whether to God or to His ways is left unclear—by 'walking in intermediate ways', that is, by cultivating 'intermediate characteristics' in one's soul, which constitute moral virtue.[75]

The train of thought is not hard to follow. Scripture amplified by the rabbis—in the *Sifrei* —commands man to walk in God's ways and teaches that those ways consist of being merciful, gracious, and the like. Mercy and graciousness are moral virtues; in fact, the rabbis called them *midot*,[76] which means psychological or moral attributes.[77] Philosophers have shown that the moral virtues are intermediate characteristics of the soul. In commanding man to walk in God's ways and make himself similar to God, Scripture must accordingly be prescribing the cultivation of intermediate psychological characteristics. The desired niche has been provided for incorporating a theory of ethical virtue in a code of religious law.

But, as before, the reasoning has something unsatisfactory about it. If God has neither intermediate, nor any other psychological characteristics, and scriptural descriptions of God are metaphors and not actual attributes, culti-

[75] *MT*, 'Hilkhot de'ot', 1: 5–6, together with 'Hilkhot yesodei hatorah', 1: 12.
[76] BT *RH* 17*b*.
[77] See above, n. 29.

vating intermediate characteristics in one's soul does not make one similar to God. Rendering oneself as free as possible of psychological characteristics, as God is free of them, would do so.

That is exactly the conclusion at which the *Moreh nevukhim* arrives when it analyses scriptural descriptions of God. Maimonides posits in the *Moreh nevukhim* that no attribute can describe God's essence, since His essence is unknowable; no attribute can refer to a component in God, since His being is simple and has no components; none can denote a psychological characteristic of God, since He has no psychological characteristics.[78] Attributes can legitimately be applied to God only if they presume to say nothing about God Himself.

Attributes of action circumvent the pitfalls. 'Whenever one of God's actions is grasped' through observation of the world, which is His product, 'God is described by the attribute through which the action in question would proceed' if an ordinary man performed it. Thus nature, being on the whole beneficent but occasionally destructive, exhibits what the human observer perceives as merciful, gracious, or wrathful actions. In the human realm, actions of the sort ordinarily proceed from the psychological characteristics *mercy*, *graciousness*, and *vengefulness*. Since God is the ultimate author of the universe, and hence of the ostensibly merciful, gracious, and vengeful events observed in nature, He is called 'merciful', 'gracious', or 'vengeful'. In reality, however, God does not act through a 'characteristic of the soul', or an 'affection', or 'anything whatsoever added to His essence'; for He has no psychological characteristics, indeed has no soul, and is 'not possessed of moral qualities' (Arab.: *akhlāq*; Heb.: *midot*). Characteristics are ascribed to God only metaphorically, because of the actions He performs, and it is incumbent on us to keep firmly in mind that the actions do not proceed from characteristics in God's being.

Maimonides spells out the implication for man more logically than in the earlier writings: God's 'ways', when understood correctly, are not characteristics of the soul; they 'are the actions emanating from Him'. If a man—Maimonides speaks in particular of a 'political leader who is a prophet', but what he writes would apply more generally—is veritably to walk in God's ways, he must act as God does. He must behave mercifully and graciously or vengefully and angrily as circumstances demand, not through 'mere mildness and commiseration', in the one instance, or 'mere anger', in the other; 'for all suffering of affection [*infiʿāl*] is evil'. He will not, in other words, be merciful, gracious, or vengeful in the sense that he cultivates mercy, graciousness, and anger, in his soul. Just as God's actions do not issue from psychological characteristics, human actions should not.

[78] *MN* i. 52.

The merciful and gracious actions of the person who walks in God's ways will outnumber the vengeful actions, but when necessary, a man whom circumstances place in authority must not hesitate to perform the latter. Maimonides' elaboration may make more than one reader uncomfortable. There are times when the person in authority has to command that someone be 'burned to death'; he will come to the decision 'without being angry . . . and without animosity', by rationally weighing the merits of the situation. When Scripture ordained the destruction of the seven nations of Canaan and ordered 'thou shalt save alive nothing that breatheth', it thus immediately explained the motive: 'that they teach you not to do after all their abominations, which they have done unto their gods, and so ye sin against the Lord your God'. The nations of Canaan were to be destroyed not out of cruelty and vengefulness, but through completely cool, rational considerations, in order to prevent them from being an evil influence.[79]

The *Moreh nevukhim* concludes its discussion of divine attributes of action by again deploying the formula: 'What is God? . . . You too . . .'. 'The ultimate virtue for man', Maimonides states, 'is imitation of God to the extent of [man's] ability'; and imitating God means 'assimilating our acts to His acts'. The rabbis explained as much when 'commenting on the verse "Ye shall be holy." They said: "What is He? Gracious. You too be gracious. What is He? Merciful. You too be merciful." The general point is that the attributes ascribed to God are attributes of His actions, not that He possesses any quality.'[80]

In the *Sefer hamitsvot* and the *Mishneh torah*, Maimonides' thinking was that God's ways are mercy, graciousness, and the like; in the case of man, mercy, graciousness, and so on are moral qualities; man therefore imitates God and walks in His ways by cultivating the desired moral qualities in his soul. The *Mishneh torah* added that it is precisely by cultivating *intermediate* characteristics in his soul that man imitates God. The *Moreh nevukhim* draws the more cogent conclusion that man imitates God and walks in His ways by acting not through a moral quality or characteristic of the soul, since all suffering of affection is evil, but, like God, dispassionately. The notion of imitating God, when pursued consistently, leads to the higher ethical standard of the *Moreh nevukhim*.

It should now be clear that the *Moreh nevukhim* does not, in its higher standard, advocate extreme psychological characteristics in place of the intermediate characteristics of the rabbinic works. Maimonides is still concerned with the source from which actions spring. But whereas his rabbinic works made

[79] *MN* i. 54 (65*a*–66*a*). The verses are Deut. 20: 16, 18.

[80] *MN* i. 54 (66*b*). Consciously or inadvertently, Maimonides now links the formula not to Deut. 11: 22–3, but instead to Lev. 19: 2: 'Ye shall be holy; for I, the Lord your God, am holy.'

intermediate psychological characteristics the locus of ethical perfection and instructed that human acts proceed from them, the *Moreh nevukhim* mandates that human acts proceed from reason, not from any psychological characteristic.

5. The Closing Paragraphs of the *Moreh nevukhim*

As was already seen, the final chapter of the *Moreh nevukhim* distinguishes four purported human perfections. Maimonides disposes of the first three, 'possessions', bodily 'constitution and figure', and 'perfection of the moral virtues', as spurious; he recognizes only the fourth, 'rational virtues', that is, the 'conceiving of intelligible thoughts that give rise to correct views regarding metaphysical subjects', as truly human perfection. The chapter, and hence the entire *Moreh nevukhim*, ends with an exegesis of a biblical passage in which he easily finds references to the four perfections.

Jeremiah 9: 22–3 reads: 'Let not the wise man glory in his wisdom, neither let the mighty man glory in his might, nor let the rich man glory in his riches. But let him that glorieth glory in this, that he hath intellectual understanding [*haskel*] and knowledge of Me, that I am the Lord who exercise loving-kindness, justice, and righteousness in the earth; for in these things I delight, saith the Lord.'[81] Four types are spoken of, the wise man, the mighty man, the rich man, and the man who has intellectual understanding and knowledge of God.

The rich man is obviously the man who excels in possessions. The mighty man is the one who has perfected his bodily constitution and figure. Maimonides' rabbinic works used the term wise (*ḥakham*) as a designation for the person who possesses moral virtue,[82] and here too, he takes the wise man to be the man of 'virtuous moral qualities'. He accordingly reads Jeremiah as admonishing that neither moral qualities, a healthy body, nor possessions should be gloried in. None of the three is genuine human perfection.

The fourth man is the one distinguished by intellectual understanding and knowledge of God, and Maimonides can hardly be faulted for construing that man as a person whose perfection consists in 'knowledge of God, which is true science', and again, in the 'cognition of God' that constitutes man's 'final goal'. In contrast, ritual worship and the 'moral qualities beneficial to men in their dealings with one another' are only 'preparations' for the goal.[83]

81 Altmann, 'Maimonides' "Four Perfections"', 24, calls attention to a less developed philosophical exegesis of the verses in Abraham ibn Daud.

82 See above, §§1–2.

83 *MN* iii. 54 (134*a*–*b*). Maimonides explains why Scripture reverses the order and places ethical perfection, which is the least spurious of the three false perfections, first, and wealth, which is the most spurious, third: since Scripture addresses mankind, it proceeds from the perfection that men ordinarily rank lowest to the perfection that they rank highest; and the ordinary run of men rank moral perfection below bodily perfection, and bodily perfection below wealth.

Scripture's pronouncement on the four purported perfections does not, however, stop there. After stating that the man who has the right to glory is he who 'hath intellectual understanding and knowledge of Me', the prophet continues: 'that I am the Lord who exercise loving-kindness, justice, and righteousness in the earth; for in these things I delight'.

Following in the prophet's steps, Maimonides likewise continues: 'In expounding the most noble of ends, Scripture did not limit itself to cognition of God.' 'Rather it says that [the grounds for] glorying are both having cognition of Me and recognizing My attributes.' God's attributes, 'as we explained earlier in connection with the verse "show me now Thy ways"',[84] are 'His actions'. Scripture accordingly exhorts the man who attains knowledge of God to 'imitate' God's ways or actions, and, specifically, His acts of loving-kindness, justice, and righteousness. Maimonides' philosophical-midrashic exegesis concludes: the 'perfection of man in which one can truly glory' is 'cognition of God to the extent of man's ability and recognition of God's providence over His creatures'. 'The way of life of such a man, following upon that cognition [of God]', is 'loving-kindness, justice, and righteousness, in imitation of God's actions.'[85]

Maimonides had a knack for opening Pandora's boxes and he has opened a small one here. In the preceding paragraphs he repeatedly belittled moral virtue and moral qualities as designed for the benefit of others and he insisted that true human perfection is intellectual and the ultimate goal of human life is cognition of God. He was pleased to uncover the same assessment in the prophet Jeremiah. Seemingly out of the blue and still relying on the prophet, he now dictates that man imitate God's acts of loving-kindness, justice, and righteousness, and he speaks of a human 'perfection' that includes imitation of those actions.

Students of Maimonides have read him as thereby adding a further perfection to the four previously spelled out, and one scholar goes as far as to call it a 'fifth perfection'.[86] Some have concluded—the initial impetus having been given by Herman Cohen a century ago—that in the final lines of the *Moreh nevukhim*, Maimonides views 'the supreme knowledge of God' as 'understanding the ethical activity of God', with the consequence that 'ethics . . . has . . . become the ultimate meaning and purpose of the knowledge of God'.[87] In a variant, others have understood Maimonides to hold that 'the only positive

[84] Exod. 33: 13.

[85] *MN* iii. 54 (134*b*–135*a*).

[86] Pines, 'The Limitations of Human Knowledge', 99–100; Berman, 'The Ethical Views of Maimonides', 18–20, 31.

[87] Cohen, 'Charakteristik der Ethik Maimunis', 89–90, 121; English trans., 69–74, 155; Guttmann, *Hapilosofiah shel hayahadut*, 164; English trans., 176; Schwarzschild, *Pursuit of the Ideal*, 151–3. The quotation is from Guttmann.

knowledge of God of which man is capable is knowledge of the attributes of action, and this leads or ought to lead to a sort of political activity, which is the highest perfection of man'.[88]

As occurs more than once in his writings, Maimonides has not expressed himself as well as he might. A reasonably careful reading of what he says here and throughout the book nevertheless shows that to represent him as making the goal of human life ethical or political badly misses the mark. Maimonides stresses that 'man's goal, insofar as he is a man, is nothing other than conceiving intelligible thoughts'; it consists in becoming 'an actual intellect' and 'knowing everything in man's power to know concerning the totality of what exists'.[89] He asserts unambiguously that the prophet Jeremiah recognized 'four perfections', that 'virtuous moral qualities' are not to be gloried in, that the perfection worth glorying in and seeking is 'cognition of God';[90] there is no hint of a fifth perfection. He does not withdraw his disparagement of moral qualities as being designed to serve others rather than the person who possesses them or his statement that moral qualities pertain to the welfare of the body and not to that of the soul.

Maimonides is exhorting the man who attains knowledge of God to imitate Him in the manner in which he interpreted imitation of God earlier in the *Moreh nevukhim*. God possesses no qualities, characteristics, or moral virtues; acts of loving-kindness, justice, and righteousness flow from Him dispassionately. Analogously, human beings should cultivate a 'way of life' in which acts of loving-kindness, justice, and righteousness flow not from qualities in the soul but dispassionately, from human reason.[91] Maimonides surely did not believe that divine acts of loving-kindness are equal in value to God's knowledge of Himself. By the same token, human acts that imitate God's actions are not ranked by him as equal to, let alone higher than, human knowledge of God. As for making political activity the highest perfection of man, when Maimonides encourages readers to 'focus their intellectual thought constantly on love of God', he adds: 'That is usually accomplished in solitude and isolation. Every virtuous man therefore isolates himself as much as he can and comes into contact with others only when necessary.'[92]

[88] Pines, 'The Limitations of Human Knowledge', 100. Similarly, Berman, 'The Political Interpretation of the Maxim', 59, and Lerner, 'Maimonides' Governance of the Solitary', 44. Kellner, *Maimonides on Human Perfection*, 8–10, gives a fuller account of the positions cited in this note and the previous one.

[89] *MN* iii. 8 (12*b*); iii. 27(60*a*). See above for additional statements in the same vein.

[90] *MN* iii. 54 (134*a*–*b*).

[91] Altmann, 'Maimonides' "Four Perfections"', 24, interprets Maimonides in a similar fashion.

[92] *MN* iii. 51 (125*a*).

A notion similar to that expressed by Maimonides is found in his fellow Cordovan, Averroes.[93]

Part of Maimonides' reason for signing off with talk of loving-kindness, justice, and righteousness may have been a desire to conclude his book on a high note. Had he chosen to conclude on a less rosy note, he could have reminded readers that dispassionate behaviour in imitation of God's actions sometimes has a different outcome. It sometimes ends with sentencing people to death by fire and wiping out entire populations.

6. Summary

Shemonah perakim and *Mishneh torah* base their treatments of ethics on the postulate that characteristics in the human soul are the locus of virtue and vice. Although human actions and characteristics in the soul are interrelated, and the former are the instrument for inculcating the latter, it is not the actions that are virtuous or vicious. Only characteristics in the soul are.

Virtuous characteristics are those lying midway between two extremes, and the extremes are vices. *Shemonah perakim* and the *Mishneh torah* recognize certain exceptions. In each pair of extremes, one is worse than the other, and both works recommend that a person depart slightly from the mean in the direction of the less harmful extreme, either as a precaution against deviating in the direction of the more harmful or as a desideratum in its own right. The *Commentary on the Mishnah*, of which *Shemonah perakim* is a part, further recommends cultivating an extreme characteristic in a single instance. Pride is so harmful that the ultra-virtuous flee to total meekness. The *Mishneh torah* takes an additional step and not merely recommends, but dictates, going to the extreme in two instances. One concerns pride, the good way being the cultivation not merely of modesty but of meekness. The other concerns anger: a man should train himself to be wholly impassive even about matters where anger is warranted. Otherwise, both rabbinic works disparage persons who cultivate extreme characteristics as fools and sinners. They decry extreme characteristics as sickness of the soul, censurable, forbidden, an evil way, and a sin requiring atonement.

Without spelling out the distinction in so many words, Maimonides' *Moreh nevukhim* plainly envisages two ethical standards. The lower standard encourages balanced behaviour and serves society by creating salutary social conditions. Since such behaviour has no intrinsic value, the person who performs it

[93] Averroes, *Compendio de Metafisica*, iv, §28; German trans.: *Die Epitome der Metaphysik des Averroes*, 118.

toils for the sake of others. The higher standard rests on the proposition that man's material side is the source of every human infirmity and evil, that the sense of touch and the claims of matter are shameful. Physical pleasures are not to be enjoyed in a balanced fashion; they are to be avoided completely. Men have to do their best to extirpate physical desire, minimize their contact with the manure of physical pleasure, and in particular shun the dirt of sexual intercourse. They must act dispassionately, solely in accordance with reason.

Despite the surface resemblance of the lower standard of ethics in the *Moreh nevukhim* to the ethics of intermediate characteristics in Maimonides' rabbinic works, he has not simply transformed the latter into the former. True, he speaks in the *Moreh nevukhim* of *moral qualities* and *moral virtues*, but he scrupulously avoids defining what moral virtue is. Even though his lower standard encourages behaviour that is neither excessive nor defective, but balanced, the *Moreh nevukhim* never speaks of characteristics of the soul that are balanced. What Maimonides wrote in his rabbinic period about characteristics of the soul and their role in ethics is jettisoned.

On one essential point, Maimonides is consistent and unequivocal throughout his writings. The goal of human life is to perfect the human intellect and to think intelligible thoughts concerning metaphysical matters and, most importantly, God. Ethical attainments, however construed, are means to the greater end.

NINE

Maimonides the Rationalist

> It is known and clear that love of God establishes itself in man's heart only when he is ravished by it constantly and forsakes everything in the world . . . except for his knowledge of God. Knowledge and love go hand in hand; when there is less of the first there is less of the second and when there is more, there is more. Consequently, a man should, as far as humanly possible, devote himself to exercising his intellect in mastery of the sciences . . . that lead to knowledge of God.
>
> MAIMONIDES
>
> *Mishneh torah*, closing lines of 'Sefer hamada'

WE HAVE FOUND THE FOLLOWING.

Maimonides expresses his commitment to the intellectual ideal in rabbinic and philosophical writings that span more than three decades. In the *Commentary on the Mishnah*, which he completed at the age of 30, he characterizes the sciences of physics and metaphysics as the *roots*—or *principles* (*aṣl*)—on which the legal and ritual part of the Jewish religion rests.[1] Prophets and philosophers, he assures us, agree that everything in the lower world exists for the single purpose of bringing forth men who excel in 'knowledge and practice' (*'ilm* and *'amal*), and knowledge in the present context means the 'conceiving of the true essences [of things] . . . and the cognition of everything a man can know'; *'ilm*, in other words, has its technical sense of *science*. 'The goal of the human species is to conceive intelligible thoughts' and it is attained by those who are 'students of science and philosophize'.[2] In a remark that some may find disquieting, Maimonides writes that human beings who are incapable of attaining the intellectual goal exist in order to supply the needs of those who have the capability.[3]

The *Mishneh torah*, Maimonides' code of Jewish law, goes further. It teaches that the first two positive commandments of the divine Law are fulfilled by mastering rational demonstrations of the existence and unity of God. Love of God is predicated on knowledge, and 'a man should, as far as humanly possible, devote himself to exercising his intellect in mastery of the sciences . . . that lead to knowledge of God'. Mastery of the sciences is a prerequisite for

[1] Maimonides, *Commentary on the Mishnah*, *Ḥag.* 2: 1 (end).
[2] Ibid., introd., 42–3.
[3] Ibid., introd., 43–5.

prophecy. Immortality is achieved through the acquisition of knowledge, specifically metaphysical knowledge, and Maimonides marks the human intellect as the part of man that survives the death of the body. He joins the prophet Isaiah in looking forward to a time when 'the earth shall be full of the knowledge of the Lord, as the waters cover the sea'.[4]

The *Moreh nevukhim* continues to hammer the point home. The ideal man, Maimonides writes there, is he who masters 'the demonstration for whatever can be demonstrated, who possesses certainty concerning metaphysical [*ilāhī*] matters where certainty is possible while approaching certainty where only approaching it is possible'.[5] 'True human perfection' consists in acquisition of 'the rational virtues', that is to say, in 'conceiving intelligible thoughts that give rise to true opinions in matters of metaphysics [*ilāhiyyāt*]'.[6] The person who finds grace in God's sight is he who knows Him, not he 'who merely fasts and recites the liturgy'.[7] Intellectual perfection 'is the ultimate end, which genuinely perfects the individual; it belongs to him alone, and it gives a man eternal existence'.[8] 'The amount of providence a person enjoys is dependent on his intellectual attainments.'[9] In the *Moreh nevukhim*, Maimonides takes the position that moral virtue, in the conventional sense, does not serve the person who possesses it, and if a man should live 'alone and not have dealings with anyone else, all his moral virtues would be idle, in vain, and useless'. 'You should therefore strive to attain that which is permanent for you and not weary yourself and toil for others' by expending effort in cultivating moral virtue.[10]

Far from conceding that he was importing foreign notions into Jewish tradition, Maimonides maintains that the Jewish 'nation was a knowledgeable, perfect nation' and possessed 'many sciences', but 'the wicked members of the ignorant nations destroyed . . . our learning, our books, and our wise men, so that we became ignorant' as they are. 'We mingled with them and adopted their opinions, their moral qualities, and their behaviour.' As a consequence, 'philosophical matters have come to appear alien to our Law. . . . The truth, however, is different.'[11]

The Mishnah and Babylonian Talmud prize the subjects that they call the account of creation and the account of the chariot. In the first instance, the two accounts are the description of the creation of the world in the book of Genesis and the depiction of a heavenly chariot in the book of Ezekiel; the terms were then extended beyond the scriptural texts themselves to include

[4] *MT*, 'Hilkhot yesodei hatorah', 1: 1–7, 4: 8–9, 7: 1; 'Hilkhot teshuvah', 8: 2, 6, 10: 6; 'Hilkhot melakhim', 12: 4–5.

[5] *MN* iii. 51 (124*a*).

[6] *MN* iii. 54 (133*b*).

[7] *MN* i. 54 (64*a*).

[8] *MN* iii. 54 (133*b*).

[9] *MN* iii. 17 (36*a*–37*b*), 18 (38*a*), 51 (127*a*–*b*). See H. Davidson, *Moses Maimonides*, 374–7.

[10] *MN* iii. 54 (133*b*–134*a*).

[11] *MN* i. 71 (93*b*), ii. 11 (24*a*–*b*).

the abstruse rabbinic exegesis of them. From Maimonides' study of 'the statements of the Rabbis', it 'became clear' to him that the account of creation and the account of the chariot—by which I assume he means the terms in their double senses—are the equivalent of the sciences of physics and metaphysics.[12] He goes on to interpret a statement in the Babylonian Talmud in a manner that makes metaphysics a 'great matter' in contrast to the legal disputations of the Babylonian Talmud, which are only a 'small matter'. The upshot, to the scandal of more than one traditional reader, is that the ancient rabbis rated the study of metaphysics higher than traditional talmudic study and indeed regarded it as the acme of their curriculum.[13]

Maimonides moreover reads statements on astronomy in the Mishnah corpus and Babylonian Talmud as reflecting expertise in that subject as well. Rabbinic literature thus discloses to him that the rabbis had a broad knowledge of science and philosophy, comprising physical science, astronomy, and metaphysics, and he finds those subjects to have been part of the talmudic curriculum. In preaching the intellectual ideal and encouraging the study of science and metaphysics, he sees himself not as a radical innovator but as a conservative restorer of a venerable patrimony. The anachronism may be jarring to us, but what we recognize as anachronistic did not necessarily appear so in an earlier age, even to a thinker of stature. Maimonides betrays no hint of being other than utterly serious, and to presume that he is being disingenuous is itself a form of anachronism.

As philosophy was pursued in the Middle Ages, an aspirant prepared himself to a much greater extent than today by mastering the philosophical writings of his predecessors. Since Maimonides views philosophy as integral to the ultimate goal of human life and a tool for restoring what time and its vicissitudes have eroded from the ancient rabbinic legacy, more than one scholar has taken for granted that he mastered the philosophical literature available to him. The evidence tells a different tale.

He could have encountered watered-down Neoplatonic notions in a few authors whose names he mentions, but all he tells us about those authors is that they purveyed inanities, wind, and vanities, and their writings serve no function apart from wasting a person's time. Motifs of Neoplatonic provenance play a role in his thought only insofar as they were appropriated by the Arabic Aristotelian school, woven into the Arabic Aristotelian quilt, and mistakenly regarded by Maimonides as authentically Aristotelian. The picture of

[12] Maimonides, *Commentary on the Mishnah*, *Ḥag.* 2: 1 (from which I have taken the quotation); *MT*, 'Hilkhot yesodei hatorah', 2: 11, 4: 10–11; *MN*, introd., 3*b*.

[13] *MT*, 'Hilkhot yesodei hatorah', 4: 13; 'Hilkhot talmud torah', 1: 12; 'Hilkhot melakhim', 12: 4–5.

the universe that he attributes to the Kalam is flawed. As for Aristotle, the philosopher *par excellence*, there is no reliable evidence that, by the age of 40, Maimonides had read a single line of any of his works. The *Moreh nevukhim* and other writings from Maimonides' later period do reveal a direct knowledge of a number of Aristotle's compositions, yet key works, notably the *Metaphysics*, are still absent. Even for the later period, there is no reliable evidence that he read any of the Greek commentaries on Aristotle.

Two of his sources for fleshing out his knowledge of Aristotle were the *Principles of the Universe* and *On Providence*, attributed to Alexander of Aphrodisias, neither of which is a commentary. It was primarily the Arabic Aristotelians who shaped his philosophical orientation.

He is to be contrasted with Avicenna, Averroes, and Aquinas, who pored over—without, in the case of Avicenna and Aquinas, accepting—every word of Aristotle's that was accessible to them, while making as much use as they could of the Greek commentators. Within the ambit of Maimonides' own scholarly activity, the short cuts he took in studying the philosophical literature stand in contrast to the thoroughness with which he studied the rabbinic and medical literatures.

Maimonides did not view human reason as all-powerful. There are, he writes, 'existent beings and matters that it is not in the nature of the human intellect to comprehend at all', for which 'the gates of comprehension [*idrāk*] are shut tight before' the human intellect. And there are 'matters of which the human intellect can comprehend [*yudrik*] part, while remaining ignorant of other parts'. He assures readers that in making these statements he has not been swayed by religious considerations. The limitations of the human intellect are 'something that philosophers have affirmed and understood' as well, and they did so 'without concern for any school or [ulterior] opinion'.[14]

Human reason, in his judgement, is capable of acquiring broad scientific knowledge of the sublunar world and a lesser level of knowledge concerning the celestial region. As regards the latter, it can demonstrate the existence of multiple spheres, each with its proper motion, and can predict where a given star or planet will be at any moment. Through proofs that fall short of apodictic demonstrations, it can arrive at a convincing determination of the factors involved in the movements of the heavenly bodies—the existence of an incorporeal mover for each sphere, the souls of the spheres, the love that their souls experience for their respective incorporeal movers, the spheres' desire to render themselves as similar as possible to their movers, and the expression of

[14] *MN* i. 31 (33*b*, 35*a*).

their desire in circular motion.[15] Progress, furthermore, occurs in astronomy. Maimonides states that Aristotle's knowledge of the heavens had been outstripped by the astronomical achievements of Maimonides' own day, and he acknowledges that astronomical problems thwarting him and his contemporaries will perhaps be solved by future generations of astronomers. Knowledge of the nature, substance, and form of the spheres nevertheless remains beyond man's grasp, with a proviso. If we take Maimonides at his word, he believed that Moses, the greatest of the prophets, was vouchsafed a cognition of the incorporeal intelligences and a level of knowledge of the celestial spheres exceeding the powers of philosophers, though there was a limit to what even Moses could attain.[16]

Human reason can conclusively demonstrate the existence of God and other propositions about Him, although knowledge of the divine essence and hence having God as the form the human intellect thinks are beyond man's power. Finally, the existence of a transcendent, incorporeal active intellect, which is the source of sublunar natural forms and actual human thought, has, Maimonides maintains, been established beyond doubt.

Maimonides' rationalism sends out tendrils in a number of directions, some of which have already been touched on at one spot or another in the book: it governs his exegesis of Scripture and of the non-legal—aggadic—side of rabbinic thought, creates hurdles that he has to negotiate in treating the halakhic—legal—side, leads him to a reconstruction of the early history of mankind, and shapes his conception of the highest form of human worship and human life. The remaining pages explore those subjects.

1. Rationalist Exegesis of Scripture

Maimonides writes in the Introduction to the *Moreh nevukhim* that he could discover no stratagem for 'imparting what is true and has been demonstrated except' by proceeding in a manner 'appropriate for a single superior person, although inappropriate for 10,000 ignoramuses'. He chose to care for the needs of the former even if he thereby left himself open to the opprobrium of the latter, for his object was to rescue 'the single superior man . . . and show [him the way out of] his perplexity, so that he might perfect himself and achieve repose'.[17]

The only person whom Maimonides is actually known to have had in view was Joseph ben Judah, who came to Egypt from the West. He studied with

[15] See above, Ch. 5, §2. [16] *MN* ii. 24 (54*a*–*b*). [17] *MN*, introd. (9*b*).

Maimonides, and although they apparently spent only a short time together, it was sufficient to establish a strong bond between them. The *Moreh nevukhim*, which was written after Joseph left Egypt for Syria, is dedicated to him, and here and there within the book Maimonides addresses him directly.

Joseph was a trained physician but he did not stay long enough to complete the scientific and philosophical curriculum that Maimonides designed for him. The dedication of the *Moreh nevukhim* reveals that when Joseph departed, he had still not been initiated into philosophical metaphysics, and it seems that he had not even reached the stage where he could be apprised of the errors of the Kalam. Maimonides recalls that Joseph had some prior knowledge of Kalam and was eager to learn whether its system rests on demonstrations, that is to say, whether it qualifies as scientific. Maimonides put him off on the grounds that he had to start at the beginning and proceed step by patient step through the programme, for only in that manner could his perplexity be properly resolved.[18] We are not told that instructor and student ever reached the subject of Kalam.

Writers on Maimonides often convey the impression that the 'perplexed' referred to in the title of the *Moreh nevukhim* were sophisticated thinkers grappling with the abstract issue of faith and reason. Maimonides' dedication of the book to someone who never completed the scientific and philosophical plan of study planned for him, together with a statement of the two objects for which he composed the *Moreh nevukhim*, reveal that the perplexity perturbing one superior person in 10,000 was more modest.

Maimonides' first stated object is to aid persons who believe in the Torah, have also studied some philosophy, and are in a dilemma. They are pulled one way by scriptural verses that depict God in physical terms and in another by the philosophical proposition that God is incorporeal, and they do not know how to choose between the two. His second object is to enlighten persons who do not realize that Scripture speaks in metaphors and allegories and who take them literally; they are thereby again reduced to perplexity.[19] Books often have a mind of their own, and as the *Moreh nevukhim* develops, its vista expands. Nevertheless, when Maimonides sat down to write the *Moreh nevukhim*, his intention was unambiguous. He was composing a book for persons—for example, Joseph ben Judah—who were perplexed because they had not been taught how to read the Bible correctly.

His guidelines in pursuing the twin tasks are put forward in connection with the account of creation but plainly apply to Scripture as a whole. Scripture, he

[18] *MN*, dedicatory letter (2*a*–*b*). Maimonides describes Joseph as *ḥā'ir*, 'perplexed', the same word that appears in the title of the book.

[19] *MN*, introd. (2*b*–3*a*).

tells us, must be read with a healthy 'intellect, after one has attained perfection in the demonstrative sciences and knowledge of the prophetic secrets'.[20] Most of the sentence is clear: in reading the Bible, one should place implicit reliance on reason, prepare oneself by studying science, and ground one's exegesis in solid scientific knowledge. What Maimonides means by *knowledge of the prophetic secrets* is less certain. He may be alluding to the thesis, laid down in the Introduction to the *Moreh nevukhim* and underlined in the chapter from which the sentence just quoted is taken, that the prophets spoke in metaphors and allegories. He may, in other words, be urging readers to keep in mind that Scripture often speaks in a figurative fashion and to interpret it accordingly.

Maimonides accomplishes his first task, rescuing those who are torn between the words of Scripture and the proposition that God is incorporeal, by drawing up a glossary of anthropomorphic and anthropopathic terms by which God is described in Scripture—words such as *heart*, *foot*, *face*, *eye*, *back*; *going*, *coming*, *going up*, *going down*, *sitting*, *standing*, *resting*; *sorrow*, *anger*, *joy*. Through citations from Scripture itself, each term is painstakingly shown to have a range of meanings including at least one that is free of physical implications and is applicable to God. For instance, Maimonides cites biblical verses to show that an extended sense of *heart* is *will*. When God announces through His prophet: 'I shall give you shepherds according to My heart, who will feed you with knowledge and understanding', the meaning is not that God has an actual heart. The prophet declares God's intention to give His people shepherds, spiritual leaders, in accordance with His *will*. The term *sitting*, to take another example, has the extended sense of a *stable and unchanging state*, and that is the sense in which it should be understood when the Psalmist describes God as Him 'who sitteth in heaven'. The Psalmist is teaching that God is unchanging.[21]

Once each of the terms is seen to have a non-physical usage appropriate to the context, the conflict between the perplexing description of God and the philosophical proposition that He is incorporeal evaporates.[22] As a watchword, Maimonides repeatedly proclaims: 'Scripture speaks in conformity with the language [Heb.: *kileshon*] of men'; that is to say, it makes itself comprehensible to a broad spectrum of readers by employing non-technical language that is similar to ordinary human speech, and its descriptions of God are therefore not always exact.[23]

[20] *MN* ii. 29 (65*b*).

[21] *MN* i. 11, 39. The verses are Jer. 3: 15 and Ps. 2: 4.

[22] *MN* i, chs. 10, 11, 12, 15, 18, 21–5, 28–30, 36–9, 43–5, 65.

[23] The rule 'Scripture speaks in conformity with the language of men' is cited on eight different occasions in *MN*. See the list in Schwarz's index to his translation of *MN*, 774.

In cleansing Scripture of anthropomorphisms and anthropopathisms, Maimonides goes over ground that had already been covered by earlier medieval Jewish rationalists,[24] and 'Scripture speaks in conformity with the language of men' had long been a motto of Jewish thinkers who do away with anthropomorphisms.[25] His treatment may be more thorough than that of his predecessors, but readers who were thrown into a quandary by biblical descriptions of God had adequate resources without him where they could seek help.

Maimonides accomplishes his second task by interpreting a large swath of Scripture allegorically, and here he breaks fresh—and controversial—ground.[26] He gives particular attention to the scriptural account of creation and the scriptural account of the chariot.

Genesis presents a multi-stage creation that lasted six days. Maimonides, in harmony with a policy of keeping divine intervention in the universe to a minimum, maintains that the universe was not in fact brought into existence through a series of creative acts extending over six days but rather by a single act, and he finds support for his stance in Scripture itself and in rabbinic literature.[27] The creator was like 'a farmer who sowed different seeds at the same moment', some of which sprouted after a day, some after two, and so on.[28]

The opening verse of Genesis relates that God 'created the heaven and the earth', and verse 2 speaks of earth, water, the wind of God, and darkness. Maimonides takes those four terms as allusions to the four elements—earth, water, air, and fire—from which, the science of physics postulates, every object in the sublunar world is constituted. Together, the two verses teach that the initial stage in the emergence of the sublunar world was the appearance of the four physical elements.

Subsequent verses in Genesis allude to the presence of water vapour in the atmosphere;[29] in the Arabic Aristotelian hierarchy of existence, water vapour

[24] Sa'adiah, *Emunot vede'ot*, ii, introd., chs. 8–10; Bahya ibn Pakuda, *Ḥovot halevavot* (Kafah), 1: 10, 77; *Ḥovot halevavot* (Ibn Tibbon), 1: 10, 45; Abraham ibn Daud, *Emunah ramah*, 51.

[25] For authors prior to Maimonides who cited the rule when interpreting away anthropomorphisms, see Bacher, *Die Bibelexegese der jüdischen Religionsphilosophen vor Maimûni*, 72, and *Die Bibelexegese Moses Maimûni's*, 19; to which add Jacob ben Nissim, cited in Kaufmann, *Geschichte der Attributenlehre*, 217; Rabbi Hai, in *Otsar hage'onim: Berakhot: Responsa*, p. 131; Ibn Ezra, *Commentary on the Pentateuch*, Gen. 1: 26 *et passim*; Abraham ibn Daud, *Emunah ramah*, 51. For the meaning that the rule originally had in rabbinic halakhic exegesis, see Bacher, *Die älteste Terminologie*, 98.

[26] Maimonides was preceded by Philo, the allegorist *par excellence*, but Philo was unknown to medieval Jewish thinkers.

[27] Isa. 48: 13: 'When I call unto them [the earth and the heavens], they stand up together.' The verse is quoted in BT *Ḥag.* 12*a* and *Genesis Rabbah* 1: 15, to establish that heaven and earth were created 'as one', like 'a pot and its lid'.

[28] *MN* ii. 30 (67*a*).

[29] Gen. 2: 6: 'There went up a mist from the earth and watered the whole face of the ground.'

and the dry exhalation arising from the earth constitute the level of existence coming immediately after the four elements. By filling in a few gaps, Maimonides is able to read the opening chapters of Genesis as reflecting the successive degrees of complexity in sublunar being. At the bottom stand the four elements; water vapour and the dry exhalation follow; they, in turn, are responsible for meteorological phenomena and the existence of minerals; plants, animals, and man complete the picture. What was latent in the undifferentiated creation unfolded stage by stage in accordance with laws known from the natural sciences until the physical world evolved into the form we see around us today. The unfolding of the different stages is depicted by Scripture metaphorically as a series of acts extending over six days.[30]

Not only are breaks in nature, or miracles, rare in Maimonides' universe; they also are short-lived. The serpent that was more subtle than the other beasts of the field, that struck up a conversation with Eve, and that induced her to sin, would, if taken literally, be a prodigious antediluvian exception to reptilian nature. Maimonides tacitly rejects such a notion. Nor could he take literally a rabbinic description of Adam and Eve as originally joined back to back and forming a single composite being or the depiction of Satan seated astride the serpent and performing the role of tempter.

Maimonides reads the scriptural story of the serpent, Eve, and Adam, together with the rabbinic elaborations of the narrative, as a web of allegories. He does not spell out his understanding of all the particulars because of ancient restrictions on access to the account of creation. But he makes clear that the allegories concern man's composite nature—a physical side symbolized by Eve and an intellectual side symbolized by Adam—and the tempting of man's higher nature by his material side and the imaginative faculty of his soul.[31]

In the other of the two accounts, that of the chariot, Ezekiel is described as having seen 'the likeness of four living creatures', four wheels (*ofanim*) 'hard by the living creatures', 'the likeness of a firmament' over their heads, 'the likeness of a throne' above the firmament, and 'a likeness as the appearance of a man' upon the throne. The four wheels represent, for Maimonides, the natural regions of the four sublunar elements, which are arranged in layers, one surrounding the other—earth at the centre, then water, then air, and then fire. The living creatures represent the celestial spheres, and the location of the wheels hard by the living creatures symbolizes the dependence of the sublunar region on the movement of the heavens.

[30] *MN* ii. 30 (67*b*–68*b*, 69*b*). The unfolding of the sublunar world was brought about through the rotations of the spheres—the 'heaven' of verse 1—together with alternating light and darkness in the world.

[31] *MN* ii. 30 (70*a*–*b*).

The rabbis placed even tighter restrictions on divulging the secrets of the account of the chariot than on divulging those of the account of creation, and Maimonides took the restrictions seriously.[32] As a consequence, the rest of his exegesis of the chariot is so allusive that it is hard to follow. The best guess is that he took the firmament over the heads of the living creatures as standing for the outermost, all-encompassing celestial sphere, and the likeness of the man upon the throne as representing the incorporeal intelligences that move the spheres. What is significant for us is that the two scriptural accounts, that of creation and that of the chariot, one encapsulating the science of physics and the other, the science of metaphysics, become, in Maimonides' reading, a figurative portrayal of the Arabic Aristotelian universe: Scripture sketches the structure of the higher and lower worlds, the interaction between the two, the nature of man, and the struggle of the human intellect with the lower faculties of the human soul.[33]

A good deal more allegorical interpretation of Scripture is found in the *Moreh nevukhim*. I limit myself to a theme in which Maimonides' rationalist approach especially stands out, namely, angels.

From the demonstrative sciences, he knew that there do not exist heavenly angels who have, or can adopt, physical characteristics and walk the earth. Angels in the true sense are, for him, the incorporeal movers of the spheres and the active intellect, although Scripture sometimes employs the term more broadly to include any intermediary through which God governs the universe, be it a prophet, a force of nature, or even the physical elements. The Psalmist thus can bless God, 'Who makest winds Thy angels, the flaming fire Thy ministers.'[34]

Scripture often relates that God or an angel spoke to one of the prophets in a vision or dream.[35] Inasmuch as the genuine angels are, like the deity, incorporeal, Maimonides lays down the rule that whether or not Scripture says so explicitly, whenever it depicts God or an angel as speaking—or appearing—to a human being, 'that occurs solely in a dream or prophetic vision' inspired by the emanation of the active intellect;[36] an exception is prophecies in which Moses received a direct communication from God.[37] The angelic figures who

32 *MN* iii. 1 (2*a*).

33 *MN* iii. 2.

34 *MN* i. 43 (48*a*), 49 (55*a*–*b*), ii. 6 (16*a*–17*b*), 42 (89*b*–90*a*). The verse is Ps. 104: 4. The underlying meaning of *malakh*, the Hebrew term for angel, like that of the Greek *angelos*, is 'messenger'.

35 For example, Gen. 15: 1, 31: 11, 46: 2; Dan. 10: 7–8, cited in *MN* ii. 41 (87*a*–88*a*).

36 *MN* ii. 41 (87*b*). Maimonides considered the point important enough to warrant reiterating it; see *MN* i. 49 (66*b*), ii. 6 (18*a*), 42 (89*a*).

37 *MN* i. 37 (44*b*), ii. 35: Moses' prophecy differed from that of the other prophets in four respects, one of which was that he heard a voice without the mediacy of an angel. *MN* iii. 45 (98*b*): his initial prophecy at the burning bush was, nevertheless, through an angel.

approached Abraham's tent, who were provided with water for washing their feet, to whom Abraham served a hearty meal, who delivered the tidings that Sarah would soon bear a son, who travelled on to Sodom and informed Lot that God was going to destroy the cities of the Plain, were not angels walking the earth in human guise. The chain of events occurred in one or more prophetic visions. The angel who at the last moment instructed Abraham not to sacrifice his son, the numinous figure with whom Jacob wrestled and who strained a sinew in Jacob's thigh, leaving him with a limp, the mysterious man who directed Joseph to the site where his brothers were camping, the angel who appeared to Moses in the burning bush, the angel who rebuked Balaam, the angelic figure whom Joshua encountered and conversed with before the battle of Jericho, the angel Gabriel who gave Daniel cryptic clues regarding the date of redemption—these and other personages and incidents reported in Scripture did not exist and take place in the external world. They were visions. The angels who spoke to Sarah's maidservant Hagar in the desert and the angel of the Lord who informed Samson's parents that they would be blessed with a son appeared to the three—who, although ordinary persons and not prophets, had imaginative faculties strong enough to receive the emanation of the active intellect in a sub-prophetic mode—as visions.[38]

The tactic of locating events in visions rather than in the external world serves Maimonides even where angels are not involved. When Scripture tells that God took Abraham outside to count the stars, that Balaam quarrelled with his she-ass, that Isaiah went naked and barefoot, that Jeremiah buried a girdle near the Euphrates and returned some time later to see what happened to it, that Hosea married a harlot, that Ezekiel was transported to Jerusalem in a trice, that he shaved his head and beard and performed additional bizarre actions—these incidents and others occurred only in visions.[39]

Maimonides' policy of interpreting away what does not meet his rationalist and philosophical criteria and of discovering philosophical truths within problematic texts carries over to his reading of rabbinic aggadah.

2. Rationalist Exegesis of Aggadah

There are, Maimonides writes, three ways of looking at the aggadic side of ancient rabbinic literature. Most readers, being ignorant of science, take rabbinic aggadah literally, and even where the surface meaning of a piece of

[38] *MN* ii. 6 (18*a*), 41 (88*a*), 42 (89*a*–90*a*).

[39] *MN* ii. 46. Ibn Ezra similarly writes, in his commentary on Hos. 1: 2, that the prophet's marrying a harlot occurred only in a prophetic vision, and he indicates in his commentary on Isa. 20: 1, that he understands the prophet's going naked also to have taken place in a vision.

aggadah is 'impossible', they accept it as 'necessarily existent' (*wājib al-wujūd*). Maimonides is thinking of the highly anthropomorphic descriptions of God and the scores of fantastic stories and descriptions found in rabbinic literature. A second group, which is also large, is made up of readers who regard themselves as educated, yet are even more ignorant than members of the first group. They too take aggadah literally, but instead of blindly embracing the surface meaning, they ridicule it as absurd and belittle the rabbinic authors responsible for it as fools. They fail to grasp something that the rabbis understood well: metaphysics is a subject that can be presented to the ordinary run of mankind only in a non-abstract, figurative guise.

A very small number have the correct approach. They perceive from the profundity of statements scattered through rabbinic literature that the rabbis were great minds who comprehended the 'verities'; and they recognize, as they are confident the rabbis did, 'the impossibility of what is impossible'. When the literal meaning of a piece of aggadah contains something impossible, perspicacious readers are confident that the aggadah has an inner meaning and they search it out.[40]

We have encountered a few of the philosophical truths that Maimonides discovers within aggadah. The righteous who, in the world to come, sit with crowns on their heads and enjoy the splendour of the divine presence symbolize 'the permanence of the soul through the permanence of its object of knowledge'. Satan seated astride the serpent in the Garden of Eden symbolizes the temptation of the human intellect by the lower faculties of the human soul. Of Rabbi Akiva's warning to his colleagues not to cry 'water water' when they 'reach the stones of pure marble', Maimonides writes: 'If you consider and grasp everything demonstrated in meteorology', you will appreciate how 'the whole issue' of the waters above the firmament in Genesis 1 is 'clarified . . . and disclosed' in a single aggadic sentence. Unfortunately, we are not told what the profound truth embodied in the single aggadic sentence is.[41]

Maimonides did not regard the ancient rabbis as infallible nor was he happy with every piece of aggadic lore.[42] On one occasion, he expresses dismay regarding statements that the rabbinic sources report in the name of single individuals and that he judges to be incompatible with the fundamental tenet of creation *ex nihilo*; he warns that the opinion of an individual rabbi is not necessarily authoritative.[43] Where natural science is concerned, he observes that

[40] Maimonides, *Commentary on the Mishnah, San.* 10, introd., 202.

[41] Regarding the inner meaning that he uncovers in one piece of aggadah, *MN* i. 70 (92*b*), he writes: 'Look how these true, abstruse matters', which superior philosophers have discovered through their lucubrations, are 'scattered through the aggadic part of rabbinic literature [*al midrashot*].'

[42] *MN*, introd. (11*b*).

[43] *MN* ii. 30 (67*a*).

the ancient rabbis did not receive their information from the prophets—in which case it would have been immune from error—and did not always even have the best available science. For instance, in their picture of the heavens, the planets and stars circle the earth by moving along the surface of a stationary sphere, whereas gentile astronomers of the time knew better. They realized that the stars and planets are in fact embedded in the celestial spheres, it is the spheres that rotate around the earth, and they carry the stars and planets with them. Astronomy, moreover, was not as well developed in earlier days as it would be in Maimonides'. And in 'theoretical matters', scientific 'demonstration' is the arbiter.[44]

Maimonides nonetheless insists that the words of the ancient rabbis should, whenever possible, be construed in a fashion that brings them into harmony with scientifically demonstrated knowledge. Anyone at all who has something to say deserves the benefit of the doubt; *a fortiori*, the rabbinic sages.[45]

To further illustrate his approach to aggadah, I offer examples of the manner in which he brings his theory of angels to bear.

In connection with the scriptural verse 'Let us make man in our image', the rabbis said: 'The Holy One does nothing, so to speak, until He looks at the supernal host'; and, in another version: 'The Holy One does nothing until He consults with the supernal host'. 'Ignoramuses' who suppose that God deliberates with His creatures before acting are dismissed by Maimonides with disdain. The twin sayings teach, on his reading, that in making the first man—and, generally, in creating the world—God acted through the intermediacy of the incorporeal intelligences, whom the rabbis called the 'supernal host'.[46] Rabbinic texts moreover refer to a being that they call 'the prince of the world'. Maimonides understands the *prince of the world* to be nothing other than the active intellect, the final rung in the supernal host, which emanates the natural forms that appear in the sublunar world.[47] On his reading, the rabbis, following in the path of Scripture, subscribed to the Arabic Aristotelian picture of the incorporeal hierarchy subject to God, comprising the movers of the spheres and the active intellect, which is known as the prince of the world.

Sometimes rabbinic statements about angels are read by him as referring not to genuine, incorporeal, angels but to natural forces whereby God governs

[44] *MN* ii. 8, referring to BT *Pes.* 94*b*; *MN* iii. 14 (28*b*). Maimonides appears to have had a different version of the *Pesaḥim* passage from the one in the printed editions of the Babylonian Talmud.

[45] *MN* iii. 14 (28*b*).

[46] *MN* ii. 6 (16*b*–17*a*). The verse is Gen. 1: 26. Maimonides' source for the first of the aggadic statements has not been traced. *MN* (Schwarz), 279 n. 15, lists sources for the second.

[47] *MN* ii. 6 (17*a*). *MN* (Schwarz), 280 n. 24 lists rabbinic texts that have the expression 'prince of the world'.

the universe. The midrashic compilation *Genesis Rabbah* records the following: 'Every day the Holy One creates a band of angels; they sing before Him and pass away.' *Genesis Rabbah* immediately acknowledges an obvious objection: Scripture recognizes angels that do not sing just once and pass away. And it resolves the apparent contradiction in typical style: 'Some angels are permanent, and some are ephemeral.' Maimonides explains: the permanent angels are the incorporeal intelligences and the forces of nature, while the angels that sing once and pass away are 'particular' instances of those forces. Although the general forces of nature are permanent, particular expressions of them pass away after performing their function. The force of gravity is permanent; its effect on a given falling object does its job and ceases.[48]

Genesis Rabbah relates at another spot that 'God and His court, as it were, have come to an agreement concerning each part' of the human body and have assigned it its role in the human organism. As long as the words are not accepted literally, Maimonides is open to taking God's court as a metaphor either for the natural forces involved in the formation of the human foetus or for the final rung in the incorporeal hierarchy. He writes, with undisguised annoyance: if you should tell people that God sends an angel that actually enters a woman's womb and there fashions the foetus, the benighted will marvel at God's wondrous ways. If, however, you should propose a rational explanation and construe the angel doing God's will as the power in the male semen that fashions the foetus, or alternatively as the active intellect, which constantly emanates a full range of natural forms and, through its emanation, endows the fertilized matter in the mother's womb with the form of a human being, the benighted will turn their backs and flee.[49]

To take one more instance: Maimonides quotes the following from *Ecclesiastes Rabbah*: 'When a person sleeps, his soul speaks to the angel and the angel speaks to the cherub.' The rabbis, Maimonides writes, here 'state clearly to him who comprehends and exercises his intelligence that the imaginative faculty is also called an angel, and the intellect is called a cherub'. 'How beautiful this is for him who understands, and how repellent for the ignoramuses.'[50] The underlying thought is plain: since angels in the strict sense are impersonal incorporeal intelligences, human beings do not converse with them, and the

48 *MN* ii. 6 (17*b*), citing *Genesis Rabbah* 78: 1. Maimonides often quotes from memory, and his version is slightly different from the version in *Genesis Rabbah* and the parallel sources. The gravity example is my own.

49 *MN* ii. 6 (17*a*), citing *Genesis Rabbah* 12: 1. Maimonides' version is again slightly different from the version in *Genesis Rabbah*.

50 *MN* ii. 6 (17*b*–18*a*), citing *Ecclesiastes Rabbah* 10: 20. Unless Maimonides had a version that was very different from the printed text, he has quoted only the segment of the passage in *Ecclesiastes Rabbah* that serves his purpose.

angel to which the human soul speaks must be an angel in an extended sense. Maimonides nominates the human imaginative faculty to fill the role.

But as happened in connection with the Rabbi Akiva passage and as often happens in his allegorizing, it is hard to make out just what Maimonides is driving at. It is unclear what he means by the soul's speaking to the imagination. It is unclear what the intellect that is called a cherub is supposed to represent; although Maimonides probably takes the cherub to be the human intellect, he could be taking it as the active intellect. In either case, it is uncertain what the imaginative faculty's speaking to the intellect signifies. Several medieval commentators on the *Moreh nevukhim* read Maimonides as intimating that when a person is asleep, the lower faculties of his soul are free of distractions and have an easier job of transmitting information to the imaginative faculty than when the person is awake; the imaginative faculty similarly finds it easier to transmit to the human intellect what it refines out of that information.[51] Perhaps, though, he is intimating that when the body sleeps, the human imaginative faculty is able to establish contact with the active intellect and with the help of its emanation, frame an inspired dream for the soul of the person who is asleep.[52]

As a matter of course, Maimonides does not allow his identification of the angels with the incorporeal intelligences to affect his outline of the Jewish liturgy. The text of the morning prayer that he sketches for daily use includes an exaltation of God 'whose ministers stand at the peak of the world, let their voice be heard', and 'grant one another permission to sanctify the deity . . . in a clear tongue and pure melody'. They 'declare in unison and aver in awe: Holy, Holy, Holy is the Lord of hosts; the whole world is full of His glory'. 'The *ofanim* and the holy living creatures raise themselves opposite them and, praising, intone: 'Blessed be the glory of the Lord from His place.'[53]

3. Rationalism and Halakhah

Almost all the foregoing instances of Maimonides' rationalizing the aggadic side of the ancient rabbinic corpus come from the *Moreh nevukhim*. The *Mishneh torah*, his law code, deals primarily[54] with halakhah. It undertakes to

[51] Narboni's commentary on *MN* ii. 6, followed by the commentaries of Efodi and Shem Tov ben Joseph.

[52] Shem Tov Falquera's commentary suggests an interpretation along these lines.

[53] Goldschmidt, 'Maimonides' Rite of Prayer' (Heb.), 192. On page 187 Goldschmidt gives solid reasons for accepting the authenticity of the attribution to Maimonides. *MT*, 'Sefer ha'ahavah', appendix, which is a much briefer sketch of the liturgy, does not include the lines I quote. It does, however, have similar passages in its text of the Kedushah prayer.

[54] Not exclusively. See H. Davidson, *Moses Maimonides*, 232–59.

'assemble the entire Oral Law', that is, the traditional elucidation of the commandments of the Written Law, 'together with the positive ordinances, customs, and negative ordinances' that were instituted up to the redacting of the Babylonian Talmud and that are recorded in that work.[55]

Maimonides' view, as just seen—and there have been more fundamentalist views among traditional Jewish thinkers—is that not everything of an aggadic hue in the literature of the ancient rabbis need be accepted as authoritative. Regarding halakhah, he endorses the standard position that legal or ritual ordinances and customs certified by the Babylonian Talmud, whether expressly or through one of its indirect devices, are binding on all Israel; those adopted by individual Jewish communities and lacking the stamp of the Babylonian Talmud are binding only on the communities that subscribe to them. All ordinances and customs certified by the Babylonian Talmud as halakhah should accordingly receive a place in Maimonides' comprehensive law code.[56]

Side by side with what it makes clear are binding regulations, the Babylonian Talmud is replete with advice and instruction on a range of topics, notably: physical safety, diet, prevention of disease, medications, family relations, business practices, etiquette, as well as such preternatural subjects as the evil eye, the evil spirit, demons, black magic, and the means whereby a person can protect himself against those sinister forces. Maimonides, like other rabbinic judges and codifiers of Jewish law, had to decide which pieces of talmudic advice are no more than helpful advice and which, if any, have legal status and rise to the level of halakhah. Sometimes, the advice takes the form: 'it is forbidden' to do such and such. The term *forbidden* would appear to bolster the claim of the designated items to legal status, but the term by itself does not settle things. It could be no more than a manner of speech designed to give the advice urgency.

On a certain occasion—the date has not been preserved—Maimonides received an enquiry from unnamed persons regarding a woman who had been married twice and whose husbands had died. The Babylonian Talmud instructs that a twice-widowed woman should not marry a third time because of her '*mazal*'.[57] The particular case had complicating circumstances, and the questioners asked Maimonides to help them adjudicate it.

In the first instance, the Hebrew term *mazal* means a *planet* or *constellation*. If that is the sense of the word in the talmudic passage, a woman whose *mazal* brings about the death of two husbands and is not to marry again is deemed to have been born under an inauspicious celestial sign. *Mazal* has the secondary

[55] *MT*, introd. [56] *MT*, introd. [57] BT *Yev.* 64*b*.

meaning of luck in general, and if that is the sense it has in the passage, the death of the husbands and the directive that the widow not marry again are ascribed to her being a bearer of bad luck. Maimonides was an implacable critic of astrology and condemned it as bordering on idolatry. If he took the talmudic passage as saying that the woman may not marry again because she was born under an inauspicious sign, he could not possibly have made his peace with it. Even if he read the passage in the second way, as I assume he did, he could not have been happy with a woman's losing the opportunity to lead a normal life because she was branded a bearer of bad luck, a vague notion redolent of superstition and astrology.

In answering the men who asked for guidance regarding the twice-widowed woman, Maimonides distinguishes between actions that the Talmud prohibits outright and those that are 'merely odious but contain no prohibition'.[58] The marriage of a twice-widowed woman is of the latter sort. 'There is no difference', Maimonides writes, between the marriage of a woman who has been twice widowed and, let us say, eating vegetables as they come bound together in bunches without undoing the string. The Babylonian Talmud warns against eating from a bunch of vegetables without removing the string because doing so renders a person susceptible to black magic,[59] and Maimonides was confident that his questioners did not take the talmudic warning to heart and perhaps were not even aware of it. As for the unfortunate woman who was the occasion of the enquiry, he writes that although the local rabbinic court should not expressly sanction her marriage because of the talmudic statements, it should allow her to enter into a marriage contract in private. The court could then accept the contract as a *fait accompli* and recognize the marriage.[60]

He thus maintains that the Babylonian Talmud sometimes labels actions as dangerous and odious without prohibiting them. If we generalize, his position is that some talmudic advice is legally binding and some is not. It would be the mandatory that should be included in a code of law. Maimonides does not give criteria for identifying which advice falls under the one heading and which under the other, and his criteria have to be inferred.

The Babylonian Talmud at one point lays down the principle that human beings have the obligation to protect life and limb; a person must consequently be even more strict in avoiding situations in which he might endanger his life than in avoiding situations where there is a possibility of a ritual transgres-

[58] Maimonides explains that the dictate of the Babylonian Talmud regarding a twice-widowed woman is a matter of 'omens, auguries, and imaginings', which might affect 'bodies of weak constitution'. I understand him to mean that the third husband might fear he is doing something dangerous and, if he is of a weak constitution, thereby undermine his health.

[59] BT *Ḥul.* 105*b*.

[60] Maimonides, *Responsa*, no. 218.

sion.[61] Maimonides creates a niche for the principle in a section of the *Mishneh torah* entitled 'Laws concerning a Murderer and concerning the Preservation of Life' ('Hilkhot rotse'aḥ ushemirat hanefesh', more literally: 'Laws of a Murderer and Preservation of the Soul'). He writes: Supplementing commandments of the Torah regarding the preservation of human life, 'the Rabbis prohibited a large number of things because they involve danger. A person who transgresses such regulations saying "I am going to place myself in danger; how is that anyone else's affair?" or "it doesn't worry me"' is not allowed blithely to go his way. He 'is subject to a rabbinically sanctioned whipping'.[62]

After stating that the rabbis prohibited a large number of things because of the dangers they involve, Maimonides records a few such items from both the Babylonian and Jerusalem Talmuds. He rules that a person should not drink water directly from a water pipe or drink at night from a stream or pond, because he might swallow a leech; a person should not put coins in his mouth, because they may have been in contact with the saliva or perspiration of someone suffering from boils or leprosy; he should not touch his underarm with his hand, because of the possibility of the hand's having come into contact with the perspiration of a leper or with some other noxious material. Maimonides repeats, in full detail, a rabbinic prohibition against drinking water and certain other beverages that were left in uncovered vessels or eating from fruits or vegetables in which puncture marks are seen. The fear was that a snake might have drunk from the open container or punctured the fruit or vegetable in order to eat from it and, in doing so, deposited venom.[63] Poisonous bites were a field in which Maimonides was later reputed to have medical expertise, and he was commissioned by Saladin's secretary to write a treatise on antidotes. He evidently took seriously the possibility that venom might be deposited in uncovered beverages or unprotected fruits and vegetables and he accepted the premiss that ingesting snake venom endangers a person's life. We have, then, instances where he recognizes talmudic advice about dangerous situations as binding and codifies the advice as halakhah.

Much of the talmudic advice relates to diet, hygiene, and medicaments. The rabbis recommend certain foods because they contribute to health while warning against others because they cause a range of ills: halitosis, catarrh, headaches, haemorrhoids, indigestion, leprosy, and blindness. They record numerous medicaments for the treatment of these maladies as well as others. And they offer instruction on the manner in which a person should conduct

[61] BT *Ḥul.* 10*a*.

[62] *MT*, 'Hilkhot rotse'aḥ', 11: 5.

[63] *MT*, 'Hilkhot rotse'aḥ', 11: 6–12: 5. Frankel's edition of the *Mishneh torah* gives the talmudic sources.

himself at meals, at stool, in the bath, in bloodletting, and during other activities.[64]

Rabbi Sherira Gaon, the leading rabbinic figure in tenth-century Iraq, once received a query about some of the medical advice in the Babylonian Talmud. In the course of his answer, he emphasizes that 'the rabbis were not physicians. They reported what they observed in individual instances during their times, and the reports do not have the status of religious commandments.' Rabbinic medical advice is not to be relied on unless a person 'reviews it and knows with certainty from expert physicians that it does no harm and that he will not endanger his life' by obeying it.[65] Maimonides makes no mention of Sherira Gaon's observation, but the *Mishneh torah* reflects the same stance.

It has an entire chapter on diet, conduct at meals, bathing, bloodletting, hygiene, and related medical matters. Those subjects, Maimonides explains, merit inclusion in a code of Jewish law because a complete code should direct men to the ultimate goal of human life, and 'it is impossible for a man to acquire understanding and knowledge when he is ill'. A person must therefore 'distance himself from things that destroy the body and do that which nourishes the body and keeps it healthy'. A very small number of items in the chapter coincide with advice offered by the Talmud: in harmony with the rabbis, Maimonides stresses that one should eat with moderation, that when someone feels the urge to evacuate his bowels or bladder he should not delay.[66]

In almost every instance, he ignores the rabbis' views. To illustrate again, the Babylonian Talmud warns that when a person 'eats without drinking, his eating is [like spilling his own] blood', whereas if one does drink enough for the food he has eaten to 'float in water', he will not suffer stomach problems. Maimonides, by contrast, instructs readers to drink no more than a small amount of water mixed with wine during meals, to limit their drinking of water after meals until the food they have eaten is digested, and never to drink unless thirst requires it.[67] The Babylonian Talmud recommends eating cabbage for both its nutritional and medicinal virtues and eating lentils once a month because they are effective in preventing croup—although not daily because they will then cause bad breath. It reports that the eating of garlic on Friday evenings was among the ten ordinances instituted by the biblical Ezra, the rationale being that garlic increases male sperm and Friday night is the time when husbands and wives ordinarily have sexual intercourse; and it enumerates additional virtues in the eating of garlic. Maimonides places cabbage,

[64] BT *Ber.* 40*a*, 51*a*, 55*a*; *Shab.* 41*a*, 81*a*, 82*a*, 109*a*–110*b*, 129*a*–*b*; *Git.* 67*b*, 70*a*–*b*; *AZ* 28*a*–*b*.

[65] Epstein, 'Rav Sherira Gaon's Commentary' (Heb.), 2.

[66] BT *Shab.* 82*a*, *Git.* 70*a*, *Bekh.* 44*b*; *MT*, 'Hilkhot de'ot', 4: 1–2.

[67] BT *Ber.* 40*a*, *Shab.* 41*a*, *BM* 113*b*; *MT*, 'Hilkhot de'ot', 4: 2.

lentils, and garlic in the category of especially unhealthy foods, which are to be avoided.[68] The Babylonian Talmud encourages bloodletting and warns that a person who undergoes the procedure must immediately eat a hearty meal or drink wine to the point where, hyperbolically, his 'spleen is floating' in it, the 'odour of the wine wafts out of his ear', or the wine 'oozes out of the incision'; otherwise he puts his life at risk. Maimonides, who in his most significant departure from Galenic medicine expressed hesitation about bloodletting in general, cautions persons who do undergo the procedure to 'eat and drink less than they usually do'.[69]

We have arrived at the following picture: the *Mishneh torah* was planned as a comprehensive law code and even more broadly as a guide for the good life. Maimonides accordingly designed it with niches in which he could treat topics of importance for human life, and among them are the avoidance of danger and matters of diet, hygiene, and medicine. Some talmudic advice on avoiding danger meets Maimonides' scientific standards: he recognizes and codifies it as halakhah and even states that rabbinic courts have the obligation to enforce it. Almost all the rabbinic dicta on diet, medicine, and hygiene fail to satisfy his scientific criteria and hence do not, in his opinion, qualify as halakhah. He feels free to ignore items of the sort and to replace them with advice—not halakhah—drawn from his knowledge of medical science.

When Maimonides confronts talmudic advice regarding the preternatural, he again allows non-talmudic criteria to determine what qualifies as halakhah and what does not. The criteria now come not from medical science but from his rationalistic outlook. I shall focus on the evil spirit and demons.

The term 'evil spirit' appears in the Hebrew Bible in two narrative contexts. One relates that 'God sent an 'evil spirit between Abimelech and the men of Shechem', with the consequence that the amity between the two sides collapsed and 'the men of Shechem dealt treacherously with Abimelech'. The other relates that the 'spirit of the Lord departed' from King Saul after he disobeyed God's command, and 'an evil spirit from the Lord terrified him'. When David took the harp and played, 'Saul found relief, and the evil spirit departed from him'.[70]

The term comes up twice in the Mishnah corpus, and the subject each time is a person who is possessed by an evil spirit that affects his faculties; the legal issue in each case is whether the person is exempt from a given religious law. In explicating one of the mishnaic passages, Maimonides explains that *evil spirit* is

[68] BT *Ber.* 40*a*, 44*b*, *BK* 82*a*; *MT*, 'Hilkhot de'ot', 4: 9.

[69] BT *Bekh.* 44*b*, *Shab.* 129*a*; *MT*, 'Hilkhot de'ot', 4: 18.

[70] Judg. 9: 23; 1 Sam. 16: 14, 23.

a term covering 'all kinds of melancholia'. In explicating the other, he writes that any impairment in a person's power of judgement is called an *evil spirit*.[71] Despite differing somewhat, the comments agree in construing the evil spirit as a psychological or mental state internal to the person and not as a power threatening him from without. In the same vein, Maimonides twice glosses obscure mishnaic terms as: an 'evil spirit' that 'terrifies' a person;[72] he plainly is using the term *evil spirit* in the sense of an unhealthy state of mind.

The tactic of construing the evil spirit as a morbid mental state, with tacit allusions to King Saul, works nicely in the above instances. It does not work in the majority of cases where the Babylonian Talmud refers to an evil spirit.

The Babylonian Talmud warns against eating garlic, onion, or an egg that have been peeled and left overnight and against drinking water on Tuesday night or Friday night because an evil spirit may have settled on the garlic, onion, egg, or water.[73] Nothing of the kind appears in the *Mishneh torah*.

A talmudic passage warns that touching one's eye with an unwashed hand can blind it, touching one's ear can render it deaf, touching one's mouth can render it dumb, touching one's nose can produce polyps, and unwashed hands can cause other damage as well. The reason is that 'it', the evil spirit, attaches itself to human hands and is 'free' to do its mischief until a person washes each hand three times after awaking.[74] The passage is the basis for the instruction, which became a ritual obligation in Jewish law codes subsequent to Maimonides and is scrupulously observed by traditional Jews today—and not exclusively by those who have an active fear of evil spirits—to pour water over each hand three times upon awakening in the morning.[75] Keeping water next to one's bed in order to wash one's hands immediately on arising is regarded as an act of especial piety.

Maimonides' *Mishneh torah* makes no mention of the damage that unwashed hands can inflict or of an obligation to wash one's hands three times upon rising in order to remove the evil spirit. Since his rationalist world-view had no place for the existence of an evil spirit that comes from without and alights on a person's hands, he did not regard the danger as real and the talmudic instructions as being of a legal nature.

He was once asked why, in recording a certain law in the *Mishneh torah*, he explained it differently from the manner in which the talmudic source seems to do and he answered that he allowed himself a degree of freedom in stating reasons. His aim in the code 'was to explain the legal regulations in the

71 Maimonides, *Commentary on the Mishnah*, *Shab.* 2: 5, *Eruv.* 4: 1.

72 *MT*, 'Hilkhot gerushin', 2: 14, 'Hilkhot biat hamikdash', 8: 16.

73 BT *Pes.* 112*a*, *Nid.* 17*a*.

74 BT *Shab.* 109*a*.

75 For example, *Shulḥan arukh*, 'Oraḥ ḥayim', 4.

most plausible fashion or in accordance with the most common situations'.[76] If he found a talmudic explanation to be complicated, he allowed himself to simplify it.

When handling a piece of advice anchored in a consideration that he felt uncomfortable with, he sometimes records the advice while changing or omitting the reason. Thus the Babylonian Talmud warns against leaving food or drink under a bed even in a covered metal container because an evil spirit might attach itself to the food.[77] Maimonides does not ignore the warning but reformulates it. He directs readers not to keep food under the bed because 'something harmful might fall in when the person is not looking'.[78] The Babylonian Talmud dictates that a person wash his hands after meals because he may have gotten a corrosive form of salt on his hands and may then rub his eyes; it prescribes that the water with which one washes is not to be spilled on the ground; and it gives two reasons: 'Abaye stated: At first I thought that the reason why one does not wash one's hands directly over the ground is because of the uncleanliness; then my teacher told me that the reason is because an evil spirit attaches itself to the water.' In the *Mishneh torah*, Maimonides records an 'obligation', hence a halakhah, to wash one's hands after eating because of the 'danger' and he directs that the water with which one washes not be spilled on the ground. He says nothing about an evil spirit and leaves it to the reader to surmise why caution must be taken with the water after it has been used.[79]

Besides the evil spirit, the Babylonian Talmud recognizes the existence of a veritable world of demons that overlies the natural world we experience around us. The demons are portrayed as usually invisible and extremely numerous, as belonging to different parties or tribes, and as ruled by a king. In contrast to the evil spirit, they have personalities; sometimes their names are given, and conversations between them and rabbinic figures are reported. They are malevolent, and their malevolence is inflamed by intruders who blunder into their haunts.[80] That other cultures of the period, notably the surrounding Persian culture, recognized the existence of demons scarcely need be said.

Most of the advice about demons in the Babylonian Talmud centres on the dangers they pose. We saw that Maimonides instructs readers not to drink

[76] Maimonides, *Responsa*, no. 252; H. Davidson, *Moses Maimonides*, 224.

[77] BT *Pes.* 112*a*; slightly different in the Jerusalem Talmud.

[78] *MT*, 'Hilkhot rotse'aḥ', 12: 5. *Shulḥan arukh*, 'Yoreh de'ah', 116: 5, which generally follows Maimonides almost step by step, departs from him at this point and explains that the danger is the possibility of the evil spirit's attaching itself to the food.

[79] BT *Ḥul.* 105*a*–*b*; *MT*, 'Hilkhot berakhot', 6: 2, 3, 16. (A curious comment in R. Joseph Karo's commentary on the *Mishneh torah* turns Maimonides' position upside down.) *Shulḥan arukh*, 'Oraḥ ḥayim', 181: 2 restores the reference to the evil spirit.

[80] BT *Ber.* 6*a*, 51*a*; *Shab.* 67*a*; *Pes.* 110*a*, 111*b*, 112*b*; *Yev.* 122*a*; *Git.* 68*a*; *Kid.* 29*b*; *Ḥul.* 105*b*.

from a water pipe or from a stream or pond at night, the fear being that one might swallow a leech. The talmudic context from which he draws the warnings also includes a blanket admonition against drinking water at night, because a certain demon might be present in it. Maimonides omits the additional admonition regarding the demon.[81]

The Babylonian Talmud warns that in the morning one must not receive the garment one is going to wear from someone else, one must not let someone who has not yet washed his hands help one wash one's own, and when drinking the morning asparagus tonic—a health drink—one must not return the cup to the person from whom one took it. It cautions against greeting a strange figure at night, sitting under a downspout, entering the shadow of various kinds of trees, entering the shadow of a privy, walking between palm trees that stand close to one another, moving one's bowels between a palm tree and a nearby wall, and placing oneself in sundry other situations, since those are locations and situations in which demons are likely to be encountered.[82] It prohibits being bled on the eve of Pentecost and pronounces 'a decree' extending the prohibition to every holiday eve. The rationale is that when the Israelites stood before Mount Sinai on the eve of the first Pentecost, a windstorm named Tavoah stood ready to shed the Israelites' blood if they refused to accept God's Law.[83] The Babylonian Talmud discusses the permissibility of turning to demons for advice, and against the background of that discussion, medieval and early modern rabbinic writers debate the permissibility of consulting with demons and asking them for help in recovering stolen property.[84] Not a hint of any of these items appears in Maimonides' code.

The Babylonian Talmud gives three reasons for not entering a deserted, dilapidated building: a wall might fall down, one might be suspected of having an assignation with a woman, and one might encounter demons. Since the danger in entering a dilapidated building is real, Maimonides records the instruction to avoid such buildings. He groups it, however, with other situations where men have the obligation to avoid danger and preserve life and limb, makes no mention of the danger from demons, and, for good measure, omits the risk of being suspected of an assignation with a woman.[85] The Talmud prescribes that a person should recite the 'Hear O Israel' verse when he goes to sleep. and it quotes a rabbi who held that reciting the verse protects one against demons.[86]

[81] BT *AZ* 12*b*. (I have simplified a bit, as will be seen by a close comparison of the talmudic passages with *MT*, 'Hilkhot rotse'aḥ', 11: 6.)

[82] BT *Ber.* 51*a*; *Pes.* 111*a–b*; *Meg.* 3*a*; *Ḥul.* 105*b*.

[83] BT *Shab.* 129*b*, codified in *Shulḥan arukh*, 'Oraḥ ḥayim', 468: 10 (gloss).

[84] BT *San.* 101*a*; Jacob b. Asher, *Arba'ah turim*, 'Yoreh de'ah', no. 179 (end), and its commentaries and successors.

[85] BT *Ber.* 3*a*; *MT*, 'Hilkhot rotse'aḥ', 12: 6.

[86] BT *Ber.* 4*b*–5*a*; *MT*, 'Hilkhot tefilah', 7: 2.

Maimonides records the obligation to recite the 'Hear O Israel' verse when going to sleep but drops the part about demons.

In short, he ignores almost every piece of talmudic advice relating to the evil spirit and all advice regarding demons, undoubtedly justifying to himself that the items in question are merely advisory, the supposed dangers are not real, and the talmudic advice is therefore not binding.[87] When he does honour a few items regarding the evil spirit, he construes them in a manner that omits any mention of sinister forces.

Although what Maimonides has done may be obvious to the sympathetic modern eye, not everyone who studied his writings over the centuries realized—or acknowledged—what he was about. A scholar recently drew up an astonishing list of almost three dozen medieval and modern traditional Jewish writers who could not accept that a man of Maimonides' calibre and standing would reject the talmudic belief in the evil spirit and demons.[88] Rabbi Elijah, the Gaon of Vilna, understood perfectly.

A passage in the Babylonian Talmud permits reciting incantations as protection against scorpions and snakes, and on the basis of the passage, Maimonides lays down the rule: 'Should someone be bitten by a scorpion or snake, it is permitted to recite an incantation over the bite . . . in order to set the person's mind at rest and raise his spirits even though the incantation has no effect whatsoever. Since the person is in danger, the Rabbis permitted reciting the incantation for him in order that he not go into a panic.'[89] Although Rabbi Elijah respected Maimonides' rabbinic expertise, he could not contain his ire at the rejection of the efficacy of incantations. He fumes: 'Everyone who came after Maimonides disagreed, for incantations are often referred to in the Talmud. He was drawn after accursed philosophy and accordingly wrote that magic, holy names, incantations, demons, and amulets are all false, but others hit him over the skull' for saying so, since the Babylonian and Jerusalem Talmuds confirm their reality and efficacy. 'Philosophy . . . seduced Maimonides into making a mockery of the

[87] On the question whether Maimonides ever omits or alters a genuine *halakhah* out of ideological considerations and whether he ever codifies his own opinion as a binding *halakhah* when there is no talmudic basis for it, see A. Levinger, 'Maimonides as a Physician' (Heb.), 151–4 (which maintains that Maimonides did), and H. Davidson, *Moses Maimonides*, 226–7 (which doubts that he did). Shapiro, *Studies in Maimonides*, 95–150, which assembles a large amount of valuable material, disregards the distinction between halakhah and mere advice (see p. 99), and is thereby able to conclude that Maimonides' rationalism led him to omit a number of talmudic *halakhot*. On p. 119, Shapiro gives what could be a single plausible instance of Maimonides' omitting a genuine *halakhah* because of rationalist considerations; even there, however, the pertinent talmudic passage may well have been read by Maimonides as non-binding advice. Shapiro complicates matters by relying on a composition that is attributed to Maimonides but that he could not possibly have written, at least in the form in which it has been preserved; see *Studies in Maimonides*, 99–103, and Davidson, *Moses Maimonides*, 494–7.

[88] Shapiro, *Studies in Maimonides*, 106–8.

[89] *MT*, 'Hilkhot avodah zarah', 11: 11.

Talmud and uprooting the plain meaning. . . . Everything, however, should be taken in its plain sense, with the proviso that it has an inner meaning—not the inner meaning of the philosophers, which belongs in the rubbish dump . . . but that of the adherents of the truth', in other words, of the kabbalists.[90]

4. Monotheism and History

To the extent that history consists of 'chronicles' and books regarding 'the ways of kings', it holds no interest for Maimonides; writings on those subjects are relegated by him to the category of human literature that is a 'mere waste of time'.[91] He nevertheless invests a good deal of thought in what he believes to have been a momentous chain of events, the struggle between monotheism and polytheism. His reconstruction of the events is given in the *Mishneh torah*, and he expands on some of the details in the *Moreh nevukhim*.

He starts with the unspoken assumption that earliest mankind, being close to the act of creation, was monotheistic and he undertakes to explain how polytheism and idolatry developed and were countered by a resurgent monotheism. Things started to go wrong, he writes, in the time of Enosh, who was the son of Seth, the son of Adam. In the days of Enosh, as Maimonides reads an ambiguous verse in Genesis, 'the name of the Lord was desecrated'.[92] Fitting bits of rabbinic aggadah together with what he learned from Arabic works on the subjects of star worship and idolatry, then viewing the composite through his personal prism, he arrives at the following scheme.

'In the days of Enosh, men made an enormous error, and the counsel of the wise men of the generation was rendered senseless.' Men reasoned that since God created the stars and celestial spheres and employed them as intermediaries in governing the universe, He must want mankind to revere them. Men accordingly built temples in which they sacrificed to the heavenly bodies and they sang the heavenly bodies' praises. With the passage of time, false prophets emerged, claiming to be messengers sent by God or the heavenly bodies themselves to instruct mankind in worship of the heavens. Images were fashioned to represent the stars and planets, and the images too became objects of worship. The upshot of the faulty reasoning and chicanery was that the incorporeal deity, who exists beyond the heavens and is the first cause of the universe, was forgotten.

[90] Elijah of Vilna, commentary on Karo, *Shulḥan arukh*, 'Yoreh de'ah', no. 179, n. 13. Regarding the correct reading of R. Elijah's comment, see Dienstag, 'Gaon of Wilna' (Heb.), 253, 255–7.

[91] Maimonides, *Commentary on the Mishnah*, *San.* 10: 1, p. 210.

[92] Gen. 4: 26. There are other ways of reading the verse, all clearly set forth in Kimhi's commentary on Gen. 4: 26.

A turn for the better came when Abraham, the father of the Israelite nation, appeared on the scene. Although raised in an idolatrous environment by an idolater father, Abraham wrested himself free of error through the strength of his intellect. He observed the movements of the heavens and on his own worked out the demonstration of the existence of a first incorporeal being who is responsible for celestial motion and 'created everything'. Abraham went on to refute the adherents of idolatry and star worship with his 'proofs', taught his 'theoretical proofs' to all with whom he came into contact, gathered a following of 'thousands and tens of thousands', and 'composed books' on the subject of the true God. He educated his son Isaac in the true doctrine, Isaac taught it to Jacob, and Jacob taught it to his sons, while appointing Levi and Levi's offspring as the primary carriers of the doctrine. Isaac and Jacob followed in Abraham's footsteps and, through theoretical arguments, spread the truth.[93]

Human beings are influenced by those around them.[94] When the Israelites went down to Egypt, they fell under the influence of the native populace, and 'the root that Abraham planted was in a very little while uprooted'; only the tribe of Levi remained faithful to the true God. At the appropriate moment, God sent Moses to rescue His people from idolatry and star worship through commandments designed to wean them away from the pernicious error.[95]

Abraham, Isaac, and Jacob enjoyed the gift of prophecy, and an inspiration from above was part of what moved them to proclaim their discovery. Their prophecy served only themselves, however, and when summoning others to their cause, they relied solely on rational persuasion.[96] Moses, for his part, was both a man of highest intellect and the greatest of the prophets, and unlike Abraham, who taught monotheism solely through rational proofs, he brought both his intellectual and prophetic gifts to the task with which he was charged. Scripture tells that before Moses started on his mission, he asked God how he should answer when asked for the name of the deity who sent him. He received the answer 'I am that I am', and Maimonides finds the enigmatic reply to be pregnant with meaning. He explains: with very few exceptions,

93 *MT*, 'Hilkhot avodah zarah', 1. The notion that Abraham brought thousands and tens of thousands to the truth goes back to Gen. 12: 5, which speaks of 'souls that they [that is, Abraham, his wife, and his nephew Lot] had gotten in Harran'. Regarding the books composed by Abraham, see BT *AZ* 14*b*: 'Abraham's [treatise on] idolatry comprised 400 chapters'. Maimonides does not explain whether a different scenario might have been possible and, if so, how it would have affected history—if Abraham had not exercised his reason and demonstrated the existence of God, if Aristotle had been the first to frame the demonstration and had not kept it within the walls of his Lyceum but announced it to the world, or if, as Kellner puts things nicely, a Navaho had worked out the demonstration and been the one to propagate the true religion. Would the Navahos have become God's chosen people? See Kellner, *Maimonides' Confrontation with Mysticism*, 81.

94 *MT*, 'Hilkhot de'ot', 6: 1; 'Hilkhot teshuvah', 4: 5.

95 *MT*, 'Hilkhot avodah zarah', 1: 3; *MN* i. 63 (81*b*–82*a*).

96 *MN* i. 63 (81*b*), ii. 39 (84*a*).

people at the time 'were imperfect intellectually' and had no inkling of the existence of a being beyond the heavens. What God conveyed to Moses was not just a name but the 'science' (*'ilm*), 'the proofs', and 'the rational demonstrations', whereby the Israelites would be convinced of the existence of the true God, whose agent Moses was. The formula 'I am that I am' is tantamount to 'the existent that is existent', that is to say, the existent being whose existence is not distinct from Himself, and hence 'the necessarily existent [by virtue of Himself]'. The formula accordingly embodies the nub of the 'demonstration' that God taught Moses.[97]

Abraham, through the power of his intellect, worked out the demonstration of the existence of a first incorporeal being who is the ultimate mover of the celestial spheres, and it was through rational proof that he won over idolaters and star-worshippers of the day; Isaac and Jacob continued Abraham's work. God imparted a different demonstration to Moses, the proof of the existence of God as a being necessarily existent by virtue of Himself, and Moses employed that demonstration to establish his credentials with the Children of Israel before undertaking the mission of emancipating them physically and spiritually. From Abraham to Moses, a line of Israelite leaders thus battled religious error, first through one, and then with the aid of another, rational demonstration of the existence of a single incorporeal deity.

5. Intellectual Worship of God

As we have seen more than once, Maimonides liked to rank things. Among them are forms of worship of God.

He views one of the main inferior forms as a concession to historical circumstances. The Israelites in Egypt had lived among idolaters and star-worshippers for more than a generation when Moses established his credentials as the prophet of the true God and led them to freedom. They now had to be re-educated. Worship in Egypt and its neighbours was centred at the time on animal sacrifice, with a sacred area, an altar to which people brought sacrifices dedicated to a star or image, and ministers who maintained the sacred area and performed the sacrificial rites. That was the milieu in which the Israelite nation had been immersed and from which it had to be extricated.

Because human nature balks at being wrenched suddenly from one extreme to another, changes in human affairs have to be brought about gradually. God, in his subtle wisdom (*talaṭṭuf*), therefore did not attempt to institute the highest form of divine worship at once. Imagine, Maimonides writes, that 'a

[97] *MN* i. 63 (81*b*–82*b*). 'I am that I am' is from Exod. 3: 14.

prophet appeared today summoning people and announcing: "God has commanded you not to recite the daily prayers, not to fast, not to cry out to Him for help in times of trouble. Instead your worship should consist solely in [meditative] thought [*fikra*], unaccompanied by any action whatsoever.'" People would be scandalized. By the same token, people would have been scandalized had Moses instructed them completely to abandon the religious rites that they had grown up with. Instead of abolishing sacrificial worship outright, God in His wisdom redesigned it. He steered it away from 'created beings and imaginary things' and redirected it 'to His own name'. A new sacred area was delineated, it had a different-style altar, a new group of men was given responsibility for performing the rites, and the Israelites were instructed to offer sacrifices exclusively to the true God.[98] In support of his thesis that animal sacrifice is not the highest form of religious worship, Maimonides quotes from the prophets Samuel and Isaiah and in particular calls attention to a passage in which Jeremiah upbraided his contemporaries with the words: 'I spoke not unto your fathers, nor commanded them in the day that I brought them out of the land of Egypt, concerning burnt-offerings and sacrifices.' Jeremiah, Maimonides contends, was not asserting that God never commanded the offering of sacrifices; after all, the divine Law contains a full sacrificial service. The prophet meant that sacrifices were not 'intended for their own sake'. They were a preliminary stage, preparing the way for the mode of worship that is the 'primary intent' for man.[99]

Worshipping God through the formal liturgy and petitionary prayer, through tying fringes to the corners of one's garments, affixing a parchment scroll containing specified scriptural verses to the doorposts of one's house, wearing phylacteries that contain parchment scrolls on which specified scriptural passages are written, and performing all the other prescribed religious practices is deemed by Maimonides to be 'closer to the primary intent' than animal sacrifice, even when sacrifice is directed to the true God. A sign that that is so is the relative scope of the two sorts of worship. The personal rituals are incumbent on everyone and everywhere. Sacrifices, when they are in effect, are by contrast restricted to a single venue and a single priestly family in order to 'minimize such worship so that it should not go beyond what divine wisdom determined not to abolish completely'.[100]

Maimonides resists the seemingly logical conclusion that inasmuch as animal sacrifices are an inferior mode of worshipping God and have accomplished their purpose, they should never be restored. His sketch of Jewish liturgy

[98] *MN* iii. 32 (69*b*–70*a*).

[99] *MN* iii. 32 (70*a*, 72*a*). The verse is Jer. 7: 22, and the other verses that Maimonides quotes are 1 Sam. 15: 22 and Isa. 1: 11.

[100] *MN* iii. 32 (71*b*–72*a*).

includes traditional prayers for the return of the sacrificial rites, and he too undoubtedly recited the prayers. He repeats, with no apparent qualms, the talmudic expectation that the messiah will rebuild the Holy Temple and reinstate the temple service.[101] How he harmonized for himself his understanding of the historical function of sacrifices, which has now passed, with the expectation that they will, or may, be reinstated in the future can only be guessed.

As for the many ceremonial practices incumbent on each and every Jew, although Maimonides ranks them below the highest form of worship, glimpses he affords of his own life reveal that he was meticulous in observing them. He expended time and effort in ascertaining how his predecessors arranged the parchment scrolls in their phylacteries, and when he became convinced that the scrolls in his own phylacteries had not been written and inserted in the correct order, he removed the scrolls and acquired a new, correctly designed set. He fulfilled the arduous commandment incumbent on every Jewish male, but only rarely observed, to write a Torah scroll once in his lifetime, and he explains how the scroll he wrote incorporated all the halakhic niceties. He informs a colleague that he always bathed (*lirḥots*) after a seminal emission—that is, after sexual intercourse—unless he was ill since it was the custom of his fathers to do so, even though bathing after a seminal emission is supererogatory and not mandatory. When eating his last meal before the fast of the ninth day of Av, he went beyond the restrictions that the Talmud places on the meal.[102] His meticulousness in performing the ritual acts was rooted in a deep-seated attachment to Jewish tradition,[103] an attachment that not every student of Maimonides appreciates, yet he had a rationale as well: the rituals play an essential role in the programme he lays out for reaching the highest level of worship attainable by man.

A person has advanced well along the path when he can 'exercise his intellect wholly in reflecting on what exists, in order to frame proofs therefrom regarding God, with the object of understanding how God's governance' of the universe is 'possible'.[104] Once someone possesses the requisite scientific grounding, he must learn to turn away from everything except God, and here is where the ritual commandments play a role: when performed properly, they train a man to focus exclusively on God and His commandments and to disregard everything else. As for persons who pray with their lips and read the Torah with their tongue while their thoughts are on their business affairs and

[101] Goldschmidt, 'Maimonides' Rite of Prayer' (Heb.), 196, 202–5; *MT*, 'Hilkhot melakhim', 11: 1.
[102] H. Davidson, *Moses Maimonides*, 542–3.
[103] Maimonides, *Commentary on the Mishnah*, introd., 16; *SM*, introd., 4–5; *Responsa*, 3: 57 (which I see no reason to read as disingenuous).
[104] *MN* iii. 51 (124*a*).

their house, or who perform ritual acts with their limbs without paying attention to what they are doing, they, in Maimonides' view, could as well be 'digging a hole in the ground or gathering firewood in the forest'.

One should accordingly start with the scientific knowledge needed to demonstrate the existence of God and then, when performing the ritual commandments, reciting prayers, reading or listening to Scripture, train oneself to disregard everything else. After that level has been achieved, a person should go on to train himself to disregard worldly matters even when not engaged in specifically religious activity. He should allow his mind to occupy itself with the 'needs and amenities of life', such as business affairs, his household, and the care of his body, only during times when he is in any event distracted, as when he is at meals, in the bathhouse, or conversing with his 'wife, his small children, or . . . the common people [*jumhūr al-nās*]'. During the precious hours when a man is alone during the day or lies awake in bed at night, his thoughts should have a single focus, the 'intellectual worship' consisting in coming near to God and placing oneself in God's presence in the true, and not in any imaginary, sense.[105]

The foregoing, Maimonides submits, lies within the power of 'men of science' who follow the programme that he outlines. There is yet a further, crowning stage, which he considers so extraordinary that he can offer no programme for attaining it. It is the state in which a man's 'cognition of the verities' (*idrāk al-ḥaqā'iq*) and 'joy in what he has cognition of' reaches a degree of intensity where 'he converses with people and attends to his physical needs while his intellect is turned towards God and he is in his heart constantly in God's presence, although outwardly he is with other people'. That was the level achieved by Moses and the three patriarchs, as shown, first, by Scripture's report of their 'union with God, that is, with cognition and love of Him' and, secondly, by the fact that God's providence was with them constantly, even as they were engaged in governing other men or attended to their personal affairs. Since providence is channelled through intellect, they must have been conducting their business solely with their 'limbs, while their intellects were in God's presence'. They never let their thoughts stray from God.[106]

A man should therefore 'make every effort to increase the times' when he is 'with God or striving to reach Him, and minimize the times' when he is 'with others and not striving to approach Him'.[107]

105 Maimonides is undoubtedly thinking of Psalm 4: 5: 'Commune with your heart upon your bed.' He had already quoted the verse as a prescript for ideal worship in *MN* i. 59 (73*b*).

106 *MN* iii. 51 (125*b*–127*a*).

107 *MN* iii. 51 (129*b*).

The Arabic–Aristotelian picture of the universe, which Maimonides embraced as the most philosophically and scientifically reputable, lent itself to his rationalist enterprise. It enabled him to demonstrate the existence of a single, incorporeal first cause. Using tools it provided, he was satisfied that he could frame strong, albeit less than apodictic, proofs of the creation of the world; and creation entailed that the divine author of the universe is possessed of will and is able to intervene in the universe. The Arabic–Aristotelian universe furnished him with rationales for the phenomenon of prophecy, for providence, and for human intellectual immortality. Maimonides' exegesis of Scripture and rabbinic texts will strike a modern reader as extravagantly far-fetched, and that was the way some of his own day saw it as well. He was nonetheless convinced that it fitted comfortably into his scientific and philosophical picture of the universe and rationalist reconstruction of Israelite history.

Celestial spheres, incorporeal movers of the spheres, and the active intellect have disappeared from today's universe. The demonstration of the existence of God from the motion of the celestial spheres lost its credibility with the Copernican and Newtonian revolutions. Although two of Maimonides' remaining demonstrations of the existence of God do not depend on a defunct physical science and astronomy, they too command little credibility among contemporary philosophers. The demise of the active intellect has taken with it the scientific basis for prophecy, the thesis that divine providence is dependent on developing one's intellect, and the thesis that the developed human intellect, and it alone, is capable of achieving immortality. Maimonides' exegesis of Scripture and rabbinic aggadah is now a quaint antique.

His rationalist enterprise was valiant, intriguing, and, I would submit, admirable, but the philosophical and scientific pillars on which it rested have crumbled. A new marriage of a wholly rational picture of the universe with traditional Jewish religious thought would seem to be possible only, oxymoron though it may be, through a sturdy act of faith.

Works Cited

ANON., *Kitāb ma'ānī al-nafs*, ed. and annotated I. Goldizher (Berlin, 1907).

AARON OF NICOMEDIA, *Gan eden* (Gozlva [= Yevpatoriya], 1866).

ABBA MARI, *Minḥat kena'ot*, in Sh. Adret, *Teshuvot*, ed. H. Dimitrovsky (Jerusalem, 1990).

ABRAHAM DE BOTON, *Leḥem mishneh*, commentary printed in standard edns. of Maimonides, *Mishneh torah*.

ABRAHAM IBN DAUD, *Emunah ramah*, ed. and German trans. S. Weil (Frankfurt, 1852).

ABRAHAM MAIMONIDES, *The High Ways to Perfection*, ed. S. Rosenblatt, vol. ii (Baltimore, 1938).

ABRAHAMS, I., *Hebrew Ethical Wills*, vol. i (Philadelphia, 1926).

ALBALAG, I., *Tikun hade'ot*, ed. G. Vajda (Jerusalem, 1973).

ALBO, J., *Ikarim*, ed. and trans. I. Husik (Philadelphia, 1946).

ALEXANDER OF APHRODISIAS, *De anima*, in *Scripta minora*, ed. I. Bruns (Berlin, 1887).

——*On Aristotle Metaphysics 1*, trans. W. E. Dooley (London, 1989).

——*On Fate*, trans. R. Sharples (London, 1983).

——[?], *Principles of the Universe* (*Mabādi' al-kull*), ed. and trans. as *On the Cosmos*, Ch. Genequand (Leiden, 2001).

——[?], *Texte arabe du peri nou d'Alexandre d'Aphrodise*, ed. J. Finnegan (Beirut, 1956).

——(Alexandre d'Aphrodise), *Traité de la providence* (*Fī al-'ināya*), ed. and French trans. P. Thillet (Paris, 2003).

ALFARABI, *Catálogo de las Ciencias* (*Iḥṣā' al-'ulūm*), ed. and trans. A. Gonzalez Palencia (Madrid, 1953). Partial English translation in R. Lerner and M. Mahdi, *Medieval Political Philosophy* (Glencoe, Ill., 1963), 22–30.

——*Commentary and Short Treatise on Aristotle's De interpretatione*, trans. F. Zimmermann (London, 1981).

——*Epitome of the De interpretatione* (*Fârâbî'nin Peri Hermeneias Muhtasari*), ed. M. Küyel, *Arastirma*, 4 (1966), 36–85.

——*Falsafat arisṭūṭālīs*, ed. M. Mahdi (Beirut, 1961).

——*Fuṣūl al-madanī* [Chapters for the Statesman], ed. and trans. D. Dunlop (Cambridge, 1961). Essentially identical with the following.

——*Fuṣūl muntaza'a* [Excerpted Chapters], ed. F. Najjar (Beirut, 1993); English translation in Alfarabi, *The Political Writings*, 11–67, trans. C. Butterworth (Ithaca, 2001).

——*L'Harmonie entre les opinions de Platon et d'Aristote* [Al-jam' bain ra'yai al-ḥakīmain], ed. and trans. M. Najjar and D. Mallet (Damascus, 1999). English translation in Alfarabi, *The Political Writings*, trans. Ch. Butterworth (Ithaca, 2001), 115–67.

——*Kitāb al-ḥurūf*, ed. M. Mahdi (Beirut, 1969).

——*Al-madīna al-fāḍila*, ed. and English trans. R. Walzer, as *Al-Farabi on the Perfect State* (Oxford, 1985). The margin of Walzer's text gives the page numbers of the edition published by F. Dieterici (Leiden, 1895).

ALFARABI, *Philosophische Abhandlungen* (Arabic), ed. F. Dieterici (Leiden, 1890); German translation: *Alfarabi's philosophische Abhandlungen*, trans. F. Dieterici (Leiden, 1892).

——*Risāla fī al-ʿaql* [Epistle concerning Intellect], ed. M. Bouyges (Beirut, 1938). Partial English translation (paralleling pp. 12–36 of the Arabic text), in *Philosophy in the Middle Ages*, ed. A. Hyman and J. Walsh (New York, 1973).

——*Al-siyāsa al-madaniyya*, ed. F. Najjar (Beirut, 1964). Najjar gives the page numbers of the edition published in Hyderabad, 1927.

ALTMANN, A. (ed.), 'Ibn Bājja on Man's Ultimate Felicity', repr. in his *Studies in Religious Philosophy and Mysticism* (Ithaca, 1969), 73–107.

——*Jewish Medieval and Renaissance Studies* (Cambridge, Mass., 1967).

——'Maimonides' "Four Perfections"', *Israel Oriental Studies*, 2 (1972), 15–24.

——*Von der mittelalterlichen zur modernen Aufklärung* (Tübingen, 1987).

——and S. STERN, *Isaac Israeli* (Oxford, 1958).

AMMONIUS, *see* PSEUDO-AMMONIUS

ANATOLI, J., *Malmad hatalmidim* (Lyck, 1866).

APOLLONIUS OF PERGA, *Treatise on Conic Sections*, ed., in modern notation, T. Heath (New York, 1896).

ARISTOTLE, *The Arabic Version of the Nicomachean Ethics*, ed. A. Akasoy and A. Fidora, trans. D. Dunlop (Leiden, 2005).

——*De anima*, ed. D. Ross (Oxford, 1962). Medieval Arabic translation: *Fī al-nafs*, ed. A. Badawi (Cairo, 1954).

——*De coelo et meteorologica* (medieval Arabic translation), ed. A. Badawi (Cairo, 1961).

——*Generation of Animals*, ed. and trans. A. Peck (Loeb Classical Library) (Cambridge, Mass., 1953); *Generation of Animals, the Arabic Translation*, ed. J. Brugman and H. Lulofs (Leiden, 1971).

——*Manṭiq arisṭū* (medieval Arabic translation of the *Organon*), 3 vols., ed. A. Badawi (Kuwait, 1980).

——*Metaphysics*, ed. D. Ross, 2 vols. (Oxford, 1953).

——*Parva naturalia*, ed. D. Ross (Oxford, 1955).

——*Posterior Analytics*, trans. J. Barnes, 2nd edn. (Oxford, 1994).

——*Rhetorica in versione Arabica*, ed. A Badawi (Cairo, 1959).

——*Al-ṭabīʿa* [medieval translation of the *Physics*], ed. A. Badawi (Cairo, 1964–5).

——*Works of Aristotle Translated into English*, 11 vols., trans. W. Ross, et al. (Oxford, 1908–24).

ASHʿARI, *Maqālāt al-islāmiyyīn*, ed. H. Ritter (Wiesbaden, 1963).

AVERROES, *Compendio de Metafisica*, ed. and Spanish translation C. Quirós Rodríguez (Madrid, 1919); German translation: *Die Epitome der Metaphysik des Averroes*, trans. S. Van den Bergh (Leiden, 1924).

——*Drei Abhandlungen über die Conjunction* (Hebrew), ed. and German trans. J. Hercz (Berlin, 1869).

——*Epistle on the Possibility of Conjunction with the Active Intellect*, ed. and trans. K. Bland (New York, 1982).

——*Kitāb al-kashf*, ed. M. Müller (Munich, 1859). German translation with pagination of Arabic indicated: *Philosophie und Theologie*, trans. M. Müller (Munich, 1875).

——*Long Commentary on the De anima* (Latin), ed. F. Crawford (Cambridge, Mass., 1953).

——*Middle Commentary on Aristotle's Nicomachean Ethics* [Habe'ur ha'emtsa'i shel ibn rushd lesefer hamidot], ed. L. Berman (Jerusalem, 1999).

——*On the Harmony of Religion and Philosophy* [translation of *Faṣl al maqāl*], trans. G. Hourani (London, 1961).

——*Tafsīr mā ba'da al-ṭabī'a* [Long Commentary on the *Metaphysics*], ed. M. Bouyges (Beirut, 1938–52).

——*Tahāfut al-tahāfut* [The Incoherence of the Incoherence], ed. M. Bouyges (Beirut, 1930); English translation with pagination of the Arabic text indicated: *The Incoherence of the Incoherence*, trans. S. van den Bergh (London, 1954).

AVICENNA, *Fī al-'ahd*, in Avicenna, *Tis' rasā'il* (Cairo, 1908), 142–51.

——*Al-ishārāt wa-al-tanbīhāt: Livre des théorèmes et des avertissements*), ed. J. Forget (Leiden, 1892); French translation with pagination of the Arabic text indicated: *Livre des directives et remarques*, trans. A.-M. Goichon (Beirut, 1951).

——*Dānesh nāmeh* [Book of Knowledge], trans. M. Achena and H. Massé as *Le Livre de science*, vol. i (Paris, 1955).

——*Manṭiq al-mashriqiyyin* (Cairo, 1910; repr. Qum, 1984–5).

——*Mubāḥathāt*, in A. Badawi (ed.), *Arisṭū 'ind al-'Arab* (Cairo, 1947), 119–239.

——*Najāt* (Cairo, 1938).

——*Réfutation de l'astrologie*, ed. and French trans. Y. Michot (Beirut, 2006).

——*Shifā': Al-af'āl wa-al-infi'ālāt*, ed. I. Madkour et al. (Cairo, 1983).

——*Shifā': Ilāhiyyāt: The Metaphysics of the Healing*, ed. and trans. M. Marmura (Provo, 2005).

——*Shifā': Al-ma'ādin wa-al-āthār al-'ulwiyya*, ed. I. Madkour et al. (Cairo, 1983).

——*Shifā': Manṭiq: Burhān*, ed. I. Madkour et al. (Cairo, 1956).

——*Traités mystiques . . . d'Avicenne*, ed. M. Mehren, vol. iii (Leiden, 1894).

——[misattributed], *Fī ithbāt al-nubuwwāt*, ed. M. Marmura (Beirut, 1968). English translation in: R. Lerner, and M. Mahdi, *Medieval Political Philosophy* (Glencoe, 1963), 112–21.

BACHER, W., *Die Aggada der babylonischen Amoräer* (Frankfurt, 1913).

——*Die älteste Terminologie der jüdischen Schriftauslegung* (Leipzig, 1899).

——*Die Bibelexegese der jüdischen Religionsphilosophen des Mittelsalters vor Maimûni* (Budapest, 1892).

——*Die Bibelexegese Moses Maimûni's* (Budapest, 1896).

BADAWI, A. (ed.), *Arisṭū 'ind al-'Arab* (Cairo, 1947).

——(ed.), *Commentaires sur Aristote perdus en grec* (Arabic) (Beirut, 1971).

BAGHDĀDĪ, *Kitāb uṣūl al-dīn* (Istanbul, 1928).

BAHYA IBN PAKUDA, *Ḥovot halevavot. Al-hidāya ilā farā'iḍ al-qulūb* [Arabic text of *Ḥovot halevavot*], ed. A. Yahuda (Leiden, 1912). Arabic text and Hebrew translation, ed. and trans. J. Kafah (Jerusalem, 1973). Hebrew translation, Judah Ibn Tibbon, ed. A. Zifroni (Jerusalem, 1928). English translation: *Duties of the Heart*, trans. M. Hyamson (New York, 1925–47).

BĀQILLĀNĪ, *Kitāb al-tamhīd*, ed. R. McCarthy (Beirut, 1957).

BASHYAZI, E., *Aderet eliyahu* (Ramleh, 1966).

BEDERSI, J., *Igeret hitnatselut*, in Sh. Adret, *Teshuvot* (Vienna, 1812), §418.

Bereschit Rabba see *Genesis Rabbah*

BERMAN, L., 'The Ethical Views of Maimonides within the Context of Islamicate Civilization', in J. Kraemer (ed.), *Perspectives on Maimonides* (Oxford, 1991), 13–32.

——'The Political Interpretation of the Maxim: The Purpose of Philosophy Is the Imitation of God', *Studia Islamica*, 15 (1961), 53–61.

BLAU, J., *A Dictionary of Mediaeval Judaeo-Arabic Texts* [Milon letekstim araviyim-yehudiyim mimei habeinayim] (Jerusalem, 2006).

BOS, G., 'Maimonides' Medical Works', *Maimonidean Studies*, 5 (2008), 243–66.

BURNET, J., *The Ethics of Aristotle* [annotated edition of the Greek text of the *Nicomachean Ethics*] (London, 1900).

CHIESA, B., 'Una fonte sconosciuta dell'Etica di Shem Tob ibn Falaquera: la *Summa Alexandrinorum*', in *Biblische und judaistische Studien*, Festschrift for P. Sacchi, ed. A. Vivian (Frankfurt, 1990).

COHEN, H., 'Charakteristik der Ethik Maimunis', in W. Bacher et al. (eds.), *Moses ben Maimon*, vol. i (Leipzig, 1908), 63–134. English translation: *Ethics of Maimonides*, trans. A. Bruckstein. (Madison, 2004).

CORNFORD, F., *Plato's Cosmology* (New York, 1952).

CREIZENACH, M., *Thariag, oder Inbegriff der mosaischen Vorschriften nach talmudischer Interpretation* (Frankfurt, 1833).

CRESCAS, H., *Or hashem* (Vienna, 1859). Corrected with the help of JTS, MS Bamberger.

DAIBER, H., *Ein Kompendium der Aristotelischen Meteorologie in der Fassung des Ḥunayn ibn Isḥaq* (Amsterdam, 1975).

DAVIDSON, H., *Alfarabi, Avicenna, and Averroes, on Intellect* (New York, 1992).

——'Further on a Problematic Passage in *Guide for the Perplexed* 2.24', *Maimonidean Studies*, 4 (2000), 1–13.

——'John Philoponus as a Source of Medieval Islamic and Jewish Proofs of Creation', *Journal of the American Oriental Society*, 89 (1969), 357–91.

——'Maimonides' Secret Position on Creation', in I. Twersky (ed.), *Studies in Medieval Jewish History and Literature* (Cambridge, Mass., 1979), 16–40.

——*Moses Maimonides: The Man and his Works* (New York, 2005).

——*Proofs for Eternity, Creation and the Existence of God in Medieval Islamic and Jewish Philosophy* (New York, 1987).

DAVIDSON, I., *Thesaurus of Mediaeval Hebrew Poetry*, 4 vols. (New York, 1933).

DEL MEDIGO, E., *Beḥinat hadat*, ed. J. Ross (Tel Aviv, 1984).

DHANANI, A., *The Physical Theory of Kalām* (Leiden, 1994).

DIENSTAG, J., 'Was the Gaon of Wilna an Opponent of Maimonides' Philosophy?' [Ha'im hitnaged hagera lemishnato hapilosofit shel harambam?], *Talpiyot*, 4 (1949), 253–68.

DRUART, TH., 'Astronomie et astrologie selon Farābī', *Bulletin de philosophie médiévale*, 20 (1978), 43–7.

——'Le Second Traité de Farābī', *Bulletin de philosophie médiévale*, 21 (1979), 47–51.

DURAN, S., *Zohar rakia* (Vilna, 1879).

ELEAZAR OF WORMS, *Hasod, hayiḥud, veha'emunah*, ed. J. Dan, *Temirin*, 1 (1972).

ELIJAH HAZAKEN, *Shirat hamitsvot*, ed. I. Meiseles (Jerusalem, 2001).

ELIJAH OF VILNA, *Commentary on Shulḥan arukh*: 'Yoreh de'ah', 3 vols. (New York, 1953).

Encyclopedia of Islam, 12 vols., 2nd edn. (Leiden, 1960–2004).

ENDRESS, G., *Proclus Arabus* (Beirut, 1973).

EPSTEIN, Y., 'Rav Sherira Gaon's Commentary on the Terms in BT *Gitin*, Chapter 7' [Tafsir alfaz mi she'aḥazo lerav sherirah], *Ginzei kedem*, 5 (1934), 1–12.

ESS, J. VAN, *Die Erkenntislehre des 'Aḍudaddīn al-Īcī* (Wiesbaden, 1966).

——'Jüngere orientalische Literatur zur neuplatonischen Überlieferung', in *Parusia*, Festschrift for J Hirschberger, ed. K. Flasch (Frankfurt, 1965), 333–50.

——*Theologie und Gesellschaft im 2. und 3. Jahrhundert Hidschra*, 6 vols. (Berlin, 1991–7).

FALAQUERA, SH.-T., *Epistle of the Debate* [Igeret havikuaḥ], ed. and trans. S. Harvey (Cambridge, Mass., 1987).

——*Sefer hama'alot*, ed. L. Venetianer (Berlin, 1894).

FLEISCHER, E., 'The *Azharot* of R. Benjamin Paytan' [Azharot lerabi binyamin paytan], *Kobez al Yad*, 21 (1985), 1–75.

FOWLER, G., 'Manuscript Admont 608' (*Summa alexandrinorum*), *Archives d'histoire doctrinale et littéraire du moyen âge*, 49 (1983), 195–263.

FRAENKEL, C., 'From Maimonides to Samuel Ibn Tibbon' [Min harambam lishemuel ibn tibon], Ph.D. diss., Freie Universität, Berlin, 2000.

——*From Maimonides to Samuel Ibn Tibbon* [Min harambam lishemuel ibn tibon] (Jerusalem, 2007).

FRANK, R., 'Knowledge and *Taqlīd*', *Journal of the American Oriental Society*, 109 (1989), 37–62.

FREUDENTHAL, G., 'Maimonides' *Guide of the Perplexed* and the Transmission of the Mathematical Tract "On Two Asymptotic Lines"', *Vivarium*, 26 (1988), 113–40.

——'Science in the Medieval Jewish Culture of Southern France', repr. in id., *Science in the Medieval Hebrew and Arabic Traditions* (Aldershot, 2005).

FREUDENTHAL, J., *Die durch Averroes erhaltenen Fragmente Alexanders zur Metaphysik des Aristoteles* (Berlin, 1885).

FUCHS, S., *Studien über Abu Zakaria Jachja Ibn Bal'ām* (Berlin, 1893).

GALEN, *Compendium Timaei Platonis*, ed. P. Krauss and R. Walzer (London, 1951).

——*De usu partium*. English translation: *On the Usefulness of the Parts of the Body*, trans. M. May, 2 vols. (Ithaca, 1968).

GASTER, M., 'Die 613 Gebote und Verbote der Samaritaner', in *Festschrift zum 75 jährigen Bestehen des jüdisch-theologischen Seminars Fraenckelscher Stiftung*, vol. ii (Breslau, 1929).

Genesis Rabbah [*Bereschit Rabba*], ed. J. Theodor and Ch. Albeck (Jerusalem, 1965).

GERSON, L., *Plotinus* (London, 1994).

GHAZALI, *Maqāṣid al-falāsifa* [Intentions of the Philosophers] (Cairo, n.d.).

——*Tahāfut al-falāsifa* (*Incoherence of the Philosophers*), ed. and trans. M. Marmura (Provo, 1997).

GINZBERG, L., *Legends of the Jews*, 7 vols. (Philadelphia, 1967–8).

GOICHON, A., *La Distinction de l'essence et de l'existence d'après Ibn Sīnā* (Paris, 1937).

——*Lexique de la langue philosophique d'Ibn Sīnā* (Paris, 1938).

GOITEIN, S., 'Abraham Maimonides and his Pietist Circle', in A. Altmann (ed.), *Jewish Medieval and Renaissance Studies* (Cambridge, Mass., 1967), 145–64.

——'Documents on Abraham Maimonides and his Pietist Circle' [Rabi avraham ben harambam veḥugo haḥasidi], *Tarbiz*, 33 (1963–4), 181–97.

GOLDREICH, A., 'Possible Arabic Sources of the Distinction between "Duties of the Heart" and "Duties of the Limbs"' [Hamekorot ha'araviyim ha'efshariyim shel hahavḥanah ben ḥovot ha'evarim [*sic*] veḥovot halevavot], *Te'udah*, 6 (1988), 179–208.

GOLDSCHMIDT, D., 'Maimonides' Rite of Prayer According to an Oxford Manuscript' [Seder hatefilah shel harambam al pi ketav yad oksford], *Yedi'ot hamakhon leḥeker hashirah ha'ivrit*, 7 (1958), 185–213.

GOLDZIHER, I., *Die Richtungen der islamischen Koranauslegung* (Leiden, 1920).

——*Streitschrift des Gazali gegen die Batinijja-Sekte* (Leiden, 1916).

——'Zurechtweisung der Seele', in D. Philipson et al. (eds.), *Studies in Jewish Literature issued in Honor of Professor Kaufmann Kohler* (Berlin, 1913), 128–33.

GOMPERZ, TH., *Greek Thinkers*, vol. iv (London, 1912).

GROSSMANN, I., *613 Gesetze der mosaischen Lehre* (Cincinnati, 1892).

GUTAS, D., *Avicenna and the Aristotelian Tradition* (Leiden, 1988).

——*Greek Wisdom Literature in Arabic Translation* (New Haven, 1975).

——'The Starting Point of Philosophical Studies', in W. Fortenbaugh (ed.), *Theophrastus of Eresus: On his Life and Work* (New Brunswick, 1985), 115–23.

GUTTMANN, J., *Hapilosofiyah shel hayahadut* (Jerusalem, 1953). English translation: *Philosophies of Judaism*, trans. D. Silverman (New York, 1964).

GUTTMANN, M., *Beḥinat hamitsvot* (Breslau, 1928).

Halakhot gedolot, ed. A Traub (Warsaw, 1875); ed. J. Hildesheimer as *Halachoth gedoloth* (Berlin, 1888); ed. N. Hildesheimer, vol. iii (Jerusalem, 1988).

HALEVI, J., *Kuzari* (Tel Aviv, 1964).

HARVEY, S., 'The Sources of the Quotations from Aristotle's *Ethics* in the *Guide of the Perplexed*' [Mekoran shel hamuva'ot min ha'etikah], *Jerusalem Studies in Jewish Thought*, 14 (1998) (Sermoneta memorial volume), 87–102.

HARVEY, W., 'Maimonides' First Commandment', in Y. Elman and S. Gurock (eds.), *Ḥazon naḥum*, Festschrift for Norman Lamm (New York, 1997), 149–62.

HAYOUN, M. R., *Mosheh Narboni* (Tübingen, 1986).

HEFETS BEN YATSLIAH, 'New Extracts from *Sefer hamitsvot* of Hefets ben Yatsliah' [Keta'im ḥadashim misefer hamitsvot lerabi ḥefets ben yatsliaḥ], ed. M. Zucker, *Proceedings of the American Academy for Jewish Research*, 29 (1960–1), Hebrew section, 1–68.

——*A Volume of the Book of Precepts*, Arabic text ed., Hebrew trans., English introd. B. Halper, (Philadelphia, 1915).

HERMES, *see* PSEUDO-HERMES

HESCHEL, A., *Heavenly Torah* [Torah min hashamayim], vol. i (London, 1962).

HOPKINS, S., 'A New Autograph Fragment of Maimonides' *Hilkhot ha-Yerushalmi*', *Journal of Semitic Studies*, 28 (1983), 273–96.

HOURANI, G., *Islamic Rationalism* (Oxford, 1971).

HYMAN, A., 'Rabbi Simlai's Saying and Beliefs Concerning God', in A. Ivry et al. (eds.), *Perspectives on Jewish Thought and Mysticism* (Amsterdam, 1998).

IBN BĀJJA, *Ittiṣāl al-ʿaql bi-al-insān*, ed. and Spanish trans. M. Asín Palacios, as 'Tratado de Avempace sobre la unión del intelecto con el hombre', *Al-Andalus*, 7 (1942), 1–47.

——*Rasāʾil falsafiyya*, ed. J. Alaoui (Casablanca, 1983).

——*Risāla al-wadāʿ* (*Risālat al-widāʿ*), ed. and Spanish trans. M. Asín Palacios, as 'La Carta de Adios', *Al-Andalus*, 8 (1943), 1–87.

——*Tadbīr al-mutawaḥḥid*, ed. and Spanish trans. M. Asín Palacios as *El régimen del solitario* (Madrid, 1946).

——*Al-wuqūf ʿalā al-ʿaql al-faʿʿāl*, in Ibn Bājja, *Opera metaphysica*, ed. M. Fakhry (Beirut, 1968). French translation: T. Druart, 'Le Traité d'Avempace . . . ', *Bulletin de philosophie médiévale*, 22 (1980), 73–7.

IBN DAUD, A., *Emunah ramah*, ed. S. Weil (Frankfurt, 1852).

IBN EZRA, A., *Commentaries on Ecclesiastes, Hosea, and Proverbs*, in *Mikra'aot gedolot*, 10 vols. (New York, 1951).

——*Commentary on the Pentateuch* [Perush al hatorah], ed. A. Vayzer (Jerusalem, 1976).

——*Yesod mora*, ed. J. Cohen (Ramat Gan, 2002). English translation: *The Secret of the Torah*, trans. H. Strickman (Northvale, NJ, 1995).

IBN GABIROL, SH., *Keter malkhut*, ed. I. Levin (Tel Aviv, 2005).

IBN KASPI, J., *Sefer hamusar*, in I. Abrahams, *Hebrew Ethical Wills*, vol. i (Philadelphia, 1926), 130–61.

IBN TIBBON, S., *Otot hashamayim* [medieval Hebrew translation of Yaḥyā ibn Biṭrīq's Arabic version of the *Meteorology*], ed. and trans. R. Fontaine (Leiden, 1995).

IBN ṬUFAYL, *Hayy ben Yaqdhân*, ed. and French trans. L. Gauthier (Beirut, 1936). English translation, with pagination of Gauthier's text indicated: *Hayy Ibn Yaqzān*, trans. L. Goodman (New York, 1972).

IKHWĀN AL-ṢAFĀʾ, *Rasāʾil* (Beirut, 1957).

ISAAC OF CORBEIL, *Amudei golah* (Ladi, 1805).

ISAAC BEN SHESHET, *Responsa* (Hebrew) (New York, 1954).

IVRY, A., 'Neoplatonic Currents in Maimonides', in J. Kraemer (ed.), *Perspectives on Maimonides* (Oxford, 1991), 116–39.

JACOB BEN ASHER, *Arba'ah turim hashalem*, 21 vols. (Jerusalem, 1990–4).

JAEGER, W., 'Aristotle's Use of Medicine as Model of Method in his Ethics', *Journal of Hellenic Studies*, 77 (1957), 54–61.

JELLINEK, A., *Beit hamidrash* [*Bet ha-Midrasch. Sammlung*], 6 pts. in 2 vols., ed. A. Jellinek (Jerusalem, 1967).

JELLINEK, A., *Kuntres taryag* (Vienna, 1878).

JONAH BEN ABRAHAM GERONDI, *Commentary on Pirkei Avot*, in standard edns. of the Babylonian Talmud.

JOSEPH IBN TSADIK, *Ha'olam hakatan*, ed. S. Horovitz (Breslau, 1903); repr. with English translation, Hebrew pagination indicated in: J. Haberman, *The Microcosm of Joseph ibn Saddiq* (Madison, NJ, 2003).

JUDAH BEN BARZILAI, *Commentary on Sefer yetsirah* [Perush sefer yetsirah] (Berlin, 1885).

KADISCH, S., *Otsar hahayim* (Prague, 1832).

KAHAN, A., *The Taryag Mitzvos* (Brooklyn, 1987).

KAHANA, H., *Birkehot ḥayim* (Berdichev, 1898).

KATZ, J., *Divine Law in Human Hands* (Jerusalem, 1998).

KAUFMANN, D., *Geschichte der Attributenlehre* (Gotha, 1877).

—— *Studien über Salomon b Gabirol* (Budapest, 1899).

KELLNER, M., *Maimonides' Confrontation with Mysticism* (Oxford, 2006).

—— *Maimonides on Human Perfection* (Atlanta, 1990).

KIMHI, D., *Commentaries on Ezekiel and Hosea*, in *Mikra'aot gedolot*, 10 vols. (New York, 1951).

—— *Commentary on Genesis*, in *Torat ḥayim*, 5 vols., ed. M. L. Katzenellenson (Jerusalem, 1986).

KLEIN-BRASLAVY, S., *Maimonides' Interpretation of the Story of Creation* [Perush harambam lesipur beriat ha'olam] (Jerusalem, 1987).

KOKHAVI, DAVID BEN SAMUEL, *Sefer habatim*, vol. ii, ed. M. Hershler (Jerusalem, 1982).

KRAEMER, J., 'How (Not) to Read the *Guide of the Perplexed*', *Jerusalem Studies in Arabic and Islam*, 32 (2006), 350–409.

—— (ed.), *Perspectives on Maimonides* (Oxford, 1991).

KRAKOVSKI, M., *Avodat hamelekh* (Jerusalem, 1971).

KREISEL, H., 'Judah Halevi's Influence on Maimonides', *Maimonidean Studies*, 2 (1991), 95–121.

KROCHMAL, N., *Moreh nevukhei hazeman*, in *Kol kitvei rabi naḥman krokhmal*, ed. S. Rawidowicz (Waltham, Mass., 1961).

LANGERMANN, TZ., 'The Mathematical Writings of Maimonides', *Jewish Quarterly Review*, 75 (1984), 57–65.

—— 'A New Source for Samuel Ibn Tibbon's Translation of the *Guide of the Perplexed*' [Makor ḥadash letargumo shel shemuel ibn tibon'], *Pe'amim*, 72 (1997), 51–74.

—— 'Supplementary List of Manuscripts and Fragments of *Dalālat al-Hā'irīn*', *Maimonidean Studies*, 4 (2000), 31–7.

—— 'The True Perplexity', in J. Kraemer (ed.), *Perspectives on Maimonides* (Oxford, 1991), 159–74.

LEBERECHT, P., *Tariack Mitzwoth* (Heb. and German) (Hamburg, 1734).

LERNER, R., 'Maimonides' Governance of the Solitary', in J. Kraemer (ed.), *Perspectives on Maimonides* (Oxford, 1991), 33–46.

—— and M. MAHDI, *Medieval Political Philosophy* (Glencoe, Ill., 1963).

LETTINCK, P., *Aristotle's Meteorology and its Reception in the Arab World* (Leiden, 1999).

LEVINGER, A., 'Maimonides as a Physician and as an Authority of Religion' [Harambam betor rofe ufosek], *Harefuah*, 9 (1935), 150–62.

LEVINGER, J., 'On the Reason for Naziritism' [Al ta'am hanezirut], *Bar Ilan Annual*, 4–5 (1967), 299–305.

LIEBERMAN, S., *Hellenism in Jewish Palestine* (New York, 1950).

LOWY, S., *The Principles of Samaritan Bible Exegesis* (Leiden, 1977).

LUZKI, S., *Torei zahav im nekudot hakasef* (Ramleh, 1978).

Ma'amar haskel (Rödelheim, 1804).

MACCOBY, H., *Philosophy of the Talmud* (London, 2002).

Maḥazor shavu'ot, ed. Y. Frankel (Jerusalem, 2000).

MAIMONIDES, *Commentary on the Mishnah* [= Mishnah im perush rabi mosheh ben maimon] (Arabic), ed. and Hebrew trans. J. Kafah (Jerusalem, 1963–8).

——*Epistle to Yemen: The Arabic Original and Three Hebrew Versions*, ed. and English trans. A. Halkin and B. Cohen (New York, 1952).

——*Epistulae* (Heb.), ed. D. Baneth (Jerusalem, 1946).

——*Fī tadbīr al-ṣiḥḥat* [Regimen of Health], ed. H. Kroner, *Janus*, 28 (1924); English translation: Maimonides, *The Regimen of Health*, trans. A. Bar Sela et al., *Transactions of the American Philosophical Society*, NS 54/4 (1964).

——*Igerot harambam*, ed. Y. Shailat (Jerusalem, 1987–8).

——*Kovets teshuvot*, ed. A. Lichtenberg (Leipzig, 1859).

——*Medical Aphorisms*, treatises 1–5 (Arabic), ed. and trans. G. Bos (Provo, 2004); treatises 6–9 (Provo, 2007). Medieval Hebrew translation: *Pirkei mosheh*, ed. S. Muntner (Jerusalem, 1959).

——*Mishneh torah*, Shabse Frankel edn. (Jerusalem, 1975–).

——*Moreh nevukhim*. Arabic text: *Dalālat al-ḥā'irīn*, ed. S. Munk (Paris, 1856–66); republished by I. Joel (Jerusalem, 1929). English translation: *The Guide of the Perplexed*, trans. S. Pines (Chicago, 1963). French translation: *Le Guide des égarés*, trans. S. Munk (Paris, 1960). Hebrew translations: *Moreh nevukhim*, trans. S. Ibn Tibbon (Warsaw, 1930); *Moreh nevukhim*, trans. J. al-Harizi (Tel Aviv, 1964); *Moreh hanevukhim*, trans. J. Kafah (Jerusalem, 1972); *Moreh nevukhim*, trans. M. Schwarz (Tel Aviv, 2002).

——*On Asthma* (*Maqāla fī al-rabw*), ed. and trans. G. Bos (Provo, 2002).

——*On the Causes of Symptoms* (*Maqāla fī bayān ba'ḍ al-a'rāḍ*), ed. J. Leibowitz and S. Marcus (Berkeley, 1974).

——*Responsa* [Teshuvot harambam], ed. J. Blau, 2nd edn. 4 vols. (Jerusalem, 1986).

——*Sefer hamitsvot* [Book of Commandments] (Arabic), ed. and Hebrew trans. J. Kafah (Jerusalem, 1971). English translation: *The Commandments*, trans. C. Chavel (London, 1967). Medieval Hebrew translations: *Sefer hamitsvot*, ed. Ch. Heller, 2nd, rev., edn. (Jerusalem, 1946); *Sefer hamitsvot*, with commentaries and Nahmanides' *Hasagot* (Frankel edn.) (Jerusalem, 1995).

——*Shemonah perakim* [Eight Chapters; *Commentary on the Mishnah*, iv. 378–407]. English translation: *The Eight Chapters of Maimonides on Ethics*, ed. and trans. J. Gorfinkle (New York, 1912).

MAIMONIDES, *Treatise on Resurrection* (Arabic and medieval Hebrew translation), ed. J. Finkel, *Proceedings of the American Academy for Jewish Research*, 9 (1939), English section, pp. 57–105; Hebrew section, pp. 1–42.

MAINZ, E., 'Zum arabischen Sprachgebrauch des Maimonides', *Islamica*, 5 (1932), 556–72.

MAKKI, A.-T., *Qūt al-qulūb*, vol. i (Cairo, 1991).

MARCHESI, C., *L'Etica Nicomachea nella traduzione latina Medievale* (Messina, 1904).

MARGOLIOUTH, M., *The Fundamental Principles of Modern Judaism Investigated* (London, 1843).

MARX, A., 'Texts by and about Maimonides', *Jewish Quarterly Review*, 25 (1935), 371–428.

MAʿṢŪMĪ, M., 'Ibn Bājjah on the Human Intellect', *Islamic Studies*, 4 (1965), 121–36.

MATTOCK, J., *Tract Comprising Excerpts from Aristotle's Book of Animals, Attributed to Mūsā b. ʿUbaid Allāh al-Qurṭubī* (Cambridge, 1966).

MCCARTHY, R., *Theology of Al-Ashʿarī* (Beirut, 1953).

MEIRI, M., *Ḥidushim* (Zikhron Ya'akov, 1976).

Mekhilta derabi yishma'el, ed. H. Horovitz and I. Rabin (Jerusalem, 1960).

MENDELSSOHN, M., *Jerusalem*, trans. A. Jospe (New York, 1969).

——*Netivot hashalom (Be'ur)*, vol. ii (Vienna, 1846).

Midrash hagadol, Genesis, ed. M. Margulies (Jerusalem, 1947).

Milot hahigayon [*Treatise on Logic*; misattributed to Maimonides], Arabic text (*Maqāla fī ṣināʿa al-mantiq)*, ed. I. Efros, *Proceedings of the American Academy for Jewish Research*, 34 (1966), English section, pp. 155–60; Hebrew section, pp. 9–42; three medieval Hebrew translations, ed. and trans. I. Efros (New York, 1938).

MONTGOMERY, J., *The Samaritans*, 2nd edn. (New York, 1968).

MOSES OF COUCY, *Sefer mitsvot gadol* (Venice, 1547).

MUBASHSHIR B. FĀTIK, *Mukhtār al-ḥikam*, ed. A. Badawi (Madrid, 1958).

MÜNSTER, S., *Catalogus omnium praeceptorum legis mosaicae* (Basel, n.d.).

NAHMANIDES, *Commentary on the Pentateuch* [Perush al hatorah], ed. Ch. Chavel (Jerusalem, 1962–3).

——*Hasagot* [Animadversions] on Maimonides, *Sefer hamitsvot*, in Maimonides, *Sefer hamitsvot* (Frankel).

NARBONI, M., *Commentary on* Moreh nevukhim [Be'ur lesefer moreh nevukhim] (Vienna, 1852).

NATHAN BEN JEHIEL, *Arukh hashalem*, ed. H. Kohut (Vienna, 1926).

Netiv mitsvotekha [*Azharot* of Yitshak ben Reuven and Solomon ibn Gabirol] (Livorno, 1841).

NEUSNER, JACOB, *Philosophical Mishnah* (Atlanta, Ga., 1988).

NICOLAUS OF DAMASCUS, *De Plantis* (Arabic), ed. and English trans. H. Lulofs and E. Poortman (Amsterdam, 1989).

Numbers Rabbah, 2 vols. (Jerusalem, 1970).

Otsar hageonim: Berakhot, ed. B. Lewin (Haifa, 1928).

PERLA, Y., *Sefer hamitsvot lirabenu saʿadyah*, 3 vols. (Warsaw, 1914–16).

PETERS, F., *Aristoteles Arabus* (Leiden, 1968).

PINES, SH., 'The Limitations of Human Knowledge According to Al-Farabi, ibn Bajja, and Maimonides', in I. Twersky (ed.), *Studies in Medieval Jewish History and Literature* (Cambridge, Mass., 1979), 82–109.

——'Les Limites de la métaphysique selon al-Fārābi, Ibn Bājja, et Maïmonide', *Miscellanea Mediaevalia*, 13 (1981), 211–25.

——'The Philosophical Purport of Maimonides' Halachic Works and the Purport of the *Guide of the Perplexed*', in Sh. Pines and Y. Yuval (eds.), *Maimonides and Philosophy* (Dordrecht, 1986), 1–14.

PLOTINUS, *Enneads*, ed. and trans. A. Armstrong, 7 vols. (Cambridge, Mass., 1966–88).

——*Opera*: *Enneades*, ed. P. Henry and H. Schwyzer, vol. ii (Paris, 1959); contains English translations of the Arabic paraphrases of the *Enneads*.

The Problemata Physica attributed to Aristotle: *The Arabic Version of Hunayn ibn Ishaq*, ed. L. Filius (Leiden, 1999).

PSEUDO-AMMONIUS, *On the Views of the Philosophers* (Arabic), ed. and trans. U. Rudolph as *Die Doxographie des Pseudo-Ammonios* (Stuttgart, 1989).

PSEUDO-ARISTOTLE, *De mundo*, in *Works of Aristotle*, vol. iii, trans. D. Ross et al. (Oxford, 1931).

——*De plantis*, in Aristotle, *Minor Works*, ed. and trans. W. Hett (Loeb Classical Library) (Cambridge, Mass., 1963).

PSEUDO-HERMES, *Hermes Trismegistus an die menschliche Seele*, ed., and German translation, H. Fleischer (Leipzig, 1870). Slightly fuller text: *Hermetis Trismegisti . . . de Castigatione animae libellum*, ed., and Latin translation, O. Bardenhewer (Bonn, 1873).

RABINOWITZ, A., *Taryag* (Jerusalem, 1967).

RAWIDOWICZ, S., *Iyunim bemaḥashevet yisra'el*, vol. i (Jerusalem, 1969).

RICIUS, P., *De sexcentum et tredecim Mosaice sanctionis edictis* (Pavia, 1510).

ROBINSON, J., 'Some Remarks on the Source of Maimonides' Plato', *Zutot*, 3 (2003), 49–57.

ROSENTHAL, F., *Greek Philosophy in the Arab World* [collected articles] (Brookfield, Vermont, 1990).

——*Knowledge Triumphant* (Leiden, 1970).

——'Maimonides and a Discussion of Muslim Speculative Theology', in M. Caspi (ed.), *Jewish Tradition in the Diaspora*, W. J. Fischel memorial volume (Berkeley, 1981), 109–12.

ROSIN, D., *Die Ethik des Maimonides* (Breslau, 1876).

RULAND, H.-J., *Die arabischen Fassungen von zwei Schriften des Alexander von Aphrodisias* (Saarbrücken, 1976).

SA'ADIAH GAON, *Emunot vede'ot* [*Amānāt wa-al-i'tiqādāt*], ed. S. Landauer (Leiden, 1880). English translation with pagination of the Arabic indicated: *The Book of Beliefs and Opinions*, trans. S. Rosenblatt (New Haven, 1948).

——*Sidur*, ed. I. Davidson et al. (Jerusalem, 1941).

SA'ADIAH GAON, *Sefer hamitsvot*, *see* Y. PERLA

SABRA, A., 'The Andalusian Revolt against Ptolemaic Astronomy', in E. Mendelsohn (ed.), *Transformation and Tradition in the Sciences*, Festschrift for B. Cohen (Cambridge, Mass., 1984), 133–53.

SCHACHT, J., and M. MEYERHOF, 'Maimonides against Galen on Philosophy and Cosmogony', *Bulletin of the Faculty of Arts of the University of Egypt*, 5/1 (1937), 53–88.

SCHEIBER, A., 'Autograph Manuscripts of Maimonides', *Acta Orientalia Academiae Scientiarum Hungaricae*, 33 (1979), 187–95.

SCHICK, M., *Al taryag mitsvot* (Munkacs, 1895).

SCHOLEM, G. (ed.), *Walter Benjamin/Gershom Scholem: Briefwechsel 1933–1940* (Frankfurt, 1980).

SCHOONHEIM, P., *Aristotle's Meteorology in the Arabico-Latin Tradition* [edition of Yaḥyā b. Biṭrīq's Arabic version of the *Meteorology* and Gerard of Cremona's Latin translation of Yaḥyā's version] (Leiden, 2000).

SCHREINER, M., 'Igeret hapetirah' (pt. 2), *Mimizraḥ umima'arav*, 4 (1899), 26–38.

SCHWARZ, M., 'Who Were Maimonides' Mutakillimūn?', pt. 1, *Maimonidean Studies*, 2 (1991), 159–209; pt. 2, *Maimonidean Studies*, 3 (1992–3), 143–72.

SCHWARZSCHILD, S., *Pursuit of the Ideal*, ed. M. Kellner (Albany, 1990).

Sefer haḥinukh, ed. Ch. Chavel (Jerusalem, 1956).

Sefer hayashar, ed. J. Dan (Jerusalem, 1986).

SFORNO, O., *Commentary on Genesis*, in *Torat ḥayim*, 5 vols., ed. M. L. Katzenellenson (Jerusalem, 1986).

—— *Or amim*, in Sforno, *Kitvei rabi ovadyah seforno*, ed. Z. Gotleib (Jerusalem, 1983).

SHAHRASTĀNĪ, *Al-milal wa-al-niḥal* [Religious and Philosophical Sects], ed. W. Cureton (London, 1846). French translation: *Livre des religions et des sectes II*, trans. J. Jolivet and G. Monnot (Paris, 1993).

SHAPIRO, M., *Studies in Maimonides and his Interpreters* (Scranton, 2008).

Sifrei Deuteronomy, ed. L. Finkelstein (Berlin, 1939).

Sifrei Numbers, ed. H. Horovitz (Leipzig, 1917).

SIMPLICIUS, *Commentary on the Physics*, ed. H. Diels (Berlin, 1895).

SIRAT, C., 'Une liste de manuscrits: Préliminaire à une nouvelle édition du *Dalālat al-Hāyryn*', *Archives d'histoire doctrinale et littéraire*, 58 (1991), 9–29.

SKLARE, D., *Samuel ben Ḥofni Gaon and his Cultural World* (Leiden, 1996).

SORABJI, R., *Time, Creation and the Continuum* (Ithaca, 1983).

SPINOZA, B., *Ethics*, in *Chief Works of Benedict de Spinoza*, trans. R. Elwes (New York, 1951).

STEINSCHNEIDER, M., *Al-Farabi* (St Petersburg, 1869).

—— *Die arabischen Uebersetzungen aus dem Griechischen* (Graz, 1960).

—— *Die hebräischen Uebersetzungen des Mittelalters und die Juden als Dolmetscher* (Berlin, 1893).

—— 'Die *Parva Naturalia* des Aristoteles bei den Arabern', *Zeitschrift der deutschen morgenländischen Gesellschaft*, 37 (1883), 477–92.

STEPANSKY DE SEGAL, R., *Preguntas y respuestas sobre judaísmo* (Buenos Aires, 1990).

STERN, J., 'The Knot that Never Was', *Aleph*, 8 (2008), 319–39.

STRAUSS, L., *Persecution and the Art of Writing* (Glencoe, Ill., 1952).

—— *Philosophie und Gesetz* (Berlin, 1935). English translation: *Philosophy and Law*, trans. E. Adler (Albany, 1995).

STROUMSA, S., 'Note on Maimonides' Attitude to Joseph ibn Tsadik' [He'arah al yaḥaso shel harambam lerabi yosef ibn tsadik], *Jerusalem Studies in Jewish Thought*, 9 (1990), Festschrift for Shlomo Pines, 33–8.

SUHRAWARDĪ, *Ḥikmat al-ishrāq* [The Philosophy of Illumination], ed. and trans. H. Ziai (Provo, 1999).

TAWḤĪDĪ, *Baṣā'ir wa-dhakhā'ir*, ed. I. Kailani, vol. ii (Damascus, 1964).

THEMISTIUS, *An Arabic Translation of Themistius, Commentary on Aristoteles 'De anima'* [Paraphrase of *De anima*], ed. M. Lyons (Columbia, SC, 1973).

——'Paraphrase of *Metaphysics* 12' (Arabic), in A. Badawi (ed.), *Arisṭū ʿind al-ʿArab* (Cairo, 1947), 12–21.

——'Paraphrase of *On the Heavens*' [*In libros Aristotelis de Caelo Paraphrasis, Hebraice et Latine*; medieval Hebrew translation of the medieval Arabic translation], in *Commentaria in Aristotelem graeca*, vol. v, pt. 4, ed. S. Landauer (Berlin, 1902).

——'Paraphrase of the *Physics*' [*In Aristotelis Physica Paraphrasis*], in *Commentaria in Aristotelem graeca*, vol. v, pt. 2, ed. H. Schenkl (Berlin,1900).

Theologie des Aristotles (Arabic), ed. Fr. Dieterici (Leipzig, 1882). English translation in Plotinus, *Opera*, vol. ii.

THEOPHRASTUS, *De ventis*, ed. and trans. V. Coutant and V. Eichenlaub (Notre Dame, Ind., 1975).

——*Metaphysics*, ed. and trans M. van Raalte (Leiden, 1993).

THOMSON, J., *The Samaritans* (Edinburgh, 1919).

TISHBY, I., *Mishnat hazohar*, vol. i (Jerusalem, 1949).

Torat ḥayim [Pentateuch with traditional commentaries], 5 vols., ed. M. L. Katzenellenson (Jerusalem, 1986).

TROUILLARD, L., *La Purification plotienne* (Paris, 1955).

TWERSKY, I., 'Did Rabbi Abraham ibn Ezra Influence Maimonides?' [Hahishpia rabʿ al rambam?], in I. Twersky and J. Harris (eds.), *Rabbi Abraham Ibn Ezra* (Cambridge, Mass., 1993).

——*Introduction to the Code of Maimonides* (New Haven, 1980).

——'Some Non-Halakic Aspects of the *Mishneh Torah*', in A. Altmann (ed.), *Jewish Medieval and Renaissance Studies* (Cambridge, Mass., 1967), 95–118.

——(ed.), *Studies in Medieval Jewish History and Literature* (Cambridge, Mass., 1979).

ULLMANN, M., *Die Medizin im Islam* (Leiden, 1970).

URBACH, E., *Ḥazal: Emunot vede'ot* (Jerusalem, 1971). English edition: *The Sages: Their Concepts and Beliefs*, trans. Israel Abrahams (Jerusalem, 1987).

VAJDA, G., *L'Amour de Dieu* (Paris, 1957).

——'A propos d'une citation non identifée d'al-Fārābī dans le *Guide des égarés*', *Journal asiatique*, 253 (1965), 43–50.

——'Langage, philosophie, et politique d'après un traité recemment publié d'Abū Naṣr al-Fārābī', *Journal asiatique*, 257 (1970), 247–60.

VAJDA, G., *La Théologie ascétique de Bahya ibn Paquda* (Paris, 1947).

WENSINCK, A., *La Pensée de Ghazzali* (Paris, 1940).

WOLFSON, H., 'Albinus and Plotinus on Divine Attributes', repr. in id., *Studies in the History of Philosophy and Religion*, i. 115–30.

——'Avicenna, Algazali, and Averroes on Divine Attributes', repr. in id., *Studies in the History of Philosophy and Religion*, i. 143–69.

——'The Classification of Sciences in Mediaeval Jewish Philosophy', repr. in id., *Studies in the History of Philosophy and Religion*, i. 493–545.

——*Crescas' Critique of Aristotle* (Cambridge, Mass., 1929).

——'The Knowability and Describability of God in Plato and Aristotle', repr. in id., *Studies in the History of Philosophy and Religion*, i. 98–114.

——*Philo*, 2 vols. (Cambridge, Mass., 1948).

——*Philosophy of the Church Fathers* (Cambridge, Mass., 1956).

——*Philosophy of the Kalam* (Cambridge, Mass., 1976).

——'The Plurality of Immovable Movers in Aristotle, Averroes, and St. Thomas', repr. in id., *Studies in the History of Philosophy and Religion*, i. 1–19.

——'The Problem of the Souls of the Spheres', repr. in id., *Studies in the History of Philosophy and Religion*, i. 22–59.

——*Repercussions of the Kalam in Jewish Philosophy* (Cambridge, Mass., 1979).

——*Studies in the History of Philosophy and Religion*, 2 vols. (Cambridge, Mass., 1973–7).

——'The Terms *Tasawwur* and *Taṣdīq*', repr. in id., *Studies in the History of Philosophy and Religion*, i. 478–92.

WRIGHT, W., *Grammar of the Arabic Language* (Cambridge, 1955).

YAḤYĀ IBN BITRĪQ, *see* P. SCHOONHEIM

YELLIN, A.,. *Yefeh einayim*, printed in standard edns. of Babylonian Talmud.

ZELLER, E., *Die Philosophie der Griechen*, 3 pts. in 6 vols. (Leipzig, 1919–23).

Zohar, 3 vols. (Vilna, 1911).

ZONTA, M., 'Maimonides as Zoologist?', in G. Hasselhoff and O. Fraisse (eds.), *Moses Maimonides* (Würzburg, 2004), 83–94.

ZULAI, M., 'The *Azharot* of R. Isaac Ibn Gikatila' [Azharot rabi yitsḥak ibn gikatila], *Tarbiz*, 20 (1950), 161–76.

Index

Printed and bound by CPI Group (UK) Ltd, Croydon, CR0 4YY

09/06/2025

14685793-0004